SITUATING MEDIEVAL INDIA

Situating Medieval India
POLITY, SOCIETY AND CULTURE

SURINDER SINGH

BOYDELL · MANOHAR

© Surinder Singh, 2023

All Rights Reserved. Except as permitted under current legislation
no part of this work may be photocopied, stored in a retrieval system,
published, performed in public, adapted, broadcast,
transmitted, recorded or reproduced in any form or by any means,
without the prior permission of the copyright owner

The right of Surinder Singh to be identified as
the author of this work has been asserted in accordance with
sections 77 and 78 of the Copyright, Designs and Patents Act 1988

ISBN 978-93-94262-77-5 (Manohar Publishers & Distributors)
ISBN 978-1-83765-125-2 (Boydell ◆ Manohar)

First published 2023 by
Ajay Kumar Jain for
Manohar Publishers & Distributors
4753/23 Ansari Road, Daryaganj
New Delhi 110 002

First published Worldwide excluding India, Sri Lanka, Nepal,
Bangladesh, Afghanistan, Pakistan and Bhutan, 2023 by Boydell ◆ Manohar
A joint imprint of Boydell & Brewer Ltd and
Manohar Publishers & Distributors
PO Box 9, Woodbridge, Suffolk IP12 3DF, UK
and of Boydell & Brewer Inc.
668 Mt Hope Avenue, Rochester, NY 14620–2731, USA
website: www.boydellandbrewer.com

A CIP catalogue record for this book is available
from the British Library

The publisher has no responsibility for the continued existence or accuracy of URLs for
external or third-party internet websites referred to in this book, and does not guarantee
that any content on such websites is, or will remain, accurate or appropriate

Typeset by
Kohli Print
Delhi 110 051

This publication is printed on acid-free paper

Contents

Acknowledgements	vii
Introduction	1
1. Appointment of Government Officers in Medieval States: The Concerns of Nizam ul-Mulk Tusi and Ziauddin Barani	9
2. Dynastic Change in Northern India: Divergent Approaches to the Exercise of Sovereign Power	36
3. Rulers, Zamindars and Sufis: Probing a Triangular Model of State Formation	60
4. Administrative Consolidation in the Delhi Sultanate: Evidence from a Collection of Letters	84
5. Scientific Temperament and Technical Innovations in North India: From the Eleventh to the Fifteenth Century	110
6. Revolt of Dulla Bhatti against the Mughal State: A Study of Oral Tradition and Modern Cultural Forms	139
7. Travelling Across Northwestern India: The State of Rivers, Bridges and Boats during the Mughal Age	163
8. Political Culture in the Mughal Empire: An Idealistic Vision and the Ground Reality	190
9. A Central Asian Visitor at the Mughal Court: Meetings of Mutribi Samarqandi with Emperor Jahangir	213
10. Pictures of Amazement in Medieval India: Looking into the Works of Mushtaqi, Jahangir and Bhandari	240

vi   *Contents*

11. Historical Dimensions of Islam in South Asia:
    Modern Writings on Polity, Religion and Culture   263

12. Cultural Ethos of Medieval Panjab: The Pathways
    of Resistance to the Structures of Dominance   289

13. Caste, Creed and Custom: North Indian Society
    Towards the Close of the Eighteenth Century   321

14. Celebration of Religious Diversity in Agra: Reading
    the Observations of Nazir Akbarabadi   348

Index   371

Acknowledgements

I am grateful to the staff of several libraries, where the research for this book was carried out. Since it is not possible to name the individuals, I will mention their institutions. These are A.C. Joshi Library and the library of the Department of History at Panjab University, Chandigarh; Shri Natnagar Shodh Samsthan, Sitamau, Madhya Pradesh; Maulana Azad Library and the library of the Centre of Advanced Study, Department of History at Aligarh Muslim University, Aligarh; Rampur Raza Library, Rampur, Uttar Pradesh; Maulana Abul Kalam Azad Arabic and Persian Research Institute, Tonk, Rajasthan; Indian Institute of Advanced Study, Shimla, Himachal Pradesh; Central Library, Jamia Millia Islamia and Institute of Islamic Studies, Jamia Hamdard, New Delhi; Prof. Ganda Singh Collection, Punjabi Reference Library, Punjabi University, Patiala; Bhai Gurdas Library, Guru Nanak Dev University, Amritsar; and Sikh History Research Department, Khalsa College, Amritsar.

I owe a debt of gratitude to a number of scholars and colleagues, who have helped me in different ways. The late Iqtidar Husain Siddiqui took a keen interest in my studies and showered his affection on me. Harbans Mukhia provided me with opportunities to learn and illuminated my path with encouraging words. Priyatosh Sharma, in spite of his onerous academic and administrative responsibilities, found time to give suggestions on the presentation of my arguments, besides offering the facilities at our departmental library. Ashish Kumar, with his natural courtesy and kindness, lent his books to me and provided printouts from online sources. Subhash Parihar, true to his saintly self, placed his impressive library at my disposal, without hesitating to send relevant materials through post. At different points of time, I have received assistance from Manohar Singh Ranawat, Azizuddin Husain, Raj Kumar Hans, Zaheer Husain Jafri and Vinod Kumar Singh.

Over the last four decades or so, my understanding of medieval India has benefited from the writings of many a stalwart. They are

viii   *Acknowledgements*

Mohammad Habib, Khaliq Ahmad Nizami, Saiyid Athar Abbas Rizvi, M. Athar Ali, Satish Chandra, Irfan Habib, Simon Digby, Muzaffar Alam, Sunil Kumar, Shuja Alhaq, Richard M. Eaton and Carl W. Ernst. I place on record my sense of gratitude to them.

At Manohar, the editorial team has taken great pains to shape this work. Ramesh Jain placed his trust in my abilities and exerted himself to attain perfection in the publication of this volume. Ajay Jain, appreciative of my academic interests and needs, has been prompt in meeting my demands for books. On the home front, I have been receiving unconditional affection from my mother, sister, wife, daughter and granddaughter. My son-in-law Pawan and nephew Lakhprit have always stood by me. Needless to add, I alone am responsible for the views expressed in the following pages.

Chandigarh   SURINDER SINGH
21 October 2022

Introduction

Medieval India, for the purpose of this book, constitutes a span of six hundred years from the thirteenth to the eighteenth century. Bureaucrats of the colonial state took the lead in writing the history of this period. Since the medieval states thrived under a ruling class that was largely Muslim, the political institutions were designated in religious terms. This facile interpretation lost ground owing to increased availability of Persian chronicles, emergence of a class of professional historians and progressive forces emanating from the anti-colonial movement. Though the historians kept their focus on ruling dynasties and important rulers, efforts were made to explore the impact of state policies on a predominantly agrarian society. Simultaneously, attention was drawn to the development of a cultural fusion, with reference to new spiritual currents and art forms. In the post-independence period, we come across a wider variety of sources and their more critical use. As a result, attention was turned to the organization of the military bureaucracy, stratification within the peasantry and growth of urbanization. While the scholarly focus moved away from the Delhi-Agra region, new light was thrown on the plurality of spiritual cultures. These trends have paved the way for fresh studies on medieval India, which have been elaborated in the following pages.

Ziauddin Barani was a distinguished historian and political thinker. His relatives held important positions in the Delhi Sultanate. In his *Tarikh-i Firoz Shahi*, he has chronicled the period from the accession of Ghiasuddin Balban to the early years of Firoz Shah Tughluq's reign. He was the only Indian writer to have dealt with the issue of the social background of government officers (Chapter 1). He has praised Iltutmish and Balban for opposing the appointment of lowborn persons, besides ignoring competence and loyalty. Barani has recorded the monologues of these Sultans, besides their comments on specific cases. He has given the names of lowborn individuals, who were appointed to high positions during the reign of Muhammad bin Tughluq (r. 1325-1351). He has attributed their appointment to contradictions in the Sultan's character. It was noteworthy that Barani has discussed this subject in his *Fatawa-i Jahandari*, which was a theoretical treatise on the art of governance. He has linked noble virtues to high birth and evil traits to low birth. He has advocated that the lowborn persons, particularly the sons of market people and artisans, must not have access to education, as it enabled them to aspire for government jobs. Barani was alarmed at the plebeianization of the bureaucracy that had resulted from socio-economic changes. He became

2   *Introduction*

a spokesperson of the established aristocracy, which was threatened by the social mobility of the underprivileged groups. Barani was not the only political thinker to express these views. Two hundred years before him, Nizam ul-Mulk Tusi, the famous Saljuqid prime minister (*wazir*) articulated similar views in his book on the principles of governance. Tusi asserted that one post must not be given to two persons and two or more posts must not be assigned to one person. He believed that prime-ministership (*wizarat*) must be reserved for the offspring of families that had held this position in the past. More importantly, Tusi laid down religious conditions for government jobs. These must be given to Khurasani Sunnis. All others – Jews, Christians, Zoroastrians, Shias, Kharijis, Batinis, Qaramatis and Dailamites – must be entirely excluded. Interestingly, the Saljuqid rulers and Delhi Sultans did not subscribe to these sectarian exhortations.

Ziauddin Barani, as compared to other historians of the Delhi Sultanate, enjoyed certain advantage. As mentioned above, some of his elders held high positions under the Balbani and Khalji regimes. This enabled him to dig out facts that were not accessible to his contemporaries. This advantage, though tinged with strong prejudices, came to the surface in his account of the reign of Jalaluddin Khalji (r. 1290-1296). Barani held that the Turkish rule was intrinsically superior to that of the Khaljis. Since modern writers, ranging from Shaikh Abdur Rashid to Iqtidar Husain Siddiqui, have expressed diametrically opposite views about this reign, it is necessary to take a closer look at Barani's account (Chapter 2). He has recorded the conversations between Jalaluddin Khalji and his principal advisor Ahmad Chap. These discussions pertained to Sultan's important measures, such as his first entry into Balban's palace, punishment to the supporters of the rebel Malik Chhajju, the retreat of the Delhi army from Ranthambhore and the return of Alauddin Khalji from an expedition to Deogiri. It was creditable for the Sultan to encourage divergent views on state policy. In addition to a record of these debates, Barani has offered two assessments of the reign. The Sultan's contemporaries, who had observed him from close quarters, acknowledged his military prowess. They found that he was wanting in statesmanship, absolutism and magnificence. In contrast, the friends of Barani's father, endowed with age and experience, admitted several merits of the Sultan's rule. This was so because they had felt the severity of Alauddin Khalji and Muhammad bin Tughluq. Barani's articulation of diverse positions enabled us to develop a fresh understanding of the reign of Jalaluddin Khalji. Since it was a transitional phase between Balban's absolutism and Alauddin Khalji's radical reforms, it was faced with its own challenges and compulsions.

After the death of Jalaluddin Khalji, the Delhi Sultanate underwent a major administrative transformation. As the territorial control expanded, the burden

Introduction

of agrarian taxation was maximized and rural intermediaries were suppressed. The state exchequer overflowed with money, which was invested in schemes of agrarian expansion and shift in the cropping pattern. The failure of these measures left important lessons. During the second half of the fourteenth century, the Delhi Sultanate adopted new strategies of state formation (Chapter 3). The focus was moved from the Gangetic plain to the southeast Panjab and Multan region. The Tughluq rulers, benefiting from the crucial support of the Khokhars, went on to forge a series of alliances with diverse local elements, particularly the *zamindars* and Sufis. Such ties were formed with Rana Mal Bhatti of Abohar, Sadhu and Sadharan of Thanesar and Karam Chand Chauhan of Darrera (Hissar). At the same time, liberal land grants were conferred on the Sufi establishments between Uch and Delhi. As these relations stabilized, agrarian expansion was undertaken with the help of canal networks and settlement of pastoral groups. Timur, during the course of his invasion, marched through these areas and grabbed huge heaps of grain. Therefore, three parallel developments – alliances with local elements, canal driven agrarian expansion and Timur's attacks – occurred in the same geographical space. The triangular model of state formation (involving the rulers, *zamindars* and Sufis), which had been built with great effort and foresight, collapsed due to the widespread dislocation following Timur's invasion and internal conflict within the ruling class. Still, its legacy was visible in the second half of the fifteenth century. Two Sufis, Haidar Shaikh and Yusuf Qureshi, emerged as the new rulers of Malerkotla and Multan respectively. Since they did not possess military resources, they stitched alliances with powerful local potentates to strengthen the roots of their authority.

Since the early thirteenth century, the Multan region had been appearing in the contemporary records with regular frequency. The Delhi Sultanate was unable to impose its authority on its semi-autonomous governors, forcing Balban to appoint his son Sultan Muhammad in the province. It was often exposed to the raids of the Mongols and Qarlughs. Lying on the Delhi-Qandhar overland route, it had access to the sea through Sind. Its Suhrawardi hospice had become a thriving centre of Islamic spirituality. Ibn Battuta, visiting the city in 1333, has left an interesting account of his experiences. During the reign of Firoz Shah Tughluq, Ain ul-Mulk Mahru was deputed as the governor of Multan (Chapter 4). A diligent scholar with a flair for writing, Mahru has compiled a volume of 133 letters. This work was an authentic source for the history of Delhi Sultanate, in general and Multan, in particular. One of the letters laid down the functions of the prime minister (*wazir*), while other epistles detailed the attempts at winning over the local elements of Bengal and acquiring elephants from Jajnagar (present-day Odisha). The nobles were required to sign an agreement (*ahdnama*) affirming their loyalty

4 *Introduction*

to the Sultan. A number of letters revealed the operation of state power in the distant province, besides illuminating the work of the provincial government. In view of the prevailing depopulation and declining economy, Mahru developed a multi-pronged strategy to revive the material conditions. In order to balance the finances, Mahru prioritized the maintenance of the army over the needs of the theologians and lower bureaucracy. A survey was carried out on the state of land grants. The grantees were provided with incentives, so that their incomes were increased and cultivated area was widened. Mahru developed a network of five canals and, for their excavation and upkeep, the local beneficiaries were assimilated into the project. With regard to essential commodities, the evil of hoarding was suppressed and prices were regulated. Some letters throw valuable light on the malpractices of merchants and complaints regarding petty functionaries. On a variety of administrative matters, Mahru kept up a correspondence with the Sufis of the region.

In the early eleventh century, Alberuni attributed the backwardness of Indian sciences to the inadequacy of Sanskrit, arrogance of the intellectuals and stranglehold of theology. Amir Khusrau, in his counter argument, asserted the superiority of India's knowledge in comparison to Greece, Persia and China (Chapter 5). A large stock of knowledge had been raised in natural sciences, mathematics, geography, logic and astrology. Foreigners came to India to learn advanced subjects. The city of Delhi attracted learned immigrants from the central Islamic lands. The Delhi Sultanate, benefiting from the availability of paper, maintained statistical records on salaries, revenues, crops, cattle and houses. Advanced technology was involved in the installation of Ashokan pillars, astrolabes and time keeping devices. Several ancient Sanskrit texts were translated into Persian. Sant Kabir and Guru Nanak, while attacking ignorance and superstitions, argued that the laws of nature governed the lives of all living beings. Moving to the Mughal period (Chapter 7), we find that technology was associated with the means of crossing rivers. A variety of travellers – soldiers, merchants and pilgrims – were required to cross flowing waters. Permanent bridges were built over seasonal streams. Perennial rivers were crossed with boats at the ferries. In hilly areas, semi-permanent structures were constructed with logs and ropes. Large armies fabricated a chain of boats and laid a passage with earth and grass. In spite of precautions, numerous lives were lost in accidents.

Abul Fazl was one of the greatest Indian intellectuals of the sixteenth century. Apart from a voluminous history of Akbar's reign, he articulated the theoretical foundations of Mughal kingship. Jahangir was committed to continue the political legacy of his illustrious predecessor. Within seven years of Jahangir's accession, his subordinate Muhammad Baqir produced a new treatise on the mode of governance (Chapter 8). The two parts of this work

Introduction 5

comprised exhortations for the emperor and his nobles respectively. The Mughal emperor dispensed justice and punished the wrong doers, so that the weak were protected. His bravery was reflected in military preparedness and firmness towards enemies. At a personal level, his forbearance and mercy percolated to the lower rungs of society. Though he was advised to consult advisors, he had to keep secrecy. He appointed four categories of employees (warriors, secretaries, administrators, and news writers) and treated them with kindness. Baqir's exhortation on the exclusion of lowborn from state services was a reiteration of Barani's stance on the issue. Baqir was candid in speaking for the nobles and, indirectly, pointed to the shortcomings of Jahangir. The nobles had become vulnerable as their colleagues carried tales to the emperor, who was urged to verify the facts himself. Nobles must realize the value of friends, though friendship itself was going downhill. Poverty led to degradation, but blind pursuit of materialism was not the answer. Since not every aim was achievable, man must learn to accept his destiny and imbibe moral values. Thus, morality was an effective antidote to frustration.

The Mughal State maintained multiple channels of communication with Central Asia. The Mughal emperors took pride in their descent from Timur. A large number of Turanis held high ranks in the Mughal nobility. Commercial relations between the two kingdoms were carried over transcontinental routes. Both were associated with the Naqshbandi mystics. In this context, Mutribi Samarqandi, a poet and musician, visited Jahangir's court in 1626. He has left a memoir of twenty-four meetings with the emperor (Chapter 9). He has enumerated the gifts from his royal host. He presented a compilation of Persian poets, *Nuskha Zeba-i Jahangir*, to the emperor, who relished reading of its excerpts. Discussions were held on the verses of Miram Siyah, Muhammad Yusuf Khwaja, Maktub Khan and Masih-ul-Zaman. Mutribi attended a number of functions, including camel and deer fights. As an accomplished vocalist, he sang two melodies and delved into the ancient roots of music. He was surprised at a massive lump of sugar from Lucknow and a European notebook that could be erased after writing. Jahangir supervised the portraiture of Uzbek rulers, besides acknowledging the deep impact of Sufi music on human minds. Mutribi made every effort to satisfy Jahangir's curiosity about the city of Samarqand. The emperor took a keen interest in the maintenance of Timur's mausoleum. He wished to know the scholars who could be invited for literary discussions. He was thrilled at some wondrous events of Samarqand. The devotional practices at the shrine of Shaikh Nuruddin Baseer were as interesting as the magical inventions of Maulana Jalali. Somewhat amusing was the mode of smuggling liquor out of Samarqand. Mutribi's memoir enables us to comprehend the Mughal elite culture.

Mutribi's memoir was not the only text to engage with the phenomena of

6   *Introduction*

amazement. In India, this literary feature had a long past. During the pre-Mughal times, Amir Khusrau described the incredible feats of the Jogis, while Shams Siraj Afif highlighted the physical deformities among humans and animals. Abul Fazl, the official historian of Akbar's reign, noted the exceptional practices in Kangra, Malwa and Kamrup. A greater presence of the wondrous element was found in the writings of Shaikh Rizqullah Mushtaqi, Nuruddin Jahangir and Sujan Rai Bhandari (Chapter 10). Mushtaqi, in view of sheer numbers and length of his stories, has excelled all Persian chronicles. His tales underscored the distinction between the merits of genuine love and negativity of lustful passion. Some of his tales revolved around heinous crimes, while others pointed to the movement of graves. His accounts have devoted considerable space to women in a variety of roles. Jahangir, in spite of his scientific bent of mind, had faith in the miraculous powers of Sufis. Invocation of Sufis helped in hunting animals, whereas some Sufis predicted their own deaths. Jahangir availed every opportunity of noting the strange behaviour in birds, animals and reptiles. Bhandari has described the miracles of Shah Shamsuddin Dariayi, a Sufi of Batala. He has recorded rare happenings pertaining to the reigns of Akbar and Jahangir. More significantly, he has described numerous tricks that a group of magicians and acrobats, who had arrived from Bengal, performed at the Mughal court. Such references are helpful in understanding medieval mentalities.

For more than a millennium, South Asia has been a fertile ground for the growth of Islam. Gaining an early foothold on the western coast, it attained an indigenous character in the Indo-Gangetic plain. Modern scholarship has produced a large body of literature on the historical aspects of Islam (Chapter 11). Since the Chishti lineage created a vast network in northwestern India, pioneering studies engaged with the organization of hospices, training of disciples and recording of spiritual discourses. More recently, the transformation of the Chishtis has been carried forward to the colonial period, with reference to its two branches, the Nizamis and Sabiris. Research on Shaikh Ahmad Sirhindi, without restricting itself to his attitude to the state and religion, has recognized his contribution to the mystical thought. S.A.A. Rizvi, going beyond the Naqshbandis and Mahdawis, examined the role of Shah Waliullah and Shah Abdul Aziz, besides exploring the polemical writings of Shia ideologues. The major Sufi shrines at Pakpattan, Ajmer and Bahraich nurtured distinct rituals and, thus, fed into Islamic acculturation. In western Panjab and eastern Bengal, the process of Islamization proceeded alongside agrarian expansion. In Kashmir, the spread of Islam was connected to immigration from Central Asia and the efforts of the Rishi order. Today, we are better informed of the relations between the Sufis and state. Some Sufis were seen as competing with the rulers for their claims to authority. Akbar shifted his

Introduction

patronage from the Naqshbandis to Chishtis, though the contestation between the two orders continued. The seventeenth century witnessed the success of Sirhindi Naqshbandis in penetrating the Mughal royal household. Moreover, the Mughal kingship did not hesitate to claim spiritual authority in different ways.

Modern historiography on medieval Panjab has been largely restricted to accounts of the rise of the Sikhs. A critical examination of contemporary evidence points to a more complex past (Chapter 12). The medieval states faced sustained resistance from the tribes, such as the Jats, Khokhars, Mandahars, Bhattis and Minas. In the post-Timurid phase, Jasrath Khokhar overwhelmed the revenue assignees and pro-state landed gentry. In the first half of the sixteenth century, the Afghan State found it difficult to impose its authority on the Gakkhars, Niyazis, Balochis and Langahs. The Mughals won over the Gakkhars, but faced frequent revolts in the hill chiefdoms. The legendary lovers struggled against patriarchy and became immortal in folklore and Sufi discourses. The tradition of Jog, emanating from the monastery of Tilla Balnath, assimilated the stories of Puran Bhagat and Ranjha Jogi. Islamic spirituality, operating through a network of hospices (*khanqahs*) and shrines (*dargahs*), gained large followings. The Sikh movement, with its scripture and congregations, raised the status of depressed castes. Thus, the Panjabi culture has evolved around the pivot of resistance. Dulla Bhatti, who led a powerful revolt against Akbar, became a perennial symbol of resistance (Chapter 6). His struggle has been commemorated in Panjabi folklore, plays, musical features and films. In each of these genres, his revolt has been interpreted in different ways.

Regarding the eighteenth century, there have been contentious debates on the decline of the Mughal State, rise of the new powers and expansion of British colonialism. Two writers, the linguist Mirza Hasan Qatil and the poet Nazir Akbarabadi, have illuminated little known aspects of the north Indian society. The former, in a prose work, discussed the social structure of the Hindus and Muslims (Chapter 13). He showed that the Rajputs, owing to their obscure origin, were inferior to the Khatris. The Panjabi Khatris were culturally different from the Purabi Khatris. The Kayasthas commanded prestige due to their expertise in Persian and accounts. Among the elite Muslims (*ashraf*), four groups – Syeds, Mughals, Shaikhs and Afghans – received members from diverse social classes. Muslim mercantile communities were identified on the basis of their regions and goods traded. Social respectability of the Hindus was built on birth (*nasb*), while that of the Muslims was based on profession (*hasb*). The Muslims were claimed to be more scrupulous in adhering to the boundaries of social purity, which was reflected in the choice of avocations, formation of marital ties and seclusion of women.

8   *Introduction*

Since Muslims were preponderant in the ruling class, many Hindus imbibed Muslim cultural etiquettes. Nearly twenty heterodox sects, falling outside Hinduism, cultivated an interface with Islam. Popular cults had grown around the saintly figures of Shah Madar, Ghazi Miyan, Sultan Sarwar and Shaikh Saddu. Qatil's picture of social structure was completed in the Urdu verses of Nazir Akbarabadi (Chapter 14). Nazir celebrated religious diversity prevailing in the city of Agra. He has paid rich tributes to Prophet Muhammad and Hazrat Ali, besides narrating the biography of Krishna. He has showered fulsome praise on Ali bin Usman Hujweri, Guru Nanak and Shaikh Salim Chishti. He has described the popular fervour associated with Id ul-Fitr, Shab-i Barat, Diwali, Holi, Janmashtami and Baldev's carnival. For commoners, physical enjoyment was more meaningful than theological tenets. However, Nazir was anguished at the growing unemployment and resultant disparity between the rich and poor.

From the above discussion, it emerges that the medieval state was not merely a military machine, which coerced the peasantry into paying tributes and taxes. Instead, it engaged with the locally dominant elements in different ways. By distributing land grants to Muslim theologians and Sufis, the state created a class of loyal supporters and, thus, sought to overpower local chiefs and legitimize its authority. Many a times, it faced resistance from armed groups (largely tribes, chiefs and intermediaries), who possessed military resources and enjoyed traditional autonomy. In some cases, a symbiotic relation between the state and locality led to agrarian expansion and social change. The state, though monarchical, was not absolute. Writings on political theory, nurturing high expectations from the rulers, did not hesitate to criticize the state policy. The rulers showed devotion to Sufi lineages and tried to bring prominent shrines in the ambit of patronage. The members of lower orders, equipped with the knowledge of Persian and accounts, secured government jobs and, with experience, rose to be governors and ministers. The established aristocracy was alarmed at the social mobility of the plebeians. The cultural interface between India and Central Asia brought in immigrants as well as ideas. In respect of science and technology, improvements were noticed in various aspects of life. The Bhakti reformers, suspicious of power and wealth, sought to enlighten the masses through their teachings. The social structure, both among the Hindus and Muslims, was marked with vigorous contestations. The celebration of popular festivals, cutting across religious boundaries, displayed material concerns. The folk traditions commemorated legendry lovers and rebel warriors, besides portraying the rulers in poor light. The medieval realities, being complex and dynamic, retained a distinct interest for its modern students.

CHAPTER 1

Appointment of Government Officers in Medieval States: The Concerns of Nizam ul-Mulk Tusi and Ziauddin Barani

Nizam ul-Mulk Tusi (1018-1092) was a distinguished statesman of the Islamic world.[1] During the early part of his career, he served the Ghaznavids as the tax collector of Tus. Following the defeat of Sultan Masud (r. 1030-1041) and consequent Seljuqid occupation of Khurasan, he entered the service of the new masters. For thirty years, he served as the prime minister (*wazir*) of the Seljuqid empire during the reigns of Alp Arsalan (r. 1063-72) and Malik Shah (r. 1072-92). At this time, the Seljuqid territories extended from the borders of Afghanistan to the shores of the Mediterranean Sea.[2] Tusi, as head of the administration, attained great authority and prestige. Towards the end of his life, he wrote the *Siyasatnama* at the instance of Malik Shah, who looked for advice on improving the state of his government and conditions of the people. A century and half after the appearance of this treatise, Ziauddin Barani, the most prominent chronicler of the Delhi Sultanate, produced two major works. In his *Tarikh-i Firoz Shahi*, he covered the political history from the reign of Ghiasuddin Balban to the early years of the rule of Firoz Shah Tughluq. In his *Fatawa-i Jahandari*, he laid down advice on the modes of governance. Tusi and Barani, though placed in different socio-political contexts, dealt with common ground of state power relating to justice, army and bureaucracy. Since both associated the state with orthodox Sunni Islam, they were disturbed at the existence of numerous sects falling outside the narrow religious groove. What is equally important, both were

10 *Situating Medieval India*

deeply concerned with the social background of government functionaries. In the following pages, an attempt is being to examine
their views on this important aspect of political power.

Tusi, in his *Siyasatnama*, holds up as an ideal the practice of the
Samanid and especially the Ghaznavid realm, where he started his
bureaucratic career. His work was composed at the end of his career
when he was beginning to lose Sultan Malik Shah's confidence.
He has made barely disguised attacks on his rivals, particularly his
archenemy in the bureaucracy Taj ul-Mulk and the latter's patron
Terken Khatun, Malik Shah's wife. He accused these enemies of
secret adherence to Ismailism, providing examples of the dangers.
The treatise was an attempt of the author to save his position in
the Seljuqid court and, to attain this aim, he discredited his enemies
and showed how only he could solve the growing administrative
and fiscal problems in the empire. The book was far from being a
simple administrative handbook. Its prescriptions were often better
evidence of what the Seljuqid practice was not, rather than what it
was. Instead of highlighting the success of the Persian bureaucrats
at acculturating the Seljuqids to their norms, the work was a testimony to their limitations.[3]

To begin with, Tusi saw appointments from the angle of efficient
work, without going into the professional and social qualifications.
In his view, enlightened kings and clever ministers never gave two
appointments to one man or one appointment to two men. As a
result, their affairs were conducted with efficiency and lustre. When
one man was given two appointments, he performed one of the
tasks with diligence and the other was spoiled and neglected. Since
he channelized his attention on either of the two, one of them was
damaged and ended in failure. Usually, the man failed in both
and, as a result, constantly suffered criticism and complaint from
his dissatisfied manager. When two men were given a single post,
each tended to shift his responsibility to the other, so that the work
remained forever undone. According to a proverb, 'The house with
two mistresses remains unswept; with two masters it falls into ruins.'
Each felt that if he took pains to do the work expediently, the master
would think that it was due to the capability and skill of his partner,
not to his own diligence and patient efforts. Since the other one

Appointment of Government Officers in Medieval States   11

had the same idea, there would be constant confusion in the work. When the manager, sought to know the cause of this inattention and inefficiency, the man would excuse himself and put the blame on the other. If one went into the root of the matter and reflected with keen intelligence, the fault did not lie with either of them. Instead, it lay with the superior authority, who gave one appointment to two persons.[4]

Tusi has drawn attention to another aspect of the problem. He was aware of cases, where one officer was given more than two posts. The number of offices could go up to three or five or seven. When the head of the ministry (*diwan*) made such appointments, it was a sign of the incompetence of the *wazir* and negligence of the king. During his days, Tusi saw men, utterly incapable, holding as many as ten posts. Their appetite for grabbing an increasing quantum of authority did not have any limit. If still another appointment turned up, they applied for it and, giving bribes if necessary, got it. Nobody cared to consider their worthiness for that post or possessed any ability whatsoever. No attempt was made to determine if they understood secretaryship, administration and business dealings. No effort was made to find if they could perform the numerous tasks they had already accepted. No one had the imagination and discernment to enquire why one person, who was unknown, incapable, lowborn and ignorant, should hold so many posts. All the time, there were men, who were capable, earnest, deserving, trustworthy and experienced, sitting idle at home. These noble and trusted men, who had no work at all, were left deprived and excluded. To these men, the present dynasty (Seljuqids) was greatly indebted for their satisfactory and meritorious services.[5] It meant that the state had employed them in the past and, for unstated reasons, they had been removed. Tusi, referring to the professional competence and moral qualities of the government functionaries, opposed the appointment of lowborn men. Unlike Barani, he refrained from discussing the adverse impact of such employees on the government and people.

Tusi was unhappy with the contemporary lack of concern with the religious affiliation of the officers. In the previous ages, a government post was given to the man of the same religion and same rite,

12   *Situating Medieval India*

as he was pure in both religion and origin. If he refused to accept it, the state coerced him to accept the responsibility. A positive impact was manifested in the political system and social fabric. The land revenue was not misappropriated, the peasants were unmolested and the assignees enjoyed a good reputation and safe existence. At the same time, the king lived a life of mental peace and physical ease. During the reigns of the previous rulers—Mahmud, Masud, Tughril and Alp Arsalan—no Zoroastrian, Christian or Rafizi (Shia) would have dared to appear in a public place or to present himself before a Turk for a job. Those who administered the affairs of the Turks were professional civil servants and secretaries from Khurasan, who were orthodox Sunnis following the Hanafi or Shafi schools of jurisprudence.[6] The Turks never allowed the heretics of Iraq to work as secretaries and tax collectors. In fact, the Turks never employed them at all. These men, in their religious affiliation, were seen as similar to the Dailamites and their supporters.[7] It was feared that if they established a firm footing, they would injure the interests of the Turks and cause distress to the Muslims. The Turks, perceiving them as enemies, thought it better to keep them out of their midst. Owing to this precaution, the Turks lived free from disaster.

Tusi, while approving the Turkish preference for Khurasani Sunnis and their aversion to the Iraqi Shias, felt disturbed at the change in this situation. In his times, all distinctions had vanished. It became possible for a Jew to administer the affairs of Turks. The same was applicable to religious sects such as the Zoroastrians, Rafizis, Kharijis and Qarmatis. This indifference was becoming dominant everywhere. Things had reached a state where the court and secretariat were full of them. Every Turk had two hundred of such individuals after him and their object was to prevent any Khurasanis from entering the service of the Seljuqid court and earning a livelihood here. The opening of state services, in the eyes of Tusi, had an adverse impact. There was no zeal for religion, no concern for the revenue and no pity for the peasants. Tusi, afraid of the evil eye, shuddered to imagine the end result of the sad state of affairs. Sure of his stance, he declared that the Turks, one day, would realize the injustice ingrained in the change and would recall his warning

Appointment of Government Officers in Medieval States 13

when the secretariat became empty of Khurasanis.[8] Thus, we find that Tusi was anguished at dwindling number of Khurasani Sunnis and increasing presence of non-Sunnis and non-Muslims from other areas. He was less worried about the lowborn, which was Barani's main worry.

Tusi approved the situation in the former times when the Turks paid due attention to the socio-religious identity of job seekers. If a man appeared before a Turk for one of the jobs—an administrator, cleaner or stirrup holder—he was questioned about his province, city and religion. If he stated that he was of the Hanafi or Shafi persuasion and hailed from Khurasan, Transoxiana or a Sunni city, he was taken into service. If he said that he was a Shia from Qom, Kashan, Aba or Ray, he was rejected and told to go away. Even if money and presents were offered, the Turk did not relent. The latter asked the candidate to take the gifts back to his own house and use them on himself. Not only this, the Turks claimed that they preferred to kill the snakes and had no inclination to nourish them. If Sultan Tughril and Sultan Alp Arsalan heard that a Turk or noble had admitted a Rafizi into his presence, they became angry and reprimanded him for the error. Once Sultan Alp Arsalan castigated Ardam for attempting to appoint Dihkhuda Abaji as his secretary. Since Abaji happened to be a Batini, the Sultan declared him as an enemy. Ardam stated that Abaji, even if he turned into pure venom, could not harm the empire. The Sultan, summoning Abaji to his court, accused him of being a Batini, as he did not accept the legality of the Caliph of Baghdad. Abaji submitted that he was not a Batini, but a Shia. The Sultan, holding that one was bad and the other worse, had him thrown out of the palace after a severe beating. The Sultan availed himself of the opportunity to explain the rationale of his rage and action. This statement was significant because, two centuries later, Balban reacted in the same manner at the recommendations for Fakhr Bauni and Kamal Mahiyar.

Since the Batinis were regarded as worse than the Rafizis,[9] a king was advised to wipe them out from the face of the earth and free the country of them. Similarly, he was forbidden from employing Jews, Christians and Zoroastrians, who could not be placed over the Muslims. Tusi, in support of this advice, offered two instances

14 *Situating Medieval India*

from the rule of the second caliph Umar bin al-Khattab. Once, Abu Musa Ashari presented the accounts of Isfahan before Umar. Every one admired the fair handwriting of the papers. Umar learnt that the writer was Ashari's Christian secretary. Umar dismissed the secretary and, quoting a Quranic verse (5: 56) forbidding friendly relations with Christians and Jews,[10] delivered a hard blow on Ashari's thigh.[11] Under the governorship of the Arab general Saad Waqqas over the area of Baghdad, Wasit and Anbar upto Basra and Khuzistan, the tax collector was a Jew. The people of these districts, in a petition to Umar, complained against excessive oppression. They demanded the appointment of a Muslim tax collector as, being of the same religion, he would not oppress them. Even if he did so, they would suffer injustice from a Muslim than from a Jew. Umar ordered Waqqas to make the change. Waqqas summoned all Muslim tax collectors, both Arab and Persian, serving in Iran. He discovered that none of them matched the ability of the Jew in various aspects of work including collecting revenue, developing the country, dealing with people and keeping up with taxes and arrears. Waqqas, informing Umar of the exercise, admitted the compulsion of retaining the Jew, lest the tax collection should break down. Umar, in his anger, wrote that the Jew's death would necessitate a new appointee and none was indispensable. Waqqas replaced the Jew with a Muslim, who was found to be more efficient, even as the public works progressed. Umar's action became a precedent, which was employed to dismiss an officer, who was able and competent, but who was extortionate, unjust or a heretic.[12]

Sultan Alp Arsalan declared that the fault did not lie with Abaji. Rather, it lay with Ardam, who had taken an infidel in his service. The Turks, who were foreigners to Khurasan and Transoxiana, had conquered the country by the sword. The achievement of the Turks was attributable to the fact that they were pure and orthodox Muslims, who did not tolerate vanity and heresy. They had an ancient enmity with the Dailamites and Iraqis because of their heresy and false religion. So long as they were weak, they would remain in submission and obedience. Once they attained power and fortunes of the Turks declined, they would wipe out the Turks both for religious and political reasons. It would be foolish for the Turks to be ignorant

Appointment of Government Officers in Medieval States 15

of their friends and enemies. When Ardam was given a few strands of horse hair, he broke them easily. When these were twisted into a rope, he could not break it. It was the case with enemies. In ones or twos or fives, they could be easily eliminated. If they became numerous and combined, they could not be rooted out. If they infiltrated the Turks one by one and were allowed to administer their business and know their affairs, they would try to destroy the Turks when a revolt broke out in Iraq or the Dailamites attacked the country. For the Turks, all administrators, secretaries and officers must be Khurasanis. The king, unlike individual Turks, was bound to be vigilant and thus protected his people. Anyone, who became friendly with the king's enemies, was himself an enemy of the king.[13]

Tusi was strongly opposed to the reduction in the number of public servants, both civil and military. Sometimes, more than one post was given to an individual or the number of soldiers was brought down. This was done to curtail the expenditure on salaries and replenish the state coffers. These measures were harmful and shortsighted, as they led to unemployment, resentment and instability. An increase in the numerical strength of the army led to an expansion in the size of the empire. If the number of soldiers increased from 400,000 to 700,000, it would be possible to occupy the lands up to Rum (modern-day Turkey) and North Africa in the west and up to India and China in the east. A *wazir*, who did not adhere to this principle was ignorant and incompetent, besides being an enemy of the king. In this regard, Tusi has drawn attention to senior officers, who had performed great tasks for the empire and earned considerable fame. Since they had been deprived of their positions, they were ruined, disappointed and dispossessed. In addition, another body of men—doctors, scholars, noblemen and men of valour—had claims on the state treasury. If their case were not placed before the king and they continued to be deprived of their salaries, they would become disaffected towards the government. In frustration, they would expose the weakness of the administration and, getting hold of troops and funds, would revolt against the king and cause disturbance in the country. Such a possibility appeared in the city of Ray during the reign of Fakhr

16 *Situating Medieval India*

ud-Daula. Every day a group of thirty or forty men assembled on the top of a tower, which was originally built for fire worshippers. The Sultan, receiving reports of their suspicious activities, carried out an investigation. It was discovered that they were a group of unemployed officers, who had been deprived of their jobs and pay. Reduced to poverty, they were exploring avenues of migrating to Khurasan, where Sultan Mahmud welcomed men of merit, learning and talent. At the instance of Fakhr ud-Daula, the minister Sahib Ismail bin Abbad gave to these men appointments along with horses, clothes and expenses. Wherever he found a man holding two posts, he relieved him of one and gave it to the seniors.[14]

Tusi treated the *wazir* as the pivot around which the polity revolved. On the one hand, he advised the king and framed administrative policies. On the other hand, he supervised the work of tax collectors. As head of the tax collectors and civil servants, he kept the kingdom in order. When the *wazir* was corrupt, treacherous, oppressive and unjust, the tax men would be similar to him and even worse.[15] A good *wazir* enhanced the fame and character of the king. The kings, who had become great rulers, enjoyed the services of good *wazirs*. In the history of powerful states—pre-Islamic Persia, Abbasid caliphate and Sejuqids—the kings were remembered in association with their *wazirs*. Tusi, after listing more than a dozen pairs, laid down the qualifications of a *wazir*. First, the *wazir* must be a man of sound faith and adhere to a good doctrinal school like the Hanafi and Shafi. Second, he must be efficient, shrewd, a fluent writer and loyal to the king. Third, it was better if he was the son of a *wazir*. This practice prevailed in Iran until the coming of Islam. The caliph Sulaiman bin Abdul Malik, in a meeting with his nobles, was adviced to have a distinguished man as his *wazir*. The candidate suggested was Jafar bin Barmak. Since the time of Ardashir Papakan, Jafar's ancestors had been *wazirs* and sons of *wazirs*. When the Iranian dynasty was displaced with the spread of Islam, Jafar's ancestors settled at Balkh. As the office was hereditary in the family, they possessed books on the duties and functions of the *wazir*. When their children learnt literature, writing and secretary-ship, they were given these books to read, learn and follow. The

Appointment of Government Officers in Medieval States 17

sons imbibed the character of their fathers in all respects. Therefore, Jafar was the most suitable man in the world to be the caliph's *wazir*.[16]

Let us turn to the Delhi Sultanate. During the early years of his reign, Ghiasuddin Balban (r. 1266-1286) took a number of measures to increase the prestige of kingship, amplify the splendour of the court and stabilize the government. Recruiting thousands of horsemen and foot soldiers, he placed them under experienced nobles. For multifarious duties in the court, he appointed a large number of dignitaries, helpers and supporters. In this regard, he laid three categories of qualifications—moral, professional and social. The appointees stood out for wisdom, competence and obedience. They were free from greed, meanness and miserliness. What was most important, they belonged to superior social classes. Throughout his reign, he did not allow worthless, mean and lowborn to hold any governmental post. In fact, he did not allow such people to come anywhere near the court. It became impossible for a person to get an appointment till his social antecedents were thoroughly known. By temperament, he was strongly opposed to the rise of the base and mean.[17] Barani has come out strongly in favour of Balban's sectarian attitude in matters of state.

Balban's aversion to the lowborn came to the forefront in the cases of Fakhr Bauni and Kamal Mahiyar. Fakhr Bauni, the chief of merchants (*amir bazariyan*), was a rich man. He wished to speak to Balban probably in connection with a matter relating to trade. In the hope of having a conversation with the Sultan, he gave valuable gifts to officers and courtiers. For many years, these people kept conveying his request to the Sultan. However, the Sultan refused to give his consent for a meeting and availed himself of the opportunity of explaining his stance. He placed Fakhr Bauni among ordinary people such as soldiers, shopkeepers, jesters and other lowly individuals. If the Sultan interacted with them, it would impair the majesty of the kingdom and lowered his dignity. His commands were obeyed only through terror. Kingship, being the vicegerency of God, could not exist with any weakness. A king, who had attained his position in heredity, did not feel the need to display his terror. In the absence of heredity, it was essential for

18   *Situating Medieval India*

him to possess prestige and terror. Otherwise, the Hindus became disobedient, Muslims indulged in immorality and religion was disregarded. Balban warned the chamberlain (*barbak*) Alauddin Kishli Khan to refrain from recommending Fakhr Bauni for a meeting, as it would undermine the prestige of kingship. Barani has put these words in the mouth of Balban who, in turn, has attributed these to the companions of his patron, Shamsuddin Iltutmish (r. 1210-1236).[18]

Barani heard the case of Kamal Mahiyar from Tajuddin Makrani,[19] an experienced accountant (*khwaja*), who was close to Balban. The Sultan, having appointed Amir Ali Sarjandar as assignee of Amroha, asked the nobles to suggest a person, who belonged to a good family and possessed the requisite experience, for appointment as accountant of the place. Alauddin Kishli Khan (*amir-i hajib*) and Nizamuddin Bazghala, the incharge of royal household (*vakil-i dar*) suggested the name of Kamal Mahiyar. On enquiry, it was found that Mahiyar was the name of his father and that he had been the slave of a Hindu. On hearing this, Balban became angry and withdrew into his privacy. In addition to the above nobles, he summoned Adil Khan Shamsi Ajami, Tamar Khan, Fakhruddin Kotwal, the army minister Imad ul-Mulk and special chamberlain Isami. Expressing strong displeasure at the recommendation of a lowborn and worthless son of a slave on grounds of his expertise in clerkship (*mard-i hunarmand wa nawisindah kardan*), the Sultan elaborated his stance. The nobles, who had served with him, knew that he had descended from Afrasiyab (the legendary ruler of pre-Islamic Persia). Owing to his noble descent, he was divinely endowed with a specific trait (*khasiyat-i afrida*). He did not tolerate base, lowborn and worthless persons to hold any position of authority. His veins shook on seeing such a person. If the nobles recommended a lowborn person for any government post (revenue assignee, accountant, auditor and intelligence officer) he would respond in an exemplary manner. He did not care if such a candidate possessed a thousand skills. During the lifetime of Balban, the officers and courtiers did not recommend any lowborn person for any post. Balban, in an attempt to seek validity for his views, argued that he had followed the footsteps of his patron Iltutmish.[20]

Appointment of Government Officers in Medieval States 19

During the reign of Iltutmish, Prince Nasiruddin was granted the revenue assignment of Qanauj, while Khwaja Bahroz was named his deputy. Nizam ul-Mulk Junaidi, the *wazir*, proposed the name of Jamaluddin Marzuq as the accountant of Qanauj. Bahroz, referring to Marzuq, asserted the impropriety of giving a pen in the hands of the lowborn. Such an act was as abominable as turning the black stone of Kaaba for the purpose of cleaning. The Sultan, accepting the intervention, asked Junaidi to reveal the origin of Marzuq. It was learnt that Marzuq hailed from an inferior social background. Junaidi, reiterating his recommendation, stated that Marzuq was not only competent and intelligent, he also possessed a good handwriting. The Sultan, annoyed with Junaidi, decreed that the appointment of the lowborn people with skills brought the government into disrepute. Refusing to conduct any business, the Sultan ordered an enquiry into the number of lowborn persons holding offices of accountant, auditor and news writer. Following investigation, it was found that 33 persons belonged to this category. The submission of a list led to their immediate dismissal. The matter did not end there. Two nobles, Aizzuddin Salari (*barbak*) and Qutbuddin Hasan Ghori (*vakil-i dar*) demanded that the antecedents of Junaidi be probed. Unless there were traces of low origin in him, he would not have appointed lowborn people to official posts. It was assumed that a dignitary of noble birth and high extraction would oppose the recruitment of lowborn persons even in the army. It followed that such nobles would also disapprove lowborn candidates for non-military positions. Rigorous investigation revealed that Junaidi had descended from the weavers. He was not only disgraced for giving offices to lowborn persons, he himself came to be reviled as a weaver. Balban, having descended from Afrasiyab, would never allow lowborn persons to hold official posts, lest his own low lineage was confirmed.[21] If we go by Barani, Balban, on becoming the Sultan, worried about his low origin. Lest he should pay a political price for it, he expressed his disdain for the lowborn and, by doing so, he was able to claim a high birth for himself.

Balban, having excluded the lowborn from his polity, urged his son Sultan Muhammad to follow the suit. During their last meeting,

20 *Situating Medieval India*

Balban delivered a comprehensive political sermon to the Prince. He regarded his thoughts as so important that he asked the Prince to note them on paper. The advice was of two kinds. The first comprised of the counsels he had heard from the nobles of Iltutmish. It was nearly impossible to follow them. The second comprised counsels that people like themselves followed and, in return, attained an exalted position.[22] In this category, one of the exhortations focused on their attitude to different social classes. Since kingship was the deputyship of God, a ruler, in public and private, was bound to maintain the prestige of kingship and dignity of his person. In pursuit of this objective, he interacted with people who were highborn, wise, pious, loyal, grateful, brave and talented. He must confine his patronage and kindness only to these people. As a reward, his credibility would rise in this world and he would be spared of repentance in the hereafter. In no case should he fraternize with the lowborn, cruel, corrupt, uncultured, ungrateful and impious. Patronage of these people yielded dishonour in this world and punishment in the hereafter. By favouring these people, he would impair his own virtues. Such people did not bring any credit to their master and, instead, they brought ignominy and remorse. If such a person did something for the ruler, he might be favoured in proportion to his service. In no case should he be made a friend and supporter. If the king gave high offices to the lowborn and raised them to prominence, he would only earn God's anger and annoyance. Promotion of the lowborn and their progeny undermined royal prestige and administrative authority. The progress of state power lay in subjecting this group to hatred. Once the king kept it way from the court, he could hope for esteem in this world and salvation in the next.[23]

Barani's account of the case of Kamal Mahiyar has not been accepted at its face value. According to Irfan Habib, Barani's addiction to the principle of birth did not derive from any theory of blue blood. It derived from a craving of security and stability for those, who were already 'in possession'. After 1236, Iltutmish's Turkish slaves established their supremacy by overthrowing the free nobility. As the upstarts rooted their authority and one of them (Balban) became the Sultan, Barani perforce accepted their claims to high birth,

Appointment of Government Officers in Medieval States 21

though established merely with the passage of time. Now, the highest nobles were those who had been fellow slaves (*khwajatashan*) of the Sultan.[24] Sunil Kumar, in an incisive analysis, holds that Barani's account of the case of Kamal Mahiyar, from the rejection of his appointment to the dismissal of Junaidi, was didactic. He shows that Balban's dispensation was composed of diverse elements. His slaves (*bandagan*) occupied a privileged place, as they were deployed as governors, military commanders and figured in the central contingent at Delhi. He employed newly purchased slaves as domestics and pages at the court. A majority of Shamsi slaves were dead, though the surviving ones continued to hold important positions under Balban. If they had aspired for association with kingship, they had to pass the test of loyalty to Balban. After the death of his old allies, Balban appointed their sons in the same posts. He also extended his patronage to non-slaves, particularly social menials such as Afghans, Sistanis, Khaljis and Mongols. With no claims to aristocratic lineage, they were entirely dependent on the Sultan. Thus, Kamal Mahiyar was rejected not because of his low origin as the son of a slave (*maulazadah*). The recommendation for his appointment as the financial administrator of Amroha was based on his skills in Persian, mathematics and accountancy. He was rejected because he had not earned Balban's support and protection. This qualification was necessary for all aspirants to governmental posts, irrespective of their social background. Throughout his reign, Balban showed no hesitation in employing plebeian elements. The sons of slaves, though excluded from the privileged slave cadre, networked their way to attention and emerged as great Maliks with large garrisons in Kaiqubad's reign.[25]

Barani, as a historian, compromised his position due to two reasons. First, he remained ardently committed to the interests of the class of old aristocracy to which he belonged. Second, he repeated his contempt for the lowborn (which prominently figured in his *Tarikh-i Firoz Shahi*) in his work on political theory entitled, *Fatawa-i Jahandari*. In this treatise,[26] he began his argument with the admission that all humans were created equal and, therefore, they were similar in form and appearance. The differences among them arose due to the effect of their character and consequences of

22 *Situating Medieval India*

their actions. At the beginning of time, merits and demerits were apportioned to them. The divine command determined their actions. God endowed them with the faculty to give expression to their goodness or wickedness. Since the first generation of the children of Adam, humans grew in numbers and inhabited the world. They needed everything for the sake of existence. God instilled human minds with the arts they needed. Some minds were inspired with different arts—horsemanship, weaving, smith craft, hair cutting and tanning—in accordance with their basic nature. The quality of minds determined the quality of arts. The aptitude for arts, whether fine or coarse, was hereditary. The descendents received a particular art from their ancestors. In every generation, the descendents, in accordance with their quickness of intelligence and acuteness of mind, added something to their legacy, so that the product attained perfection. Barani divided humankind into two broad categories. The highborn, who adopted nobler professions, possessed numerous virtues including kindness, loyalty, justice, equality, recognition of rights, protection of other classes, gratitude for favour and fear of God. The lowborn, practicing baser arts and meaner professions, were capable of vices including immodesty, falsehood, miserliness, misappropriation, wrongfulness, lies, ingratitude, injustice, cruelty, dirtiness, shamelessness, impudence, blood shedding and Godlessness. Dirty by birth, the lowborn included the bazaar people, base, mean, worthless, plebeian and shameless.[27]

Barani asserted that the king, while making appointments, should not deviate from the wisdom of creation. He was advised to adorn government offices with the highborn, who possessed virtuous behaviour and good actions. Because of the just dealings of these officers, the king could hope for good reputation in this world and salvation in the next. The appointment of the lowborn, owing to their meanness and wickedness ingrained in them and developed through heredity, resulted in a variety of losses. The people were distressed and scattered, while the government failed to achieve its objectives. The king was disgraced in this world and faced punishment on the day of judgement. He had to refrain from placing the people of God under their command. He must not let them come

Appointment of Government Officers in Medieval States   23

near his administrative and religious offices. He should not be captivated by their intelligence and agility, as their excellences were imitative and not real. Barani, while linking the highborn and lowborn with opposite qualities, has garnered support from the Quran and Prophetic traditions. Further, a majority of ancient and modern thinkers, relying on observation and experience, had declared that the lowborn officers had failed to properly perform the great administrative duties. If a lowborn man became a ruler, he had striven, as far as he could, to elevate the lowborn and overthrow the highborn. The work of the lowborn did not produce beneficial results. They were incapable of showing loyalty in any contingency. In cases where the rulers were captivated by flattery, agility, outward jugglery of the lowborn and made them their colleagues and confidential officers, they had suffered in both the worlds and failed to diminish their repentance during all eternity. If the lowborn, including the bazaar people and cowards, were established in high offices and succeeded in their work, they associated their own kind in the consultation and administration. They would make the lowest and meanest their partners and intimates, assigning a part of their authority to them. Owing to the promotion of one lowborn, many of their kind would get offices and honour. On the other hand, the highborn would be overthrown, disgraced and persecuted.[28]

In order to confer respectability on his abhorrence for the lowborn, Barani has dug out a incident from the Ghaznavid State. Once, a group of 50 or 60 women, all in a pitiable condition, appeared before Sultan Mahmud. They complained against the *wazir* Abdul Abbas Isfraini, who was alleged to have wrongfully locked their sons, brothers and husbands in the prison of the revenue ministry (*diwan-i wizarat*). The Sultan, disturbed at the complaint, held an assembly (*mahzar*) in which the women repeated their allegation in the presence of Isfraini. At his suggestion, the male relatives were produced in the assembly. The accused, who were all revenue officers, confessed their gross irregularities. Isfraini had not done any injustice to them as they had duly received their salaries. Instead, each of them owed sums ranging from fifty to seventy thousand. Apart from consumption and pleasure, they had

24 *Situating Medieval India*

used the money in false display, so that they could make the highborn give their daughters in marriage to them. At Isfraini's request, an investigation was done into the origin of the culprits. It was revealed that they were the sons of tavern keepers, butchers and weavers. Isfraini, who had been deceived by their cleverness and efficiency, admitted that he had not been cautious about their origin and birth. He agreed to pay a fine for his fault, while the Sultan took steps to undo the damage. Though the officers were set free, they were directed to submit a deed promising that they would never come near the ministry of revenue, that they would devote themselves to agriculture and that they would spend the rest of their lives as villagers.[29] Barani, owing to his deep rooted contempt for mercantile and artisanal work, believed that people should cease to follow these professions, as they were intrinsically bad.

Barani's observations on the Ghaznavid State did stand before the evidence on the career of Tilak. This prominent Ghaznavid general performed distinguished service for the kingdom. The son of a barber, he was handsome in appearance and eloquent in speech. He wrote an excellent hand, both in Hindi and Persian. For a long time, he lived in Kashmir, where he attained proficiency in disguise, eroticism and witchcraft. He served under Qazi Shirazi, the Ghaznavid civil administrator at Lahore. He gained proximity with the *wazir* Hasan Maimandi and, becoming his secretary, handled correspondence and difficult matters. He entered the good books of Sultan Mahmud (r. 999-1030), who attached him as an interpreter with Prince Bahram. During the reign of Sultan Masud (r. 1030-41), Tilak brought the Hindu chiefs under the Ghaznavid rule. He was promoted as the commander of an army and granted a golden robe and jewelled dagger, besides a tent and umbrella. In accordance with the custom of Hindu chiefs, kettledrums were beaten at his abode, while gilded tops ornamented his banners. He sat amidst nobles in the privy council and conducted administrative duties. Baihaqi has argued that Tilak did not suffer any setback on account of his being the son of a barber. If, with his character and wisdom, he had been gifted with a good social background, he would have risen still further in the bureaucratic

Appointment of Government Officers in Medieval States 25

structure.[30] During the revolt of Ahmad Niyaltigin in Panjab, Tilak volunteered to lead the punitive expedition, while other nobles developed cold feet. He was regarded as fit for the job, as he could wield the sword and possessed men and material. The Sultan approved his plan for the campaign and issued documents regarding his appointment, authority and privileges. Reaching Lahore, he separated the Jats from Niyaltigin, who was defeated and killed.[31] With his competent generalship and astute management, he saved the Ghaznavid State from a major crisis.

Drawing on the Quran and Prophetic traditions, Barani argued that the orders of the king had been placed on the same pedestal as those of God and Prophet Muhammad. Moreover, a king was answerable about the state of his people (*raiyyat*) on the day of judgement. On his own, a king could not discharge his onerous duties of conducting the government in accordance with the Shariat. It was necessary for him to delegate the administrative work among helpers, supporters and partisans. He assigned the official positions to governors and nobles, who were closest to him. The strangers, owing to their doubtful loyalty and lack of concern for state business, were ruled out. The same was true of the lowborn as, owing to their ignoble qualities, they were unable to accomplish the state enterprises. As a result, the affairs of state and religion fell into disorder. Though they enjoyed the privileges of authority, the king was answerable for their misdeeds to God. If the supporters of the king were highborn, their virtuous character produced praiseworthy results. On the day of judgement, the king would have no difficulty in answering questions on the welfare of his subjects. Such a king would acquit himself better than the Sufis, who would be unable to answer for themselves. If the kings suffered in matters of state and religion, it was due to his bad supporters. Some rulers, in the intoxication of power, were blinded by the sincerity and loyalty of the lowborn. Even if the king was given to vices and his supporters were men of high extraction, the work of administration retained stability and order. Barani has attributed the long rule of Persian kings (Kisras) from Kaimurs to Khusrau Parvez to the exclusion of the lowborn from the state offices.[32]

Barani, while discussing the market regulations of Alauddin

26 *Situating Medieval India*

Khalji, betrayed his aversion for the class of merchants. In the *Tarikh-i Firoz Shahi*, he noted that the cruel officers subjected the merchants to beating, imprisonment, chaining and cutting of flesh. The harshness was justified because the bazaar people were shameless, impudent, deceitful, foolish and liars. It was easier to cut distant jungles and suppress distant rebels than bring the merchants to obedience.[33] In the *Fatawa-i Jahandari*, he adopted a similar attitude against the merchants. The government, while enforcing price regulations, should not allow the shopkeepers, grocers, artisans and other 'shameless' people to tyrannize over the hapless masses. They resorted to strange ways of business, knavery, rough handling, impudence and shamelessness. They were found selling glass beads at the price of diamonds. Regrating, which was the profession of Hindus, Magians, infidels and polytheists, was a social sin, which the kings must suppress. If the prices of grain and other means of livelihood were cheap, every group, class, caste and community devoted itself to its own specific work, craft, art and profession, leading to stability of the government and improvement in administration. If profit was seen in regrating, people discarded their own professions by a natural instinct. Soldiers took to agriculture; cultivators took to trade; regraters, owing to the influence of their wealth, extended their hands to high posts; shopkeepers tried to become officers; men of noble birth became merchants; transport merchants aspired to become government officers and army commanders. In other words, the evil of regrating engendered political instability and social disorder.[34]

Barani has castigated Alauddin Khalji for appointing Hamiduddin Multani, the chief of merchants (*malik ut-tujjar*), as the chief judge of the Delhi Sultanate. Prior to him, distinguished persons—Qazi Sadruddin Arif, Qazi Jalaluddin Walwalji and Maulana Ziauddin—held this office because of their learning, lineage and piety. Multani did not bear these qualities. He had served in the royal palace as a domestic servant, holding charge of the curtains and keys. The Sultan took into account his long service and that of his father. Multani appeared to possess knowledge, but this was not enough. The essential qualification was piety (*taqwa*), which meant withdrawal from the world and abstaining from sins

Appointment of Government Officers in Medieval States   27

(*shart qaza ilm mujarrad nest balkeh az lawazim shart qaza taqwa ast*). A king could not hope for salvation until he assigned the chief judgeship to the most pious scholar of the kingdom (*ba mutaqi tarin ulama-i bilad mamalik khud*). If the king did not regard piety as essential condition for this exalted post and, instead, assigned it to the greedy, irreligious and worldly, he undermined his status as the protector of faith. This appointment of the Sultan became a precedent, so that the condition of piety was entirely dropped.[35] Barani would have us believe that he was not the only one to raise the objection. Maulana Shamsuddin Turk, an Egyptian scholar of Prophetic traditions, who had arrived in Multan to explore the possibility of settling in Delhi, wrote a letter to the Sultan.[36] He praised the Sultan for humiliating the Hindus, lowering the prices of grains and other goods, checking the irregularities of merchants and suppressing immoral practices. However, he censured the Sultan for appointing an unworthy person like Multani as the chief judge. Owing to the negligence of Multani, who was a confidant of the Sultan, the theologians of Delhi issued dubious legal opinions and, thus, violated the rights of Muslims. Bahauddin Dabir concealed this letter from the Sultan due to the fear of Multani. The Sultan, learning of the letter from Saad Mantaqi, wished to punish Dabir for his misconduct.[37]

Barani's reference to the lowborn officers serving Muhammad bin Tughluq (r. 1325-51) was made in the context of disturbances in western India and the Sultan's personal contradictions. Barani disapproved the recall of Qutlugh Khan from Deogiri, the division of the Maratha land into four districts and the fixation of a new revenue estimate. He was equally critical of the appointment of Aziz Khammar as the governor of Malwa and his killing of eighty centurion nobles (*amiran-i sadah*), leading to the spread of disaffection among this particular class of bureaucrats. A large part of Barani's disdain for Aziz Khammar was clearly attributable to the governor's lowly social origin. Not attempting to conceal it, Barani exposed the Sultan's conflicting attitude in the matter. According to him, the Sultan often expressed his contempt for the people, who were lowborn, ignoble, uncouth, faithless, wicked and ill-mannered. The Sultan appeared to hold the lowborn as a

28 *Situating Medieval India*

greater enemy than the idols. Yet, he had appointed numerous lowborn persons to high posts.[38] Barani was so full of scorn for them that he refrained from giving their formal names. In order to ridicule them, he mentioned their menial castes along with only half of their names. He has deliberately ignored their education and experience. Evidently, these officers could not boast of an illustrious pedigree. Barani made no attempt to find out the facts about their fathers, grandfathers and uncles. This did not mean that they were illiterate and unmeritorious. They must have been learned and competent. On the basis of their professional credentials, they must have served at the lower and middle rungs of the administration. While rising from the ranks, they must have given enough proof of their abilities and trustworthiness before earning promotion to high posts. Barani's contempt for the lowborn became even more galling when compared with his respectful references to nobles hailing from elite backgrounds.

Najba, the son of a lowly musician (*mutrib bacha bad asl*), was assigned Gujarat, Multan and Badaun and, as a result, his status was raised higher than that of all the nobles. In the same manner, numerous lowly persons—Aziz Khammar and his brother, Firoz the barber, Manka the cook, Masud the distiller, Ladha the gardener and many others, who really were gems among the lowborn (*jawahar-i latrah*), were entrusted with high offices and corresponding assignments. The Sultan elevated the rank of the ignoble and base Shaikh Babu Naik, the son of a weaver and, thus, made him a close confidant. Pira the gardener, who was the lowest among the lowborn in entire Hind and Sind (*sufla tarin wa razala tarin sufalgan wa razalgan hind wa sind*), was appointed the head of the finance ministry (*diwan-i wizarat*) and placed over the nobles, governors and assignees. Kishan Bazran Indari, the lowest of the low, was assigned the territory of Awadh. Muqbil, who was the slave of Ahmad Ayaz and who, owing to his appearance and qualities, a blot on the name of all slaves, was given the deputy governorship of Gujarat, an office that was bestowed only on prominent nobles.[39]

Barani, after listing the names, caste and post of the officers, has tried to explain the Sultan's action. In his view, these people were not only lowborn, but they were born out of illicit sexual contacts.

Appointment of Government Officers in Medieval States 29

The Sultan, by giving them high posts and big assignments, placed authority in their hands. As a result, a large number of people came to depend on them. The Sultan, in doing so, appeared to rival the Supreme Sovereign. God, owing to His autonomy, often conferred power and wealth on people, who were ignoble and unworthy. Sometimes, God bestowed the authority over entire world to idolaters and polytheists like Firaun (Pharaoh) and Nimrod. However, the Sultan could not be placed in this undignified company in view of his conformity to Islamic injunctions, adherence to etiquette, respect for his teacher Qutlugh Khan and obedience to his mother Makhdumah-i Jahan. Barani, admitting his failure to understand the Sultan, stated that God had created him as a wonder among His creatures.[40] Endowed with a pathological hatred for the lowborn and unmitigated inability to see any merit in them, Barani attributed their appointment to the Sultan's contradictory traits. As a matter of fact, the problem did not lie with the Sultan. Rather, it lay with Barani, who failed to comprehend the social processes that enabled the lowborn to enter state services and, thus, posed a challenge to the old aristocracy. This process, according to his own admission, had begun a hundred years earlier under Iltutmish. It had reached a high point during the reign of Muhammad bin Tughluq, provoking Barani to adopt a scornful attitude towards the lowborn. Irfan Habib has characterized the change as plebeianization of the nobility, which was an inevitable product of the political development of the Delhi Sultanate, the process reaching its veritable apex under Muhammad bin Tughluq.[41] Iqtidar Husain Siddiqui prefers to place the appointments in the context of the larger process of social mobility occurring throughout the Sultanate period.[42]

Barani, in the *Fatawa-i Jahandari*, stated that education must be out of reach of the lowborn. In support of this advocacy, he has quoted an order of caliph al-Mamun, who succeeded Harun al-Rashid. The decree was designed to check two great evils of immoral practices and rationalistic philosophies. Barani saw the restriction as a device to prevent the rise of the lowborn in the polity of the Delhi Sultanate. The teachers of every kind were sternly advised to refrain from thrusting precious stones down the throats of dogs or

30 *Situating Medieval India*

putting collars around the necks of pigs and bears. They had to desist from imparting education to the mean, who included the lowborn, shopkeepers, ignoble and worthless. They could be given some rudimentary forms of learning such as the rules about prayer, fasting, religious charity and Haj pilgrimage. To these could be added some chapters of the Quran and a few doctrines of the faith. Without these fundamentals, their religion would not be correct and valid prayers would not be possible. They were to be taught nothing else, lest it should bring honour to their mean souls. They were not to be taught reading and writing, as plenty of disorders arose owing to the skill of the lowborn in knowledge. If the affairs of religion and state fell into disorder, it was due to acts and words of the lowborn, who had become skilled. Because of their skill, they became governors (*wali*), revenue collectors (*amil*), auditors (*mutasarrif*), officers (*farman deh*) and rulers (*farman rawa*). If the teachers were disobedient and, during investigation, it was found that they had imparted knowledge or taught letters or writing to the lowborn, they must be inevitably punished for their disobedience.[43]

The Delhi Sultanate did not employ the lowborn only in the reign of Muhammad bin Tughluq. More than a century earlier, they were seen holding government jobs at all levels of the administration. Apart from the knowledge of Persian and accountancy, they commanded expertise in clerkship. With the steady expansion of agrarian taxation and measurement of land, there was an exponential increase in the number of revenue officers including clerks, collectors and accountants. Alauddin Khalji had reduced 10,000 revenue officers to destitution in Delhi, while Qutbuddin Mubarak Shah Khalji released 17,000-18,000 people languishing in jails or condemned to exile. By the time of Muhammad bin Tughluq, many of them were elevated to the highest rung of the bureaucracy. Their rise to prominence could not have been sudden. Relying on hard work, competence and promotion, they earned the confidence of Muhammad bin Tughluq. The Sultan, having assimilated elite foreigners and members of Sufi families in the polity, had no reason to deny high posts to the long serving officers on any ground whatsoever. Barani belonged to a class that had

Appointment of Government Officers in Medieval States   31

enjoyed power and wealth in the late thirteenth century. Slowly and surely, it was losing ground to highly competent men, who were seen as upstarts. Barani assumed the impossible task of reversing the trend. He employed a number of devices in pursuit of this aim. On the one hand, he demonized the lowborn officers, who were solely identified with their castes and denied their professional credentials. On the other hand, he distorted religious texts, fabricated historical events in the Caliphate and Ghanznavid State, and attributed his personal sectarian prejudices to Ghiasuddin Balban and Muhammad bin Tughluq. He closed his eyes to the process of social mobility among the depressed classes, particularly petty traders, artisans and menials. The process was essentially rooted in technology, production and commerce, besides the proliferation of Islamic schools in the cities and towns. Barani, standing against the inexorable tide of social forces, ended up covering himself in controversy and impairing the credibility of his classic works on contemporary developments and political theory. Though his references on the lowborn were derogatory and offensive, they provided crucial insights into the social processes unfolding in the thirteenth and fourteenth centuries.

NOTES

1. A preliminary version of this paper entitled, 'Public Appointments in Medieval States: Theoretical Precepts and Political Processes', was presented at the National Seminar on *State and Society in Medieval India* at the Centre of Advanced Study, Department of History, Aligarh Muslim University, Aligarh, 3-5 April 2006.
2. Towards the middle of the eleventh century, the Seljuqids emerged as champions of Sunnism, which was upheld by the Baghdad caliphate. This happened when Shiaism had been steadily gaining ground. When the Ghaznavids enlisted Seljuqids to defend Khurasan (eastern Iran), they were still closer to their nomadic and military origin. During their rule (1038-1194), the Seljuqids dominated Transoxiana, Iran, Iraq and Anatolia. The restoration of Sunni supremacy witnessed the emergence of institutional and architectural model of *madrassa* (colleges for the study of religion and jurisprudence) and innovative organization of Sufi mystics into *tariqat*

32   *Situating Medieval India*

(ways). Francoise Aubin, 'The Turco-Mongol Period', in *History of Humanity*, vol. IV: From the Seventh to the Sixteenth Century, ed. M.A. al-Bakhit et al., Paris: Unesco; London and New York: Routledge, 2000, pp. 286-7.

3. A.C.S. Peacock, *The Great Seljuk Empire*, Edinburgh: Edinburgh University Press, 2015, pp. 66-7.

4. Nizam ul-Mulk Tusi, *Siyasatnama*, Eng. tr. Hubert Darke, entitled *The Book of Government or Rules for Kings*, Richmond, Surrey: Curzon Press, rpt., 2002, p. 158. (Hereafter cited as Tusi).

5. Ibid., pp. 158-9.

6. The four schools of Islamic jurisprudence (*fiqh*) were known after their respective founders. The Hanafi, relying on personal opinion (*ray*) and analogy (*qiyas*), prevailed among a third of all Muslims in the world. The Maliki added the practice of the Madinese to other known sources of law, besides taking notice of prevailing conditions and customs. It was regarded as the most dynamic and comprehensive of all schools. The Shafi placed Islamic law on the four roots of Quran, Sunnah, consensus of opinion and reasoning by analogy. The Hanbali laid emphasis on the Hadis, with little use for analogy. Adopted by the puritanical Wahabis, it was predominant in Saudi Arabia. A school did not imply a definite organization, formal teaching or official status. Nor was there a strict uniformity of doctrine within each school. Mohammad Hashim Kamali, *Shariah Law: An Introduction*, Oxford: Oneworld Publication, 2009, pp. 68-86; for comparison, see, Khaliq Ahmad Nizami, *Religion and Politics in India during the Thirteenth Century*, New Delhi: Oxford University Press, new edn., 2002, pp. 38-40.

7. Dailamites hailed from the mountainous part of Gilan. The area was bound on the north by Gilan proper, in the east by Tabaristan (Mazandran), in the west by Azerbaijan and Al-Ran, and in the south by Kazwin, Tarm and Rai. The rulers belonged to the Jastan family and resided in Tarm. The Dailamites, being heathen, were exposed to slave hunters until they elected a Alid, Hasan bin Zaid, as their suzerain. Another Alid, Hasan bin Ali Otrush, converted a section of them to Islam. The Dailamites rendered assistance to Mardawij. They supplied mercenaries to the armies of the Abbasid caliphs. Led by Ahmad bin Buwaih, they deposed the caliph Mustakfi. Khorzad, whom Khusrau the First entrusted with the task of conquering Yemen, had been a Marzban of Dailam. M.T. Houtsma et. al., eds., *The Encyclopaedia of Islam*, vol. I, Leyden: E.J. Brill and London: Luzac and Co., 1913, p. 896.

8. Tusi, pp. 159-60.

9. Batinis, also known as Ismailis, were a major Shia community. Currently numbering several million, they were scattered as Muslim minorities in some 25 countries of Asia, Middle East, Africa, Europe and North America. They

Appointment of Government Officers in Medieval States 33

have been named after Ismail, the eldest son of Jafar al-Sadiq (d. 765), in whose progeny they recognized a continuous line of Alid Imams. They have elaborated specific literary and intellectual traditions based on a fundamental distinction between the exoteric (*zahir*) and esoteric (*batin*) aspects of religious scriptures and prescriptions. They have made important contributions to Islamic civilization, especially during the Fatimid period of their history, when they possessed an important state over which the Ismaili Imams ruled as Fatimid caliphs. The Ismailis have been subdivided into a number of major branches and minor groupings. The Nizari and Mustali-Tayyibi Ismailis of South Asian origin were commonly designated respectively as Khojas and Bohras. John L. Esposito, *The Oxford Dictionary of Islam*, Karachi: Oxford University Press, rpt., 2007, p. 151.

10. According to the Quranic verse 5: 51, 'O you who believe! Take not Jews and Christians as protectors. They are the protectors of one another. And whosoever takes them as protectors, surely he is of them. Truly God guides not wrongdoing people.' Although this is the only verse in the Quran in which believers are urged not to take Jews and Christians, specifically, as protectors, believers are elsewhere urged to avoid taking as protectors those who disbelieve, those who mock their religion, God's enemies, and even close relatives who prefer disbelief to belief. Seyyed Hossein Nasr et. al., ed., *The Study Quran: A New Translation and Commentary*, New York: Harper One, 2015, pp. 302-3.

11. Tusi, p. 164.

12. Ibid., pp. 171-2.

13. Ibid., pp. 161-2.

14. Ibid., pp. 165-9.

15. Ibid., p. 170.

16. Ibid., pp. 173-4.

17. Ziauddin Barani, *Tarikh-i Firoz Shahi*, Persian text, ed. Sir Syed Ahmad, Aligarh: Sir Syed Academy, Aligarh Muslim University, rpt., 2005, pp. 29-30.

18. Ibid., pp. 33-5.

19. Born in 1285, Barani belonged to an aristocratic family, which served the Ilbaris, Khaljis and Tughluqs. His maternal grandfather Sipahsalar Husamuddin was attached as an officer (*vakil-i dar*) with Malik Bektars, the chamberlain (*barbak*) of Balban. He was deputed as a police officer (*shahna*) to Lakhnauti during Balban's Bengal campaign. Barani's father Muwaiyyud ul-Mulk, a descendent of the Syeds of Kaithal, served as a deputy (*naib*) to Prince Arkali Khan and, during the reign of Alauddin Khalji, received Baran as assignment. Barani's uncle Ala ul-Mulk, a confident

34 *Situating Medieval India*

of Alauddin Khalji from his Kara days, was rewarded with Kara and Awadh. He rose to be the Kotwal of Delhi. Barani, owing to his knowledge of history, served Muhammad bin Tughluq as a consultant for 17 years. During his last years, he lived in disgrace and poverty. Khaliq Ahmad Nizami, *On History and Historians of Medieval India*, New Delhi: Munshiram Manoharlal, 1983, pp. 126-7.

20. Ziauddin Barani, *Tarikh-i Firoz Shahi*, pp. 36-7.

21. Ibid., pp. 38-9.

22. Ibid., p. 70.

23. Ibid., pp. 75-6.

24. Irfan Habib, 'Barani's Theory of the History of the Delhi Sultanate', *The Indian Historical Review*, vol. VII, nos. 1-2, July 1980 – January 1981, p. 107.

25. Sunil Kumar, *The Emergence of the Delhi Sultanate 1192-1286*, Ranikhet: Permanent Black, 2007, pp. 305-20.

26. The *Fatawa-i Jahandari* was not exactly a typical example of the 'Mirror for Princes' literature due to three reasons. First, the views of Barani in it were not abstract and normative ideas, though parallels can be drawn from the works of classical Islamic political theory, some of which was known to him. Second, his views on many issues, including the status of non-Muslims, are scattered all over the *Tarikh-i Firoz Shahi*. Third, the tone of his views in the *Tarikh* was not different from that of the *Fatawa*. At several places, the language of the *Tarikh* was harsher than the one in his *Fatawa*. Raziuddin Aquil, 'On Islam and *Kufr* in the Delhi Sultanate: Towards a Reinterpretation of Ziya al-Din Barani's *Fatawa-i Jahandari*', in *Rethinking a Millennium: Perspectives on Indian History from the Eighth to the Eighteenth Century (Essays for Harbans Mukhia)*, ed. Rajat Datta, Delhi: Aakar Books, 2008, pp. 168-9.

27. Ziauddin Barani, *Fatawa-i Jahandari*, Eng. tr., (*The Political Theory of the Delhi Sultanate*), Mohammad Habib and Afsar Umar Salim Khan, Allahabad: Kitab Mahal, n.d., pp. 97-8.

28. Ibid., pp. 98-9.

29. Ibid., pp. 99-100.

30. Abul Fazl Baihaqi, *Tarikh-i Subuktigin*, Eng. tr., H.M. Elliot and John Dowson, *A History of India as Told by Its Own Historians*, vol. II, Allahabad: Kitab Mahal, rpt., n.d., pp. 127-9.

31. Ibid., pp. 132-4.

32. Ziauddin Barani, *Fatawa-i Jahandari*, pp. 91-3.

33. Ziauddin Barani, *Tarikh-i Firoz Shahi*, pp. 316-7.

34. Ziauddin Barani, *Fatawa-i Jahandari*, pp. 36-8.

Appointment of Government Officers in Medieval States   35

35. Ziauddin Barani, *Tarikh-i Firoz Shahi*, p. 352.

36. Ibid., pp. 297-8.

37. Maulana Shamsuddin Turk must have been disappointed with Alauddin Khalji for rejecting his application for a judicial post in the Delhi Sultanate. Being a total alien, he would not have dared to write a highly controversial letter to the Sultan without the concurrence of his Suhrawardi hosts. He might have realized his mistake and, therefore, refrained from going to Delhi for a meeting with the Sultan. The Sultan's secretariat, knowing the contents of the letter, did not deliver it to the Sultan. Barani might have learnt about the contents from his sources in the government. It was strange that three entities—the Suhrawardi establishment, Shamsuddin Turk and Barani—were on the same page on the appointment of Hamiduddin Multani, the state of Islam in Delhi and the Sultan's indifference to Islamic injunctions. We need not be surprised at Shamsuddin Turk's aspiration for making a career in the Sultanate. Less than two decades later, Muhammad bin Tughluq patronized numerous foreign notables, including Ibn Battuta who was made the Qazi of Delhi. For details, see, Surinder Singh, *The Making of Medieval Panjab: Politics, Society and Culture c. 1000—c. 1500*, New York & London: Routledge, 1919 / New Delhi: Manohar, 2020, pp. 335-9.

38. Ziauddin Barani, *Tarikh-i Firoz Shahi*, p. 505.

39. Ibid., p. 505.

40. Ibid., pp. 506-7.

41. Irfan Habib, op. cit., p. 109.

42. The social composition of the governing class kept on changing with the entry of new groups. From Central Asia and Persia, the Mongol invasions drove a large number of migrants—scholars, mystics, philosophers, merchants and artisans—to settle in Delhi. The Khaljis and Afghans, who made their careers in the Delhi Sultanate during the thirteenth century, faced competition from the sons of Hindu converts. The expansion of the Sultanate created the need for educated people to run the administration, whereas the old aristocratic families could no longer supply sufficient officers. Numerous followers of Haji Maula hailed from plebeian backgrounds. The ruling class, through the maintenance of workshops (*karkhanas*) and educational institutions (*madrassas*) contributed to social mobility. The process promoted new groups such as Parwaris, Kalals, Kambohs, Jains and Khatris. Iqtidar Husain Siddiqui, *Delhi Sultanate: Urbanization and Social Change*, New Delhi: Viva Books, 2009, pp. 98-121.

43. Ziauddin Barani, *Fatawa-i Jahandari*, p. 49.

CHAPTER 2

Dynastic Change in Northern India: Divergent Approaches to the Exercise of Sovereign Power

The reign of Sultan Jalaluddin Firoz Khalji (r. 1290-96), on the face of it, did not boast of spectacular achievements.[1] It was overshadowed by the awesome deeds of a predecessor like Ghiasuddin Balban and the brilliant accomplishments of a successor like Alauddin Khalji. As a result, its role in the making of the Delhi Sultanate has remained subdued. The problem partly lay with the nature of evidence at our disposal. Medieval writers—Amir Khusrau, Abdul Malik Isami and Yahya Ahmad Sirhindi—were quite reticent. Averse to delving deep into the political developments, they had left behind extremely concise summaries of the subject. In contrast, Ziauddin Barani has provided a detailed account of the Sultan's response to the challenges facing the sovereign power. Barani enjoyed several advantages. A number of his elders (father, uncle and maternal grandfather) held important positions during the reigns of Ghiasuddin Balban and the Khaljis. He availed every opportunity of comprehending the political thinking of the ruling elite. He worked hard to dig out facts that were skillfully woven into his narrative. He had imbibed the best of the vibrant cultural milieu of Delhi, which was imbued with Sufism, literature and arts. His advantages were tinged with deeply rooted prejudices. He employed his pen to prove that the Turkish regime was intrinsically superior to that of the Khaljis, who faced strong opposition from long entrenched interests. To be fair to him, he recognized the personal qualities of Jalaluddin. The Sultan was not only simple

Dynastic Change in Northern India 37

and humble, he was also far from vindictiveness and tyranny. Even in the case of controversial measures, he did not resort to royal privilege. Instead, he believed in explaining the necessity of a decision with logical reasoning. Since Barani was a staunch supporter of monarchical absolutism and social privilege, his reconstruction has ended up showing that the Sultan lacked qualities essential to kingship. His record of conversations between the Sultan and his advisors has added a considerable charm and spice to his narrative. However, his occasional rhetorical flourishes demanded caution on the part of the reader.

Modern writers have assessed Jalaluddin's reign in different ways. Rashid argued that the Sultan, with his impolitic public debasement on entering the royal palace, inflicted a permanent damage on his authority. He could never reconcile the constant inner struggle between sentiment and realism, duty and power, renunciation and action. He lacked the essential qualities of kingship besides the awe and majesty essential in a sovereign. Referring to the Sultan's murder, Rashid held that if a man crawled like a worm, he should not cry if he were trodden upon.[2] In contrast to this view, Ishwara Topa has painted a bright picture of Jalaluddin. The Sultan's approach to kingship was peculiar, as he effected a harmony between the throne and people. He believed that the exercise of despotic power resulted from anti-Islamic actions and, therefore, he built his state policy on Islamic precepts. Rejecting the Balbanite school of political thought, which associated kingship with op-pression and cruelty, the Sultan transformed kingship through its rehumanization and spiritualization. In introducing a new code of morality in politics, the Sultan was far too enlightened and ahead of his times.[3] The Sultan's attempt was not novel, as he gave a final shape to tendencies introduced during the reign of his Ilbarite predecessor Kaiqubad.[4] Tripathi has approved the change up to a point. The Turkish monopoly over power caused resentment among quasi-Turkish and non-Turkish nobility that comprised of foreigners as well as converted Hindus. The Khalji Revolution dealt a heavy blow to the loyalty growing around the throne of Delhi and was likely to bear good results. If allowed to grow to its full stature, the element of militarism would have minimized, while traditions of

38 *Situating Medieval India*

rights and duties, of command and obedience would have crystallized as in some other countries of the world.[5] Lal held that Jalaluddin Khalji, owing to his tactless behaviour and inability to harbour any ill, was most unsuited to wear the crown. The Sultan cursed his enemies not so much for plotting against him, but for making him strive for defending his throne.[6]

Barani's cryptic remarks on the opposition to Jalauddin Khalji generated confusion. An impression was created as if the Turks had ruled over the Delhi Sultanate for 80 years and, therefore, the ascendency of the Khaljis was intolerable.[7] The power struggle within the ruling class has been portrayed as a tussle between elements belonging to two distinct races, the Turks and Khaljis. The confusion would disappear if the word 'Ilbari' was added to the 'Turks'. This would be perfectly in keeping with Barani's style, as he used the generic terms where specific ones were required. Here, a brief discussion was needed on two points, the ethnic origin of the Khaljis and racial composition of the two warring factions. A perusal of the statements of early writers—the anonymous author of *Hudud ul-Alam*, Ibn Hauqal, Istakhari, Al-Masudi, Ibn Khurdazbih, Kashghari and Fakhr-i Mudabbir—showed that the Khaljis were one of the numerous Turkish tribes. From their original habitat in the steppes of Turkistan, they migrated to the districts around Ghazni in Afghanistan. Accordingly, the Khaljis served in the armies of the Ghaznavids and Ghorids.[8] A large number of Khaljis sought greener pastures in Bengal, which Muhammad bin Bakhtiar Khalji conquered in the early thirteenth century. Two modern writers, A.B.M. Habibullah and Iqtidar Husain Siddqui, saw the accession of Jalaluddin Khalji as more than a dynastic change. Characterizing the change as revolutionary, they asserted that the Turkish monopoly of the state came to an end, as the Khaljis seized power with the help of the non-Turks and Indians. The doors of higher government offices were opened to all, irrespective of race, birth and also creed to some extent.[9] However, Sunil Kumar has shown that the Turks did not monopolize Balban's dispensation, as it contained plebeian elements such as Afghans, Sistanis, Khaljis and Mongols. He also had no hesitation in promoting the sons of freed slaves (*maulazadahs*). During Kaiqubad's reign (1286-90), they emerged as great *maliks*

Dynastic Change in Northern India 39

with large garrisons and were used to counter the baleful influence of Balban's slaves.[10] In this light, it appeared that the two contending parties were not built around any particular race. Instead, they were organized around political interests involving distribution of prized posts and lucrative assignments. This manifested in Jalaluddin Khalji's earliest set of appointments.

Shortly before his formal accession, Jalaluddin secured an initial advantage in the conflict between two major factions of the nobility. With the active support of his kinsmen, he eliminated a few leading members of the dominant Turkish group, including Aitmar Surkha and Aitmar Kachhan. Having acted largely in self-defence, he retained the boy king Kaimurs on the throne. He offered regency to two kingpins of the Balbanite regime, first to Malik Chhajju, the nephew of Balban, and then to Malik Fakhruddin, the long serving *kotwal* of Delhi. He himself volunteered to administer the frontier districts of Multan, Bhatinda and Dipalpur.[11] On their refusal, Jalaluddin initially assumed the regency and, after adequate preparation, ascended the throne. While he quietly consolidated his position, some Turkish nobles shifted their loyalty to him. His exercise of government formation, involving the filling of administrative posts and distribution of revenue assignments, demonstrated a striking continuity with the Balbanite regime. It was true that the Sultan's extended family—three sons, a brother, an uncle and four nephews—constituted the inner core of the new dispensation. His three sons were given the titles of Khan-i Khanan, Arkali Khan and Qadr Khan. His brother Malik Khamosh received the army ministry (*diwan-i ariz*) with the title of Yaghrash Khan. His nephews Alauddin, Almas Beg, Ulugh Khan and Ahmad Chap were charged with important departments. Alauddin was chosen as the keeper of the royal insignia (*amir-i tuzuk*), while Ulugh Khan was made the master of the royal stables (*akhur beg*). His uncle Malik Husain was honoured with the title of Taj ul-Mulk. The Sultan, averse to breaking with the past, included nobles of the Ilbari era in the highest rungs of the administration. Most significant was the continuation of Khwaja Khatir and Malik Fakhruddin as the *wazir* and *kotwal* of Delhi respectively.[12]

In continuation of the above approach, Qutbuddin Alavi received

40 *Situating Medieval India*

the exalted rank of the deputy to the government (*naib-i mumlikat*). Malik Chhajju was assigned, as per his request, the governorship of Kara-Manikpur, where the surviving members of Balban's family departed. Amir Ali Sarjandar was confirmed in the governorship of Awadh. Two Indian converts, Ainuddin Ali Shah and his brother Ikhtiaruddin Kuhrami, who had served under Balban, found a place in the arrangement. Ikhtiaruddin Hindu Khan-i Ghiasi, who appeared to be the son of one of Balban's slaves, was given the post of deputy controller of the royal household (*naib vakil-i dar*).[13] Fakhruddin Kuchi, the new administrator of the department of justice (*dad beg*) and his brother Tajuddin Kuchi, the governor of Awadh (probably after the removal of Amir Ali Sarjandar) belonged to a family whose bureaucratic pedigree could be traced to the reign of Iltutmish.[14] A list of Jalaluddin's nobles showed that a third of them had been in the service of Kaiqubad.[15] Since very few of them jumped into the bandwagon of Malik Chhajju, their appointment was a vindication of Jalaluddin's attitude to the Ilbarite regime.

The inhabitants of Delhi, who had lived under the Ilbarite rule for eighty years, did not accept the ascendency of the Khaljis. They did not express their stance in any violent upheaval. There was an undercurrent of opposition, which Jalaluddin could discern with ease. Since he gave priority to assimilating diverse interests in the polity, he decided to avoid any conflict with the people of Delhi. The most appropriate course was to maintain a respectable distance from them and, at the same time, ensure the security of the nobles and functionaries. In a sensible, though unprecedented move, he did not enter the metropolis for one year. Instead, he established a temporary capital (*dar ul-mulk*) at Kilugarhi on the banks of the Yamuna. He completed Kaiqubad's unfinished palace and laid a magnificent garden (*bagh-i benazir*) in front of it. He directed his supporters—relatives, nobles, theologians and prominent citizens (*akabir-i shahr*)—to reside at the new site after building houses for themselves. He invited mercantile groups (*bazariyan*) to set up a market for meeting the needs of the residents. For the purpose of security, a massive stone wall (*hisar*) was constructed around the complex, providing tall towers (*burj-ha buland*) at appropriate

Dynastic Change in Northern India 41

points. Nobles were charged with guarding its portions. The new township was given the name of the New City (*shahr-i nau*).[16] In the initial stages, the elite faced difficulties in constructing their houses. Once the Sultan began to reside in the palace, houses came up in all directions and brisk business was transacted in the bazaars. The chasm between the government and people was bridged. The Sultan earned their confidence because of his virtuous character, justice and piety (*mukarim akhlaq wa adl wa ahsan wa deendari*). The Delhi Sultanate, irrespective of its strength, could win over recalcitrant elements with the distribution of patronage. Leaders of various social classes—commoners, nobles, scholars, theologians and merchants—went to Kilugarhi in groups and offered allegiance to the Sultan, who conferred robes of honour on them. During his stay here, he was engaged in strengthening his supporters with troops and assignments.[17]

Jalaluddin was not the first Sultan to have shifted his capital to Kilugarhi. His predecessor Muizzuddin Kaiqubad (r. 1286-90) left Delhi's Red Palace (*kushk-i lal*) and, moving to Kilugarhi on the banks of the Yamuna, built a palace and laid out a garden. Members of the elite—nobles, courtiers, officials and employees—constructed their bungalows near the palace. Following the Sultan's example, every one began hosting social gatherings marked with gluttony, drinking, gambling and music. Various categories of entertainers (musicians, singers, courtesans, jesters, mimics and storytellers) emerged from their isolation and congregated in Kilugarhi to meet the growing demands. The royal convivial parties, unforgettable for their opulence and liberty, were sought after. Here, the entertainers were given robes, awards and horses. Depraved sinners, in order to make easy money, trained young girls in the tricks of seduction, music, chess, riding horses and throwing javelins. The elite pursuit of pleasure spilled across the distant towns of the kingdom.[18] The pursuit of pleasure became so entrenched in the life of the ruling class that Jalaluddin did not try to suppress it. In fact, he allowed it to continue, though with some modifications. If Barani is relied upon, Jalaluddin's assemblies appeared to be heavenly. The Sultan abolished stern formalities and created a relaxed atmosphere. The leading boon companions

42 *Situating Medieval India*

were the poet Amir Khusrau and philosopher Saaduddin Mantaqi. The other nobles, reputed for their bravery on the battlefield, were also the masters of conversation, history and poetry. Comely beardless youth served wine with amorous playfulness. Female singers, Fatuha and Nusrat Khatun, brought down birds with their melodies. Two dancers, the daughters of Nusrat Bibi and Mehr Afroz, bewitched the beholder with their coquettish movements. Every day, Amir Khusrau recited a fresh sonnet (*ghazal*) in praise of beauty.[19] Yet, Jalaluddin's assemblies were different from those of Kaiqubad. They were private affairs restricted to the confines of the palace. They were bereft of the earlier licentiousness and extravagance. Instead, there was a calculated streak of sophistication and intellect.

Having thus spent a year in consolidating his position, the Sultan felt confident to enter the metropolis. On this crucial public occasion, he conducted himself like a noble and not a king. Instead of riding into Balban's palace (*kushk-i lal*), he dismounted at the entrance and went inside on foot. He refused to occupy the Sultan's exalted throne and took his seat among the nobles. He was reminded of the days when he had stood before Balban as a subordinate officer and, overwhelmed with emotion, started weeping loudly. Besides offering an appropriate justification for his actions, he articulated his innermost thoughts on the existing nature of state and the procedure of succession. Jalaluddin asserted that he had never nurtured any political ambition. He had not inherited the pride and arrogance (*nakhwat wa kibr*) associated with royalty. He believed that kingship was sheer deception. It was attractive from outside, but hollow from within. He was forced to destroy the households of Aitmar Surkha and Aitmar Kachhan only to save his own life. The circumstances had induced him to occupy Balban's palace, but the building continued to be the rightful inheritance of the latter's offspring. Balban exercised power for forty years and enabled numerous supporters—sons, nephews and nobles—to strike their roots deep in the polity. Yet, only a few of them were alive three years after his death. Despite Balban's immense power and vast experience, kingship did not survive in the hands of his successors. It was not possible for Jalaluddin, a mere servant of

Dynastic Change in Northern India 43

Balban, to claim the support of eminent nobles and aspire for a throne that could be bequeathed to his progeny. He could not endanger the lives of his sons, soldiers and supporters for the sake of a possession so transient. In other words, sovereign power was so unstable that vast military resources and innumerable supporters could not guarantee its stability.[20]

In his second regnal year, Jalaluddin faced the revolt of Malik Chhajju, the governor of Kara-Manikpur. Assuming the title of Sultan Mughisuddin and other symbols of royalty, he built a wide base of support. Amir Ali Sarjandar, the governor of Awadh, and nobles holding assignments in the districts of Hindustan joined him. In addition, the Hindustani feudatory commanders (*rawats*) and footmen (*paiks*), as numerous as ants and locusts, promised on oath to fight against the Sultan. In and around Delhi, a large number of people, who had benefited from the Ilabarite rule during the previous two generations, felt that Malik Chajju was the rightful claimant to the throne, while the Khaljis had usurped it from Balban's offspring. The Sultan, leaving Khan-i Khanan in Delhi, marched to Rohilkhand via Badaun. Arkali Khan crossed the Rahib and, doing the bulk of fighting, forced the rebels to disperse. Barani, glorifying the Khaljis as lions, lampooned the vanquished as 'lazy Hindustanis', who were addicted to wine drinking as well as eating rice and fish. Malik Chhajju took shelter in an unpacified tract (*mawasat*). The headman (*muqaddam*) of the village sent him to the Sultan in captivity.[21] The Sultan, during his return to Delhi, penetrated the countryside of Tarsiya, Kahsun, Amethi and Khatrak. The jungles were cut and rebellious villages terrorized. Numerous local chiefs were chastized and forced to pay the tribute. Two chiefs, Rupal and Bhim Deo Kotla, were put to death.[22] The recent alliance between Malik Chhajju and his local adherents broke up.

The leading rebels—Amir Ali Sarjandar, Malik Ulughchi, Malik Tajudar, Malik Ahjan and others—were brought before the Sultan. Barani learnt the proceedings from Amir Khusrau, who was present at the site. The captives were seated on camels, with their necks clamped in pillories and hands tied behind their backs. Their faces were covered with dust and clothes soiled. It was hoped that they would be paraded around the camp before a punishment was

44 *Situating Medieval India*

pronounced. Contrary to these expectations, the Sultan ordered them to be brought down from the camels. Their pillories were removed and hands untied. The rebels, who had occupied high positions during the reigns of Balban and Kaiqubad, were separated from other prisoners and treated with special consideration. The imperial servants helped them wash their heads and hands, besides providing them with royal clothes and perfume. They were consoled at a convivial party (*majlis-i sharab*), where they were served cups of liquor. All the prisoners were released and none of them was punished. Malik Chhajju was permitted to leave for Multan, where a palatial bungalow was reserved as his residence.[23]

Disapproving the Sultan's clemency, Ahmad Chap invoked the Balbanite practice and advocated death penalty for the rebels, who were guilty of the most heinous of crimes. If the vanquished faction had made them prisoners, they would have wiped out the very name of the Khaljis from Hindustan. On the other hand, Jalaluddin defended his action on political, religious and ethical grounds. The rebellious nobles had not committed any crime, but had merely shown their loyalty to the son of their former master. The Khaljis, having usurped the throne by force, did not have any legitimate claim over it. Since Balban had patronized the Sultan and his brother, the former ruler had a prior claim to their loyalty. During the previous reigns, the accused nobles had been providing hospitality to Jalaluddin, who had warmly reciprocated these gestures. The Sultan could not violate the Shariat by ordering the execution of Muslims for the sake of a transient kingdom. The Sultan was answerable to God for his actions on the day of judgement. The rebels, having been shamed into submission through clemency, would not repeat their act in the midst of Muslims.[24] This explanation failed to silence the criticism of Sultan's supporters. They gave unrestrained expression to their censorious views in drinking parties. In a gathering held at the house of Malik Tajuddin Kuchi,[25] they crossed all limits in a state of inebriation and, declaring the host as their sovereign, threatened to slice the Sultan's head like a melon. An outraged Sultan summoned the revellers with a view to punish them.[26] Malik Nusrat Sabah, who was famous for his sense of humour, sought forgiveness on the grounds of drunkenness.

Dynastic Change in Northern India 45

The Sultan, instead of taking strict action, ordered them to leave for their fiefs and forbade their entry into Delhi for a year. Justifying his measure, he asserted that kingship did not mean tyranny and vendetta (*jabbari wa qahhari*). Nor did it denote the power to kill and imprison. As a practicing Muslim, he knew that Prophet Muhammad had instituted capital punishment for Muslims only in cases of apostasy and adultery, not for their objectionable thoughts and bad actions.[27]

Barani has provided a few instances of Jalauddin's magnanimity. These passages indirectly exposed his unsuitability for the kingly office. During the reign of Balban, Jalaluddin served as the Sultan's bodyguard (*sarjandar*) and deputy (*naib*) of Samana, besides holding the revenue assignment (*iqta*) of Kaithal. The Samana-based agents of Jalaluddin extracted the land tax (*kharaj*) from a land grantee named Maulana Sirajuddin Savi. This famous local poet was treated on a par with other peasants. His laudatory verses in Jalaluddin's praise, submitted at the assignee's (*muqti's*) office, secured him no respite from harassment. Hurt at the official apathy, he composed the *Khalji Nama*, which contained a severe condemnation of Jalaluddin. During the same period, Jalaluddin ravaged a village in Kaithal that was inhabited by the Mandahars. In a close encounter, a Mandahar attacked Jalaluddin with his sword, leaving a permanent scar on his face. When Jalaluddin had been ruling in Delhi for a year, the poet and the tribesman began to fear that they might be put to death. Bidding farewell to their relatives, they appeared at the royal court with ropes around their necks. The Sultan embraced Savi and conferred a ceremonial robe on him, besides appointing him as a special companion (*nadim-i khas*). The Sultan not only restored his grant (*inam*) of one village, but also added another to it. In fact, he ordered the concerned document (*misal*) to be prepared immediately and sent through special couriers to Savi's sons at Samana. A similar treatment was accorded to the tribesman. Declaring that he had not encountered a warrior like the Mandahar in the countless battles of his career, the Sultan favoured him with a robe of honour and a horse. In addition, the Mandahar was appointed as the household manager (*vakil-i dar*) of Malik Khurram at a salary of one lakh *jitals*, with permission to

46   *Situating Medieval India*

appear at the royal court with other nobles. On another occasion, the Sultan desired to assume the title of warrior in the way of God (*mujahid fi sabil allah*) in the Friday sermon, as he had fought against the Mongols for many years. The Sultan's wife, at the instance of her husband, secured the approval of the clerics. He changed his mind at the eleventh hour. Speaking to the clerics, he revealed that he had himself prompted his wife to broach the subject. He had fought against the Mongols to gain fame, never to exert in the way of God.[28]

In spite of his best efforts, the Sultan could not absorb all the former adherents of Balban's regime in the political structure. A large number of Balbanite freedmen (*maulazadas*), who were the sons of nobles (*amirs* and *maliks*), had been reduced to poverty in the absence of any suitable employment and a decent source of income. Prominent among them were Biranjtan Kotwal and Hatiya Paik, two renowned wrestlers, who formerly enjoyed a stipend of one lakh *jitals*, but subsequently pushed to the brink of starvation. These disgruntled elements, including Qazi Jalaluddin Kashani and some dismissed officers, began to frequent the hospice (*khanqah*) of the controversial Sidi Maula and hatched a conspiracy to overthrow the Khalji regime. Prince Khan-i Khanan was quite close to Sidi Maula, who treated him like a son. In addition to his active involvement in politics, Sidi Maula acquired wide notoriety for the large multitude of visitors at his hospice, the consumption of huge quantities of provisions, the lavish distribution of cooked food and the mysterious sources of income.[29] A group of Sufis, who were jealous of Sidi Maula, circulated misinformation about him. Allegedly, he indulged in alchemy, controlled the demons, secretly collected troops, gave cash to the nobles and aspired to be the king in the absence of the Sultan.[30]

According to the plot, Biranjtan Kotwal and Hatiya Paik would kill the Sultan in a suicidal attack. Sidi Maula was to be installed as the king and married to a daughter of the late Sultan Nasiruddin Mahmud. The matrimonial bond would link him with the family of Iltutmish and strengthen his claim to the throne. Qazi Jalaluddin Kashani was to be assigned the fief of Multan with the title of Qazi Khan. The dispossessed officers (*khanzadas* and *maulazadas*)

Dynastic Change in Northern India

were to be rewarded with high posts and prized assignments. However, one of the conspirators betrayed the secret, so that all of them were brought before the Sultan. It became difficult to prove the charges because the accused pleaded their innocence. More importantly, the practice of extracting a confession through physical torture was not prevalent. The Sultan decided to determine the truth by making the accused undergo the ordeal of fire. A huge fire was lit in a wide plain at Baharpur, where prominent citizens, including nobles, Sufis and clerics, were present. In a legal opinion (*fatwa*) delivered in the open court (*mahzar*), the theologians unanimously rejected the move on the grounds that the Shariat did not permit the procedure and that fire, owing to its inherent nature, was bound to destroy the truthful and liars without discrimination. They also asserted that the prosecution in such a major crime could not be built on the testimony of a single approver.[31] According to Sirhindi, the Sultan's Mongol son-in-law Alaghu revealed the conspiracy to the Sultan and advised the arrest of the accused.[32]

Ultimately, the Sultan exercised his supreme judicial authority, but did not inflict punishments on a large scale. He pronounced different punishments for various categories of the accused. Biranjtan Kotwal and Hatiya Paik, who had conspired to murder the Sultan, were put to death. Qazi Jalaluddin Kashani, the chief conspirator, was merely transferred as the judge of Badaun. The sons of Balbanite nobles (*maulazadas* and *malikzadas*) were let off with banishment after confiscating their lands (*imlak*). It is important that Abu Bakr Tusi,[33] the famous Haidari Qalandar Sufi of Delhi,[34] and his followers were present during the interrogation. The Sultan, failing to pronounce Sidi Maula guilty of treason, turned to these mendicants. He asked them to take his revenge from Sidi Maula. Bahri, a fanatical Haidari, stabbed Sidi Maula with a knife and injured him with a large packing needle. At the angry intervention of Arkali Khan, Sidi Maula was trampled under the feet of an elephant. Barani, who was expected to praise the Sultan for his stern action, did not do so. He was rather mildly critical of the Sultan and attributed this criticism to the elder contemporaries. The death of Sidi Maula not only undermined the authority of

48   *Situating Medieval India*

the Sultan, but also caused a draught, famine and rise in grain prices.[35] Unlike Barani, Isami was more categorical in stating that Sidi Maula was an innocent victim of false charges. The resulting famine caused distress, starvation and mortality. A large number of people, including mystics and theologians, prayed to God under the leadership of Alam Diwana. Their collective repentance of their sins and prayer for forgiveness caused abundant rainfall.[36]

Jalaluddin succeeded in crushing two major rebellions. It was difficult for him to decide the punishment of political offenders. The problem was not new. The rulers, before and after him, were required to deal with similar situations. Barani, while discussing the issue at theoretical level, fell in line with Jalauddin's important decisions. Since the Shariat and theologians were silent on political punishments, the king was held entirely responsible for them. In cases where the conspiracy of the rebellion was discovered before it was put into practice, the king generally sentenced the accused to death, without accepting their repentance and without considering their religious affiliation. In view of the king's anxiety to put the things right (*siyasat*), the punishment appeared necessary. Yet, it was troublesome from the religious perspectives. If the rebels got killed in military action, there was no problem. If they were captured alive, things were not clear. According to one opinion, not all of them should be put to death. A distinction must be drawn between the wholesome and wicked. The former, including camp followers, slaves, servants and bazaar people, joined a rebellion due to necessity or deception. The wicked were divided into two categories. If they were repeat offenders, their repentance was rejected and they were put to death. If they had not rebelled in the past, their repentance was accepted and they were imprisoned or exiled. A Muslim king, being firm in his faith, was careful in punishing the Muslims and generally refrained from applying the same penalty on all. If the innocence of a person was proved after his death, the king paid blood money to the heirs and nurtured them under his wings. In no case did he touch the innocent relatives. It was improper to punish many for the sins of one. If a large number of persons were hauled up for the same offence, the king delivered different punishments—fines, imprisonment, clamping in fetters, beating

Dynastic Change in Northern India 49

with kicks and exile to distant places—in accordance with the character of each. In case of political punishments, a door was kept open for intercession (*shafaat*), which widened the support base of the king and filled his opponents with hope. The intercessor had to be neutral and honourable, while the intercession could not be easy and frequent.[37]

Jalaluddin sent military expeditions to Panjab, Rajasthan and Malwa. After crushing Malik Chajju's revolt, the Delhi army defeated the Mongols at Barram on the banks of a river. In a bloody battle between the two vanguards, the Mongols were routed and a few of their captains were captured. The Sultan exchanged emissaries and presents with the Mongol chief Abdullah, who was permitted to return in peace. He allowed Alaghu, a grandson of Chengiz Khan, to stay back along with his *hazara* and *sadah* commanders, all of whom embraced Islam along with their followers. He gave his daughter in marriage to Alaghu, enrolled the Mongol immigrants in the army and settled them with their families at colonies (Kilugarhi, Ghiyaspur, Indraprastha and Tiloka) in Delhi.[38] Early in his reign, the Sultan led an expedition against Ranthambhor in order to curtail its expansion. Marching for two weeks, he passed through Rewari and Narnaul. From here, a hundred camels were employed to carry water across the dry tract. Mandor, occupied with ease, yielded much booty. An advance guard, targeting Jhain, overpowered 500 defenders. Next day, a larger force pierced through the hills, causing panic in Jhain. Rai Hammir Dev deputed Gardan Sahini at the head of 10,000 soldiers to fight the invaders. Following a fierce battle, the defenders fled into the defiles, while thousands of feudatory commanders (*rawats*) were killed. The fort was razed down, the temple vandalized and gold idols carried away. The Sultan, in order to occupy the fort of Ranthambhor, constructed covered passages and installed siege engines, only to withdraw from the site. The Delhi army compensated itself by plundering parts of Malwa.[39]

Ahmad Chap found fault with the Sultan's retreat from Ranthambhor. In the past, the great rulers, who undertook any military expedition, did not turn back without achieving their aim. In the instant case, the Rai would be emboldened to entertain hostile

50   *Situating Medieval India*

designs. The prestige of the Sultan would be lowered in the eyes of the people. The Sultan ought to follow the example of Sultan Mahmud and Sultan Sanjar, who not only conquered different parts of the world, but also strengthened Islam in their territories. These views were in the interest of the kingship of Delhi. The Sultan, however, did not agree with Ahmad Chap. All through his long life, he had been a keen student of history. Every day, a few pages from history were read out to him. He was aware of kings who, in order to gain fame as world conquerors, endangered the lives of thousands of men. They blindly pursued their ambition, unmindful of the immense price, suffering and destruction. There was a wide gulf between the teachings of prophets and the concerns of autocratic rule. As a devout Muslim, he had faith in the prophetic injunctions and the day of judgement. He was unimpressed with rulers who, for attaining transient power, employed tyranny and oppression. He looked at kingship from the perspective of Islam. It was impossible for him to follow Sultan Mahmud and Sultan Sanjar. In their kingdoms, Islam had reached the pinnacle of glory. But, he did not have the kind of soldiers and servants, who served them. They were a hundred times superior to his own. In Delhi, the Hindus lived in great prosperity and openly performed the rituals of their creed. If the rulers of Delhi really possessed power, they would not have permitted the Hindus to flourish in this manner. Instead, they remained satisfied with a few coins in alms (*sadqah*) from them.[40] They were not more than the slaves of Sultan Mahmud and Sultan Sanjar. The Sultan meant to say that a ruler, who was unable to prevent the Hindus from acquiring wealth and enjoying religious freedom, could not perform the bigger tasks of conquering distant kingdoms. Ahmad Chap, overwhelmed with the Sultan's logic, fell at his feet.[41]

Jalaluddin, like his predecessor Kaiqubad, organized frequent social gatherings that exuded magnificence and grandeur. Outstanding musicians, singers, dancers, poets and humourists provided entertainment. Female dancers mesmerized the beholders with their beautiful physiques and coquettish expressions. Handsome cup bearers maintained an endless flow of liquor, while fresh lyrics (*ghazals*) were recited by Amir Khusrau, Hamid Raja and Amir

Dynastic Change in Northern India 51

Khasa. The Sultans companions (*nadims*)—Tajuddin Iraqi, Amir Khusrau, Muiyyad Jajarmi, Muiyyad Diwana, Sadr Ali, Amir Arsalan Kulahi, Ikhtiar Bagh and Taj Khatib—distinguished themselves in the knowledge of poetry, prose, history, politics and art. The Sultan also invited a galaxy of nobles—Tajuddin Kuchi, Aizzuddin Ghori, Malik Qeer, Nusrat Sabah, Ahmad Chap, Kamaluddin Abul Maali, Nasiruddin Kuhrami and Saaduddin Mantaqi—who had surpassed their contemporaries in the art of conversation, narration of jokes and recitation of poetry. For our purpose, it was important to focus on the Sultan's attitude towards his nobility. He discarded the conventional royal arrogance (*nakhwat-i badshahi*) and treated the nobles as his equals. He permitted them to arrive at social gatherings wearing the informal clothes instead of the formal court attire. He played the games of dice and chess (*nard wa shatranj*) with them. The nobles interacted freely with each other and engaged in light-hearted banter, without any inhibition from the Sultan's presence. The fear of imprisonment and torture did not trouble them.[42] Jalaluddin's attitude stood in sharp contrast to Balban's, who had created a wide gulf between himself and the nobility, which was terrorized through various draconian methods, including cruel punishments and espionage network. Jalaluddin utilized these social gatherings to erase the social distance between the monarchy and nobility, so that the bridges of mutual understanding and trust were built. He envisioned the Delhi Sultanate as a collective enterprise in which the nobility had as much stake as the Sultan.

The Sultan found no reason to suspect the intentions of Alauddin Khalji, who held the revenue assignment of Kara. He had received the booty Alauddin had brought from an attack on Bhilsa. He had permitted Alauddin to retain the surplus revenue of Kara and Awadh, so that a fresh army could be fitted out against Chanderi. He had felt reassured on receiving favourable reports of Malik Ala ul-Mulk (Barani's uncle), who served as Alauddin's deputy at Kara. During an expedition to Gwalior, the Sultan learnt that Alauddin, who had invaded Deogiri without permission, was returning with a vast booty. Owing to his simplicity, the Sultan celebrated the triumphant return of Alauddin. In this context, he convened a confidential meeting of his advisors, who were endowed with expertise in matters of statecraft. They discussed the Sultan's response to Alauddin's return with the huge spoils of Deogiri. Ahmad Chap argued that a number of dubious characters—rebels, flatterers and wicked people, who were formerly associated with Malik Chhajju—had gathered around Alauddin. Ancient rulers believed that sedition and treasure were inseparable. Alauddin might be nurturing treacherous designs. The Sultan must intercept him at Chanderi and take the entire booty from him. Thereafter, he could reward Alauddin with a part of the booty and an additional revenue assignment. The matter did not permit the consideration of kinship. If this was not done, the Sultan's government and its supporters would be exposed to grave danger. Another advisor Fakhruddin Kuchi realized the correctness of Ahmad Chap's advice and, at the same time, noted the Sultan's opposition to it. He argued that the reports of Alauddin's treasure and elephants remained unconfirmed. The advance of the Sultan's army would force Alauddin to flee into the jungles and, during the monsoon, his pursuit was impossible. Since Ramzan was around the corner and the sweet melons had ripened, the Sultan must return to Delhi and watch the situation. If suspicions against Alauddin were substantiated, the imperial army could destroy him with ease. Ahmad Chap, countering Fakhruddin, warned that if Alauddin reached Kara with the treasure and elephants, he would be able to occupy Lakhnauti. No one would be able to chase him. The Sultan accused Ahmad Chap of opposing Alauddin without reason. He would never suspect one whom he had brought up like a son.[43] The subsequent developments, revealing the treachery of Alauddin, vindicated the plea of Ahmad Chap.

For the reign of Jalaluddin Khalji, Barani has offered two assessments that stood in sharp contrast to each other. The first opinion had been expressed by the Sultan's contemporaries—nobles, ministers, clerics and influential persons—who had observed his functioning from close quarters. They felt that he had been an efficient general, second to none in courage and bravery. He had distinguished himself in fighting against the Mongols. But, he was totally ignorant of matters relating to statecraft (*jahandari*).

Dynastic Change in Northern India 53

His administration had acquired strength owing to the competent services of a host of supporters and kinsmen, who were knowledgeable and experienced. He lacked in two important respects. He did not spend lavishly on the royal workshops (*karkhanas*) and charities. He did not display absolute despotism in the form of terror and magnificence (*qahr wa satwat*). These qualities enabled a ruler to subdue opponents and convert rebels into loyalists.[44] Evidently, these views were articulated by a particular section of the ruling class, which had been conditioned to regard Balbanite statecraft as the only valid political norm and felt scandalized at Jalaluddin's attempt to deviate from it.

The second assessment, separated from the first by almost half-a-century, was made by the friends of Barani's father in their social gatherings and elsewhere. In their younger days, they were critical of Jalaluddin's mild policies. Disillusioned with the subsequent regimes, they were filled with nostalgia for the past, which was manifested in unrestrained admiration for Jalaluddin's rule. The Sultan and his officers, while performing their administrative duties, adhered to the Shariat and were guided by the principles of benevolence and sagacity. Acts of oppression—confiscation of land grants, appropriation of hereditary property and extortion of the wealth of Muslims after torture and imprisonment—did not occur. The lowborn were not appointed to positions of authority, providing no cause for the established elite to feel alarmed. Non-conformist intellectuals, including philosophers and atheists, were not patronized. Unfortunately, the people, owing to ingratitude and wickedness, failed to thank God for providing them with a noble ruler like Jalaluddin. Without any rhyme or reason, they pinpointed a hundred faults in him. Not surprisingly, they were afflicted with divine wrath. They were made to suffer under a ruler (Alauddin Khalji) who was autocratic, tyrannical and irreligious. The highborn gentry was marginalized and artists were ignored, while the lowborn and wicked were promoted.[45] Barani, speaking through his father's friends, has expressed his hatred against two groups, the lowborn officers and atheistic philosophers, who had gained ascendency during the reign of Muhammad bin Tughluq.

Barani has recorded four conversations between Jalaluddin and

54   *Situating Medieval India*

his principal advisor Ahmad Chap. These dialogues were rooted in the contemporary political developments—the Sultan's first entry into the royal palace, the treatment of Malik Chajju's adherents, the Sultan's retreat from Ranthambhor and the return of Alauddin Khalji with the spoils of Deogiri. Barani had little opportunity of injecting his own ideas into the statements of the discussants. His account of the conversations, both in approach and semantics, was substantially different from his descriptions of the overtly didactic monologues such as the sermon of Nuruddin Mubarak Ghaznavi to Iltutmish, the advice of Balban to his sons and the counsel of Qazi Mughisuddin to Alauddin Khalji. The Jalaluddin-Ahmad Chap exchanges provide valuable insights into the political concerns of the Khalji regime, with reference to its aims, methods and limitations. Jalaluddin, conscious of the transitional nature of his reign, fought throughout on two fronts. On the one hand, he tried to win over the members of the Balbanite regime and faced two major revolts from it. On the other hand, he tried to curtail the growing disillusionment among his own supporters such as Ahmad Chap, Tajuddin Kuchi and Alauddin Khalji. Employing his knowledge, eloquence and experience, he endeavoured to bring them around to his own understanding. This method succeeded only so long as the criticism remained within the confines of discussion. When his detractors became desperate and resorted to treacherous intrigue, Jalaluddin lost his throne and life. Since he refrained from acting against his wily nephew and son-in-law Alauddin, he might have expected him to be kind to his own sons. Unfortunately, these hopes were shattered soon after his murder. Alauddin not only purged the Khalji government of the Ilbarite remnants, but also eliminated the surviving members of Jalaluddin's family and the Jalali nobles who had deserted to his camp. The new dispensation, both in theory and practice, buried Jalaluddin's expediency, benevolence and morality. Ahmad Chap, who had differed with Jalaluddin on several occasions, remained loyal to the late Sultan's family and, in the bargain, suffered blindness and imprisonment. Ironically, Alauddin followed in the footsteps of Jalaluddin in vital aspects of state policy such as territorial expansion, Mongol invasions and rural intermediaries.

Dynastic Change in Northern India   55

NOTES

1. An earlier version of this paper appeared as 'Political Culture in the Delhi Sultanate: Compulsions of a Transitional Phase', *Proceedings of the Indian History Congress*, 63rd Session, Amritsar, 2002, pp. 251-62.

2. Shaikh Abdur Rashid, 'Jalaluddin Firoz Khalji,' *Muslim University Journal*, vol. 1, no. 1, 1931, pp. 146-9.

3. Ishwara Topa, *Politics in Pre-Mughal Times: A Study in the Political Philosophy of the Turkish Kings of Delhi up to circa 1400 AD*, Delhi: Idarah-i Adabiyat-i Delli, rpt., 1976, pp. 100-19.

4. It has been argued that Kaiqubad, in his attitude to kingship and welfare of people, was diametrically opposite to Balban. He believed that pleasure could not be confined to upper classes. The ordinary people were equally entitled to enjoy life in all aspects. It indirectly raised their status and brought them closer to kingship as never before. Kaiqubad's kingship permeated the entire social fabric. The reign witnessed the birth of a new India on the basis of a fusion of cultures, Hindu and Islamic. The culturalized kingship counteracted the absolutism and foreign element in Balban's kingship. The power of the state, thus freed from discriminatory motives, became broadbased. Ibid., pp. 88-9.

5. R.P. Tripathi, *Some Aspects of Muslim Administration*, Allahabad: Central Book Depot, rpt., 1974, pp. 40-1.

6. Kishori Saran Lal, *History of the Khaljis*, New Delhi: Munshiram Manoharlal, rev. ed., 1980, pp. 17-18.

7. Ziauddin Barani, *Tarikh-i Firoz Shahi*, Persian text, ed. Sir Syed Ahmad, Aligarh: Sir Syed Academy, Aligarh Muslim University, rpt., 2005, p. 175. (Hereafter cited as Barani).

8. Khaliq Ahmad Nizami, *Royalty in Medieval India*, New Delhi: Munshiram Manoharlal, 1997, pp. 5-6; Iqtidar Husain Siddiqui, *Authority and Kingship under the Sultans of Delhi: Thirteenth-Fourteenth Centuries*, New Delhi: Manohar, 2006, pp. 91-3.

9. A.B.M. Habibullah, 'Jalauddin Firuz Khalji', in *A Comprehensive History of India: vol. V, The Delhi Sultanate, AD 1206-1526*, ed. Mohammad Habib and Khaliq Ahmad Nizami, New Delhi: People's Publishing House, rpt., 1982, p. 311; Iqtidar Husain Siddiqui, op. cit., p. 96.

10. Sunil Kumar, *The Emergence of the Delhi Sultanate 1192-1286*, Ranikhet: Permanent Black, 2007, pp. 314-15, 320.

11. Yahya bin Ahmad bin Abdullah Sirhindi, *Tarikh-i Mubarak Shahi*, Persian text, ed. M. Hidayat Hosain, Calcutta: Asiatic Society of Bengal, 1931, p. 59. (Hereafter cited as Sirhindi).

56 *Situating Medieval India*

12. Barani, p. 177.
13. Sirhindi, pp. 62-3.
14. Peter Jackson, *The Delhi Sultanate: A Political and Military History*, Cambridge: Cambridge University Press, 1999, pp. 83-4.
15. S.B.P. Nigam, *Nobility under the Sultans of Delhi*, New Delhi: Munshiram Manoharlal, 1968, p. 196.
16. This important reference may be read with modern studies on the growth of Delhi as an urban centre. Muhammad Habib, 'The Urban Revolution in Northern India', in *Politics and Society during the Early Medieval Period: Collected Works of Professor Mohammad Habib*, ed. K.A. Nizami, vol. I, New Delhi: People's Publishing House, 1974, pp. 80-4; M. Athar Ali, 'Capital of the Sultans: Delhi during the Thirteenth and Fourteenth Centuries,' in *Delhi Through the Ages*, ed. R.E. Frykenberg, New Delhi: Oxford University Press, rpt., 1992, pp. 21-31; Hamida Khatoon Naqvi, *Agricultural, Industrial and Urban Dynamism under the Sultans of Delhi 1206-1555*, New Delhi: Munshiram Manoharlal, 1986, pp. 134-76; H.C. Verma, *Dynamics of Urban Life in Pre-Mughal India*, New Delhi: Munshiram Manoharlal, 1986, pp. 183-266.
17. Barani, pp. 175-6.
18. Ibid., pp. 129-31.
19. Ibid., pp. 197-200.
20. Ibid., pp. 179-80.
21. Ibid., pp. 181-2.
22. The official account of the military expedition described the march of Arkali Khan towards the east, the initial skirmishes of the advance guard and arrangement of the royal forces on the battlefield. This was followed by an account of a pitched battle spreading over two days, the imperial attack under Malik Kik of Kol and the defeat of the rebels. It also narrated the march of the Sultan to Bhojpur via Kabar, construction of bridges on the Ganga and Yamuna and finally the punishment of the rebels. Amir Khusrau, *Miftah ul-Futuh*, Persian text, ed. Shaikh Abdur Rashid, Aligarh: Aligarh Muslim University, 1954, pp. 9-23.
23. Barani, pp. 183-4.
24. Ibid., pp. 184-7.
25. Fakhruddin Kuchi was one of the three leading nobles, who were chosen by Barani for special mention, the other two being Ahmad Chap and Nusrat Sabah. Tajuddin Kuchi surpassed other nobles in dignity, grace and humour. Destiny had endowed him with perfections expected of nobles in the battlefield and social gatherings. He was unmatched in discernment of people and patronage of skills. He was an unlimited source of generosity

Dynastic Change in Northern India

57

and sophistication. Along with his brother Fakhruddin Kuchi, he was a companion and counsellor of the Sultan. Eminent people of Delhi took pride in associating with them. People, reputed in Delhi for different arts, were always present in their establishments. After them, their qualities were never seen in nobles. Barani, pp. 203-4.

26. Sirhindi has portrayed the episode as a revolt of Malik Mughlati, who enjoyed the support of Tajuddin Kuchi, Hiranmar and Malik Mubarak. That night, the Sultan remained alert. Next morning, he held a public audience, where all the nobles assembled to pay their respects. The Sultan, confronting the conspirators, asserted that God had not granted him the kingdom with their help. They could not deprive him of it even if they tried hard. They must identify his specific wrong, which had induced them to revolt in this manner. When he did not get a suitable reply, he changed their offices. Malik Mughlati was sent to the fief of Badaun, while Malik Mubarak was deputed to that of Bhatinda. The office of the chief bodyguard was taken away from Hiranmar and given to Bughra Kandhali. Sirhindi, pp. 64-5.

27. Barani, pp. 190-3.

28. Ibid., pp. 194-7.

29. The personal piety of Sidi Maula did not match his politics, wealth and ambition. Originally hailing from northwestern highlands (*vilayat mulk-i bala*), he migrated to Delhi in the early years of Balban's reign. On his way to Delhi, he stopped at Ajodhan and stayed with Baba Farid for a few days. The Chishti saint, finding that Sidi Maula intended to earn fame for himself in Delhi, advised him to keep away from the nobles. The visits of nobles to his hospice must be seen as perilous. Any dervish, who associated with nobles, was bound to end in disaster. Though Sidi Maula did not follow this advice, he was sincere in his devotions. Unlike the devout, he did not pray at the Jama Masjid in Friday congregations. He undertook hard spiritual exercises. Clad in a coarse sheet and eating simple food, he did not keep a wife or maidservant. Averse to physical pleasures, he did not take a penny from anyone in alms. Barani, pp. 208-9.

30. Abdul Malik Isami, *Futuh us-Salatin*, Eng. tr., Agha Mahdi Husain, vol. II, Aligarh: Aligarh Muslim University and Bombay: Asia Publishing House, 1976, pp. 380-1.

31. Barani, pp. 210-11.

32. Sirhindi, p. 65.

33. During the thirteenth century, Abu Bakr Tusi had built a beautiful hospice on the Yamuna near Indarpat. Admired for his piety, he enjoyed a privileged place in the Chishti circles. He had an intimate friendship with Shaikh

58   *Situating Medieval India*

Jamaluddin Hansavi, who had given him the title of white falcon (*baz safed*). Whenever Hansavi came to Delhi, he called on Tusi. On the occasion, Husamuddin Indarpati, who was the chief judge and sermonizer, organized lavish feasts and musical sessions. Nizamuddin Auliya also attended these meetings. However, Tusi did not allow a mystic Nuruddin Malik Yar Parran to construct a hospice besides his own till he had brought a royal order (conferring four villages) from Sultan Balban. According to Jamali, the Haidaris passed through their male organs iron rods that were sealed at both ends. Amir Khurd, *Siyar ul-Auliya*, Persian text, Delhi: Matba-i Muhibb-i Hind, 1885, pp. 181-2; Hamid bin Fazlullah Jamali, *Siyar ul-Arifin*, Persian text, Delhi: Rizvi Press, 1893, pp. 66-7; Abdul Haq Muhaddis Dehalvi, *Akhbar ul-Akhyar*, Urdu tr. Subhan Mahmud and Muhammad Fazil, Delhi: Noor Publishing House, 1990, pp. 163-4.

34. A recent study traces the history of the Tusi shrine during the twentieth century, besides describing the unique practice of hanging earthen pitchers of water on the trees. Kumkum Srivastava, *Wandering Sufis: Qalandars and Their Path*, Bhopal: Indira Gandhi Rashtriya Manav Sangrahalaya & New Delhi: Aryan Books International, 2009, pp. 124-33.

35. Barani, p. 212.

36. Abdul Malik Isami, *Futuh us-Salatin*, vol. II, pp. 383-6.

37. Ziauddin Barani, *Fatawa-i Jahandari*, Eng. tr. (entitled *The Political Theory of the Delhi Sultanate*), Mohammad Habib and Afsar Umar Salim Khan, Allahabd: Kitab Mahal, n.d., pp. 58-63.

38. Barani, pp. 218-19; for details of the campaign, see, Abdul Malik Isami, *Futuh us-Salatin*, vol. II, pp. 372-8.

39. Amir Khusrau, *Miftah ul-Futuh*, pp. 24-34.

40. Barani, in his work on political theory, exposed the weakness of the Delhi Sultanate on three counts. (i) In Delhi and other Muslim cities, infidelity (Hinduism) was freely practised. Adorning idols, the Hindus celebrated their festivals with fanfare and taught from their scriptures. In lieu of paying the poll tax (*jaziya*), the Hindus were raised to eminence. They were appointed governors, lived in luxury and employed Muslims as servants. (ii) The Muslim rulers allowed Muslims to run taverns, brothels and gambling houses and to hold music parties. Content to levy taxes on these groups, they permitted immoralities in every lane and bazaar. (iii) In the city of Delhi, the philosophers freely propagated their doctrines, giving preference to reason over Islam. They denied the cognition of God, transience of the world, the day of judgement and the existence of heaven and hell. Ziauddin Barani, *Fatawa-i Jahandari*, pp. 48-9.

Dynastic Change in Northern India 59

41. Barani, pp. 214-18.
42. Ibid., pp. 198-9.
43. Ibid., pp. 223-8.
44. Ibid., pp. 188-9.
45. Ibid., pp. 205-7.

CHAPTER 3

Rulers, Zamindars and Sufis: Probing a Triangular Model of State Formation

During the early thirteenth century, the Delhi Sultanate sought to control the conquered areas through military governors, who were assigned chunks of land in lieu of maintaining troops.[1] Owing to frequent revolts among the nobility and recurring Mongol invasions, the state could neither assert its authority in the countryside nor undertake territorial expansion. It took some tentative steps to supervise the finances of its assignees who, finding it difficult to collect the land tax, resorted to the moneylenders for meeting their expenditure. During the first half of the fourteenth century, the ruling class felt strong enough to measure the cultivated land and produce per unit of area. As the magnitude of land tax increased, the rural intermediaries were coerced into submission. Failure of a scheme of loans and incidence of famine triggered a major peasant uprising in the Gangetic plain and, to a lesser extent, in the southeast Panjab. In these circumstances, the Tughluq rulers realized the supreme importance of the *zamindars* and Sufis in a new strategy of state formation. In tandem with these steps, they initiated canal irrigation and agrarian expansion in two arid zones, southeast Panjab and the Multan region. Ghazi Malik, the governor of Dipalpur, emerged as pioneer in this regard.

Before delving into the subject under discussion, we would do well to consider an interesting development in the middle of the thirteenth century. The ruling class realized the significance of the local chiefs dominant in the countryside, which was quiet free from the control of the Delhi Sultanate. The issue came to the

Rulers, Zamindars and Sufis

forefront when Qutlugh Khan, a strong rival of the minister Ulugh Khan, found sanctuary in the sub-Himalayan principality of Sirmur, giving rise to what has been termed as the Rana-Malik condominium.[2] If the disgruntled nobles could survive with the support of local chiefs, the loyal provincial governors could do the same in order to strengthen the foundations of their authority. Ghiasuddin Balban, on ascending the throne, appointed his elder son Sultan Muhammad as the governor of Sind. The Prince, functioning from the city of Multan, strengthened the defences against the Mongols. Autonomous for all practical purposes,[3] he thought it prudent to marry the daughter of Rai Kalu. Nothing was known about the Rai's services to the state. The implications of the marriage manifested after the death of the Prince at the hands of the Mongols. Separated from his troops during a battle, he rode to a rivulet. A Qaraunah soldier shot an arrow at the Prince, who fell from his horse and instantly died. The Qaraunah, ignorant of the identity of the fallen foe, took away his horse, sword and bow. One of the Prince's musicians, who had fallen into the hands of the Mongols, recognized his master's equipment and cried out in sorrow. The Mongols came to the rivulet and took the Prince's body in their custody. They were amazed on seeing the marvellous body, with broad shoulders and stature. Treating it as a trophy, they intended to take it back to their native land. At this moment, Rai Kalu learnt of the tragedy and rushed to the site. When his eyes fell on the body of his son-in-law, he cried, shrieked, sighed and howled in accordance with the four vents of mourning. The spirited Rai Kalu, paying a huge ransom to the Mongols in gold, redeemed the body. Though it has not been recorded, he might have buried the body with all marks of honour, which was commensurate with the status of the Prince and the heir apparent.[4]

Ghazi Malik, the Khalji governor of Dipalpur, organized the marriage of his brother Sipahsalar Rajab with the daughter of one of the local magnates. In this matter, he sought the advice of the administrator of Abohar, Malik Saad ul-Mulk Shihab Afif, the great grandfather of the historian Shams Siraj Afif, who held the administrative charge of Abohar. It was learnt that Bibi Naila, the daughter of Rana Mal Bhatti, the chief of Abohar, possessed physical

62 *Situating Medieval India*

beauty and noble qualities. The tribes of the Bhattis and Minhas inhabited the town of Abohar and its forested hinterland, which was included in the jurisdiction of Dipalpur. Ghazi Malik sent a marriage proposal to Rana Mal Bhatti. The latter rejected the proposal and even used improper words. Ghazi Malik, after a second round of consultations with Shihab Afif, entered the ancestral lands (*talwandi*) of the Bhatti chief and demanded the land tax in cash in a single instalment (*mal salinah naqd talbid*). Pressure was exerted on the village headmen (*chaudharis* and *muqaddams*), so that the entire population was brought to the verge of destruction. Since Alauddin Khalji wielded supreme authority, no one dared to protest.[5] The old mother of Rana Mal Bhatti intended to convey the tale of woes to her son. She told Bibi Naila that she was the root cause of the crisis. If she had not existed, Ghazi Malik would not have oppressed the people in such a cruel manner. In order to diffuse the situation, Bibi Naila agreed to marry the brother of the governor. She urged everyone to understand that the Mongols had abducted her (*bayad danist keh yak dukhtar ra mughlan burdand*). Pleased at her initiative, Rana Mal Bhatti conveyed his acceptance of the proposal through Shihab Afif. Following the solemnization of the marriage, the bride was renamed Bibi Kadbanu and escorted to Dipalpur. This marriage led to the birth of a son, who grew up to be Firoz Shah Tughluq. When the boy was seven, his father died. Bibi Kadbanu was worried about the upbringing of her son. Ghazi Malik assured her that he would treat the boy as his own son and as a part of his own body until he was alive.[6]

At the time of the marriage, it was impossible to predict that its offspring would ascend the throne of the Delhi Sultanate and, ruling for 37 years, bring about a major shift in the ongoing process of state formation. A number of factors converged in the career of Firoz, paving the way for his rise to sovereign power. Since Ghazi Malik kept his promise in its true spirit, Firoz did not face any discrimination on account of his birth from a Hindu Rajput mother. His uncle, stepbrothers and cousins treated him with utmost affection. He received appropriate education and training under the fraternal care of two kings, Ghiasuddin Tughluq and Muhammad bin Tughluq. As a result, he excelled his contemporaries in his

Rulers, Zamindars and Sufis 63

knowledge of administrative affairs. From Ghiasuddin Tughluq, he received the office of *Naib Amir Hajib* and the title of *Naib Barbak*. He had 12,000 horsemen in his retinue. Muhammad bin Tughluq always kept Firoz by his side and groomed him in statecraft. When he divided the kingdom in four parts, he assigned one to Firoz, so that he could understand the intricacies of governance. In due course, Firoz ascended the throne despite the presence of two elder stepbrothers, Malik Qutbuddin and Malik Naib Barbak, who were born of two other wives of Sipahsalar Rajab.[7] Firoz enjoyed cordial relations with his mother's Rajput family. On his accession to the throne, Khudawandzada Begum (a uterine sister of Muhammad bin Tughluq) conspired to assassinate him. At this critical moment, the presence and support of his maternal uncle Rai Bhiru Bhatti was one of the factors that saved his life.[8] This little known man might have been living in the Tughluq household ever since his sister was married to Rajab. It was not clear if he was assigned any office. His position, as would be seen, was quite similar to that of Sadhu and Sadharan, whose sister was married to Firoz.

A period of ten years from 1296 to 1306 stood out for the frequency of Mongol invasions. During this period, they repeatedly ravaged Panjab, twice besieged Delhi and even penetrated the Ganga-Yamuna Doab and northern Rajasthan. The cessation of these invasions after 1306 was attributable to Alauddin Khalji's defensive arrangements and internal conflict among the Mongols. However, the most important factor was the military genius of Ghazi Malik. Operating from his headquarters in Dipalpur, midway between Delhi and Multan, he repulsed the Mongols several times, apparently from the banks of the Ravi. In an inscription at the principal mosque at Multan, he proclaimed, 'I have fought twenty nine battles with the Tartars (Mongols) and have defeated them. Hence I have been named Malik ul-Ghazi.'[9] He did not limit his defence to the Ravi and, instead, undertook a sustained military offensive, which continued until his enthronement at Delhi. Every winter, he marched out of Dipalpur and, crossing the Indus, entered the hills of Afghanistan and raided Kabul, Ghazni, Qandhar and Garmsir. Plundering these areas, he extracted tributes from

64 *Situating Medieval India*

the inhabitants. He struck such terror in the minds of the Mongols that they did not turn to the western limits of Panjab. The fear of the Mongols was erased from the minds of the people inhabiting the region through which the military routes passed, i.e. the fertile plains of Panjab. These people engaged themselves in agriculture, which had been disrupted in the Mongol depredations.[10] Ghazi Malik, during his campaigns to Afghanistan, marched through the Salt Range, which was under the sway of the Khokhars. Out of expediency, he appeared to have built friendly relations with the Khokhars and, as a result, recruited them in his army and received logistic support from them. This enabled him to employ the Khokhars in his fight against Khusrau Khan and assume power in Delhi. In addition to the Khokhars, he had recruited a number of non-indigenous tribes hailing from the upper country (*iqlim-i bala*) embracing Khurasan and Transoxiana. They comprised the Ghuzz, Turks, Mongols of Rum and Rus, besides the Khurasanis of pure stock. Skilled in warfare, they were entirely devoted to their master.[11]

During his long service on the frontier, Ghazi Malik welded diverse groups including his kinsmen, the Khokhars and non-indigenous tribes into an efficient military machine.[12] His dependence on these elements increased when he could not get the support of fellow officers posted at Uch, Multan, Samana, Sind and Jalor. A convergence of interrelated developments—Ghazi Malik's alliance with the Khokhars, the inclusion of non-indigenous tribes, his sustained offensive against the Mongols and revival of agriculture in central Panjab—catapulted the Tughluqs to sovereign power in Delhi. Mohammad Habib insightfully observed that Ghazi Malik's Delhi bound army comprised of the same ethnic groups that had often fought with him against the Mongols.[13] Ghazi Malik, occupying the area up to Sarsuti, fought a pitched battle against Khan-i Khanan, the brother of Khusrau Khan. The Khokhars, led by Gul Chand and Sahij Rai, formed the vanguard. In a furious charge, they scattered the opponents, killed the captain of the rival vanguard and wrought havoc with their swords and arrows. Gul Chand slew the parasol bearer of Khan-i Khanan and raised the parasol over the head of Ghazi Malik.[14] The victors, controlling the territory up to Hansi, camped at Lahrawat between the Yamuna and the

Rulers, Zamindars and Sufis

65

city of Delhi. Khusrau Khan, mobilizing 10,000 Baradus, appeared at Hauz Khas and fought a tough battle near Koh-i Jud. The Delhi army secured an upper hand due to a fierce Baradu charge and a volley of arrows. Ghazi Mailk, rallying his leading men, made an assault from the front. Gul Chand, who led the vanguard, attacked the rear of the opponents with a unit of 100 fighters. The tide of the battle turned, forcing Khusrau Khan to flee from the site. Gul Chand, while pursuing the fugitives, repeated the act he had performed at Sarsuti. He slashed the head of the rival parasol bearer (*chhatardar mukhalif*) and, seizing the parasol, presented it to Ghazi Malik. The victors acquired the keys of two forts from the police chief.[15] The Khokhar chiefs and their retinue played a pivotal role in the military effort. On two occasions, Gul Chand crowned Ghazi Malik as the Sultan, and, in a symbolic manner, anticipated the choice of nobles.

Firoz Shah Tughluq, since his days as a prince, was extremely fond of hunting. Through this pursuit, he gained intimate knowledge of the countryside in Panjab. This enabled him to plan canal irrigation, agrarian expansion and urban development. He had a particular interest in hunting onagers (*gorkhar*). These animals were found in jungles lacking water. Such a habitat was available in the wilderness between Dipalpur and Sarsuti. The land was so arid that water could not be extracted even after digging a hundred yards. The onagers, in their search for water, covered stretches of land up to eighty leagues and, after quenching their thirst, returned to their original habitat. It was possible to hunt onagers only during summers when they tended to collect at one spot. While hunting, Firoz established his camp (*bungah*) between Abohar and Sarsuti. He left behind those with weak horses. Accompanied by those with stout horses, he marched out carrying large stocks of water. Travelling throughout the night, he organized hunting circles (*parah*) with a radius of fifteen leagues, which was gradually reduced to four, so that the onagers were trapped in it. The next day, from morning till evening, was spent in hunting. Thereafter, he broke the hunting circle. Travelling for two days with his companions, he returned to the camp on the third day and, thus, covered a distance of seventy leagues.[16] A hunting expedition, apparently a

66 *Situating Medieval India*

royal diversion, was similar to a military campaign. A vast establishment had emerged to supervise the hunt. A large number of birds and animals—lions, tigers, dogs and falcons—were trained to assist the exercise. Two or three servants, riding on horses, looked after each animal or bird. Apart from princes and nobles, the entourage comprised forty banners and a variety of tents. Besides the chief of hunt (*amir-i shikar*) Malik Dailan and his deputy Malik Khizr Bahram, there were numerous officers (*faujdars* and *bazidgars*).[17]

During the reign of Muhammad bin Tughluq (r. 1325-51), the Delhi Sultanate formed an alliance with two *zamindars* hailing from a village near Thanesar. This development took place in the context of a hunting expedition that culminated in a marital union. Once, Firoz was hunting deer in the suburbs of Thanesar and got separated from his retinue. At sunset, he began looking for a place to spend the night. He entered a village and met a group of *zamindars*. One of them, who was an expert in chiromancy (*ilm-i qifayat wa fan-i firasat*), removed the shoes of Firoz. On seeing the underside of the feet, he declared that the visitor was either a king or likely to become one. This person and his brother, Sadhu and Sadharan, busied themselves in playing the host. The wife of Sadhu, an intelligent woman, disfavoured trusting a stranger on the basis of his noble bearing. On her advice, a drinking party was organized to test the qualities of the guest. The sister of Sadhu and Sadharan, who was extremely beautiful (*jamal surat wa kamal husn*), served liquor to the guest. Sadhu's wife saw that the guest was entrapped in the maiden's beauty. She sought to know the identity of the guest, who could be offered the girl in marriage. Firoz revealed that he was the cousin of Sultan Muhammad bin Tughluq and, as such, the heir apparent to the throne of Delhi. Sadhu's wife stated that a marriage could take place, as Firoz was enamoured by her sister-in-law's beauty, while their family would gain material benefits from the alliance. The brothers readily agreed and the marriage ceremony (*nikah*) was duly performed. The marriage was consummated on the same night. Next morning, the armed contingents arrived from different directions. Firoz returned to Delhi with his bride. Sadhu and Sadharan shifted to Delhi and remained with Firoz like a shadow. Firoz fell madly in love with his

Rulers, Zamindars and Sufis

wife. In a short time, the two brothers embraced Islam. Sadharan was granted the title of Wajih ul-Mulk.[18]

The author of *Mirat-i Sikandari* would have us believe that the marriage emanated from love at first sight, which occurred in dramatic and accidental circumstances. However, the episode deserved contextualization in the process of state formation. There was a considerable similarity between the two marriages, that of Rajab and that of his son Firoz. It must be recalled that Ghazi Malik, as the governor of Dipalpur, had used coercion in the countryside of Abohar to (a) collect the land tax from the village headmen and to (b) force the local chief to marry his daughter to the governor's brother. These actions were interrelated and complementary. Firoz, an offspring of this marriage, must have been conscious of the implications of political collaboration between the Delhi Sultanate and the traditional heads of rural communities. When Firoz decided to wed a woman of a village near Thanesar, he must have been pleased to learn that she belonged to a family of *zamindars*, who were not only men of influence and exercised control over their locality, but could also muster thousands of horsemen and footmen by a mere hint.[19] They could facilitate, like Rana Mal Bhatti of Abohar, the consolidation of the Delhi Sultanate in their domain, particularly with reference to the collection of land tax from the peasantry. This suggested that the marriage might have been preceded by prolonged negotiations between the two parties. The two brothers might have agreed to the proposal of their sister's marriage and their conversion to Islam in return for high posts in Delhi and suitable prospects for the promotion of their progeny. The marital unions of the father and son, Rajab and Firoz, appeared somewhat dissimilar in outward form. However, they were similar in substance, i.e. the social classes involved, the objectives nurtured and the results achieved.[20]

Firoz Shah Tughluq, as Sultan, negotiated an alliance with Mote Rai Chauhan, the *zamindar* of Darrera near Hissar. In a poetic work, Kavi Jan has reconstructed the episode. Karam Chand Chauhan, the son of Mote Rai Chauhan, was hunting along with his companions. While searching for animals, he sat under a tree and fell asleep. Firoz, who was hunting along with Syed Nasir, the *faujdar*

68   *Situating Medieval India*

of Hissar, was astonished to see the boy. The shade covering the boy remained fixed, while the other trees did not cast any shadow at high noon. The visitors could not understand the boy's boon as, in their perception, the Hindus did not possess miraculous powers. Syed Nasir imagined that the boy would adopt the path of a Turk in the end. The Sultan, renaming the boy as Qiyam Khan, took him to Hissar. Mote Rai Chauhan was assured that the Sultan would treat the boy like a son and that he would be given a high rank on attaining maturity. Qiyam Khan was placed under the care of Syed Nasir, who brought him up along with his sons. On the completion of his education, Qiyam Khan embraced Islam after initial reluctance. Syed Nasir took Qiyam Khan to Delhi and, presenting him as his successor, secured the Sultan's approval for the change. On Syed Nasir's death, his rank, lands and goods passed on to Qiyam Khan, who became a trusted noble of the Sultan.[21]

The heroic ballad indicated that the ruling class had developed an effective mechanism, comprising a combination of negotiation and coercion, to secure the collaboration of the powerful class of rural aristocrats. For the administrative control and economic development of Hissar, the Sultan benefited from the cooperation of Mote Rai Chauhan. A matrimonial alliance was ruled out, perhaps because the Chauhan household did not have a young maiden to be offered as a bride. The only alternative was to keep the *zamindar's* son as a hostage with the local administrator of Hissar. Qiyam Khan played a role, which Bibi Kadbanu played in the household of Ghazi Malik and the sister of Sadhu and Sadharan played in the household of Firoz Shah Tughluq. In the long-run, Qiyam Khan reached the highest political rung of the Delhi Sultanate and, in due course, his descendants founded the autonomous principalities of Fatehpur and Jhunjhunu. In this sense, their rise was similar to that of Sadharan's son Zafar Khan.

By the end of the thirteenth century, Pakpattan had emerged as a premier centre of Chishti mysticism and popular pilgrimage. Baba Farid (1175-1265), apart from training a host of disciples, developed a tradition of Islamic devotionalism on the basis of the amulet-offering (*tawiz-futuh*) system. A large number of devotees

Rulers, Zamindars and Sufis 69

visited the shrine to receive amulets that were supposed to cure physical ailments. These were believed to serve as a protection against evil and a boon for good fortune. The devotees made offerings, generally in kind, which were distributed among the visitors. After the demise of Baba Farid, a series of rituals—death anniversary (*urs*), community kitchen (*langar*), devotional singing (*qawwali*), succession to the spiritual seat (*dastarbandi*) and annual entry into the sanctum sanctorum (*bihishti darwaza*)—were gradually institutionalized.[22] The Tughluq household, based in the neighbouring Dipalpur, could not remain immune from the growing popularity of the shrine in the countryside. In these circumstances, four Chishti saints, in different sets of circumstances, made prophecies regarding the rise of the Tughluqs to power.

Ghiasuddin Tughluq, as the governor of Diplapur, paid a visit to the shrine of Baba Farid at Pakpattan. His son Muhammad and nephew Firoz, both of whom were minors, accompanied him. Shaikh Alauddin, the grandson of Baba Farid, was the spiritual head of the shrine. He gifted a long piece of unsewn cotton cloth (*jama-i kirpas ghair dokhta*) to each of the three Tughluqs—three and a half yards to Ghazi Malik, twenty-seven yards to Muhammad and the remaining forty yards to Firoz. He directed them to tie the turbans around their heads and prophesied that all three would be crowned as rulers of the kingdom (*sahib-i taj wa takht*). The three Tughluqs visited Shaikh Sharfuddin at Panipat. The Shaikh offered a bowl of food to them. When they extended their hands to eat, the Shaikh remarked that three kings were eating from the same bowl. Firoz, during his days as a minor, paid his respects to Shaikh Nizamuddin Auliya at Ghiaspur in Delhi. In response to a question, he said that his name was Kamaluddin, which was his title. The Shaikh blessed Firoz with a long life of good fortune and material prosperity. On the death of Muhammad bin Tughluq at Thatta, Firoz ascended the throne. Shaikh Nasiruddin Mahmud Chiragh-i Delhi, who was present in the royal camp, prayed for a forty year long reign in favour of Firoz, provided he promised to rule with benevolence and justice.[23] In this manner, Afif has attributed the rule of Tughluq kings to the blessings of the Chishti lineage of Panjab and Delhi including Baba Farid, Shaikh Alauddin,

70 *Situating Medieval India*

Shaikh Sharfuddin Panipati, Shaikh Nizamuddin Auliya and Shaikh Nasiruddin Mahmud.

Firoz, following his acceptance (24 March 1351) of the Sultan's position, travelled from Siwistan to Delhi. Marching through the towns of southern Panjab, he tried to win over various sections of the society, who were important in view of the opposition of Khwaja-i Jahan at Delhi. As he entered a town, he visited the old Sufi shrines, revived the crumbling hospices, assured support to the descendants of dead Sufis, restored the old grants of the beneficiaries and gave stipends to the needy. Between Bhakkar and Uch, he received a delegation from Multan including Sufis, theologians, rural intermediaries, village headmen and ordinary folk. He accepted their petitions regarding the confirmation of land grants. At Uch, he restored land grants, stipends and allowances that had been cancelled years ago. He revived the dilapidated hospice of Shaikh Jamaluddin and conferred villages on his sons.[24] On reaching Multan, Firoz honoured the Sufis with rewards and presents.[25] For a few days, he stayed at Dipalpur, where he had spent his childhood. He went to pay homage at Baba Farid's shrine at Pakpattan. He organized the affairs of the saint's family, which had fallen on bad days. He honoured the descendants of Baba Farid with land grants, robes and rewards.[26] On reaching Sarsuti, he acted on the advice of Shaikh Nasiruddin Mahmud and approached Shaikh Qutbuddin Munawwar for his blessings. As a result of the new Sultan's outreach, the families of eminent Sufis—Baba Farid, Shaikh Bahauddin Zakariya, Shaikh Ruknuddin Abul Fateh, Shaikh Jamaluddin Uchi, Shaikh Nizamuddin Auliya and some others—experienced a revival owing to the grant of villages, lands and orchards.[27]

Firoz, in spite of a slew of measures favouring the Sufi institutions, could not win over the Chishti exemplars of Hansi. When he reached this town, Shaikh Nasiruddin Mahmud said that they had covered the distance up to the place because of his prayers. Since the spiritual domain of Shaikh Qutbuddin Munawwar started from Hansi, Firoz was advised to write to him. Accordingly, Firoz sent such a letter. In response, the Shaikh prayed for the victory of Firoz over Delhi.[28] When Firoz reached Fatehabad, Khwaja-i Jahan offered his

Rulers, Zamindars and Sufis 71

submission and allegiance. Afif noted that the prophecy of the Shaikh, 'Delhi itself will reach this place with folded hands', turned out to be true.[29] Since Firoz was in Hansi, he decided to call on Shaikh Munawwar. Unfortunately, the meeting ended on a sour note. It being a Friday, Firoz wished to meet the saint before the congregational prayer. By the time Firoz reached the hospice, the Shaikh had left for the mosque. The Shaikh, nonplussed at the sudden meeting, wished to go back and indirectly indicated that Firoz had arrived at an inopportune time. In a short sermon, he advised the Sultan to give up alcohol and minimize hunting. Firoz requested the Shaikh to pray for him, so that he remained away from hunting. The Shaikh was dissatisfied with the answer, as Firoz did not promise to abjure his bad habits. The Shaikh went to the mosque and offered his prayer. Firoz, returning to the fort, sent for the Shaikh a costly red and black cloak, which bore an ornamental lining. The Shaikh did not accept the cloak, as he learnt from his son Shaikh Nuruddin that it was made of stuff that the Shariat forbade. Since Firoz was still looking in the direction of Shaikh Munawwar, Shaikh Nuruddin ensured that the departure of his father was not seen. He directed two persons to hold the cloak as if it were a screen. Firoz sent a message to the Shaikh apologizing for his mistake. The Shaikh was free to ignore the unlawful garment. According to Afif, the presence of pure and exalted saints in Hansi had guaranteed its safety from the Mongol invasions.[30] The Shaikh, owing to his friendship with Shaikh Nasiruddin Mahmud, prayed for the success of Firoz, but he did not acquiesce in the violation of religious protocol.

In the narrative of Afif, the image of Firoz has been transformed from a seeker and recipient of blessings from Shaikhs to a producer of his own charismatic religious authority. Afif, through subtle and overt ways, merged the image of the Sultan into that of a Shaikh. Firoz, as Afif's ideal ruler, was claimed to possess ten attributes, each of which coincided with one of the ten mystical stages (*maqamat*) common in Sufi discourses. Firoz, on his accession, did not merely possess the characteristics of a Shaikh. Rather, he was himself a Shaikh. Qutbuddin Munawwar, the Chishti saint of Hansi, designated Firoz as one of the Shaikhs of the path (*mashaikh-*

72 *Situating Medieval India*

i tariqah).[31] Firoz developed a perpetual contact with the leading Sufi shrines. After every month or two, he visited such sacred sites in Delhi and its suburbs. On these occasions, he followed a specific pattern. For example, when he arrived at the tomb of Nizamuddin Auliya, he prostrated himself at its feet and placed his head on the ground. Besides the grave, he recited the *Fatiha* prayer. After this, he held the ornamental covering and sought blessings of the saint. He deployed an official of the public treasury (*bait ul-mal*) to distribute stipends to the attendants. He also appointed the most senior noble to look into the needs of the caretakers. Firoz, before embarking on the military expedition to Thatta, paid homage at this shrine. During the course of his long journey, he registered his devotion at the mausoleum of Baba Farid at Pakpattan.[32] In 1374, Firoz travelled all the way to Bahraich and spent some time at the shrine of Salar Masud Ghazi. That night, the saint appeared to Firoz in a dream and, making a sign, indicated that he had become old and, therefore, must prepare for the hereafter. Next morning, Firoz got himself tonsured (*mahluk*) in the manner of Sufi initiation. At this moment, he looked like an eminent Shaikh. This blessing flowed out of his reverence for the Sufis and scholars. Following his example, a number of nobles also got their heads shaved. This act conformed to a similar procedure that Prophet Muhammad and his companions had undergone centuries back. Afif would have us believe that Firoz's step marked the suppression of practices that the Shariat had forbidden.[33]

If Firoz, in the eyes of Afif, was a Sufi, then he had to portray the Sultan as displaying miraculous powers. Such an opportunity came in the way of the Sultan when he led his army to Sind. While marching through an arid forest in Kuchiran (Rann of Kutch), the soldiers were on the verge of death owing to an acute scarcity of water. Firoz was in the midst of a calamity that Hazrat Musa had faced in a waterless tract during his wanderings. The Sultan, in his desperation, withdrew into privacy and prayed for divine mercy. As a result, the sky was overcast and, because of a heavy downpour, rivulets appeared all around. The troops quenched their thirst and, storing water for the march, emerged out of the deadly forest. Afif held that the prayers of the Sultan had brought about a miraculous

Rulers, Zamindars and Sufis 73

end to the crisis. Afif compared the Sultan's miracle to a similar wondrous act of the famous Egyptian mystic Zu ul-Nun Misri (d. 859) as recorded in Fariduddin Attar's *Tazkirat ul-Auliya*. Firoz, having prayed for divine mercy like the Shaikh, caused torrential rain and brought satisfaction to the people.[34] In this narrative, Afif has placed his patron in the larger cultural universe of Islam in which eminent prophets and saints occupied a prominent place. Afif also asserted that the three major administrative measures during the latter part of Firoz's reign—release of prisoners, renovation of mosques in Delhi and justice to the oppressed—were inspired by the example of Prophet Muhammad. This enabled Afif to make a categorical statement that Firoz not only possessed all the qualities of the previous rulers, but also bore the virtues of saints.[35]

The alliance between the Delhi Sultanate and the Tak *zamindars* of Thanesar received the blessings of Syed Jalaluddin Bukhari, the famous Suhrawardi saint of Uch.[36] Firoz Shah Tughluq had cultivated intimate relations with Bukhari, who stayed in Delhi for extended periods. Sadharan, at the advice of the Sultan, became a disciple of Bukhari. The Sultan was pleased with the act, while Bukhari began to shower his grace on the two brothers. Once a number of mendicants (*fuqra*) assembled in Bukhari's hospice, but there was no food for them. Zafar Khan, the son of Sadharan, who was also a disciple of Bukhari, learnt about the dire need. Gathering food and sweets from his house and the market, he went to the hospice and served meals to the visitors. Bukhari, learning of the generosity, summoned Zafar Khan and, in lieu of the feast, conferred on him the kingdom of Gujarat along with the covering of his own bedstead. When Zafar Khan returned to his house, his wife was not impressed. Since he was old and could not rule for long, he must seek a boon for his descendants. Zafar Khan, carrying a fresh bundle of gifts, went back to the hospice. The Shaikh gave a handful of dates to Zafar Khan and told him that his descendants would rule over Gujarat for several generations equal in number to the dates. Some people believed that the number of dates was twelve or thirteen or more.[37]

The above linkages had far-reaching consequences. They enabled Firoz to bring about a canal based agrarian expansion in two areas,

74　　　　　　*Situating Medieval India*

southeast Panjab and Multan. Ghazi Malik, while serving as the governor of Dipalpur, had made a beginning in this regard when he excavated a canal from the Ravi to Jhelum.[38] Firoz laid a network of six canals that flowed across the zone between the Ghaggar and Sarsuti on the west and Yamuna on the east. According to Afif, the Rajabwah and Ulughkhani carried water to the newly established city of Hissar Firoza. Taken together, the canals appeared to have irrigated lands in places such as Ambala, Mustafabad, Shahabad, Thanesar, Kuhram, Samana, Kaithal, Tohana, Safedun, Atkhera, Jamalpur, Ahroni, Sirsa, Khanda, Barwala, Agroha, Hansi, Jind and Dhatrat. At the onset of monsoon, special officers travelled along the canals to monitor the flow of water and prevent the flooding of villages. In addition to the monsoon crop (*kharif*), the land of Hissar Firoza began to produce winter crops (*rabi*) including wheat and different varieties of sugarcane. With the rise of subsoil water, wells yielded water at the depth of four yards. The new administrative division of Hissar Firoza comprised the subdistricts of Hansi, Agroha, Fatehabad, Sarsuti, Salora and Khizrabad.[39] In the neighbourhood of Delhi, 1,200 fruit orchards were planted and 30 old gardens were revived. It was hoped that groups of pastoralists, hitherto living in clusters of bullock carts and wandering in search of water, would settle as sedentary cultivators. Apart from increasing the cattle population, the canals would benefit the movement of travellers and encampment of armies.[40]

After the new city of Hissar Firoza had been built, Firoz visited the neighbouring town of Hansi. He paid his respects to Shaikh Nuruddin, who was the spiritual mentor of the historian Afif. The Shaikh succeeded to the Chishti seat of Hansi following the death of his father Shaikh Qutbuddin Munawwar. Firoz, on reaching the hospice, did not allow the Shaikh to get up from his seat and walk out to welcome him. After exchanging pleasantries and shaking hands, they sat in conversation. The Shaikh, following in the footsteps of eminent Sufis, delivered a sermon on spirituality. The Sultan stated that he had founded the city of Hissar Firoza for the benefit and comfort of the people. It would be appropriate if the Shaikh, owing to his grace, settled in the new city. A hospice would be built for the pious and necessary funds sanctioned for its

Rulers, Zamindars and Sufis

75

maintenance. It would be easy for the people of Hansi to visit the Shaikh, as the distance was not more than ten leagues. Because of the Shaikh's blessings, the inhabitants of Hissar Firoza would be protected from hardships, while the city would become populous and prosperous. However, the Sultan clarified that it was his appeal, not a command. The Shaikh, while declining the request, asserted that he would continue to reside in Hansi. It had been the spiritual domain (*vilayat*) of his grandfather (Shaikh Burhanuddin) and father (Shaikh Qutbuddin Munawwar). It had been bestowed on them by Shaikh ul-Islam Shaikh Fariduddin Ganj-i Shakar and Mahbub-i Ilahi Shaikh Nizamuddin Auliya. The Sultan conceded that it was proper for the Shaikh to continue residing in Hansi and hoped that his blessings would protect Hissar Firoza from all calamities. Afif would have us believe that when the cruel invaders (under Timur) attacked Delhi and destroyed the property of Hindus and Muslims, the inhabitants of Hansi as well as the part of Hissar Firoza, which had been included in Hansi, remained safe due to the blessings of Shaikh Nuruddin.[41]

The agrarian expansion, as undertaken in southeast Panjab, was replicated in Multan. Ain ul-Mulk Mahru, whom Firoz appointed to govern the region, piloted the project. During the previous governor Imad ul-Mulk, outmigration of inhabitants had reduced the cultivated area and agricultural production. The crisis was compounded with a slump in grain prices, increase in land grants and abolition of numerous taxes. Mahru, while prioritizing upkeep of the army, acknowledged the need to maintain the religious classes (Syeds, theologians and Sufis) through a generous distribution of land grants. The measure was advisable because Islam had been existing in Multan for 700 years and Firoz enjoyed a considerable support from it. Mahru, carrying out a survey in land grants, laid down fresh rules for their management. Steps were taken to ensure that the grantees did not suffer due to fluctuations in grain prices and they brought barren land under the plough.[42] Mahru laid a network of canals including Nasirwah, Qutbwah, Khizrwah, Qabulwah and Hamruwah. It was clarified that works on large rivers were financed from the public treasury. In case of smaller canals, the cost of construction and maintenance was borne by the

76 Situating Medieval India

local beneficiaries including the chiefs and peasants (*ahali wa arbab*). All of them were bound to share the expenditure, so that the burden of some did not fall on others.[43] The village headmen, who offered active cooperation, were rewarded. Babdujah, a headman who had displayed great energy in digging Qutbwah and Hamruwah, was rewarded with the superintendence (*danagi*) of these canals. The headmen and peasants of the subdivision were directed to assist Babdujah in performing his duties regarding the canals.[44] Those who abstained were threatened with exile and death. Mahru condemned the land controlling elements, who did not participate in the repair of canals, though these passed through villages where they had been allotted land grants. Firoz, as seen above, distributed land grants to the Sufis in Multan immediately after his accession. In order to ensure the productivity of these lands, the state developed canal irrigation with the collaboration of intermediaries and beneficiaries.

Timur, during his invasion, marched through areas experiencing agrarian expansion and acquired a rich booty comprising grain and cattle. The political structure, which the Tughluqs had carefully raised on linkages with *zamindars* and Sufis, collapsed and disappeared. As the Delhi Sultanate was unable to control its territories and collect the land tax, it faced the autonomy of chiefs, the defiance of its assignees (*muqtis*) and threat of foreign invasions. Jasrath Khokhar, during his numerous raids on central Panjab, targeted the district governors and their local allies. The Delhi Sultanate, managing to rope in the *zamindars* between Bhatinda and Kalanaur, unleashed punitive measures against the rebellious Turkbachas. Bahlol Lodi, relying on the Indo-Central Asian horse trade and migration of Afghan tribes to Sirhind, laid the foundation of the Afghan State. Ibn Syed, a dervish (*majzub sahib kashf*) of Samana, was said to have conferred the kingdom of Delhi on him in return for an offering of 1,600 *tankahs*.[45]

During the second half of the fifteenth century, Panjab witnessed an unprecedented development. Two Sufis became rulers in Malerkotla and Multan. Though their principalities were widely separate from each other, they displayed some common traits. Both belonged to the Suhrawardi lineage and sought to emulate the Tughluqid model of state formation. On the one hand, they stitched alliances

Rulers, Zamindars and Sufis 77

with powerful rural magnates and, on the other hand, they were matrimonially linked with the Sultan of Delhi, Bahlol Lodi. Shaikh Sadruddin Sadr-i Jahan (1434-1508), popularly known as Haidar Shaikh, carved out the principality of Malerkotla near Sirhind. His rise to prominence has been narrated in different ways. According to an Afghan chronicle, Haidar Shaikh was an eminent mystic, who had a large following. Displaying his miraculous power, he forced the Sultan of Delhi to accept his saintliness.[46] Another version portrayed Haidar Shaikh as a military commander in the service of Delhi. Since he performed his official duties through miraculous powers, he was allowed to retire and serve the cause of Islam.[47] According to another version, Bahlol Lodi sought the blessings of Haidar Shaikh in his bid for the throne of Delhi. He promised to give his daughter in marriage to him if he achieved his aim. Since Bahlol Lodi met with success, he married his daughter (Taj Murassa Begum) to the saint and gave 69 villages in dowry. Haidar Shaikh, being an eminent mystic and benefiting from his kinship, emerged as a *zamindar*. He formed an alliance with Rai Bahram Bhatti, a *zamindar* of Kapurthala and, as part of the agreement, married his daughter. In due course, he contracted the marriage of his daughter Bibi Mangi in the family of a *zamindar* of Tohana. Following the demise of Haidar Shaikh, his son Shaikh Hasan, who was born to Taj Murassa Begum, inherited the spiritual legacy and Shaikh Isa, who was born of Bahram Bhatti's daughter, inherited the landed estate.[48]

In Multan, the political developments proceeded along a slightly different course. The Syed dispensation, facing internal and external challenges, failed to assert its authority in Multan. The local chiefs, both the Langahs and Balochis, were not inclined to assume the burdensome task. In this vacuum, the inhabitants and *zamindars* persuaded Shaikh Yusuf Qureshi, a descendant of Shaikh Bahauddin Zakariya, to hold the reins of the government. In order to consolidate his control, he began to win over the local chiefs and recruit fresh retainers. Rai Sehra, the Langah potentate, who held Sewi and neighbouring areas, feared the growing power of Bahlol Lodi and formed an alliance with Qureshi. Promising military assistance in all future expeditions, he gave his daughter in marriage to Qureshi. Owing to a mutual lack of trust, Qureshi did not

78 *Situating Medieval India*

permit Rai Sehra to acquire a mansion in the city of Multan. Rai Sehra displaced Qureshi after a rule of two years. He grabbed power under the name of Sultan Qutbuddin, so that his descendants ruled over Multan until the Arghuns displaced them at the instance of Babur. Sultan Qutbuddin did not allow the Suhrawardi establishment to play any role in the exercise of power. Qureshi, forced to leave Multan, became a fugitive at Delhi. Bahlul Lodi gave his daughter in marriage to Qureshi's son, but could not reinstate his guest in Multan. Barbak Shah (Sikandar Lodi) failed to snatch Multan from the Langahs, who went on to consolidate their rule with the support of the Balochis and Thattawas. Through a series of local alliances, the Langahs achieved what Qureshi and the Lodis could not.[49]

The Tughluq rulers, owing to their roots in Panjab, were intimately familiar with its topographical features and social structure. From the middle of the fourteenth century, they shifted the political focus from the Gangetic plain to Panjab. By this time, the dominant local elements, particularly the *zamindars* and Sufis, had gradually shed their aloofness from the state and showed ample willingness to collaborate with the ruling class. As a result, the Tughluqs stitched alliances with a number of *zamindars*, who possessed military resources and commanded influence in their localities. They also paid homage at prominent Sufi shrines and, through generous land grants, assimilated them in the polity. In this manner, ground was prepared for agrarian expansion based on canal networks in two semi-arid zones of southeast Panjab and Multan. By the end of the fourteenth century, the resettlement, productivity and prosperity of these tracts attracted the whirlwind movement of Timur. Three developments—the alliances between the rulers and intermediate groups, agrarian expansion and Timur's plunder—occurred in the same areas. During the course of Timur's invasion, the well-knit agricultural communities were scattered and thriving socio-economic enclaves were dislocated. However, the Tughluqid model of state formation appeared again in the second half of the fifteenth century. A close collaboration between the prominent Sufis and powerful *zamindars* led to the emergence of autonomous principalities in Malerkotla and Multan.

Rulers, Zamindars and Sufis

NOTES

1. Parts of this paper appeared in the larger exercise of my Presidential Address (Medieval Section) entitled 'The Making of Medieval Punjab: Politics, Society and Economy, c. 1200–c. 1400', Punjab History Conference, 40th session, Patiala: Punjabi University, 14-16 March 2008.

2. Sunil Kumar, *The Emergence of the Delhi Sultanate 1192-1286*, Ranikhet: Permanent Black, 2007, pp. 282-6, 297-8.

3. Balban organized the western and eastern provinces of the Sultanate into autonomous appanages that were left under the command of his two sons. At the outset of his reign, the province of Sind was assigned to his elder son Prince Muhammad, while the younger son Bughra Khan was assigned to Samana to oversee the Panjab region. In 1281, the rebellion of Tughril forced Balban to redeploy Bughra Khan as the governor of Lakhnauti. After this, Balban did not make any appointment in the western and eastern provinces. The two princes were required to remit tribute and supplies periodically to Delhi. However, for all practical purposes, the two domains of Panjab-Sind and Lakhnauti were autonomous. Sunil Kumar, 'Balancing Autonomy with Service: Frontier Military Commanders and Their Relations with the Delhi Sultanate in the 13th and 14th Centuries', Presidential Address: Medieval Section, *Proceedings of the Punjab History Conference*, 39th session, 16-18 March 2007, p. 97.

4. Abdul Malik Isami, *Futuh us-Salatin*, Eng. tr. Agha Mahdi Husain, Aligarh: Department of History, Aligarh Muslim University and Bombay: Asia Publishing House, 1976, vol. II, pp. 309-11. (Hereafter cited as Isami).

5. The rural aristocracy, comprising *rais* and *ranas*, possessed military resources and resisted the Turkish warlords in the thirteenth century. After the initial Turkish conquest, the new rulers allowed the rural aristocracy to exist and imposed a tribute on it. A lower class of village headmen, designated as *khuts* and *muqaddams*, collected land tax from the peasantry and enjoyed numerous privileges. Ghazi Malik's action indicated an advanced stage in the subversion of the rural aristocracy. The Sultanate ruling class still needed an intermediary class in the countryside to appropriate the agricultural surplus. This emerging superior class, of which the *chaudhari* was the first representative, was created out of elements of old rural aristocracy and some village headmen. Tapan Raychadhari and Irfan Habib, eds., *The Cambridge Economic History of India, vol. I: c. 1200–c. 1750*, New Delhi: Orient Longman, rpt., 1982, pp. 55-7.

6. Shams Siraj Afif, *Tarikh-i Firoz Shahi*, Persian text, ed. Maulavi Wilayat Husain, Calcutta: Royal Asiatic Society of Bengal, 1890, pp. 37-40. (Hereafter cited as Afif).

80 *Situating Medieval India*

7. Ibid., pp. 40-3.
8. Ibid., pp. 101-4.
9. Mahdi Husain, *The Rehla of Ibn Battuta: India, Maldive Islands and Ceylon,* Baroda: Oriental Institute, 1976, p. 48.
10. Ziauddin Barani, *Tarikh-i Firoz Shahi,* Persian text, ed. Sir Syed Ahmad, Aligarh: Aligarh Muslim University, rpt., 2005, pp. 322-3. (Hereafter cited as Barani).
11. Amir Khusrau, *Tughluq Nama,* Persian text, ed. Syed Hashmi Aurangabadi, Aurangabad: Urdu Publishing House, 1933, p. 84.
12. The antecedents of Ghazi Malik have been open to debate. Three contemporary writers (Amir Khusrau, Ibn Battuta and Shams Siraj Afif) state, with minor differences, that Ghazi Malik entered the service of Alauddin Khalji in a humble position and, attaining promotions, distinguished himself as a military commander on several fronts. Muhammad Qasim Firishtah and Sujan Rai Bhandari, writing in the seventeenth century, discovered that Ghazi Malik was born to Malik Tughluq (a slave of Balban) and his Jat wife of Panjab. Peter Jackson suggests that Ghazi Malik, hailing from Mongol or Turko-Mongol stock, might have been a follower of Mongol chief Alaghu, who took employment with Jalaluddin Khalji. Sunil Kumar places Ghazi Malik in the fluid conditions on the frontier, where ambitious military commanders gathered large retinues and built impressive local reputations as warriors and patrons. Sunil Kumar, 'Ignored Elites: Turks, Mongols and Persian Secretarial Class in the Early Delhi Sultanate', in *Expanding Frontiers in South Asian and World History: Essays in Honour of John F. Richards,* ed. Richard M. Eaton et al., New Delhi: Cambridge University Press, 2009, pp. 48-9.
13. Mohammad Habib, 'Nasiruddin Khusrau Khan', in *A Comprehensive History of India, vol. v: The Delhi Sultanate, AD 1206-1526,* ed. Mohammad Habib and Khaliq Ahmad Nizami, New Delhi: People's Publishing House, rpt., 1982, p. 452.
14. Isami, II, pp. 580-1.
15. Ibid., pp. 585-90.
16. Afif, pp. 319-21.
17. Ibid., pp. 317-18.
18. Shaikh Sikandar bin Muhammad urf Manjhu bin Akbar, *Mirat-i Sikandari,* Persian text, ed. S.C. Misra and M.L. Rahman, Baroda: The Maharaja Sayajirao University of Baroda, 1961, pp. 6-10.
19. Ibid., p. 7.
20. A modern writer has linked the social attitude of the two brothers to their low caste. For material gains, they used their sister to beguile Firoz Tughluq,

Rulers, Zamindars and Sufis 81

wedded her outside their caste and even abjured their religion. Such practices were not current among Rajputs, whose reaction was more accurately reflected by Rana Mal Bhatti, who refused to surrender his daughter to Ghazi Malik. According to another scholar, 'From the perspective of the Taks, offering women and military allegiance represented a potential means of upward mobility. The transformation of the Tak peasants into independent Sultans within a generation is a prime example of the benefits that manpower rich groups derived from association with the Sultanate'. S.C. Misra, *The Rise of Muslim Power in Gujarat: A History of Gujarat from 1298 to 1442*, New Delhi: Munshiram Manoharlal, 1982, pp. 139-40; Samira Shaikh, *Forging A Region: Sultans, Traders and Pilgrims in Gujarat 1200-1500*, New Delhi: Oxford University Press, 2010, pp. 200-1.

21. Nupur Chaudhary, 'A Vanished Supremacy: The Qiyamkhanis of Fatehpur Jhunjhunu', in *Popular Literature and Pre-modern Societies in South Asia*, ed. Surinder Singh and Ishwar Dayal Gaur, New Delhi: Pearson Longman, 2008, p. 64; Cynthia Talbot, 'Becoming Turk in the Rajput Way: Conversion and Identity in an Indian Warrior Narrative', in *Expanding Frontiers in South Asian and World History: Essays in Honour of John F. Richards*, ed. Richard M. Eaton et. al., New York: Cambridge University Press, 2013, p. 203.

22. Richard M. Eaton, 'The Political and Religious Authority of the Shrine of Baba Farid', in *Essays on Islam and Indian History*, New Delhi: Oxford University Press, 2000, pp. 204-7.

23. Afif, pp. 27-9.

24. Barani, pp. 538-9.

25. Afif, p. 60.

26. Barani, p. 543.

27. Ibid., p. 560.

28. Afif, pp. 61-2.

29. Ibid., p. 71.

30. Ibid., pp. 78-82.

31. Blain H. Auer, *Symbols of Authority in Medieval Islam: History, Religion and Muslim Legitimacy in the Delhi Sultanate*, New Delhi: Viva Books, 2013, pp. 99-100.

32. Afif, pp. 194-8.

33. Ibid., pp. 371-3.

34. Ibid., pp. 216-119.

35. Ibid., pp. 509-13.

36. Syed Jalaluddin Bukhari (1308-84), famous as Makhdum-i Jahaniyan,

82   *Situating Medieval India*

was a grandson of Syed Jalaluddin Surkhposh, who founded the Uch branch of the Suhrawardis. Bukhari received higher education in Multan under the care of Ruknuddin Abul Fateh. Receiving a Chishti affiliation from Nasiruddin Mahmud Chiragh-i Delhi, he declined Muhammad bin Tughluq's offer of managing 40 Sufi lodges of Sind. During seven years (1341-8), he travelled in different parts of west Asia and received 40 robes associated with six Sufi orders. Retuning to Uch, he rejuvenated the hospice with the addition of a vibrant seminary. His regimen for trainees comprised knowledge (*ilm*) of Islamic jurisprudence and action involving devotional practices (*amal*). Active in politics, he brought peace between the Delhi Sultanate and the Samma chiefs of Sind. Ziauddin Barani and Ain ul-Mulk Mahru sought his intervention in administrative matters. Afif has devoted the last chapter of his chronicle to highlight his friendly bond with Firoz Shah Tughluq. Amina M. Steinfels, *Knowledge before Action: Islamic Learning and Sufi Practice in the Life of Sayyid Jalal al-Din Bukhari Makhdum-i Jahaniyan*, Columbia: University of South Carolina, 2012, pp. 15-143.

37. Shaikh Sikandar bin Muhammad urf Manjhu bin Akbar, *Mirat-i Sikandari*, pp. 10-11.

38. Amir Khusrau, *Tughluq Nama*, p. 63.

39. Afif, pp. 125-8.

40. Barani, pp. 567-71.

41. Afif, pp. 131-3.

42. Ain ul-Mulk Ainuddin Mahru, *Insha-i Mahru*, Persian text, ed. Shaikh Abdul Rashid, Aligarh: Aligarh Muslim University, 1954, Letter no. 31, pp. 63-8.

43. Ibid., Letter no. 114, pp. 176-7.

44. Ibid., Letter no. 11, pp. 20-1.

45. Abdullah, *Tarikh-i Daudi*, Persian text, ed. Shaikh Abdur Rashid and Iqtidar Husain Siddiqui, Aligarh: Aligarh Muslim University, 1969, pp. 3-4; Shaikh Rizqullah Mushtaqi, *Waqiat-i Mushtaqi*, Persian text, ed. Iqtidar Husain Siddiqui and Waqarul Hasan Siddiqi, Rampur: Rampur Raza Library, 2002, p. 3.

46. Khwaja Niamatullah bin Khawaja Habibullah al-Haravi, *Tarikh-i Khan Jahani wa Makhzan-i Afghani*, Persian text, ed. Syed Muhammad Imamuddin, Dacca: Asiatic Society of Pakistan, 1962, vol. II, pp. 787-8.

47. Anna Bigelow, *Sharing the Sacred: Practicing Pluralism in Muslim North India*, New York: Oxford University Press, 2010, pp. 46-7.

48. Nawab Iftikhar Ali Khan, *History of the Ruling Family of Sheikh Sadruddin*

Rulers, Zamindars and Sufis   83

Sadr-i Jahan of Malerkotla (1449 AD to 1948 AD), ed. R.K. Ghai, Patiala: Punjabi University, 2000, pp. 2-10.

49. Khwaja Nizamuddin Ahmad, *Tabaqat-i Akbari*, Eng. tr., Branjendranath De and Baini Prashad, Calcutta: The Asiatic Society, rpt., 1996, vol. III, pp. 788-96.

CHAPTER 4

Administrative Consolidation in the Delhi Sultanate: Evidence from a Collection of Letters

Ain ul-Mulk Mahru was one the most important nobles of the Tughluq era.[1] The evidence about his early career was uncertain. During the reign of Muhammad bin Tughluq, he was appointed as the governor of Awadh and Zafarabad.[2] He rose to prominence when he supplied grain and money to the Sultan, who was staying in Sargdawari during a severe famine. Impressed with his efforts, the Sultan raised his status to that of a courtier and companion. He was deputed to the Deccan in the wake of financial mismanagement at the hands of Qutlugh Khan and his associates. Mahru, treating the move as detrimental to his future, raised the banner of revolt. The Sultan, in order to meet the challenge, marched with the contingents from Samana, Amroha, Baran and Kol. Barani, who associated Mahru and his brothers with clerks and traders, stated that they had no experience of fighting battles.[3] Ibn Battuta has informed us that Mahru, being an Indian, was the target of hostility from the Khurasani nobles and foreigners. At the same time, the people of India hated the foreigners because the Sultan favoured them.[4] In an encounter at Bangarmau near the Ganga, the rebels were routed. The followers of Mahru fled across the river into the countryside, while his two brothers were killed. The Sultan, discerning administrative talent in Mahru, restored him to his former dignity. Muthar of Kara, the famous poet, has showered fulsome praise on his generous patron Mahru, who had gathered a number of scholars and artists around himself. In his assemblies, the subtleties of poetry, music and science were discussed.[5] On

Administrative Consolidation in the Delhi Sultanate 85

the accession of Firoz Shah Tughluq, Mahru was assigned the exalted office of *Mushrif-i Mumalik*. A serious discord erupted between him and Khan-i Jahan, the *wazir*, on the question of jurisdiction between the branches of income and expenditure. With every passing day, the quarrel became uglier and personal. The Sultan recognized the indispensability of both. He allowed the *wazir* to dismiss Mahru, but sent the latter as the governor of Multan, Bhakkar and Siwistan. A group of senior nobles expressed their anguish at the growing arrogance of the *wazir* and his unfair treatment of Mahru. They could face a similar fate in the future. The Sultan, showing sagacity and discernment, convened a meeting of the nobles and heard Mahru's apprehensions. Mahru, as per his request, was permitted to submit the accounts of his assignment directly to the Sultan and, thus, was exempted from the control of the finance ministry. The Sultan summoned the *wazir* and, erasing the remaining signs of rancour, made the two officers bury the hatchet in the interest of the state.[6]

In a preface to his collection of letters (*Insha-i Mahru*), Mahru has described the circumstances in which he completed the task. Since he was dedicated to learning and intellect, he wrote books on complex themes in perfect prose. By doing so, he wished to fulfil the needs of readers, who were thirsty for knowledge. He himself remained oblivious to the defects if any. The increasing criticism of contemporary scholars served as an obstacle to his enterprise. Demoralized, he was impelled to put his work on hold. In the meanwhile, he received the subtle approval of Firoz Shah Tughluq and retrieved his own sense of determination. He resolved to compile the letters in the form of a treatise. He hoped that the book, with the infectious gaze of experts (*nazr kimiya asr*), would attain currency in the domain of learning. If this hope did not materialize, such a work would remain unpublished and ultimately forgotten. In the end, he prayed that his efforts would bear fruit only with divine grace.[7]

This collection comprised 133 letters in all. The first 12, drafted for the Sultan, were notifications (*manshurs*) announcing the appointment of officers ranging from the provincial governor to the local judge. The remaining letters, emanating from Mahru's

86   *Situating Medieval India*

pen, were addressed to different individuals and dealt with diverse subjects. The important ones pertained to the administrative jurisdiction of Multan. They revealed the wide scope of governor's authority. They spoke of the unfavourable material conditions of the region and measures for agrarian revival through canal irrigation. They delved into the state of land grants, besides the steps to streamline their management. Apart from price regulation, they uncovered commercial practices and incidence of taxation. Some letters were written to the local Sufis regarding the complaints against petty functionaries. Since Mahru served for some time in Gujarat, a few letters referred to the situation of its towns, particularly Khambayat. Some letters pointed to Delhi's weak control over Sind, with reference to the opposition of Samma chiefs and inability of Mahru's subordinates to deal with the rural magnates. At times, Mahru took interest in the socio-religious practices, but did not hesitate to criticize the ideological positions of the philosophers. A large number of letters were entirely personal. On one occasion, he recommended a man for a specific post and, at another, felt anguished at the lack of interaction with an acquaintance. If one letter felicitated an addressee for an achievement, another expressed condolences at a bereavement and still another offered advice on family matters. In a few letters, addressed to his sons, he stressed the value of education and conveyed his happiness on the birth of his grandsons. Unfortunately, the letters (except one on land grants of Multan) did not bear any date. In most cases, it was possible to fix the chronology because of the context, events and names. In conformity with the contemporary literary patterns, Mahru often tended to be obscure and verbose.

The reign of Muhammad bin Tughluq witnessed widespread disturbances and anarchy due to the revolts amongst the nobles. In order to strengthen the position of Firoz Shah Tughluq and ensure political stability of the dispensation, an agreement (*ahdnama*) was signed by prominent nobles, well-wishers of the court and officers of the state. It opened with an assertion that God and Prophet Muhammad had prescribed the execution of bonds and agreements. Since the ancient times, the adherents of devout kings had taken oaths of allegiance to express their fealty and morality

Administrative Consolidation in the Delhi Sultanate   87

(*izhar ikhlas wa sharf khud*). On account of this, the signatory tendered his submission with willingness, honesty and good faith. He made this declaration in the name of God, who made it obligatory for men to keep their promises as laid in a Quranic verse relating to the covenant with Him. He bound himself to be loyal, obedient and well-wisher of Firoz Shah Tughluq, the king of kings and the deputy of the Caliph. God would always preserve his kingdom, command and dignity, as he was vested with sovereignty in accordance with the Shariat and Imam of the land. The signatory would regard the Sultan's friends as his friends and the Sultan's enemies as his enemies. He would honour this obligation throughout his life. Under no circumstances, he would oppose the armies, adherents and servants of the court. He would not be friendly with the opponents of the throne. He would not entertain the thought of harming the Sultan, overtly or covertly and through action, word or writing. Conforming to his orders, he would always offer obedience and submission. Openly or secretly, he would never oppose the Sultan even if his sons and brothers did so. He would abandon them and strive to punish them. He regarded it as a divinely ordained duty, which had been inscribed in the Quran 'Obey Allah and obey the Apostle and those in authority among you.'[8] He would always express gratitude to the court for its bounties. If ever he transgressed this agreement and broke even one of the stipulations, he would treat it as a violation of his covenant with God and, as a result, be amenable to punishment on the day of judgement. In such a situation, he would be divorced from his wife and lose possession of his slaves. He accepted these conditions in the presence of God, His angels and witnesses, so that this agreement became a proof of his oath of allegiance.[9] The agreement produced the desired result, as Firoz Shah Tughluq did not face any serious opposition from the nobles.

In 1353, Firoz Shah Tughluq led his first expedition to Bengal (Lakhnauti).[10] He addressed a letter to the various social classes of the region including nobles, Syeds, Sufis, clerics, soldiers, rural intermediaries and the entire populace. The Sultan exposed the misrule of Haji Ilyas and enumerated a number of corrective measures. At the outset, the Sultan expressed his gratitude to God,

88   *Situating Medieval India*

who had chosen him to administer justice, besides establishing peace and prosperity for the people. Since the province of Lakhnauti had been under his predecessors and, by way of inheritance, had passed into his hands, he was bound to ensure the welfare of people. For a long time, Haji Ilyas was obedient to the Sultan and his predecessors. He used to send his letters of allegiance along with gifts. Later on, he broke out in open revolt and began to oppress the people. His cruelty reached such an extent that he killed Hindu women. Such an act was not permitted in any religion. Without authorization and permission of the Shariat, he extracted money from the people, unmindful of their life and property. In these circumstances, the Sultan had marched to Lakhnauti at the head of a large army. His aim was to free the region from oppression, besides providing justice and kindness (*adl wa ihsan*). First, he assured all people of Lakhnauti—*khans, maliks,* Syeds, Sufis, *imams* and *sadrs,* eminent persons, soldiers and functionaries—that their assignments and grants were being doubled, provided they expressed their allegiance to the court with personal presence. Second, the various categories of *zamindars* from river Kosi to Lakhnauti—*muqaddams, mafrozis* and *maliks*—who would appear in the court, were exempted from land tax (*kharaj wa mahsul*) of that year. In the next year, the dues would be collected in accordance with the practice of the late Sultan Shamsuddin Iltutmish. A variety of imposts (*qismat wa awarizat wa faroi wa muhaddisat*) were abolished. The possessions of the *zamindars,* who would appear with their retinues, were doubled. One bringing half of his retinue would get an increase of 50 per cent. The one coming alone would retain his original land as such. The Sultan, owing to his unlimited kindness, would not displace them. In the end, he advised the people to continue living in their homes without any worries.[11]

Firoz, returning from Bengal after his second expedition, arrived in Jaunpur and marched to Jajnagar (Odisha). Mahru has acknowledged the receipt of a letter of victory (*fatehnama*) over Jajnagar. The document revolved around the well-being of the Sultan, the defeat of Gajpat Rai and return march of the Delhi army. On its basis, he prepared a statement for an unknown person.[12] For years, the Rai of Jajnagar had been sending letters of his allegiance

Administrative Consolidation in the Delhi Sultanate   89

(*husn-i bandagi*) to the Sultan. Reacting to the Sultan's expedition to Lakhnauti and taking advantage of the long distance between Delhi and Jajnagar, the Rai discarded obedience and, rising in open revolt, refused to send elephants. His officers (*mehatgan*) assured him that Delhi was far from Jajnagar and the routes were difficult, making it impossible for the royal army to survive through it. The Sultan, advancing from Jaunpur, killed his enemies, destroyed idols and hunted elephants near Padam Talao. At the outset, he occupied the Rai's towns and the strong fort of Salmin Sikhan. Thereafter, he captured the citadel of Tinah at Tasram. The Delhi army, attaining wealth and cattle beyond calculation, reached as far as Benaras and Sarang Garh. The Rai, before his flight, had sent his select elephants to a fortified place. Ahmad Khan and Baki Patar, who were sent with treasure and gifts for the Sultan, fled before fulfilling their task. The invaders deputed detachments in pursuit of the local potentates such as Sahas Mal, Dahir Chand and Ahmad Khan. The Rai's superintendent of elephant stable was made captive. As the Rai agreed to submit through Raghav Jaita Pandit, it was learnt that he had a total of fifty-four elephants. He had already sent eight. He dispatched another batch of eighteen, while Ahmad Khan was expected to bring the remaining. One elephant, meant for the Rai, could also be surrendered. He promised to send elephants from Benaras every year to the governors of Bihar and Kara.[13] The Sultan received the submission of the Rai and his men, who were given robes of honour. In the concluding portion of the letter, Mahru has praised the region for its fertility and prosperity, besides the vibrancy of its villages and towns. He lamented that the Rai's submission before the invasion would have saved the region from destruction. Before returning to Delhi, the Sultan visited the coast and pulled down the temple of Jagannath.

Khan-i Jahan, entitled, Masnad-i Aali Azam Humayun, received a royal charter (*manshur*) on his appointment as *wazir*. It communicated the expectations from an ideal *wazir*, besides underscoring his role as an axis around which the administration revolved. The *wazir* had to be better than the nobles who held this exalted post in the past. First and foremost, he had to be loyal to the Sultan from the core of his heart. Both inwardly and outwardly, he

90   *Situating Medieval India*

had to be faithful to the Sultan's dispensation. He must be intelligent enough to quickly comprehend all matters pertaining to the kingdom. His intervention enabled the proper organization of the army, which ensured the welfare of the state and religion. He ensured the regular inflow of taxes into the public treasury, which had to possess ample funds at its disposal. This measure, in turn, went a long way in improving the administration. He must pay special attention to the well-being of Shaikhs, Syeds and scholars. To attain this result, he must continue their grants, pensions and stipends. He must see that the state did not inflict oppression on the people. He must dismiss an oppressive officer, who had somehow grabbed a governmental post, but turned out to be cruel. He must consult wise and competent persons and, thereafter, act on their advice. If the deliberations revealed that a certain measure would he harmful to the state, he must present this reality before the court with honesty and effectiveness. Never should he seek the counsel of the foolish and ignorant. He must possess a number of personal qualities. He was advised to shun arrogance. At all times, he must practice the principles of forbearance and forgiveness. In the end of the document, the Sultan urged all categories of people—nobles, governors, officers, courtiers and ordinary individuals—to be subordinate to the *wazir*. They were asked to treat the *wazir's* orders as those of the Sultan.[14]

Mahru, on his appointment as the governor of Multan, received a royal mandate (*manshur*) from the government.[15] It revealed the attitude of the Delhi Sultanate towards its nobles and, noting the qualities of Mahru, laid the scope of his functions. The state aimed at bestowing high honour and kindness on people, who were loyal to the court and received high ranks. The great nobles, owing to their knowledge, loyalty and faith, had attained positions of trust and earned the confidence of the authorities. With bright intellect and robust judgement, they had solved difficult problems and managed the affairs of the kingdom. The state, as its principal duty, trained the officers who, with their skill and honesty, illumined the country and religion. In this context, the state had showered its bounties on Ain ul-Mulk Mahru who, as the lord of the east, had conquered infidelity and destroyed the wicked and

Administrative Consolidation in the Delhi Sultanate   91

rebellious. He was a master of sword and pen, embodied knowledge and endurance, besides commanding the Persians. Endowed with eminence and zeal, he had won laurels in the domain of bravery. Accordingly, he was permitted to assume the government of Multan. With regard to its people, he was authorized to release or bind, appoint or dismiss, confiscate or grant. With his experience and understanding, he would build cities. He was entrusted with the welfare of people in this world and, regarding them, he would be answerable in the next world. He would act according to the demands of knowledge, wisdom and intelligence. Justice and generosity, as his guiding principles, would be the pillars of his government (*arkan jahandari*). These principles strengthened the foundations of the state and conformed to the Quranic verse, which emphasized the need for justice and beneficence. The people of the district—nobles, assignees, intermediaries, clerks, soldiers and inhabitants—were required to obey the orders of the mandate, so that they attained contentment and God's grace.[16]

Mahru, while analysing the economic crisis in Multan, kept a close watch on settlement patterns and agricultural production. He found that during the governorship of his predecessor Imad ul-Mulk, a large number of inhabitants had left for other places. As a result, the cultivated area had shrunk to one-tenth of the better times. In spite of the economic reconstruction being carried out under Firoz Shah Tughluq, only a few migrants returned. It was felt that unless the population reached the previous levels, there was little hope of achieving the past magnitude of revenue collection. Second, a number of taxes—*mandwah, tarkah, mal-i maujud, chahar bazaar, zaraib, guzarha* and *kharaj-i muhtarifa-i musallam*—which were bringing in a considerable money into the provincial coffers, had been abolished.[17] Third, a sum of three lakh *tankahs* had been assigned as land grants (*inam*) and cash pensions (*idrar*), whereas during the reign of Alauddin Khalji, when grain and cloth were cheaper, less than a tenth of the amount had been granted. Owing to an exponential increase in expenditure, the provincial treasury did not possess even a paltry sum of 500 *tankahs*. Fourth, Multan had suffered in the past owing to multiple factors— negligence of officers, poor quality of land and poverty of the

92   *Situating Medieval India*

peasantry and villagers. Mahru, who had been serving as the governor for the last three years, had undertaken vigorous administrative measures. As a result, the economic conditions were gradually returning to normal. The local chiefs (*rangahan*), who had been brought to submission in the first year, had again risen in revolt, forcing Mahru to march against them.[18]

In addition to establishing peace in his territorial jurisdiction, the governor was required to manage the provincial finances in a manner that a reasonable balance was achieved between income and expenditure. The task involved maintaining three classes— soldiers for warfare, theologians for piety (*ifadat*) and religious opinions (*ijtihad*) and lower bureaucracy (*ahl-i qalam*) for collecting taxes. These classes had competing claims on the financial resources of the province, which were often subject to fluctuations. Mahru's attention was drawn to a particular year when prices of foodgrains fell to one-tenth of the earlier rates. The prices of foodgrains, earlier sold at 80 *jitals* per maund, slumped to 8 *jitals* per maund. As a result, the common people enjoyed prosperity and contentment. Nevertheless, the revenue receipts of the province and income of the land grantees declined as the land, earlier yielding a revenue of 50 *tankahs*, offered just 5 *tankahs*. It had to be understood that if the agricultural produce doubled, the revenue would not increase by five times. Since in that particular year, the land tax of eight villages in the suburbs of Multan amounted to 38,000 *tankahs*, the income of land grantees ranged in the same proportion. It was not proper for them to demand cash compensation from the land tax flowing into the treasury.[19]

From the perspective of the provincial administration, its prime function was to maintain an efficient army. Accordingly, Mahru had set aside a separate head (*wajh*) of expenditure to organize the affairs of the army. While doing so, he did not overlook the preachers and Sufis. If a disproportionate amount of land tax was diverted to them, it would not be possible to achieve the aim of defending the territories. In other words, if a sufficient army was not in place, even the land grantees (preachers and Sufis) would not be able to gather revenue from the producers. It was only due to the fear of the army and blows of the sword (*ba mahabat-i lashkar wa zarbat-*

Administrative Consolidation in the Delhi Sultanate 93

khanjar) that the *zamindars* and peasants paid their taxes and the external enemies were kept in check. Any negligence with regard to the army encouraged the *zamindars* to rise in revolt. In the recent past, the *zamindars* had acquired strength owing to an excess of wealth and weapons. Mahru could not permit the *zamindars* to regain their erstwhile supremacy in the countryside. Nor could he allow the powerful enemies on the frontier to disturb peace in his jurisdiction. Therefore, the maintenance of the army commanded precedence over nourishing the religious intelligentsia.[20]

Mahru endeavoured to muster troops in accordance with his wishes and took concrete steps to ensure their welfare. Owing to the falling revenue inflows, he devised a solution by which half of a soldier's salary was paid in cash and half in kind. Though he enjoyed the privileged position of a noble, he also claimed his salary in the same manner. He treated himself on a par with his soldiers, with reference to any gain or loss in their respective remunerations. He was averse to any dishonest concealment and arrogant display. In this context, Mahru was a participant in discussions on the income of the state and imposition of new taxes. Apart from rulings of the Shariat, he relied on legal texts such as *al-Kafi*, *Siyar-i Shahan* and *al-Maheet*. It was desirable to bring income and expenditure in conformity with the Shariat. In practice, the canonical principles were not applicable. So long as war booty was available to the Muslims, there was no need to remunerate them for joining a holy war. When the Muslims faced danger, the finances could be drawn from the public treasury (*bait ul-mal*) for undertaking a crusade. If this source did not include war booty, the ruler could resort to a new tax during the course of the war. A small evil was permissible to fight a bigger evil. In emergency, the Shariat allowed a ruler to levy a new tax. This was only a temporary expedient. As a precaution, the collection had to be entrusted to officers who were guided by justice and truth. If such officers were not available, there would be injustice and oppression. In such times, one could adopt the principle that legalized the impermissible in times of need. The ruler was advised to charge only the land tax, which was levied since old times and which was familiar to the people. Such a course could not cause any damage, while a

94 *Situating Medieval India*

tax on something non-existent could instigate a revolt. Thus, it was appropriate for the wise to adopt a course, which did the least harm. Evidently, some losses were less damaging than the others.[21]

In 1361-2, Mahru carried out a survey into the land grants in the Multan region. The information pertained to the original conferment, subsequent development, amount of income and economic potential. Passing on these details to the finance ministry (*diwan-i wizarat*), he sought clarifications on controversial legal aspects and made fresh recommendations. The exercise led to the identification of two types of land grants—the endowments made by former rulers (*auqaf salatin maziya*) to pious foundations (mosques and seminaries) since the early thirteenth century and land grants bestowed on individual scholars, Sufis and nobles (*auqaf danishmandan wa mashaikh wa umara*), who had brought about agricultural improvements.[22] In the former category, it was found that Muizzuddin Muhammad bin Sam of Ghor had endowed the Jama Masjid of Multan with two villages. The income from these lands was spent on maintenance of the building and providing for teachers, students, reciters of the Quran and servants who gave the call for prayers, spread the carpets and lighted the lamps. This Sultan had also endowed the Jama Masjid of Talbina with one village and its income was spent in the manner described above. Khan-i Shahid, the son of Ghiasuddin Balban, had assigned two villages for the maintenance of a seminary, teachers, reciters and students. Sultan Shahid (Muhammad bin Tughluq) carved out a land grant in the Multan region for a prayer enclosure (*namazgah*) and mosque. The income from this source was utilized to repair the former sacred space and pay the salary of the person, who gave the call for prayers. It appears that these institutions could draw funds directly from the state treasury, if the income from their respective endowments turned out to be inadequate.[23]

However, such a privilege was not extended to the second category of beneficiaries, particularly when their incomes declined with fall in grain prices. The provincial administration undertook to compensate them with grain, but in direct proportion to the quantity as they acquired before the slump. In the first place, they were placed in properly settled villages, where some lands were cultivated and

Administrative Consolidation in the Delhi Sultanate 95

others were not. Their grants were delineated in a manner that during the years of famine (*salha-i qehat*), they did not suffer owing to the rise in grain prices. They were expected to meet their household needs with the income (*mahsul*) accruing from the cultivated lands. The remaining lands were supposed to be utilized for effecting improvements in the total grant.[24] With the reclamation of barren lands by the grantees, the respective claims of *waqf* and *diwani* came under dispute. Mahru recommended that the share of *diwani* be merged with that of *waqf* because the income from the latter was not large. Besides, Islam had been existing in Multan for the last 700 years. The process of rehabilitation of the region had begun with the return of former inhabitants. The concerned intellectuals and Sufis (*danishmandan wa mashaikh*) were just mendicants (*faqir*), who were particularly loyal to Firoz Shah Tughluq. Mahru had made these recommendations because the rehabilitation of Multan was a personal achievement (*karnama*) of the Sultan. He looked forward to the central government for final orders regarding the land grants in Multan. Looked at in totality, the intention of the governor was to transfer the gains of agrarian expansion to the grantee, rather than to the state.[25]

During the reign of Firoz Shah Tughluq, canal-based agrarian expansion was successfully undertaken in southeast Panjab. Mahru, during his governorship of Multan, implemented a similar project in his jurisdiction. As a result, a number of canals—Nasirwah, Qutbwah, Khizrwah, Qabulwah and Hamruwah—were excavated in the region. We know only the names of the canals. Unfortunately, nothing is known about the spot from where they were cut or the specific areas that they irrigated. It was probable that two rivers—the Chenab after uniting with the Jhelum at Shorkot and the Ravi flowing south of Multan—offered ample scope for the development of irrigation. Our information was clear on two points, the financial principles governing the excavation of the canals and role of the local beneficiaries in the enterprise. It was clarified that in case of works on large rivers—like Sihun, Jihun, Dajla, Ravi and Beas—money could be spent from the public treasury. If this source was short of funds, the ruler could turn to the people (*khalq*). In case of smaller canals like Nasirwah, Qutbwah and Khizrwah, the

96 *Situating Medieval India*

cost of construction and maintenance was bound to be borne by the local beneficiaries, including the peasants and chiefs (*ahali wa arbab*). Mahru advocated that the obligation be shared equally between the two classes, so that the burden of one was not shifted to the other. He condemned the refusal of land controlling elements—Sufis, clerics and intermediaries including Kamal Taj—to contribute to the repairs of Nasirwah, despite the fact that this canal passed through the villages where they had been assigned land grants. He warned of a fall in agricultural output if both, the state treasury and local beneficiaries, failed to provide financial support for the maintenance of the canals.[26]

In the task of constructing and maintaining the canals, the provincial administration sought the active cooperation of the local community, which acted through its traditional headmen. Those who performed this role were rewarded, while those who abstained were punished. A headman (*muqaddam*) named Babdujah had displayed much initiative and energy in digging two canals (*ju-i shahi*), Qabulwah and Hamruwah, when the other headmen and soldiers had run away. Mahru raised the status of Babdujah from an ordinary village headman to an exalted officer and granted him the superintendence (*danagi*) of these canals, so that he continued to exert himself in the service of the governor. The local population, comprising the village headmen and peasants of the concerned subdivision (*khutan wa muqaddaman wa riaya-i parganat*), was directed to serve and consult this new officer in the tasks related to his office. Those who refused to participate in the digging of canals and who had become fugitives were threatened with death and exile.[27]

In a public proclamation addressed to the peasantry, Mahru declared that cultivation had made a tremendous progress due to the ample availability of water. In that year, the agrarian conditions had reached a level unheard in the past. Therefore, the peasants must work hard. Regarding the magnitude of land revenue and its collection, Mahru assured them of adhering to the past practice (*rasm-i qadeem*). The old cultivators would pay half of their dues in grain and half in cash on the basis of official grain prices (*nirkh*). The new settlers would pay the entire amount in grain.[28] Mahru,

Administrative Consolidation in the Delhi Sultanate 97

turning his gaze towards Thanesar, pointed to the state of peasants with regard to their ownership rights over land.[29] From the perspective of the state, the peasants were expected to carry on cultivation in the villages they had settled in. They could not leave their traditional settlements. Such an action was bound to result in the abandonment of the existing cultivation, besides depriving the Delhi Sultanate of its share of the produce. Ziauddin, a soldier holding a village in revenue assignment, did not have any control over the person of the peasants, who were free by birth. Nevertheless, he had the right over the land tax due from them and, on this matter, the order of the Sultan was final. The *qazis* of Thanesar, the landholders (*maliks*) of a neighbouring locality, enticed away the peasants to their villages. They betrayed an ignorance of the Islamic jurisprudence (*fiqh*) and, therefore, liable to punishment. It was stipulated that the lands, whose revenue had been assigned, could not be left without crops. The *qazis* were guilty of keeping the land uncultivated and even laying claims to its land tax. On their part, it was unlawful to assert that the peasants were engaged in cultivation and that their location was immaterial. The *qazis*, deviating from the correct path, had resorted to oppression. In addition to these illegal acts, they used harsh language and berated Ziauddin for disregarding the law. In view of the interests of the oppressed, the *qazis* should have submitted their case in writing. The rights over the village had been clearly laid out. As the truth would prevail in the end, the *qazis* were advised to retrace their path. If they had any doubt, they could consult the legal texts. Otherwise, they must be prepared to face the consequences.[30]

One of the letters recorded a discussion among the nobles on the legality of price control and its impact on the common people. They took into account the opinions expressed in legal texts. According to *al-Kafi*, the state must ban the regrating (*ihtikar*) of commodities essential for humans and animals. These goods were identified as wheat, barley, grapes, dates and apricots. This position was based on the views of Imam Abu Hanifa and Imam Muhammad Idris. Abu Yusuf defined regrating as the act of blocking and stocking a commodity, including gold and silver, which harmed the common people. Abu Hanifa and Muhammad Idris did not

98   *Situating Medieval India*

empower a ruler to determine the prices of food items. Their argument was based on the authority of Prophet Muhammad, who stated, 'Do not determine the prices, because it is God who determines, controls and announces the same.' It was not proper for a ruler (*imam*) to interfere in the work of the seller, though he could do so if the common people were harmed. For example, if a person purchased a piece of land for 50 and sold it for 100, the ruler could stop the transaction and, thus, prevent any suffering of the people (Muslims). Imam Malik advocated fixation of prices during the time of a famine, so that relief could be provided to the common people. The author of *Siyar-i Shahan* argued that regrating was forbidden because it was harmful to the common people and anyone involved in such an activity deserved punishment.[31]

Mahru, keeping an eye on the merchants and artisans (*saudagaran wa muhtirfa*) observed the regrating of ghee, cloth, sugar and fuel. The malpractice varied with each commodity. The merchants brought ghee from Sarsuti paying seven *jitals* per *ser*, but stocked it till they could sell it for ten *jitals* per ser. They brought cloth from Huka and hoarded the stock until they sold it for double their cost. They brought sugar from Lahore and Delhi, but concealed it for many years to make big gains. Cartloads of fuel were brought from the neighbouring countryside (*mahals*) and sold at 8 *jitals* per maund. Initially, the merchants were made aware of the rulings of the Shariat. Owing to their greed, they showed no fear of punishment.[32] This caused suffering to all the people, including preachers, soldiers and destitute. Mahru purchased these four commodities at prices the regraters paid. He arranged their sale at reasonable prices, so that regrating was eliminated and some profit flowed into the provincial treasury. The merchants resented the measure, but to no avail. Mahru remained firm, as the Shariat approved a transaction if both the buyers and sellers were satisfied. Moreover, the common people, including the above groups, received the benefit.[33]

Mahru did not refer to the price control under Alauddin Khalji, though he must have been aware of the unprecedented measure. Barani has offered an account of the Khalji ruler's ordinances for different markets as well as their theoretical underpinnings.

Administrative Consolidation in the Delhi Sultanate   99

According to him, the stability of the army and people depended on low prices. It was obligatory for a king to reduce the prices of corn, cloth, horses and arms. During famine, a king reduced the taxes and helped people from his treasury. During plentiful harvests, the transporter-merchants and market-merchants took to regrating. In these circumstances, the king must control prices through whatever means. First, he fixed prices of all commodities on the principle of production costs. Second, the state officers—agents, police chiefs and superintendents—suppressed regrating and, confiscating the grain, sold it to consumers, as the Prophet had done. The regraters were punished with confiscation of property and exile. The regulations produced ten benefits. The army became strong and stable. The treasury remained full, as there was no need to provide relief. Money was freely spent on the army. The king attained a good reputation. The transactions were based on justice. The poor did not face distress. The divine purpose of transferring wealth from the rich to the poor was achieved. Since regrating was the profession of Hindus and Magians, the suffering consumers were essentially Muslims. If the king lowered prices, the Muslims were honoured, while Hindus and Magians were humiliated. If prices were low, every caste devoted itself to its craft. The resultant stability led to improvement in administration. In case of regrating, people discarded their professions and adopted others, resulting in disorder. Owing to increasing greed and lack of divine fear, there was regrating and suffering. The sole solution, particularly during plenitude, was royal intervention. Only the ignorant refrained a king from regulating prices. After all, a king was answerable to God on the day of judgement.[34]

The government functionaries were expected to create conditions conducive for the movement of commerce, because it brought revenues for the provincial administration in the form of taxes. The merchants were required to be honest in their dealings with the state officers. Both sides were advised to cultivate cordial relations based on mutual respect. In practice, this ideal was not realized. Mahru has recorded two cases of dispute. A merchant Khizr Abu Bakr lodged a complaint against Muizzuddin, the administrator (*hakim*) of Uch. This officer issued permits (*sajal*) regarding the

100   *Situating Medieval India*

payment of alms tax (*zakat*),[35] which was locally known as *batta*. He had refused to issue this document to Khizr Abu Bakr ever since the latter received assistance from another officer Kamal Taj. It was also alleged that the nephew and other relatives of Muizzuddin had inflicted cruelties on the merchant, who was given a beating with shoes. Mahru, in his intervention, argued that Muizzuddin should have reported the matter to him. Now, he was directed to investigate the conduct of Kamal Taj and act in accordance with the findings. If Muizzuddin delayed the issuance of the permit due to personal enmity, this would squeeze the inflow of revenues and harm the interests of the merchants. Such a situation violated both the Shariat and the ideal of wisdom.[36] In another case, Mahru exposed the deceit of two merchants, Ahmad and Yasin, the sons of Malik Shahu. They falsely claimed that they had been issued a royal order (*farman aali*) permitting them to pay *zakat* and *danganah* at Delhi and not at Multan.[37] They alleged that Mahru had ignored the royal order and extracted 20,000 *tankahs* as payment for the two taxes. Mahru, in a strong rebuttal, uncovered the dishonesty of the brothers. His subordinates had treated the brothers with respect. In contrast, they misused their eminent position in the mercantile class and failed to reciprocate the gesture. Mahru had acted in accordance with the royal order and charged only 1,700 *tankahs* as *zakat* and *danganah*. They had tried to sow the seeds of dissension between the provincial officers and the Delhi-based bureaucracy. In the sale deed (*bainama*), they had included the slaves to be carried to Khurasan for sale and sold horses to the local chiefs (Hindus) in violation of state orders. Mahru claimed that he was not one of the officers, who took bribes, ignored royal orders and connived at illegal commercial activities.[38]

The central government appointed a man for the administration of justice and enforcing the rules of public censor (*dadbegi wa ihtisab*) in Multan.[39] The letter of appointment (*manshur*), while exposing an illegal practice, gave instructions to the appointee on the basis of the Quran and Hadis. It was reported that some villagers of Multan married women, who had not been divorced from their previous husbands. The officer was advised to promote religious affairs (*amur deeni*) and, thus, traverse the path of the Shariat and

Administrative Consolidation in the Delhi Sultanate 101

justice. Dealing firmly, he must act in the manner of a *qazi* and restrain people, who violated the Shariat and religious injunctions. God had instituted legal marriage to fortify the self, produce children and continue the human race. The Quran had prohibited fornication as an indecent evil, while Prophet Muhammad had validated marriage as his practice (*sunnat*). This had to be brought home across the villages of Multan, so that the sinful act was erased and correct religious beliefs implemented.[40] If the people stated that they were merely following in the footsteps of their forefathers, they were entirely misguided. First, they must divorce the women they had kept in their houses. Thereafter, they should observe the period of waiting (*iddat*), so that the children born were deemed as legitimate and they were saved from the fires of hell. Such people could be given a month to mend their ways, desist from the illegal act and adopt obedience instead of sin. After this, if a complaint was received and the act proved, the guilty must be given adequate punishment.

Before laying down the above instructions, the letter has built a proper context. It stated that the aim of sending prophets, apostles, preachers and saints was to ensure the welfare of Muslims. The statement of Umar bin al-Khattab, the second pious caliph, regarding the prohibition of illegal acts was based on a Quranic verse on the subject. Only a few selected people understood the Quran, while the ordinary folk did not fear God, kings or saints. As a result, the crimes took place, exposing the life and property of Muslims to destruction. According to the Shariat, this was the handiwork of wicked men, who were slaves to their carnal passions. The Shariat advocated strict action against such people, so that the evil acts were outlawed and commendable practices were instituted.[41]

The provincial administration maintained correspondence with prominent Sufis and, utilizing their mediation, sought to tackle administrative problems at the local level. In a letter to Syed Jalaluddin Bukhari, Mahru stated that the Shaikh's grace could save all Muslims from inner and outer infirmities. Though Mahru prayed for the state functionaries to be free from the taint of oppression, his prayers remained unanswered. The Sufis, owing to their virtues—asceticism, faith, truth, purity and submission—were

102 *Situating Medieval India*

bound to pray that the officers worked for justice and refrained from oppression. They were not expected to malign the officers in any manner and, on this point, there was concrete evidence. There was no harm in admitting the misconduct of officers, as it would pave the way for their forgiveness from God. Having expressed himself on the role of Sufis, Mahru sought Bukhari's mediation in a specific case. Some Syeds, having violated their written undertaking at the tomb of Shaikh Kabir, refused to pay the land tax and became habituated to paying penalties. Bukhari was requested to advise the Syeds to give up their defiance, obey the government, pay their dues and treat people well. The collection of revenue enabled the authorities to pay the soldiers, scholars and poor. Mahru had the means to ensure compliance of the rules. Still, he looked forward to Bukhari's mediation to warn the Syeds of punishment if they persisted in their indiscretion.[42]

In four letters addressed to Shaikh Raziuddin, Mahru discussed a variety of administrative matters and sought his assistance in solving the problems. For example, the officers of Uch, particularly governor Khwaja Kamaluddin, extracted unpaid forced labour (*begar*) from the local inhabitants and confined their victims to dark cells to extort 2,000 *tankahs* or even more.[43] Mahru was cautious in the case of two officers Badruddin Qimaz and Kamal Taj, who were accused of imposing a new tax (*muhaddis*), subjecting the people to harassment and forcing them to protest. Mahru, who had not authorized the collection of the new tax, asserted that the merchants and artisans were quite prosperous, as they made good earnings and prices of foodgrains were low. In another case, the sermonizer (*khatib*) of Uch had allegedly made an interpolation in the call for prayer and, as a result, developed serious differences with the judge (*qazi*). The controversy degenerated to an extent that it could lead to violence. In the first instance, the sermonizer should have sought the permission of Mahru. Alternatively, he should have consulted Shaikh Raziuddin and Shaikh Sadruddin, besides taking the blessings from the tombs of Shaikh Bahauddin Zakariya and Shaikh Jamaluddin Uchi.[44]

Two letters revealed the difficulties of the Delhi Sultanate in Sind and its neighbouring regions. In the first one, Mahru discussed

Administrative Consolidation in the Delhi Sultanate 103

political matters with the auditor general, who was addressed as Malik ul-Sharq Iftikhar ul-Mulk Sahib Diwan Istifa-i Mamalik. Mahru hoped to revive his own fortune with the grace of the addressee. The letter drew attention to the strife of Banbhaniya who, having invited the Mongols, ruined the country. Once, he even intruded into the vast realm of Panjab along with the Mongol hordes. The Multan troops, in a valiant offensive, forced him to flee. Before and after this, Banbhaniya ravaged the province of Gujarat, wherefrom he abducted the village headmen. Firoz Shah Tughluq had resolved to extirpate the rebel and settle the disturbed areas. For this purpose, he entrusted Gujarat to Ruknuddin Hasan, the brother of the addressee. The latter was asked to mobilize the people of Gujarat, support the efforts of Hamir Duda and send reinforcements to that region.[45] In the second letter, written to a unnamed notable, Mahru countered the explanations that had been advanced. The notable was accused of enabling the Mongols to plunder Sind. The Sultan had issued an order to local elements— *muqaddams, shahnas* and *gumashtas*—regarding land grants. The notable, failing to implement the Sultan's decree, had deprived the locals of their wealth and cattle. The notable should have written to Mahru about the attitude of the village headmen before resorting to violence. The notable, knowing that the Delhi army had marched to Lakhnauti and proud of his large following, had indulged in contumacy. If he were loyal, he would have prevented Banbhaniya's flight from Siwistan to Thatta. For long, the notable had thrived under the Sultan's patronage. He must adopt obedience towards Delhi like the previous governors, lest he should face punitive action. Mahru justified the execution of certain Muslims guilty of plunder, but disapproved their sale as slaves.[46]

Mahru was in correspondence with a senior noble Malik Kamaluddin Jajarmi, entitled Malik ul-Umara, on the theme of Islamic mysticism. The writer has enumerated the qualities of Jajarmi, criticized the philosophers and explained the fundamentals of spirituality (*ishq*). Jajarmi had attained worldly success and, being a recluse at heart, he was bound to explore the divine secrets. Quran states that God is closer to the seeker than his jugular vein. Yet, he must understand that the philosophers, including Mutazzalis and

104 *Situating Medieval India*

Hissis, remained fixated on the pursuit of worldly knowledge and physical phenomena (*majaz*). They were incapable of seeing the spiritual light (*nur irfan*), as love could not be captured in the vessel of physicality. Since they denied the reality of love (*haqiqat muhabbat*), they designated the spiritual path as the prime evil. Since there was a basic difference between knowledge and spirituality, the two could not be merged. With this premise, it was possible to comprehend the intricacies of spirituality. A seeker, placing his foot on the righteous path (*sirat-i mustaqim*), entered the circle of mystics. As proof of this, his heart became the abode of God. Wherever he looked, he recognized nothing but the Friend (*dar har cheh nigah kunam tu ra mi binam*). Though the tongue became dumb, it continued to praise God. In the early stages, the seeker described the attributes of the Beloved. When attraction reached the station of love, he encountered the successive stages of wonder and fear. With prayer and steadfastness, the seeker climbed the heights of spiritual progress. Moving beyond the confines of the body and soul, he realized the inevitability of decay in both the worlds. Having swallowed the worldly ocean (*darya-i hasti*), his body was imbued with divine light. He saw nothing, but God. In fact, he died before death and attained eternal life like Idris, who became a resident of heaven before dying.

NOTES

1. An earlier version of this paper appeared as 'Dynamics of Statecraft in the Delhi Sultanate: A Reconstruction from the Letters of Ain ul-Mulk Mahru', *Proceedings of the Indian History Congress*, 61st session, Kolkata, 2000-01, pp. 285-93.

2. Some writers (Maulavi Abdul Wali, Shaikh Abdul Rashid, K.S. Lal, Agha Mahdi Husain, S.B.P. Nigam and K.A. Nizami) have confused Ain ul-Mulk Mahru with Ain ul-Mulk Multani. Peter Jackson and I.H. Siddiqui have shown that they were two different nobles. Multani, starting his career as a secretary of correspondence (*dabir*) during the reign of Alauddin Khalji, rose to prominence due to his role in the conquest of Ranthambhore. Following his occupation of Malwa, he was made the governor of the province. Transferred to Deogiri in 1313, he settled the turmoil in Gujarat early in the

Administrative Consolidation in the Delhi Sultanate   105

reign of Qutbuddin Mubarak Shah Khalji. He remained neutral in the Khusrau Khan-Ghazi Malik conflict and participated in the Warangal expedition of 1322. Peter Jackson, *The Delhi Sultanate: A Political and Military History*, Cambridge: Cambridge University Press, 1999, p. 329; Iqtidar Husain Siddiqui, *Authority and Kingship Under the Sultans of Delhi*, New Delhi: Manohar, 2006, pp. 283-6.

3. Ziauddin Barani, *Tarikh-i Firoz Shahi*, Persian text, ed. Sir Syed Ahmad, Aligarh: Aligarh Muslim University, rpt., 2005, pp. 486-7, 489-90.

4. Mahdi Husain, *The Rehla of Ibn Battuta: India, Maldive Islands and Ceylon*, Baroda: Oriental Institute, 1976, p. 105.

5. Iqtidar Husain Siddiqui, op. cit., p. 288.

6. Shams Siraj Afif, *Tarikh-i Firoz Shahi*, Persian text, ed. Maulavi Wilayat Husain, Calcutta: Asiatic Society of Bengal, 1890, pp. 406-18.

7. Ain ul-Mulk Ainuddin Abdullah bin Mahru, *Insha-i Mahru*, Persian text, ed. Shaikh Abdur Rashid, Aligarh: Department of History, Aligarh Muslim University, 1954, pp. 1-2. (Hereafter cited as Mahru).

8. With reference to this verse (4:59), different views have been expressed regarding the identity of those in authority. Some refer to the commanders of the Prophet sent on military campaigns. Others identify them as Muslim religious and legal scholars. Some Muslims viewed obedience to unjust rulers as preferable to chaos and social harm resulting from a revolt. Many argue that the command applied only to just rulers, who command obedience to God. Shias interpret the verse as a reference to the Shia Imams and a proof of their spiritual infallibility. In Sufi tradition, the verse points to the Sufi Shaikhs as well as to the gnostics. If the individual Muslims or groups of Muslims disagreed with authority, they are to refer the matter to God by consulting the Quran or to the Messenger by bringing it to him personally. However, a verse (5: 83) added the liberty of resorting to the Messenger and those in authority itself. Seyyed Hossein Nasr et. al., ed., *The Study Quran: A New Translation and Commentary*, New York: Harper One, 2015, pp. 219-20.

9. Mahru Letter no. 12, pp. 21-2.

10. Shamsuddin Ilyas Shah gave offence to Delhi Sultanate because he attacked Tirhut and even marched to Bahraich on the pretext of visiting the shrine of Salar Masud Ghazi. Firoz, at the end of a long military campaign (1353-4), occupied the fort of Ikdala in a river island. The Sultan abandoned the expedition owing to the lamentations of local Muslim women and his refusal to follow the predatory practices of the Mongols. A second campaign (1359) proceeded along similar lines. Firoz accepted the overtures of Sikandar, but failed to establish Zafar Khan in Sonargaon. Modern writers,

106   *Situating Medieval India*

pointing to Firoz's military incompetence, perceived the Bengal expedition in the same class as his involvement in Jajnagar, Kangra and Thatta. For the official version of the Bengal campaigns, see Afif, pp. 114-24, 137-62.

11. Mahru, Letter no. 6, pp. 13-15.

12. Ibid., Letter no. 14, pp. 24-30.

13. The Delhi Sultans acquired elephants through plunder and tribute, besides purchase from outside territories or trapping directly from a wild state. In the early fourteenth century, the Sultans might have possessed 750-1,000 elephants. During the reign of Firoz Shah Tughluq, this number was below 500, though his major preoccupation was acquisition of elephants. During his first expedition of Bengal, he captured 47 out of the 50 elephants Ilyas Shah drew up for battle. In 1359, the Sultan was incensed at the small number of 5 elephants arriving from Bengal as tribute. In the negotiations after the second expedition of Bengal, he received 40 elephants from the local ruler and a promise of a yearly tribute of 40 elephants. During the Jajnagar campaign, he captured 8 elephants in a hunt and received another 20 from the Rai. Simon Digby, *War Horse and Elephant in the Delhi Sultanate: A Study of Military Supplies*, Oxford: Oxford Monographs, 1971, pp. 59-65.

14. Mahru, Letter no. 2, pp. 8-10.

15. Ibid., Letter no. 3, pp. 10-11.

16. Since the days of Sultan Muizzuddin, the Delhi Sultanate issued mandates to governors on the eve of their appointment. Malik Qutbuddin Aibak issued the first such mandate to fellow noble Malik Husamuddin Ughalbak in connection with his posting at Kol (Aligarh). In 1217, Iltutmish issued a royal order to Prince Nasiruddin Mahmud on his appointment as the governor of Lahore. On behalf of Alauddin Khalji, Amir Khusrau drafted a lengthy mandate for Prince Farid Khan, who was entrusted with the region from the head of River Maabar to the coast of Malabar. Firoz Shah Tughluq, during his expedition to Sind, issued a mandate to the new governor Prince Fateh Khan. Iqtidar Husain Siddiqui, *Perso-Arabic Sources of Information on the Life and Conditions in the Sultanate of Delhi*, New Delhi: Munshiram Manoharlal, 1992, pp. 167-84.

17. Firoz Shah Tughluq has listed 26 uncanonical taxes that he abolished, while Afif has enumerated four such imposts, viz., *danganah*, *mustghil*, *jazaari* and *dori*, resulting in a loss of 30 lakh *tankahs* to the exchequer. Firoz Shah Tughluq, *Futuhat-i Firoz Shahi*, Persian text, ed. Shaikh Abdul Rashid, Aligarh: Aligarh Muslim University, 1954, p. 5; Afif, pp. 375, 379.

18. Mahru, Letter no. 31, pp. 67-8.

19. Ibid., pp. 63-4.

Administrative Consolidation in the Delhi Sultanate   107

20. Ibid., pp. 64, 68.
21. Ibid., Letter no. 30, pp. 58-9.
22. Mahru's measures must be seen in the context of Firoz Shah Tughluq's land grants on an unprecedented scale. The grants had lapsed during the first half of the fourteenth century. Firoz, as a matter of policy, attached the beneficiaries to the state. As soon as he ascended the throne at Thatta and marched through Panjab on his way to Delhi, he visited numerous Sufi shrines and restored their land grants. Besides the Sufis, Syeds and scholars, the beneficiaries included teachers, students, preachers, Quran-reciters and custodians of pious establishments. Many deserving persons began receiving stipends and pensions. In many cases, the grants had been made in the last 170 years. For unstated reasons, they had been confiscated and deleted from the official records. Firoz permitted the beneficiaries to submit proofs of the grants, along with the subsequent confiscations, in the legal department (*diwan sharai*) and, issuing fresh grants, enabled them to take charge of their lands. Barani, pp. 537, 543, 558-60; Afif, pp. 60-1; Firoz Shah Tughluq, *Futuhat-i Firoz Shahi*, p. 16.
23. Mahru, Letter no. 16, pp. 32-3.
24. Ibid., Letter no. 31, p. 68.
25. Ibid., Letter no. 16, p. 33.
26. Ibid., Letter no. 114, pp. 176-7.
27. Ibid., Letter no. 11, pp. 20-1.
28. Ibid., Letter no. 121, p. 184.
29. Fragmentary evidence permitted only a tentative reconstruction of agrarian relations. It appeared that there was little question of peasants claiming property rights over any parcel of land. Since land was abundant, the peasant could normally put up with a denial of his right over the land he tilled. On the contrary, he feared a claim of superior classes over his crop and more still over his person. The dispute, as Mahru narrated it, indicated that the peasants were not masters of their domicile and, in effect, were no better than semi-serfs. Like serfs, they could own seeds, cattle and implements. They also sold their produce in order to pay the land revenue in cash. Tapan Raychaudhuri and Irfan Habib, eds., *The Cambridge Economic History of India, vol. I: c. 1200–c. 1750*, New Delhi: Orient Longman, rpt., 2004, p. 54.
30. Mahru, Letter no. 28, pp. 52-4.
31. Ibid., Letter no. 30, pp. 59-60.
32. During the reign of Alauddin Khalji, prices of different commodities— grain, cloth, horses, cattle and slaves—were regulated through different methods. In case of horses, the brokers were expelled and prices were fixed

108 *Situating Medieval India*

according to the grade of the animals. In the market for non-agricultural goods at Sarai Adl, the Multanis received state finances to bring goods from distant places. In order to ensure a regular supply of grain at low prices and storage in state granaries, major changes were introduced in the magnitude of agrarian taxation and mechanism of its collection. It followed that the area of price regulations coincided with the area of agrarian reforms, i.e. from Dipalpur and Lahore to Kara and Katehar. Irfan Habib, 'The Price Regulations of Alauddin Khalji: A Defence of Zia Barani', *Indian Economic and Social History Review,* vol. XXI, no. 4, 1984, pp. 398-402.

33. Mahru, Letter no. 30, pp. 60-2.

34. Ziauddin Barani, *Fatawa-i Jahandari,* Eng. tr. (*The Political Theory of the Delhi Sultanate*), Mohammad Habib and Afsar Umar Salim Khan, Allahabad: Kitab Mahal, n.d., pp. 34-8.

35. The *zakat* was one of the dozen taxes that Shariat validated. The Shariat determined it according to the valuation of property. God fixed it on all Muslims, who were major, in full senses and possessed the legal minimum (*nisab*) of property. This property should be free from debt and a year should have elapsed over it. It was of two kinds. Tax on apparent property was levied on quadrupeds that always grazed in plains and pastures. Tax on hidden property was levied on gold, silver and articles of commerce. In case of horses, it became due if males and females were pastured together. The owner had the option of paying a *dinar* for every horse or, appraising their value, paid 5 *dirhams* for every 200 *dirhams*. According to another report, no *zakat* was due on horses. Abdul Hamid Muharrir Ghaznavi, 'Dastur ul-Albab fi Ilm ul-Hisab', Eng. tr. Shaikh Abdul Rashid, *Medieval India Quareterly,* vol. I, nos. 3 & 4, 1950, pp. 62-3.

36. Mahru, Letter no. 26, pp. 50-1.

37. Firoz Shah Tughluq abolished a few practices that were found violative of the Shariat. Apart from paintings in the sleeping chamber and decorations on royal vessels, they included unlawful taxes such as *mustghil, jazari, dori* and *danganah.* In particular, Afif has identified the problems related to *danganah* in Delhi. When the goods were brought to Sarai Adl, the merchants paid *zakat* in accordance with the prescribed limit. Thereafter, the merchants carried the entire stock of goods to the treasury. Here, these were weighed again and charged *danganah* at the rate of one *dang* for each *tankah.* The state was able to collect a huge amount of money. The functionaries, owing to their caution, became oppressive in practice and put off outstanding matters. Since the merchants were forced to stay in the treasury for long, they were put to a lot of inconvenience. Afif, pp. 374-8.

38. Mahru, Letter no. 120, pp. 182-3.

Administrative Consolidation in the Delhi Sultanate 109

39. The department of *amir-i dad* played an important part in the administration of justice. Looking after the executive side of justice, it ensured that the verdicts of the Qazi were carried out and the sentence was enforced. In case of miscarriage of justice, it drew the attention of the Qazi to the fact or delayed the execution of the decision till a higher court reconsidered it. It kept an eye on the local police and public censor (*muhtasib*). The duties of the public censor were wide. Using the power of spontaneous intervention, he suppressed illegal practices and enforced public morality. He ensured that the Muslims observed religious injunctions. He came down on intoxicants, gambling and indecency. He supervised the maintenance of public utilities, besides checking maltreatment of servants and cruelty towards domestic animals. Ishtiaq Husain Qureshi, *The Administration of the Sultanate of Dehli*, New Delhi: Munshiram Manoharlal, rpt., 1971, pp. 161-5.

40. It is not clear if Mahru received any instructions from Delhi on the above matter. Apparently, his measure conformed to Firoz Shah Tughluq's formal statement of policy, which sought to implement Sunni orthodoxy. Firoz took credit for a number of interconnected steps to weed out the innovations (*biddat*) that had crept into the lives of the people (Muslims). On the legal front, he banned the infliction of unlawful punishments including amputation of limbs, crushing of bones, hammering nails into hands and feet, burning in fire, plucking of eyes and ears, pouring molten lead in the throat, beating with a barbed whip and sawing the body into two parts. During the previous reign, punishments resulted in deaths, mutilation of limbs and loss of body parts. Firoz compensated the victims with money and, securing deeds of reconciliation (*khatut-i khushnudi*), placed them in a box at the former Sultan's grave in Dar ul-Aman. Firoz Shah Tughluq, *Futuhat-i Firoz Shahi*, pp. 2, 16.

41. Mahru, Letter no. 7, pp. 15-17.

42. Ibid., Letter no. 22, pp. 44-7.

43. Ibid., Letter no. 20, pp. 41-2.

44. Ibid., Letter no. 19, pp. 38-9.

45. Ibid., Letter no. 46, pp. 86-9.

46. Ibid., Letter no. 133, pp. 198-203.

CHAPTER 5

Scientific Temperament and Technical Innovations in North India: From the Eleventh to the Fifteenth Century

There were several ways of assessing the cultural level of a society.[1] One of them was to delve into the attitudes towards science and technology. The present exercise focuses on the geographical space of the Indo-Gangetic plain and five centuries of the pre-Mughal times. The region, following the Ghaznavid occupation of Panjab, opened to cultural influences from Afghanistan and Central Asia. Alberuni, in his voluminous study, examined the Indian social structure and religious customs, besides the state of geography, literature, philosophy, astronomy and astrology. Amir Khusrau, a romantic poet and official historian, took a keen interest in the Indian contribution to learning, science and arts. Persian chroniclers, ranging from Minhaj-i Siraj Juzjani to Yahya Ahmad Sirhindi, traced the political history of the Delhi Sultanate. While doing so, they discussed the increasing systematization of the administration and schemes of agrarian expansion. In their attempts to legitimize the authority of the rulers, they threw light on the construction of lasting memorials and introduction of novel devices. At the same time, the Bhakti reformers brought about a fundamental change in the thinking of the ordinary masses. Though they were essentially rooted in India's spiritual and philosophical traditions, they did not confine themselves to the non-material aspects of life. They were deeply interested in the concrete living conditions of their contemporaries. On the one hand, they raised the people out of the morass of superstition and blind faith. On the other hand,

Scientific Temperament and Technical Innovations... 111

they engendered a spirit of enquiry, overturning the received knowledge on questions of nature, caste, gender, polity, and custom. In the five centuries, extending from Alberuni to Guru Nanak, a steady and definitive progress was made in the attitudes to science and technology.

Alberuni observed that it was difficult to learn Sanskrit,[2] because it had an enormous range, both in words and inflections. Instead of being an advantage, it was a defect. Owing to a peculiar vocabulary, Sanskrit had many words to denote a single phenomenon and, conversely, a single word to denote a variety of phenomena. It was possible to distinguish between the various meanings of a word only through the use of qualifying epithets, besides comprehending the context in which it occurred. The language was divisible into two major types. The common people used the vernacular that was neglected. The upper and educated classes used the classical one, which was more cultivated and subject to the rules of grammar, etymology and rhetoric. In Sanskrit, two or three consonants might follow each other without an intervening vowel, creating difficulties in pronunciation and, therefore, hindered intellectual exchange. Indian scribes, who were engaged in the production of books, did not take pains of collation. The successive copies, acquiring incremental faults, became entirely different from the original text. The enormous mental effort of the author was spoiled due to scribal negligence. Scientific books were composed in particular forms of poetry, as they were meant to be memorized. In the eyes of the learned classes, only the knowledge learnt through the heart was authoritative. They did not attach the same value to knowledge existing in the written form. The requirements of the poetic meter introduced a constrained phraseology and, serving as a kind of patchwork, added a certain amount of verbosity. The text, having become corrupt through additions and omissions, did not permit the accurate dissemination of learning.[3]

Indians, in the perception of Alberuni, suffered from arrogance, vanity and conceit. This particular trait, deeply rooted in them and easily manifest to everyone, was integral to their national character. They believed that everything associated with them—country, kings, religion and science—was superior to that of all

112 *Situating Medieval India*

other countries and races. They were extremely reluctant to share what they knew. They withheld it not only from foreigners, but also from men of another caste among their own people. Any person, informing them of a science or scholar in Khurasan and Persia, was treated as an ignoramus or a liar. If they had travelled and interacted with other nations, they would have been constrained to change their minds. Alberuni felt that this attitude was confined to his contemporaries, whereas their ancestors did not have such a narrow outlook. In earlier times, they acknowledged that the Greeks had made a greater contribution to science than themselves. In the times of Alberuni, this had changed. When he explained some rules of logical deduction and scientific methods in mathematics, they asked if he had learnt from an Indian master. Hearing a denial, they almost regarded him as a sorcerer.

Alberuni held that the Greeks and Indians, in matters of religion, were both heathens. However, the Greek philosophers, in contrast to the Indians, worked out the elements of science, not of popular superstition. When Socrates opposed the idolatry of the commoners and denied the status of gods to the stars, he was sentenced to death. The Indians did not have men of his stamp, who were capable and willing to bring sciences to a classical perfection. Their scientific theorems were in a state of confusion. Devoid of any logical order, they were mixed up with the vulgar notions of the crowds in term of immense numbers, enormous time spans and religious dogmas. Their mathematical and astronomical literature was a mixture of pearl shells and sour dates, or of pearls and dung, or of costly crystals and common pebbles. In their eyes, both were identical, as they could not raise themselves to the methods of scientific deduction.[4]

Alberuni berated the stranglehold of theology on Indian sciences. The Puranas, replete with assertions on the shape of the earth, were opposed to the scientific truths known to Indian astronomers. A majority of Indians consulted these books while performing religious rites and, in the process, remained entangled in unscientific astronomical calculations and astrological predictions. In consequence, the masses held astronomers in high regard. The astronomers, with a view to repay the people for public adulation,

Scientific Temperament and Technical Innovations. . . 113

accepted popular notions on scientific truths. They conformed themselves to ordinary standards of scientific knowledge and churned out spiritual stuff that the people required of them. With the passage of time, two theories, the vulgar and the scientific, were intermingled.[5]

There was a wide belief in witchcraft, which deluded the senses into seeing something different from reality. One of its aspects was alchemy that was believed to change the substance of matter. Though its existence did not prove intelligence or ignorance, its adepts tried to conceal it. In a discussion, they spoke of the processes of sublimation, calcinations, analysis and waxing of talc. Similar to alchemy was *Rasayana* which, employing plant extracts as medicines, claimed to restore youth, virility and longevity. Nagarjuna,[6] who lived near Somnath a century before Alberuni, excelled in the subject and composed a rare book on it. Alberuni heard several tales about the practice of *Rasayana.* Vyadi, who lived in Ujjain during the reign of Vikramaditya, despaired of his experiments and turned matter into gold through accident. A man, living in Dhar during the reign of Bhojadeva, tried to bestow immortality on the ruler, but ended up turning himself into an oblong piece of silver. Ranka, a fruit seller, used the golden body of a Siddha to purchase an entire town and fought a battle against the King Vallabha. The Indians had a firm belief in the efficacy of charms and incantations. A book on the subject was regarded as the work of Garuda, a bird on which Narayana rode. Most charms were intended for the victims of snakebite. In the absence of a charmer, the victim was bound to a bundle of reeds. Over him, a leaf was placed with a blessing for the person who would accidentally appear to save him. Musical chants were used as an antidote to poisoning and catching wild animals.[7]

The Indian scientific temper could be gauged from the understanding of astronomers on the solar and lunar eclipses. Varahamihira,[8] in his *Samhita,* affirmed that the former occurred when the moon covered a part of the sun and the latter happened when the earth covered a part of the moon, during their movement in the respective orbits. When the moon approached the sun from the west, it covered the sun like a portion of a cloud. The size of

114   *Situating Medieval India*

the covering differed in different regions. That covering the moon, being large, its light waned when half of it was eclipsed. That covering the sun, being small, its rays continued to be powerful in spite of the eclipse. Varahamihira complained that some people believed that the eclipse was caused by the Head, which resembled the sun and moon or a black serpent. It intruded into the heaven and, appearing among the angels, managed to have a share of the nectar (*amrit*), which Vishnu distributed. It did not die even after receiving a fatal blow from Vishnu. Accepted as an inhabitant of heaven, it appeared only on the occasion of the eclipse. It was surprising that Varahamihira, having demolished the popular notion of the Head as the cause of the eclipse, ended up accepting the Head as a celestial body and, thus, compromised with the traditionalists. Alberuni recognized Brahmagupta as the most distinguished of Indian astronomers, but censured him for accepting Head as the cause of the eclipse. Alberuni attributed the basic mistake to Puranic literature, which placed moon above the sun, so that any higher celestial body could not cover the lower one, particularly in the sight of those who stood lower than the both. They required a being that devoured the sun and moon, causing them to appear in shapes which their eclipsed parts appeared in reality.[9]

From the early thirteenth century, the metropolis of Delhi evolved as a great cultural centre. The Mongol devastation of Central Asia forced droves of Muslims to turn east. Under Iltutmish, Delhi became a haven for Muslim refugees. The Sultan went out of his way to welcome the Muslim migrants, who received a warm shelter and comfortable living. At this time, innumerable migrants—Syeds from Arabia, traders from Khurasan, painters from China and theologians from Bukhara—arrived in Delhi. Craftsmen of every kind and from every country relocated here. These entrants included assayers, jewellers, philosophers, ascetics, devotees and physicians of the Greek school. They were attracted to Delhi just as the moths gathered around a candle. In its cultural excellence, the city roused the jealousy of paradise.[10] Since astrology and astronomy had attained prestige in Central Asia, the two subjects found a fertile ground in India. Three eminent writers—Saduddin Muhammad Awfi, Tajuddin Hasan Nizami and Amir Khusrau—were familiar

Scientific Temperament and Technical Innovations. . . 115

with the planetary movements. During Balban's reign, Hamiduddin Mutriz emerged as leading expert in medicine and astrology, not far behind Buqrat and Jalinus.[11] In the times of Alauddin Khalji, Badruddin Damishqi diagnosed ailments by feeling the pulse and examining the urine. His proficiency in the classic works of Bu Ali Sina enabled him to teach medical aspirants with great ability. Other eminent physicians were Sadruddin Marigali, Yamani Tabib, Alamuddin, Izzuddin Badauni, Mah Chander and Jaja Jarrah. Nagoris, Brahmins and Jayatis also cured the sick. In every street of Delhi, Hindu and Muslim astrologers were found proficient in preparing horoscopes. The ruling elite, before performing any ritual, consulted the astrologers, who were compensated with lands and stipends.[12] Muhammd bin Tughluq, an erudite scholar of rational sciences, interacted with rationalist philosophers like Saad Mantaqi, Ubaid Shair, Najm Intishar and Maulana Alamuddin.[13]

Alberuni's observations on educated Indians indicated a dual attitude—scientific and unscientific—towards the natural phenomena. After the passage of three centuries, this outlook was manifest in Amir Khusrau (1253-1325), the prolific poet and historian. While asserting the superiority of India in a long poem, 'Nine Skies' (*Nuh Sipihr*), he built a case that was a curious mixture of fact and fiction, having fused factual information with legendary tales.[14] The poet derived his inspiration from the greatness of Saturn (*zuhl*), the presiding planet of earth and the seventh sky. India, owing to the magic of its cultural accomplishments, was superior to Rum (Greece), Khurasan (Persia) and Khotan (China). It was the land of his birth (*maulud*). A saying of Prophet Muhammad held that love of the motherland (*hub al-watn min al-iman*) was an essential part of the true faith. Since Shaikh Nizamuddin Auliya belonged to this land, it had become an attraction for the world. India's climate was similar to that of paradise. That was why Adam, after his banishment from heaven, found shelter in this country.[15] As he had been brought up in paradise, it was necessary to dispatch him to a similar habitat. During his separation from Eve, he did not ease himself in India, as such acts were not permitted in an heavenly place. Only in the desert of Damascus, his bodily excretions formed the town of Ghotah. Though the peacock was a bird of heaven, it

116 *Situating Medieval India*

was found in India. The snake, who had intruded heaven through stratagem, was also found here. Since it possessed the un-Indian habit of biting, it was made to live beneath the earth.[16]

Unlike Khurasan, India's winter was not cruel and a single garment was sufficient to keep warm. Its summer did cause discomfort, but the shade of a single branch of some tree provided protection against the blazing sun. According to a Hadis, the cool breeze felt in Hijaz blew from the direction of India. The spring, with its profusion of wine and flowers, lasted throughout the year. The flowers blossomed for a long time and retained their fragrance even after drying up. Juicy fruits included mango, banana and sugarcane. Dry spices included cardamom, camphor and cloves. Betel leaves, an accompaniment of food, was relished by the nobles and their sons. Even the poor people of India were not avaricious, being satisfied with a mere blanket. An Indian peasant, wearing a single worn out sheet, spent the night in a pasture and grazed a single animal.[17]

Amir Khusrau felt that the contemporary Muslim elite were prejudiced about the religion of Hindus and the state of their sciences. He assumed the task of putting the record straight. Having cultivated the friendship of Brahmins and having won their confidence, he undertook independent research into the secrets of their learning. Whatever he grasped from the Brahmins could not be contradicted. Some factors hampered the dissemination of Brahmanical learning on a wide scale. Most branches of this knowledge were excessively complicated, so that the mediocre did not dare to pursue them. The Brahmins, owing to their humility, were not eloquent about their learning. Some people, apparently orthodox Muslims, regarded the Hindus as unbelievers and did not acknowledge their virtues. The Hindus, being pantheists, believed that an omnipotent God sustained the universe and His will determined every action in the world. Even while the Hindus worshipped several physical objects—idols, sun, stones, cattle and plants—they regarded these things to be the creation of God and discerned the divine spirit in them.

India was superior to the whole world in learning and mental illumination. A huge wealth of knowledge had been created in

Scientific Temperament and Technical Innovations... 117

natural sciences, mathematics, geography, logic, astrology and poetry. The Brahmins surpassed Aristotle and Rumi in their contribution to philosophy. Such was their perfection in various sciences that they did not go to other lands to improve their knowledge and seek judgement on it. Instead, the foreigners travelled to India from all parts of the world to learn different subjects. A Brahmin named Asa developed mathematics, which the Greeks borrowed. A foreigner, Abu Maashar, resided in Benares for ten years and attained proficiency in astrology. The wonderful book of wisdom *Kalila wa Dimna* (*Panchtantra*) was translated into major languages of the world and inspired scholars across the globe.[18] The fascinating game of chess, with its countless moves and innumerable possibilities, did not permit any one to grasp its technique. The Indian music charmed the beasts, but it was so complex that foreigners could learn it only after staying in India for thirty and forty years.[19] In a sense, the case of Khusrau, as an insider imbued with patriotism, stood in contrast to the unfavourable judgements of the alien Alberuni.

Khusrau claimed that some Indians had acquired supernatural powers and, thus, performed miracles. Conscious of the improbability of such feats, he admitted that certain things were achieved through magic, while others were just popular stories. One who had seen them could not forget them, while one who had not seen them did not believe them. A person bitten by a snake was revived even after six months, as he was flown east to Kamrup (Assam) for treatment with magic. Brahmins, specializing in occult, revived the dead man with the recitation of incantations (*mantras*), provided that the vital organs of the dead had not decomposed. Some Jogis achieved extraordinary long lives through breath control. Inhabiting the mountainous caves of Kashmir, they transferred the soul from one body to the other. They could assume the form of different animals, draw out the blood of a person and refilled it again, controlled the minds of the young and old, flew in the air, remained under water without sinking, sat cross-legged on the surface of water and crossed the river in that posture, became invisible with the application of collyrium to the eyes, made the clouds shed or stop the rain and so on.[20]

118   *Situating Medieval India*

The birds and animals of India, being intelligent, performed a variety of wondrous feats. The parrot talked like humans and spoke what it heard. Myna (*sharak/sarika*) was more distinct and accurate in speech than the parrot. The crow flew high into the sky singing aloud and returned making the same noise. Skylark, a small black bird, who soared high, concealed hidden meanings in its flying, hopping and chattering. The peacock displayed its unique beauty in the form of a three yard long tail, which spread out as a canopy. Endowed with a crown on its head, its black feet repelled the evil eye. When it danced in a state of sexual arousal, it showered pearls from its eyes. The peahens, fascinated by the dance, swallowed the pearls to conceive and procreate. Three different types of birds— parrot, myna and swan—were trained to join each other in an astonishing act. In Bengal, a water drawing bird (*suqqa*) pulled a string with its beak to draw water from a clay vessel. A pigeon, though scared of the cat, could be trained to play with it. A number of quadrupeds were trained to behave like humans. A horse kicked the earth with different steps, while a goat could balance its feet on a wooden stick. The monkey used its hands like humans. The elephant, in spite of its bulk and strength, was intelligent and obedient. Devoted to its trainer, it could discriminate between good and bad. During sickness, it was treated with medicines administered to humans. Owing to these qualities, it adorned the courts of kings. Khusrau's observations, essentially restricted to domesticated birds and animals, pointed to a class of professionals, who trained various creatures for the amusement of upper classes. There were biologists who engaged in research and experiments on animal behaviour. They studied the chirping of birds, prancing of deer and howling of jackals. They were reputed to have written several books on the subject.[21]

The Delhi Sultanate, with regard to scientific temper, experienced a disjuncture between the thirteenth and fourteenth centuries. During the thirteenth century, the ruling class had inadequate knowledge about the indigenous society including topographical features, patterns of production, movement of trade and basis of urban centres. It failed to institutionalize the collection of statistics and maintenance of records, owing to limited availability of paper

Scientific Temperament and Technical Innovations. . . 119

and trained personnel. Instead of assessing the land tax on the individual peasant, the state extracted irregular tribute from local chiefs with the use of military force. From the early fourteenth century, the Delhi Sultanate entered a higher stage of state formation. The social base of the bureaucracy was broadened with the inclusion of social upstarts. With the marginalization of the orthodoxy, the rationalist philosophers (Ubaid Shair, Saad Mantaqi, Najm Intishar and Maulana Alimuddin) were encouraged. A new intellectual environment was created in which traditional modes of thinking were undermined and creative solutions were applied to governance, magnifying the role of state in the restructuring of the agrarian economy.

The increasing centralization and systematization of administration necessitated the production of statistics and maintenance of records. The salary of a horseman was fixed at 234 *tankahs*, while a soldier possessing an extra horse was entitled to an additional sum of 78 *tankahs*. The ruling class familiarized itself with the relative position of various social classes in the rural areas. The intermediaries, deprived of their traditional privileges, were converted into semi-official components of the revenue collection machinery. An enormous exercise was undertaken to collect information regarding the area under cultivation, yield per unit of area, the number of houses in a village and even the cattle in the possession of the peasants. Much of this data appeared to have been recorded in the account books (*bahis*) of the village accountants (*patwaris*). Since the land tax was increasingly collected in cash, the agricultural prices became crucial.[22] The entire system entailed the employment of a virtual army of functionaries—clerks, writers, accountants, assessors and agents—who were adept in Persian as well as the local language, besides possessing the knowledge of new revenue regulations and requisite skills in writing. In consequence, large sections of society from the mighty nobles to the lowly peasant—central revenue department, military commanders, assignment holders, land grantees, revenue officials, grain merchants, moneylenders, local chiefs, village headmen and of course the primary producers—were drawn into the vortex of mathematical calculations, revenue statistics and official records.

120 *Situating Medieval India*

The ruling class imbibed useful lessons from the painful experience of droughts, famines, scarcity of foodgrains, exorbitant prices, starvation deaths and abandonment of villages. Agricultural production, sustaining a burgeoning state structure, could no longer be left to the vagaries of nature. Building on its recent success in political centralization, the ruling class sought to tame the natural forces to boost agricultural production and revenue resources. Muhammad bin Tughluq (r. 1325-51) created a department for the promotion of agriculture (*diwan-i amir kohi*), which laid a series of regulations for the purpose. Under an elaborate scheme of agrarian expansion, liberal loans were given to designated officers (*shiqdars*) who promised to bring thousands of acres of wasteland under the plough, along with a shift in the cropping pattern—wheat in place of barley, sugarcane in place of wheat, and grape and dates in place of sugarcane.[23] In the wake of the failure of this scheme, the state shifted its focus of agrarian expansion from the Ganga-Yamuna Doab to the Satluj-Yamuna Divide and Multan. During the reign of Firoz Shah Tughluq (r. 1351-89), a network of canals, taking off from the Satluj, Ghaggar and Yamuna, irrigated the cis-Satluj tract, so that the spring crop (*rabi*) began to be raised in Hissar, where the rain grown autumn crop (*kharif*) had been the practice.[24] Though Barani did not live long enough to observe the definitive transformation in the countryside, his speculation on the subject demands a close attention. A diehard conservative in socio-political matters, Barani showed a remarkable capacity for scientific thinking on the restructuring of the agrarian economy.

Barani anticipated a wide range of improvements in the area south of the Satluj. Groups of pastoralist, moving from place to place in search of water along with their families and herds, would settle as sedentary cultivators. Owing to the availability of water, superior crops like wheat, gram and sugarcane would be raised in places where pulses, lentils and sesame were produced. A variety of fruit—grapes, mangoes, pomegranates, apples, melons, figs, lemons and gooseberries—would be grown. Trees like *pipal, jamun,* tamarind, dates and wild cotton (*simbal/Gosaypium aberasum*) would grow. Cattle population would increase a thousand times. The process of colonization would be set in motion, so that

Scientific Temperament and Technical Innovations. . .   121

numerous new villages would be settled and revenue assignees (*muqtis*) would be able to regularly collect the land tax from them. Large armies would be able to camp for decades on the banks of these canals, owing to the easy availability of water. Due to general prosperity and improved living standards, people would be able to consume superior goods—wheat, gram and sugar—that were earlier enjoyed only on festive occasions, being brought only from Delhi and its neighbourhood. Since a surplus of these commodities would be produced, they would be transported to deficit areas for commercial purposes. People would be able to travel across the waterless tract without carrying any stock of drinking water. The wayfarers, forced to perform ablutions with sand, would offer five prayers after taking proper baths. They would also be able to travel in boats through the new canals that were 50 or 60 leagues in length. A desert like area, where nothing grew except acacia and thorny bushes, would be covered with gardens, where a variety of fruit and flowers would grow. The birds and animals would no longer suffer due to the scarcity of water.[25]

As we have seen, Delhi Sultanate did not hesitate to mould natural resources to attain agrarian expansion. Firoz Shah Tughluq, encouraged by initial success, planned a more ambitious project. In 1360-1, he paid a visit to Sarsuti. It was observed that this river constituted two large streams that were always flowing. A high mound (*pushtah buland*) was located between them. If the mound could be dug through, the water of one stream could flow into the other. As a result, it would be possible to irrigate the tract of Sirhind, Mansurpur and Samana. The Sultan enrolled the services of 50,000 labourers (*beldars*) equipped with spades. While digging, they obtained many bones of elephants and human beings. With age, these had partly converted into stone and partly had remained as bones. The discovery generated curiosity even after two centuries. However, the water could not be diverted as envisaged. The setback did not erode Sultan's interest in scientific matters. After the Nagarkot expedition, the observers saw high flames rising from the temple at Jawalamukhi. At this sacred site, as many as 1,300 books of the Brahmins were discovered. The Sultan summoned the Brahmins and, apparently, inquired about the content of the literature. He

122 *Situating Medieval India*

ordered his translators to translate some of them into Persian. Izzuddin Khalid Khani, a poet and record keeper (*munshi*) of the reign, produced the versified translation of a book on the movement of seven planets, besides auguries and omens. Entitled *Dalail-i Firoz Shahi*, Abdul Qadir Badauni read it in Lahore (1591-2) from beginning to the end. He found it moderately good, comprising both beauties and defects. On earlier occasions, Badauni had seen some other translations in the name of Firoz Shah Tughluq. Some of these were on the science of music, while others dealt with musical performances (*ilm pinkal yani fan mausiqi wa iqsam akhara keh aan ra paturbazi me-goyend*). Badauni was not impressed as, in his view, the themes were rather trivial and it was difficult to explain them in another language.[26]

Firoz Shah Tughluq, through his knowledge and intellect, invented a number of devices. Following his return from Thatta, he consulted astrologers for many days and established a gong (*tas ghariyal*) on the palace at Firozabad.[27] A large number of spectators, belonging to all classes and ages, went to see the wonder, which was a unique memorial in the area extending from Khurasan to Bengal. Though it served a worldly purpose, its gains extended to the hereafter. Afif has enumerated seven benefits. Its sound informed the people of the departure of the day and arrival of the night. It made them conscious of the perpetual decrease in their spans of life, besides instilling the concerns for the hereafter. When it became dark due to dust and clouds, it was not possible to distinguish between early afternoon (*zuhr*) and late afternoon (*asr*) prayers. The gong enabled the people to ascertain the correct time for three prayers. The same was applicable to the midnight (*tahajjud*) prayer. During the month of Ramzan, cloudy weather caused confusion regarding the beginning and breaking of fast. People, offering night (*isha*) prayer after the passage of a third of the night, faced a similar difficulty. The difference of opinion among the theologians compounded the confusion. The gong saved the people from the multifarious obstacles.[28]

A devout Muslim was required to recognize the true nature of shadow, which kept on changing in accordance with the varying durations of the day and night. In a single year, the duration varied

Scientific Temperament and Technical Innovations... 123

from 1.5 steps to 10.5 steps. The difference was discernible only through divine knowledge. The gong, following the direction of experts was struck as per the number of passing hours. Every month, it was possible to know the location of the sun in a particular zodiac sign. The entire procedure obviated the need of astrology, which Prophet Muhammad had forbidden to the Muslims. The gong, on the one hand, provided practical convenience for devout Muslims and, on the other hand, ensured conformity with Islamic orthodoxy, particularly on the question of astrology.[29]

During the reign of Firoz Shah Tughluq, two massive Ashokan pillars were brought to Delhi from Tavera (near Khizrabad and Salora) and Meerut. This feat of engineering comprised three stages—uprooting the pillars from the ground, transporting them on a wheeled cart and erection in Kotla Firoz Shah and Kushk-i Shikar. At this time, it was believed that the pillars were the two staffs that Bhima employed to graze his cattle. One of the five Pandava brothers, Bhima was noted for his giant stature and physical strength. The Sultan, using his intelligence and taking precautions, called his horsemen, foot soldiers and slaves. He also summoned a large number of people from the villages of the Doab and beyond. Ropes made of the cotton of Simbal trees were used to prevent the pillar from falling. Digging down carefully, it was found that the pillar stood on a wide rectangular base. From top to bottom, the pillar was wrapped with wooden boards and raw hides, while big bundles of cotton were stacked around the base. As soon as the base was dug out, the bundles were removed one by one and the pillar was brought down without any damage. A long carriage of 42 wheels was put together. Two ropes, weighing ten maunds each, were attached to the wheels. Two hundred men pulled each rope, so that the carriage was brought to the Yamuna under the watchful eyes of the Sultan. The pillar was placed on a train of large boats, each of which could carry 2,000-7,000 maunds of grains. It was carried to Firozabad and placed besides the Jama Masjid. Skilled artisans built a structure of stones (*ghor sang*) that were provided with pulleys at successive levels. One end of the ropes was tied to the edge of the pillar, while the other end was passed through the pulleys. The pillar was again wrapped in wooden

124   *Situating Medieval India*

boards and raw hides. Thousands of labourers pulled hard to raise the pillar and, supporting it with iron columns, fixed it on the rectangular base straight like an arrow. The top of the pillar was surrounded with black and white stones. The pinnacle comprised a gold plated copula of copper. The height of the pillar was 32 yards, 24 of which were above the plinth and eight yards below in the foundation.[30] There was a Hindawi inscription on the pillar, but the Brahmins and Sewras could not decipher it.[31]

The second pillar was discovered in the town of Meerut in the Ganga-Yamuna Doab. The Sultan, employing numerous techniques and efforts, relocated it on a hillock at the Khusk-i Shikar. Since Afif had already described the entire procedure in the previous case, he has refrained from repeating it. Following the installation of the pillar, the Sultan ordered a celebration to mark the occasion. The inhabitants of the city were in a joyous mood. Countless pitchers of sherbet were placed at the site. People arrived without any hindrance and, seeing the marvel, returned after drinking the sherbet. With the completion of the palace, a new city sprang up. All the nobles constructed beautiful bungalows in it. Every Sultan had left behind a monument, which became a lasting memory of his creative ability. For example, Shamsuddin Iltutmish had raised a magnificent tower (Qutb Minar) near the premier mosque in Delhi. Firoz, through the relocation of two pillars, left a precedent, which was without any parallel in history. Amir Timur, during the course of his invasion and sojourn in Delhi, visited the monuments of every ruler. On seeing the two pillars, he was amazed. He had visited many countries. He found that the kings had left behind buildings that had perished with time. However, he asserted that the two pillars of Firoz would last until the day of judgement. At the orders of Firoz, the details of the two pillars, along with the important events of his reign, were inscribed at their base. With the passage of time, the visitors, on beholding the pillars, felt that the task was beyond human capacity.[32]

Afif points to the interest of Firoz Shah Tughluq in astrolabes. The Sultan always carried a small astrolabe with him. However, he installed a majestic astrolabe at the top of the golden tower (*minar zareen*). In this brief statement, Afif did not explain the

Scientific Temperament and Technical Innovations. . . 125

manner of its functioning. He implied its connection with the gong, which was struck every hour even with an overcast sky. The time keeping devices, along with paper and magnetic compass, constituted a set of innovations that contributed to intellectual development in different ways. The accuracy of these devices was important for the regulation of economic activity. Their improvement, effected through the astrolabes and clepsydras, attained a high degree of sophistication in the Islamic world. The astrolabes were truly multipurpose precision instruments on which the Muslim mathematicians and craftsmen lavished so much of their learning and art. On the top of a tower at Firozabad, Firoz Shah Tughluq installed a number of astrolabes, a sundial and possibly a clepsydra, for the time was said to have been accurately kept even when the sky was overcast. The Delhi citizenry regarded the 'time clock' as a unique wonder of the age. Unfortunately, by adjusting time-lengths to the variations in the length of the day and night, such devices perpetuated the notion of unequal hours.[33] It may be noted that the astrolabes had a complex history of diffusion. Following the traditions of the Abbasid caliphs, the Central Asian kingdoms (Khawarizm, Ghazni and Samarqand) patronized science and learning, particularly the construction of astrolabes. Alberuni has explained the working of a flat astrolabe, while Muzaffar bin Muzaffar al-Tusi (d. 1213) developed a linear astrolabe. In the Delhi Sultanate, astrolabe became a favourite instrument of scientists and a curiosity for the elite. Firoz Shah Tughluq oversaw the construction of an astrolabe, which could be used both in northern and southern hemisphere. Large in size, its components included a disc (*halqah*), hook (*urwah*), throne (*kursi*), chamber (*umm*), tablet (*sufaf*), flagstone (*safaih*) and net (*ankabut*). It was possibly a modified form of the astrolabe associated with al-Tusi.[34]

The Bhakti reformers occupied a considerable space in the cultural landscape of northern India. Here, we are concerned with the content of their socio-religious ideologies, besides the manner of their articulation and dissemination. Pleading for devotional monotheism and social equality, they sought to demolish the hegemony of the priestly classes. Their message was meant for the socially depressed groups—peasants, artisans, labourers and petty

126 *Situating Medieval India*

traders—who suffered from economic exploitation and denial of access to education. They tried to rescue the underprivileged from the stranglehold of ignorance and superstition, which the Pandit-Mulla regime had perpetuated. Serving as stern teachers and loving mentors, they communicated with their followers in the common dialects and avoided complex philosophical jargons. They found that the masses had been fed on myths and miracles regarding the creation of universe and evolution of life on earth. The Bhakti reformers explained the laws of nature in scientific terms and illustrated their arguments with examples from the ordinary experiences of the common masses, who could verify them through simple observation. Sant Kabir and Guru Nanak induced the oppressed and illiterate, both directly and indirectly, to adopt a scientific attitude towards their immediate surroundings as well as the wider universe.

Sant Kabir was an acute observer of nature.[35] His observations were based on scientific principles. He argued that the characteristics and behaviour of living creatures, both plants and animals, was governed by the laws of nature and these could not be altered by any external agency through the application of force. Nature was supreme in its wide domain and did not brook any interference. It was incumbent on human beings to form a correct understanding of natural phenomena, particularly those touching the human life. The truth regarding the laws of nature was self-evident. For example, the cloves did not bear fruit. The sandalwood tree did not produce flowers. Fish did not hunt in the forest. The lions did not swivel in the sea. Castor oil plant could not turn into Mysore sandal. A blind man could not see. A cripple could not leap over the Mount Sumeru. A dumb person could not express his knowledge in speech. There could be no tree without roots. Plants could not bear fruit without flowers. Nobody could dance without using one's feet. Praise could not be sung without using the tongue.[36] In a brilliant contrast, Sant Kabir argued that the social status of an individual could not change due to worldly factors. However, the same could not be said regarding matters that were in the hands of nature.

In a series of sharp arguments, Sant Kabir has demolished the claims of Brahmins that their lives remained insulated from flesh.

Scientific Temperament and Technical Innovations... 127

The Brahmin's house was made of clay in which dead bodies of human beings and animals had been decomposing for thousands of years. He drank the water of the Ganga and regarded it as pure, though it was contaminated with the flesh and blood of thousands of creatures—fish, turtles and crocodiles—that had been breeding on its banks. Every day he consumed milk after lunch, but it was produced in the organs of cattle that were made of flesh and blood. Therefore, he was advised to discard his scriptures that had failed to note the glaring realities of life.[37] The Brahmins claimed ritualistic purity, as they practiced untouchability with regard to the Shudras. The claim was false because the Brahmins consumed foodgrains that the Shudras produced with their hands.[38] Sant Kabir was strongly opposed to animal sacrifice as an act of religious merit. He condemned both the Pandits and Mullahs for this widespread cruelty. How could the Brahmins claim that the animals were slaughtered to please the gods? Had it been so, the gods themselves would have gone to the jungles to hunt the beasts. Instead of reaching the gods, the meat ended in human bellies. Brahma, the divine potter, created the animals in the manner he shaped other forms of creation. But, man was engaged in the mass killing of animals, as if they grew season after season like grass. People ate flesh to please their tongues, but ultimately the flesh came back to eat the people.[39]

Muslims too slaughtered cattle as a part of their religious rituals. They converted a living creature into a corpse and still claimed that it was a holy rite. They asserted that the practice was in conformity with the preaching of their ancestors and that it had been sanctified by long tradition. The blood, being shed since then, was on their head. They must share this huge backlog of guilt. They did not know that the animals were born through the same process of sexual reproduction (merger of blood and sperm) as found in all other creatures. Despite an entire life spent in continuous prayers, they had failed to comprehend the true basis of religion. The association between animal killing and religious merit was untenable, as the real purpose was to satisfy the hunger for taste. Both the Pandits and Mullahs, owing to their cruelty towards animals, would go straight to hell. Day and night, the Qazi chanted

128   *Situating Medieval India*

the same words without putting forth an original idea. He cherished his authority at the ritual circumcision of male children. If God favoured circumcision, how was the Qazi born uncut? If this particular rite made him a Muslim, the religious state of Muslim women became uncertain. Since they were seen as man's other half and remained without circumcision, such members of the community were not Muslims, but Hindus. Similar was the case of the Brahmins. If wearing the thread made them Brahmins, the religious identity of their wives remained unclear, as they were not required to wear this prime caste symbol.[40]

Since Sant Kabir believed in the universal brotherhood of man, he rejected the divisions on the basis of religion and caste.[41] All humans beings passed through the same life cycle from birth to death. Nobody read the Vedas in the womb and no Turk was born circumcised. Every human embryo grew from a single seed, while every foetus grew in the mother's womb for ten months. When the babies were born, they were composed of the same material such as skin and bone, flesh and blood, urine and faeces. It was not possible to distinguish between a Brahmin and Shudra, or between a Hindu and Turk.[42] During their active life, all human beings showed the same traits of hunger, anger and lust. When they died, their corpses ended up in the same fashion irrespective of the mode of final disposal. If the dead man was cremated, his burnt ashes mingled with the dust. If he was buried, the maggots ate his dead body. If it was neither cremated nor buried, but left unattended, then it became the food for pigs, crows and dogs. These were hard facts of life from which there was no escape. Since death was the supreme and universal reality, it did not recognize any social distinction. If one tried to look at death in a thousand different ways, the human body was still found ending in dust.[43]

Guru Nanak (1469-1539) came out strongly against the priestly classes for misguiding the common people regarding food habits, eating of meat and vegetarianism.[44] In the Brahmanical religious discourse, references to flesh occupied crucial place. The Brahmins propagated that abstaining from flesh was an essential component of religious practice and that it led to spiritual betterment. Such beliefs were not only opposed to human experience, but also came

Scientific Temperament and Technical Innovations. . . 129

into conflict with the laws of nature. They generated superstition, ignorance and intellectual oppression. The Brahmins wrongly equated the distinction between virtue and vice with that between vegetables and meat. The ethical qualities of human beings could not be determined by the preference for particular types of food. The Puranas allowed the eating of flesh. The Semitic books permitted it. It was consumed during the four ages. It was customary for the gods to kill the rhinoceroses and burn libations of their flesh in the sacrificial fires. Flesh had been an esteemed food in the ritualistic sacrifices, marriage feasts and religious rites. Nevertheless the Brahmins abjured flesh and sat holding their noses in the semblance of meditation. They were born of the blood of their parents, but refused to eat flesh or fish. Only fools wrangled over the eating of meat. Human beings could not escape from their association with flesh. Sex was a basic human need, but copulation was nothing but meeting of the flesh of two persons. When man and woman met at night and engaged in sexual intercourse, conception took place in the flesh. All humans—man and women, kings and emperors—were not only born of flesh, they were also composed of flesh. If association with flesh led the concerned person to hell, why did the Brahmins accept offerings from him? It was ironical that the giver of charity went to hell, while the recipient of charity went to heaven. They were ignorant of the manner in which flesh was produced. The process was not dissimilar from the cultivation of crops—grain, sugarcane and cotton—that were raised with the help of water.[45]

The changes in human life, in the eyes of Guru Nanak, accorded with the laws of nature. He perceived them in terms of ten stages, each of which reflected its own characteristics. In the first stage, a child was attracted to milk from the breast. In the second, he developed an understanding of his mother and father. In the third, he recognized his brother, brother's wife and sister. In the fourth, he developed a love for playing. In the fifth, he ran after food and drink. In the sixth, he nurtured the sexual desire, and, in his lust, did not inquire the woman's caste. In the seventh, he resided in his house and amassed wealth. In the eighth, his body was wasted due to anger. In the ninth, his hair turned grey and breathing became

130   *Situating Medieval India*

difficult. In the tenth, he died and, following his cremation, turned into ash. His companions, escorting the corpse, gave vent to loud lamentations. He came into this world and, after his departure, even his name disappeared. Following his demise, food was offered on leaves and crows were called in.

Guru Nanak has explained the changes in human life in another way. Assuming that a person would live for ninety years, each decade denoted a distinct activity and, ultimately, underscored a progressive physical decay. At the age of ten, the individual was a child. At twenty, he was a youth. At thirty, he was called handsome. At forty, he was seen as complete. At fifty, his feet did not match his gait. At sixty, his old age set in. At seventy, he lost his intellect. At eighty, he was unable to perform his duties. At ninety, he lay on a cot, making him weak enough to be oblivious of strength. The human life, owing to its propensity to degenerate, was comparable to a mansion of smoke. Living creatures, found in different forms and colours, passed through the stages of birth, growth and death. One who experienced these three stages understood that God had designed this play. The Creator, having created the human body, made suitable arrangements for its protection and survival. A human being saw with his eyes, spoke with his tongue, heard with his ears, walked with his feet and worked with his hands. He wore and ate what was given to him. Once the pitcher broke, its frame crumbled and it could not be moulded again. Same was true of human beings.[46]

Guru Nanak held that female biological processes, particularly menstruation, deserved unconditional acceptance.[47] Regarding the origin of humans, the mother preceded the father.[48] In the first stage of its life, it was lodged in the mother's womb through divine will. The foetus, with its body reversed, performed penance and prayed to the Lord with fixed attention. It came naked into the world and departed naked from it.[49] The first attraction of the child was to the milk of his mother's breast. Even if it had little understanding, it quaffed the milk. The mother and father had intense love for it. Like Krishna in the house of Jasodha, it was tossed with affection from hand to hand.[50] All men were conceived in a woman and, in due course, they were married to a woman. He

Scientific Temperament and Technical Innovations. . . 131

felt impelled to contract friendship (*dosti*) with a woman. The human life, during the past ages, was propagated through women. A woman could not be called inferior, as the kings were born from her. A woman, who gave birth to life, was herself born out of a woman. Without a woman, none could take birth. Only the True Lord, who is one and eternal, remained without a woman. Guru Nanak, throughout this hymn,[51] referred to the woman as a vessel (*bhandu*), as he saw her as a cornucopia from which the entire creation poured forth. In the Sikh scripture, the validation of the female was advanced through the imagery of conception, gestation, giving birth and lactation. Here, the woman was mother, who actually went through a sequence of biological processes. She was neither goddess worshipped in temples nor a temptress worthy of segregation.[52]

Guru Nanak, in a composition entitled 'Twelve Months' (*bara mah*), voiced the mental state of a bride during the change of seasons and, in the process, validated the natural concerns of female sexuality. *Chet* (March-April), the first month of the year, was the time of spring when vegetation flowered in front of the bride's door. The cuckoo sang in the mango tree, bumble bees hummed in rapture and black bees hovered around the bush. In contrast, the bride was not at peace. Since her husband was away from home, she suffered the pangs of separation and her body wasted away. She would experience equanimity only if she obtained the spouse in her house. In *Vaisakh* (April-May), new leaves sprung from plants. The bride was anxious to see the Beloved at her door and inside her house. Without Him, she was not worth a shell. If she pleased Him, her worth would rise beyond computation. Her Beloved was not distant, but present in her interior. In the months of *Jeth* (May-June) and *Asarh* (June-July), the earth burnt like a furnace. The bride, without her Spouse, was deprived of peace. Since she knew the Lord, she became like Him. Attaining virtue through His grace, she hoped to dissolve in Him. A bride, who recited the name of the True Lord, attained eternal happiness. During *Savan* (July-August), the rains enabled the bride to anticipate a shower of joy. She loved the Spouse with her body and soul. Since He was away to foreign lands, the bride was scared of lightning. More terrifying

132   *Situating Medieval India*

was the pain of separation, which had brought her close to death. She was distressed because her bed (*sej*) was lonely. She lost interest in food, sleep and clothes. During *Bhadon* (August-September), the rain filled the plains and ponds. The peacocks and frogs shrieked, while the cuckoo cried for her beloved. The snakes and mosquitoes went about with their stings. In the dark night, the rain set the stage for merriment. The bride, in the absence of her Spouse, found no comfort. At the advice of the Guru, she would go after Him.[53]

In the month of *Assu* (September-October), falling between summer and winter, there was greenery all around and shrubs bore white flowers. A bride, hopeful of meeting her Spouse, believed that the plant that ripened slowly turned out to be sweet. During *Katak* (October-November), the lamps were lit with the oil of love, which would pave the way for the cherished union. The bride prayed that He would open His door for her entry, as a single moment of her life had stretched to six months. During *Maghar* (November-December), the virtuous bride (*gunwanti*) recited the praise of the Lord in song, music and poetry, dissipating her sorrow. In the month of *Poh* (December-January), winter was manifested in ample snowfall and drying vegetation. The bride, conscious of the Lord's light in the procreation of living beings, felt His presence in her body and soul. The Spouse enjoyed the bride, who was in love with Him. In *Magh* (January-February), the bride became pure on realizing the pilgrimage sites in her interior. Her recitation of the divine name yielded the merit of bathing at sixty-eight sacred sites. In *Phalgun* (February-March), the bride's soul blossomed. In order to please Him, she adorned herself with silks, garlands, pearls and perfumes. When the Spouse met her, the varying spans of time became sublime. The Spouse not only settled her affairs, but also beautified her with numerous embellishments. As a result, she met Him and enjoyed His love. In her house, the bed (*ghar sej suhavi*) attained splendour only when He enjoyed her. By the Guru's grace, her destiny was awakened. She became jubilant due to the perpetual union. Her marital life was placed on an even keel.[54]

Scientific Temperament and Technical Innovations. . .   133

NOTES

1. An earlier version of this paper entitled, 'Scientific Attitudes in Medieval North India: Context, Nature and Articulation (AD 1000-1500)', was presented at a seminar on 'The History of Science and Technology in India', at the Department of History, School of Social Sciences, University of Hyderabad, Hyderabad, 1-3 September 2005. It was published in *History of Science and Technology: Exploring New Themes*, ed. Rattan Lal Hangloo, Jaipur: Rawat Publications, 2011, pp. 211-27.

2. Abu Raihan Muhammad bin Ahmad Alberuni hailed from the city of Khwarazm. As a versatile intellectual, he was associated with the courts of Abu Abdullah Muhammad Khwarazm Shah (d. 995) and Abu Nasr bin Ali. After the fall of the Al-i Iraq dynasty, he shifted to Jurjan and Tabiristan, where he thrived under the ruler Shams ul-Maali and lived here until the Ghaznavid occupation (1017). Sultan Mahmud brought him to Ghazni along with other prisoners. He was allowed to proceed to India where he lived for 13 years. He travelled across Panjab, Sind and other places. Learning Sanskrit and interacting with scholars, he translated many books into Arabic, including a treatise (*Karna Tilak*) on astronomy and astrology. He returned to Ghazni towards the end of Mahmud's reign and basked under the favour of Masud. He was interested in astronomy, astrology, mathematics, geography, history and religion. Important among his works are *Kitab ul-Hind, Asar ul-Baqia, Qanun-i Masudi, Nihayat ul-Amakin, Masamir ul-Khwarazm* and *Lavazim ul-Harketain.* Iqtidar Husain Siddiqui, 'Abu Raihan Alberuni: His Life and Works', in *Medieval India: Essays in Intellectual Thought and Culture*, New Delhi: Manohar, 2003, pp. 17-25.

3. Edward C. Sachau, *Alberuni's India*, New Delhi: Rupa Publications, rpt., 2002, pp. 1-3. (Hereafter cited as Alberuni).

4. Ibid., p. 8.

5. Ibid., pp. 256-7.

6. A Buddhist philosopher, Nagarjuna, was born to Brahmin parents from Andhra. Part of his early life was spent in the land of the Nagas from whom he learnt the secrets of alchemy. He became the reputed author of an alchemic treatise *Rasaratnakara*, which laid the foundation of this science in India. A profound metaphysician and acute dialectician, he was eventually converted to Buddhism and founded the Madhyamika School of Mahayana. He was regarded as the first patriarch of many Buddhist sects. Three treatises attributed to him were *Madhyamaika Sastra, Dvadasa Sastra* and *Sata Sastra.* Benjamin Walker, *Hindu World: An Encyclopedic Survey of Hinduism*, vol. II, New Delhi: Harper Collins, rpt., 1995, pp. 110-1.

134   *Situating Medieval India*

7. Alberuni, pp. 175-82.
8. Varahamihira, who lived in the sixth century CE, was associated with the court of Vikramaditya of Ujjain. In his work, a growing interest in horoscopy and astrology was included in the study of astronomy and mathematics. Aryabhatta might have questioned this addition, because Varahamihira's emphasis was on astrology rather than astronomy. His *Panchasidhantika* discussed the five currently known schools of astronomy of which two reflected a close knowledge of Hellenistic astronomy. His *Brihatsamhita* had chapters on iconography, materials for making images and methods of their installation. It had sections on omens, natural and celestial events, astronomy and mathematics. Two of his works, *Hora Sashtra* and *Laghu Jataka*, were still used in astrology. Romila Thapar, *The Penguin History of Early India: From the Origins to AD 1300*, New Delhi: Penguin Books, 2003, p. 307; Roshen Dala, *Hinduism: An Alphabetical Guide*, New Delhi; Penguin Books, 2010, p. 445.
9. Alberuni, pp. 513-18.
10. Abdul Malik Isami, *Futuh us-Salatin*, vol. II, Eng. tr. Agha Mahdi Husain, Aligarh: Centre of Advanced Study, Department of History, Aligarh Muslim University and Bombay: Asia Publishing House, 1976, p. 227.
11. Barani, p. 112.
12. Ibid., pp. 362-4.
13. Ibid., p. 465.
14. A modern writer has judged *Nuh Sipihr* as a masterpiece of Amir Khusrau. One of his five historical poems (*masnavis*), it was written in 1318. Comprising 4,500 hemistiches, it was divided into nine unequal parts, each of which was associated with one of the nine heavenly bodies. The poem opened with the praise of God, Prophet Muhammad and Shaikh Nizamuddin Auliya. The first two sections described the military achievements of Qutbuddin Mubarak Shah Khalji and the buildings in Delhi. The fourth to ninth sections, exploring diverse themes, included the festivities at the birth of Prince Muhammad and excellence of Indian poets. The third section, which formed the basis of the present analysis, was unique. It celebrated the characteristic features of India, with reference to its climate, flora and fauna, sciences, religions and languages. Overall, it shows the superiority of India over other countries. Muhammad Wahid Mirza, *The Life and Works of Amir Khusrau*, Delhi: Idarah-i Adabiyat-i Delli, rpt., 1974, pp. 181-9.
15. Adam was regarded as the first human and first prophet. His banishment from heaven along with his wife Eve figured three times in the Quran (2: 34-9, 7: 19-25 and 20: 117-24). God ordered the two to dwell in

Scientific Temperament and Technical Innovations. . .   135

the garden of heaven, where they would not suffer from hunger, thirst and heat. They were free to eat anything except from a specific tree. The Satan, acting through deception, lured them to the tree of immortality and a kingdom that never decayed. The two disobeyed God and ate from the forbidden tree. Becoming conscious of their nakedness, they began to sew the leaves to cover themselves. They expressed their repentance before God and asked for forgiveness. God banished them to a dwelling place on earth, where they could enjoy for a while. They would live there, die there and brought forth from there. According to the moral of the story, whosoever followed the guidance of God would not go astray. One who did not, he would lead a miserable life and rise up blind on the day of resurrection. Seyyed Hossein Nasr et. al., ed., *The Study Quran: A New Translation and Commentary*, pp. 23-5, 413-5 and 805-6.

16. Amir Khusrau, *Nuh Sipihr*, Persian text, ed. Muhammad Wahid Mirza, London: Oxford University Press, 1949, pp. 151-3. (Hereafter cited as Amir Khusrau).

17. Ibid., pp. 158-61.

18. A collection of popular tales and fables, *Panchatantra* was compiled by Vishnu Sharman. Traced to the early centuries of Christian Era, its versions emerged from the northwest, Kashmir, Nepal and south India. The stories, originating as myths relating to cosmogonic phenomena, exceptional topographical features and animals endowed with human qualities, such tales were prototypes of later works like Jatakas, Puranas, romances, dramas and epics of post-Vedic period. A single fable was enlarged into a succession of them, each subtly related to its predecessor. Intended initially for entertainment, some contained moral lessons. Many entered the literature of Middle East and Europe. From sixth century, the tales were translated from Sanskrit into Persian, Arabic, Hebrew, Latin, Syriac, Spanish and Italian. Margaret and James Stutley, *A Dictionary of Hinduism: Its Mythology, Folklore and Development 1500 BC-AD 1500*, Bombay: Allied Publishers, 1977, pp. 217-18.

19. Amir Khusrau, pp. 161-72.

20. Ibid., pp. 191-4.

21. Ibid., pp. 182-91.

22. Ziauddin Barani, *Tarikh-i Firoz Shahi*, Persian text, ed. Sir Syed Ahmad, Aligarh: Sir Syed Academy, Aligarh Muslim University, rpt., 2005, pp. 287-9. (Hereafter cited as Barani).

23. Ibid., pp. 498-9.

24. Shams Siraj Afif, *Tarikh-i Firoz Shahi*, Persian text, ed. Maulavi Wilayat

136 *Situating Medieval India*

Husain, Calcutta: Asiatic Society of Bengal, 1890, pp. 127-8. (Hereafter cited as Afif).

25. Barani, pp. 567-71.

26. Abdul Qadir Badauni, *Muntakhab ut-Tawarikh*, vol. I, Persian text, ed. Maulavi Ahmad Ali, Aligarh: Centre of Advanced Study, Department of History and Publication Division, Aligarh Muslim University, rpt., 2018, pp. 248-9.

27. The gong must have been established after the inscription of the *Futuhat-i Firoz Shahi*. Otherwise, it must have figured in this formal statement of state policy, which affirmed Firoz Tughluq's strong commitment to Sunni orthodoxy. It enumerated a series of steps designed to stop the practices that the Shariat forbade. In the royal palace, pictorial embellishments were banned on ceremonial robes, utensils and weapons. The names of past Sultans, who had served the cause of Islam, were reintroduced in the Friday sermon. A large number of unlawful taxes were abolished. A number of religious innovations (*bidat*) penetrating the lives of Muslims were put down. Religious persecution was inflicted on Shias, Hindus and other heretical groups such as Mulahids and Ibahatis. Women were forbidden from visiting the Sufi shrines. Apart from the construction of mosques, seminaries and Sufi lodges (*khanqahs*), repairs were carried out in the tombs of Sultans, nobles and saints. Canals were dug, trees were planted and a hospital was established. Land grants confiscated in the past were restored. Finally, the Sultan received an investiture from the Amir ul-Mominin, the title of Syed us-Sultan and a number of gifts including the Prophet's footprint. Firoz Shah Tughluq, *Futuhat-i Firoz Shahi*, Persian text, ed. Shaikh Abdur Rashid, Aligarh: Aligarh Muslim University, 1954, pp. 1-19.

28. Afif, pp. 255-7.

29. Ibid., pp. 258-60.

30. Ibid., pp. 305-12.

31. The pillar stood on a pyramid, which consisted of three terraces that provided a progressively stepped appearance. Each terrace bore a series of vaulted cells surrounding the solid core of the structure into which the foot of the tower was built. A sand monolith, the tower was 42.7 feet in height. Its 35 feet were polished, while the remainder was rough. The buried portion measured nearly 4 feet. The diameter was 25.3 feet at the top and 38.3 feet at the base, so that the diminution was 39 inches per foot. It was said to weigh 27 tons, while its colour was pale orange flecked with black spots. In dimension, it resembled the Allahabad pillar more than any other. Since it tapered more rapidly towards the top, it was less graceful.

Scientific Temperament and Technical Innovations... 137

R.C. Jauhri, *Firoz Tughluq (1351-1388 AD)*, Jalandhar: ABS Publications, rpt., 1990, p. 175.

32. Afif, pp. 313-15.

33. Irfan Habib, 'Technological Changes and Society: 13th and 14th Centuries', Presidential Address, Medieval Section, *Proceedings of the Indian History Congress*, Varanasi, 1969, p. 157.

34. Iqtidar Husain Siddiqui, 'Scientific Developments in the Sultanate of Delhi', in *Delhi Sultanate: Urbanization and Social Change*, New Delhi: Viva Books, 2009, pp. 127-9.

35. While reconstructing the life of Sant Kabir, one is faced with problems of chronology, parentage and religious identity. Modern accounts of his life are based on two Kabirpanthi works, *Kabir Kasauti* and *Kabir Charitra*, both full of wonders and miracles. Some episodes revolve around his initiation under Ramanand, complaint of Brahmins of Kashi to the Qazi, persecution at the hands of Sikandar Lodi, a meeting with Guru Nanak and a double funeral. The author of *Akhbar ul-Akhyar* testified to the popularity of Sant Kabir's verses, while the writer of *Dabistan-i Mazahab* placed him in the category of worshippers of Vishnu called Bairagis. Legendary biographies included his imaginary conversations with Gorakhnath, Prophet Muhammad and Guru Nanak. Charlotte Vaudeville, *A Weaver Named Kabir*, Delhi: Oxford University Press, 1993, pp. 39-51.

36. Sant Kabir, *The Bijak of Kabir*, Eng. tr. Linda Hess and Sukhdev Singh, Delhi: Motilal Banarsidas, rpt., 2001, p. 49.

37. Ibid., pp. 57-8.

38. Ibid., p. 69.

39. Ibid., p. 64.

40. Ibid., p. 69.

41. It was nearly impossible to discern the impact of existing religious traditions on Kabir. Close to his times, he was seen as a monotheist, who rejected caste rules. His frequent use of the term Ram for God and words from Yogic terminology did not prove his affiliation to Vaishnavism, Shaivite Nath Yogi tradition and Shankaracharya's Vedanta. In Kabir's verses, the theme of love as cornerstone of man-God relation was rather weak. Going beyond the limits of orthodox Islam, Kabir preached monotheism, which denoted a surrender to God, besides rejection of rituals and caste. Irfan Habib, 'Kabir: The Historical Setting', in *Religion in Indian History*, ed. Irfan Habib, New Delhi: Tulika Books, 2007, pp. 149-52.

42. Sant Kabir, *The Bijak of Kabir*, p. 69.

43. Ibid., p. 65.

44. Guru Nanak (1469-1539) was born in central Panjab in the house of a

138　　　　　*Situating Medieval India*

Khatri village accountant. Following his education under a Pandit and Maulavi, he served in a revenue office (*modikhana*). He attained spiritual enlightenment at river Bein in Sultanpur. During his long travels, he was believed to have visited Pakpattan, Kurukshetra, Haridwar, Gaya, Kamrup, Puri, Ceylon, Mansarovar, Hasan Abdal, Baghdad and Mecca. Erudite and argumentative, he delivered sermons in poetry sung to the accompaniment of Mardana's rebeck. He rejected the dominant religious paths, oppression of women and social inequality. He had the courage to expose the oppressive character of the Lodi regime and Babur's atrocities on the hapless masses. Credited with 973 compositions, his teachings were recorded as *Japuji*, *Asa di Vaar* and *Sidh Gosht* in the Sikh scripture.

45. Bhai Jodh Singh, *Gospel of Guru Nanak in His Own Words*, Patiala: Languages Department, Punjab, 1969, pp. 138-9.
46. Manmohan Singh, *Sri Guru Granth Sahib*, Text with Eng. and Pbi. Tr., Amritsar: Shiromani Gurdwara Prabandhak Committee, 2nd edn., 1982, pp. 137-8. (Hereafter cited as *SGGS*).
47. Ibid., p. 140.
48. Ibid., p. 989.
49. Ibid., p. 74.
50. Ibid., p. 75.
51. Ibid., p. 473.
52. Nikky Guninder Kaur Singh, *The Feminine Principle in the Sikh Vision of the Transcendent*, Cambridge: Cambridge University Press, 1993, pp. 30, 58-9.
53. *SGGS*, p. 1108.
54. Ibid., p. 1109.

CHAPTER 6

Revolt of Dulla Bhatti against the Mughal State: A Study of Oral Tradition and Modern Cultural Forms

Dulla Bhatti was a famous hero of medieval Panjab. Absent in the official chronicles of the sixteenth century, he has attained a prominent presence in the Panjabi collective memory.[1] For centuries, the Panjabis have been celebrating the festival of Lohri in the peak of every winter. Groups of young boys moved from door-to-door, collecting contributions for a common bonfire. In a specific chorus, they glorified the chivalry of Dulla Bhatti. According to a popular folk singer Ashiq Husain Jatt, the Panjabi mothers related the story to little children as soon as they acquired the ability to memorize incidents. Another noted folk singer Sharif Ragi observes that the young men, on listening to the narrative, feel so enthused that they start twirling their moustaches. The present paper aims at revealing the diverse retellings of the story. At the outset, it delves into two ballads, one composed by the balladeer Kishan Singh Arif and the other acquired by Ahmad Salim from a folk singer Ghulam Muhammad Ruliya of village Bholewal, district Lyallpur (Faisalabad). It pays due attention to the *Qissa Dulla Bhatti* of Babu Rajab Ali (1894-1979), who has been hailed as the 'King of Kavishari'. The second part of this paper is devoted to the modern cultural products including literature, music and films. Three Marxist writers—Ishaq Muhammad, Najm Hosain Syed and Gursharan Singh—have seen Dulla Bhatti as leading a widespread uprising of the toilers against the Mughal State. Two Panjabi films (1956 and 1984) have portrayed Dulla Bhatti as a faithful ally of the Mughal State, not as a

140   *Situating Medieval India*

rebel against the contemporary power structure. In contrast, modern Panjabi folk singers like Ashiq Husain Jatt, Kuldip Manak and Sharif Ragi see Dulla Bhatti as a brave Rajput warrior, who shook the foundations of the Mughal State and, in the process, became a perennial symbol of resistance.

In the second half of the sixteenth century, the authority of the Mughal State was confined to the urban centres and their hinterlands. In the countryside, the warrior lineages ruled over the peasantry. The domination was traceable to conquest, migration and settlement.[2] The local elites, having played a key role in settlement, retained their militancy that was reflected in local warfare. The lineage chief dominated the subdistrict (*parganah*), which was a miniature kingdom comprising between 20 and 200 villages. The lineage head, residing in a fortified town in the centre of his domain, maintained a miniature court, armoury and treasury. Relying on a retinue of footmen, horsemen and muskets, his hereditary claim in the produce varied from 15 to 20 per cent of the land revenue. The Mughal State, in order to penetrate the hard shell of this structure, reshaped the *zamindars* into a quasi-official service class in the countryside or they were destroyed.[3] From 1567 onwards, the Mughal State moved to a uniform system of assessment on the basis of statistics on cultivated area, revenue estimate, variety of crops, size of land grants and agricultural prices. Still, the land tax was collected through the intermediacy of the *zamindars*. The Mughal State also assessed the military resources of the *zamindars* in terms of their infantry, cavalry, forts and boats. The most important function of the executive officer (*faujdar*) was to ensure that the *zamindars* duly paid the land tax in their jurisdiction, failing which they were chastised and even expelled.[4] This increasing pressure of the Mughal State on the rural society became the context for the revolt of Dulla Bhatti.

Sandal and Farid, father and son, held the *zamindari* of twelve villages (*pindis*) in the Sandal Bar (Rachna Doab). As great warriors, they carried out raids. They neither paid the land tax nor obeyed the royal summons.[5] The Mughal army tied them in ropes and brought them to Lahore. Akbar asked them to resolve the dispute regarding the state dues. They began to abuse the Emperor, who

Revolt of Dulla Bhatti against the Mughal State 141

ordered their execution. Their bodies were filled with straw and hung at the gate of the Lahore fort. Four months later, Farid's widow Ladhi gave birth to a son, who was named Dulla. The midwife prophesied that he would be a great warrior. On the same day, Akbar was blessed with the birth of prince Salim, who came to be known as Shaikhu. At the advice of astrologers and Pandits, Akbar chose Ladhi as the wet nurse for the Prince. Ladhi brought up the boys together at Pindi.[6] At the end of twelve years, Shaikhu was found lagging behind Dulla in riding, wrestling and archery. Akbar advised Ladhi to educate Dulla, who could be taken in Mughal service. Ladhi took Dulla to the mosque and placed him under the *qazi*. Following a quarrel, Dulla beat up the *qazi*, who kept the grudge in his mind. Dulla acquired slings (*gulel*) from the village carpenter and, gathering a band of boys, engaged in mischief. They broke the pitchers of women, who fetched water from the well. The women asked Ladhi to restrain Dulla, failing which they would lodge a complaint at Lahore. Ladhi distributed metallic containers among the women. Dulla went to the blacksmith brothers, Kahna and Saun, and acquired balls of metal. Since the new missiles pierced the metallic containers, Dulla became a terror for women.[7]

Sick of the attacks, Nandi, the wife of a Mirasi, took up the cudgels on behalf of hapless women. She castigated Dulla for displaying his bravery against women. He had forgotten the practice of his forefathers, who had confronted the Mughal State. If he was a real warrior, he must avenge himself against Akbar, who had hung the bodies of his elders outside the fort. This remark, having pierced Dulla's heart, became a turning point in his life. He went to his mother and asked her to reveal the circumstances of his forefathers. Ladhi's detailed reply revolved round the might of the Bhatti *zamindars*, their refusal to pay the land tax and their cruel punishment. For the first time, Dulla saw seven cellars that stored swords, spears, daggers, shields, matchlocks, pistols and gunpowder. He also discovered a drum and began to beat it. The sound, spreading across twelve leagues, marked the revival of Bhatti revolt against the Mughal State. Dulla gathered a retinue of 500 young men and distributed weapons among them from the ancestral armoury.

142   *Situating Medieval India*

Before undertaking their first raid, they decided to distribute the entire booty, keeping nothing for themselves. They marched to Chiniot and, attacking Dulla's maternal uncles (Chanddars), took away their herd of cattle. The villagers, divided and confused, did not have the courage to fight the large Bhatti horde. On returning to Pindi, Dulla distributed the booty among the poor. To the Brahmins and Mirasis, he gave one head of cattle each and, to the carpenters and blacksmiths, he gave four heads of cattle each. Dulla, having established his authority as a premier chief in the locality, became more ambitious with every passing day.[8]

A brief account of Dulla's acts revealed the nature of his revolt. Ali, a trader of Lahore, brought 500 horses from Qandhar and encamped at Pindi. Dulla provided accommodation to Ali and sheltered the horses in a stable. At midnight, Dulla took charge of the horses and distributed them among his followers. At daybreak, he denied the presence of horses. Admitting his avocation of highway robbery, he declared that he did not fear Akbar. Ali reached Lahore and complained to Akbar. Shaikhu argued that Dulla had been wrongly identified with one of the many dacoits operating in the Rachna Doab. Akbar turned a deaf ear to the lamentations of Ali. After some time, Medha Khatri, a rich banker (*sahukar*) of Lahore, fitted out a caravan for Bokhara and camped at Pindi for the night. Dulla provided all facilities to the travellers, including the storage of goods. At midnight, Dulla captured the merchandise and mules. When Medha reminded Dulla of the punishment of Sandal and Farid, Dulla slashed his beard and moustaches. Medha, returning to Lahore, complained to Akbar about his huge loss, but failed to get any help. Flushed with a series of gains, Dulla extended his defiance to the Mughal royal family. One of the wives of Akbar, who was Shaikhu's mother, left Lahore to perform the Haj. Dulla enabled the royal entourage to camp at a pleasant site in Pindi. He placed all resources at the disposal of the guests. At midnight, Dulla took away the valuables. The Begum expressed her anguish at the deceit of Dulla, whom she treated like her own son. Dulla, denying any kinship with the Begum, slashed her ponytail.[9]

Akbar was horrified at his wife's humiliation. While condemning Shaikhu, he declared his intention of deputing an army to destroy

Revolt of Dulla Bhatti against the Mughal State   143

the entire tribe of the Bhattis. Shaikhu volunteered to examine the ground reality and, if anything were wrong, he would haul up Dulla's clan to the Mughal court. Accompanied by a detachment of 500 horsemen, Shaikhu rode to Pindi and found Dulla hunting in a jungle. He awarded twenty-five horses to Dulla for killing a lion. He persuaded Dulla to appear before Akbar and secure a pardon for his crimes. Dulla, leading a retinue of 500 horsemen, reached Lahore. He was expected to enter the court through a small entrance. This was a device to make him bow before Akbar. Dulla first inserted his feet and then his head through the passage. Face-to-face with Akbar, he struck his spear in the floor and, thus, terrified the courtiers. Shaikhu explained that Dulla was not familiar with the court etiquette and escorted him out of the palace. Dulla and his followers, fanning out in the bazaar, deprived the confectioners of their sweets and cash. He received a complaint against the butchers from Tulsi Ram, a Brahmin. He fell upon the butchers and killed twenty-four of them. The widows and confectioners went to the court and demanded action against Dulla. Shaikhu, speaking to Akbar, attributed the protest to a conspiracy of Medha and a dispute among the butchers. Akbar ordered the closure of meat business, but the public anger kept on rising. Akbar and Birbal, wearing the garb of Bhatts, rode to the Sandal Bar. Dulla gave an Iraqi horse to them in alms. The mendicants cut off its tail. Dulla, in retaliation, removed their beards and moustaches. Akbar returned to the palace and whipped Shaikhu with his own hands.

Dulla paid no heed to the growing Mughal interest in his domain. One day, a caravan from Kashmir arrived with horses, dry fruit and Palam rice. Dulla not only looted the commodities but also killed Bagga Malkira, a high-ranking noble who held the military rank of 12,000. As if this was not enough, he asked Medha to carry the officer's head to Akbar, with a message to worry about the stability of his throne. When Medha reached the court, Akbar was presiding over an assembly of numerous nobles, Rajput chiefs and fifty-two merchants. Medha uncovered the head and narrated the crimes of Dulla. Ever since Dulla had risen up, Akbar was not receiving land tax from twelve villages of the Bhattis. Dulla had looted several caravans. Owing to his misdeeds, the queens were

144 *Situating Medieval India*

crying and wives of traders were wailing. He had captured a consignment from Kashmir, though a commander of 12,000 was escorting it. He had the audacity to send the head of a leading noble as a souvenir. The Emperor must pay immediate attention to Dulla, as his banditry had become a threat to the Mughal authority. Akbar realized that he could no longer delay a drastic action against Dulla. Placing a betel roll and sword in front of the courtiers, he asked any warrior to step forward and lead a military expedition against Dulla. None of the nobles had the courage to accept the challenge. Mirza Nizamuddin, who had just returned from Ghazni and was unaware of Dulla's revolt, picked up the sword and chewed the betel roll. Akbar promised to raise his rank and give an additional revenue assignment (*jagir*) if he captured Dulla. He mobilized an army of 12,000 soldiers, five pieces of artillery, gunpowder and bundles of arrows along with numerous horses and camels. On the other hand, Ladhi pleaded with Dulla to stop his lawlessness and live indoors in submission. Recalling the fate of Bhatti elders, she feared the destruction of their bungalow and humiliation of the womenfolk. Dulla, proud of his attacks on Akbar's cargoes, asserted his right to the land tax of four villages.[10]

Nizamuddin established his camp on the edge of Pindi. Sundari, a Gujjar woman of the village, entered the Mughal ranks to sell milk. She caught Nizamuddin in an iron device, which was meant to entrap Dulla. She informed Ladhi about the emergence of the Mughal cantonment. Ladhi asked Dulla to pick up his sword and sacrifice his life in fighting the Mughals. An astrologer (*nujumi*) and Pandit advised Dulla to postpone the battle for three days to win a victory. Dulla prepared to leave for Chiniot, the territory of his maternal uncles. Ladhi reprimanded her son for his flight from the battlefield and disgracing the name of his forefathers. His wife Bhulran, while castigating him for leaving them in the lurch, declared her resolve to lead his men in the impending fight against the Mughals. Dulla, turned a deaf ear to the pleas and rode out of Pindi with a retinue of 500 men. On reaching Chiniot, he pretended that he was out on a hunting trip and sought forgiveness for taking away the cattle. His uncles, satisfied with the apology, provided hospitality to the entire company.[11]

Revolt of Dulla Bhatti against the Mughal State 145

Ladhi and Bhulran assumed the reins of the Bhatti defence. They tried to bring Nur Khan, the eighteen years old son of Dulla, into the battlefield. Bhulran explained to him the situation in which they were caught. The boy, having married only two days back, kept on sleeping and did not even open the door. Ladhi turned to her elder son Mehru Posti, a notorious drug addict. Initially, he refused to act, as Ladhi had always favoured Dulla over him. He relented when Ladhi referred to the blot on the Rajputs if the women were dragged to Lahore as hostages. He moved his limbs when Ladhi provided him with his ample dose of drugs. Accompanied by twelve addicts, Mehru launched a series of attacks on the Mughals, inflicting many casualties. He bravely fought for two days and, owing to the loss of four associates, refused to fight on the third day. Ladhi accused Bhulran of manipulating the exit of Dulla and concealing Nur Khan from the conflict. Bhulran accused Ladhi of protecting Dulla from the Mughals and argued that the turn of Nur Khan came only after his father. Nur Khan, taking the advice of Ladhi on military tactics, fought the Mughals as if a Jat slashed bushes and raised heaps of grass. The *qazi*, meeting Nizamuddin in secrecy, revealed that Dulla was not present in Pindi, while his son had been leading the defence. The Mughals captured Nur Khan, plundered Pindi and destroyed Dulla's bungalow. They captured all the women and children including mother Ladhi, wife Bhulran, two sisters Bakhto and Takhto, daughter Salemo, a daughter-in-law, two concubines and the Gujjar woman Sundari. Ladhi cried that the Mughals had stained the glorious name of the Rajputs. If Dulla was a seed of the Rajputs, he must free the hostages. Otherwise, his reputation would be destroyed for all times.[12]

In this crisis, Mehru disguised as a Suthra and, hoodwinking the Mughals, rode to Chiniot. He informed Dulla of the Mughal destruction of Pindi and the fate of the Bhatti women. Dulla, along with uncle Jang Khan and nephew Sher Khan, rushed back to Pindi that was in ruins. In order to get the hostages released, he mobilized the people of his *zamindari* and marched towards Lahore. On the way, he encountered Destiny (*honi*), who was disguised as a woman. She sought Dulla's help in lifting a basket of dung cakes.

146   *Situating Medieval India*

Dulla expressed his willingness to do the needful. Revealing her identity, she declared that he would lose his head if he failed to do so. In spite of his best efforts, Dulla could not move the basket. He was bound to surrender his life after a reprieve of three days.[13] Apart from Destiny, Dulla was faced with other problems. It was difficult for him to garner the support of neighbouring *zamindars*, though they belonged to the same caste and clan. They were perpetually engaged in petty warfare to attain local dominance. Dulla's maternal uncle Rehmat Khan had not forgiven Dulla for taking away the cattle of his clan (Chanddars). He had made Nizamuddin his foster brother by exchanging turbans with him and, in doing so, had overlooked the long-standing Rajput-Mughal enmity and the struggle of his nephew Dulla against the Mughal State. Dulla's threat to kill Rehmat Khan forced him to join his nephew with 500 men. Lal Khan Bhatti, an old *zamindar* enjoying great influence between Pindi and Lahore, rallied his sons, grandsons and nephews to attack the Mughals and free the hostages. Initially his kinsmen opposed the move as Dulla had beheaded their father and, therefore, was a sworn enemy. Lal Khan argued that they could avenge themselves against Dulla on some other occasion. At the moment, the honour of Bhatti women was at stake, while Dulla did not matter. Even before Dulla's arrival, the kinsmen of Lal Khan attacked the Mughals and, inflicting heavy losses, paved the way for the release of the hostages.[14]

Babu Rajab Ali was the only folklorist to trace the cause of a feud within the Bhattis. Two brothers, Lal Khan and Jalal Khan, were Bhatti elders. Each of them was blessed with a son, Rai Ali and Rai Farid. As they grew up, they joined hands in looting merchants and jewellers. Though outwardly they appeared united, the spark of their mutual jealousy magnified into enmity. Two swords could not coexist in a single scabbard. Rai Ali was forced to leave the ancestral domain and establish himself at Gandhali. Keeping the grudge in his mind, he went to Lahore and, meeting Akbar, revealed that Rai Farid did not pay the land tax and spent it on his household. A Mughal contingent reached Pindi at midnight and captured the inebriated Rai Farid and his father. The Mughals pulled out their skins and filled the bodies with straw. Not only

Revolt of Dulla Bhatti against the Mughal State 147

this, the Mughals forced Ladhi to stay in the Lahore fort and be a wet nurse (*chungawi*) for Shaikhu. Since Ladhi knew the complicity of Rai Ali in the tragedy, she looked for an opportunity to avenge herself. The moment arrived when Dulla, following his denunciation at the hands of Nandi, met his mother. Ladhi narrated the villainous role of Rai Ali. She asked Dulla to kill Rai Ali, cut his body into pieces and use his head like a ball in a game with boys. As the Bhatti chief, Dulla was morally bound to continue the feud. He searched out his enemy in the Bar, where he was engaged in hunting. In a bloody duel, Dulla killed his uncle. He placed the dead body of his rival (*sharik*) on his horse and brought it to his door as a trophy. Ladhi patted Dulla on his back. The body was cut into pieces and thrown in a furnace (*bhathi*) to be burnt to ashes. Cotton yarn was wound around the head that was shaped into a ball. In the playground, 60 young men knocked it around with their sticks (*khunda*), so that half of it was torn away. A jubilant Ladhi distributed sugar puffs (*patasey*) in the village. The episode not only became an integral part of the local history, but it was duly added to the growing list of Dulla's crimes. The victims of Dulla's excesses, in their complaints to the Mughal authorities, never failed to mention the murder of Rai Ali and the barbaric treatment of his body parts. In view of this cruelty, old Lal Khan and Rai Ali's widow used every argument to persuade their young men to get the Bhatti women released from the Mughal clutches.[15]

Dulla caught up with Nizamuddin and, before the battle, agreed that one Bhatti be pitted against four Mughals. On the first day, Dulla sent three warriors—uncle Jang Khan, nephew Sher Khan and friend Kehar Khan—to attack the Mughals, who remained on the receiving end. On the second day, Dulla's younger maternal uncle Jalal Khan killed four Mughals, but lost his life through deceit. Dulla fell upon the Mughals as if he was a wolf among goats. Displaying extraordinary skill in the use of various weapons, he gained an upper hand. Nizamuddin fell at the feet of Ladhi and, at her instance, Dulla spared his life. The hostages were released, while the Mughal camp withdrew from Pindi. Nizamuddin persuaded Dulla to accompany the Mughal troops to Lahore, promising to arrange a meeting with Akbar. Despite opposition

148   *Situating Medieval India*

from Ladhi and Mehru, Dulla joined the Mughal cavalcade, as he pinned his hopes on Shaikhu. On his arrival at Lahore, he was lodged in the residence of Nizamuddin. The latter, in a message to Akbar, claimed to have accomplished the task, which was not possible without deceit. At night, Nizamuddin entertained Dulla to a feast of liquor, which was laced with poison. Destiny announced that his life ended with the expiry of the three-day reprieve. Dulla surrendered his life to Destiny and, thus, did not die at the hands of the Mughals. Since Nizamuddin had failed to capture Dulla in a fair fight, a frustrated Akbar withdrew the prospective award. As the tragic news reached Pindi, the Bhatti household was plunged in grief.[16]

Ishaq Muhammad, in his play *Ququas*, shows that Dulla's struggle was not only political, it also had a social dimension.[17] While fighting against the Mughals, he was bringing about a social change in his locality. People, who belonged to lower castes and outcastes, formed the core of his armed retinue. Gahna Lohar the closest confidant of Dulla, was intelligent and articulate. Besides heading the anti-Mughal resistance of Pindi in the absence of Dulla, he understood the intricacies of the conflict and delineated the changes in the form of their endevour. Dulla, who was aware of Gahna's brilliance, valour and steadfastness, had made him the pivot of his movement. Masto Gujjari, penetrating the Mughal ranks, brought information about them and performed incredible deeds at great personal risk. Dulla's reliance on low castes caused a strong resentment in the minds of higher castes, but he stuck to his position. Dulla was not a pleasure-loving lord, who kept the toilers under a tight leash. An astute planner and fearless warrior, he was open to fresh ideas. He learnt from his conversations with Medha Khatri and a mysterious mendicant Babaji. He was in regular touch with Shah Husain and kept a permanent informer Ramza in Lahore. He did not go to Chiniot at the advice of the Qazi and Pandit. In accordance with an ingenious tactic, he left his family as bait for the Mughals and, making a great sacrifice, fell upon them in a lightning attack. From Medha Khatri, he learnt that he, with his base in Pindi, had disrupted the main transcontinental Badakhshan-Delhi highway. The big merchants, who made huge profits from

Revolt of Dulla Bhatti against the Mughal State   149

long distance trade, raised kings and supported the priestly classes. The Mughals, reacting to their setback in Pindi, took a number of steps. Ramza was hanged, a reporter was placed over Shah Husain and military outposts were erected from Lahore to Pindi.

Dulla, following introspection, laid down a blue print for the future. It was a good opportunity for uniting and organizing people at the grassroots. They must assess the losses in the recent conflict and distribute weapons among themselves. Since they had a long struggle ahead, they had to start preparations without delay. So far, their fight had been restricted to Pindi. In order to widen the scope of their movement, they must create bases in the countryside. A beginning had already been made, as Nur Khan had mobilized boys from neighbouring villages. Forming cultural troupes, they must travel to every corner of Panjab and comprehend cultural diversities. They would oust the Mughals and, keeping the trade routes open, build a new Panjab. Since the Mughals had constructed a powerful polity by forming alliances with numerous feudatories, the people must adopt an opposite course. They must mobilize the entire populace, particularly the low castes. They must keep an eye on changes taking place in the oceans beyond the Indian subcontinent. With the retreat of feudal lords and decline of traders, the intellectuals and artisans had joined hands to employ scientific knowledge for social development. The discovery of America had brought to light new crops like potato, sweet potato, maize and tobacco. Dulla admitted that the days of his own class, which was attuned to courts and palaces, were over. In the new society, people like Gahna, who were rooted in the soil and distant from power, were bound to play a significant role. The fate of three generations—Sandal, Farid and Dulla—indicated that the rural magnates were in an advanced stage of degeneration. But, the people had still not come out of their primordial loyalties to the local lords and, therefore, time was not ripe for the rise of artisans like Gahna. Dulla was astute enough to understand that he formed only a transitional link in the inexorable march of time. Looking into the future, he saw the unnamed and anonymous mass of toilers, particularly the artisans, providing leadership to the next phase of the movement. However, he advised them to evade immediate

150 *Situating Medieval India*

conflict with the Mughals and, instead, migrate into the hills, waiting for internal contradictions to overwhelm the mighty structure of the Mughal State. Instead of repairing the old dam, they must construct a new one.

Najm Hosain Syed, in his play *Takht Lahore*, has kept Dulla Bhatti entirely absent.[18] He uncovers the nature his revolt through its impact on his supporters and opponents. His revolt was not restricted to the rural areas of Sandal Bar, but had penetrated the city of Lahore, particularly the artisans and lowly placed employees of the Mughal State. The seminary (*madrassa*) of Shah Saadullah and royal workshops became the epicentres of the revolt. The two were linked through the subversive activities of the servant Ramza and the Sufi poet Shah Husain. Ramza, with his ability to wear different guises, gained access to the high-ranking Mughal nobles and enabled Dulla to escape from prison. Shah Husain, while studying under Shah Saadullah, educated the artisans about the weaknesses of the Mughal State and merits of Dulla's revolt. Owing to his suspicious conduct, the Mughal aristocracy tried to stop his degree (*sanad*) of education. Though big officers were involved in corruption at the royal workshops, a weaver Bhag and tailor Ratta were unjustly arrested. Ramza and Shah Husain helped them escape and became instrumental in organizing a strike of the workers.[19] The highest nobles—provincial governor Khizr Khan, military commander Mirza Nizamuddin and head of the royal stores (*toshakhana*) Bahar Khan—took stock of the volatile situation. The Mughal administration, both civil and military, was not equipped to deal with the elusive guerrilla bands. It could not treat Dulla as a plunderer, as plundering was merely his mode of resistance. He was a sworn enemy of everything associated with the Mughal State such as the kingdom, palaces, nobility, luxurious living, elite culture, religious customs and magnificent monuments. In order to protect these, the provincial authorities took strong steps. The Mughal troops, camping in the Bar, were cutting at the roots of the revolt. Any village, smelling of the revolt, was destroyed. Teams of scholars and preachers were engaged in convincing the people that Dulla was an enemy of religion, while the Mughal State was its protector. Yet, the supplies did not reach Lahore, while the fort

Revolt of Dulla Bhatti against the Mughal State   151

itself became vulnerable. Disruption of trade routes forced the Panjabi traders to shift their operations to Gujarat and Deccan. Leading merchants, including Mehta Manik Chand and Painda Beg, extended their support to the Mughal State only to revive their own profits.

The Mughal bureaucracy took emergency measures to retrieve its prestige. Since the city of Lahore was imbued with mutiny (*balwa*), it was placed under the army. Malik Ali, a classmate of Shah Husain, was appointed as the new Kotwal due to his familiarity with the seditious elements. Though many rebels including Dulla, Bhag and Ratta were untraceable, a trial was held in the court of Qazi Mohiuddin. Dulla was charged with fomenting an armed insurrection against Akbar, inducing peasants to withhold the land tax, attacking Mughal outposts, taking away horses and provisions, looting bankers and moneylenders, destroying their records and finally breaking jail to escape on the eve of his execution. In the *qazi's* verdict, Dulla and Ramza, along with Bhag and Ratta, were sentenced to death. Shah Husain, who had made an abortive attempt to rescue Ramza, was recognized as a promising poet, whose verses Bahar Khan would compile. The Mughal State did not dare to touch Shah Saadullah, who had taught three generations of students. Malik Ali, following royal orders, conveyed the last words of Dulla at the time of his execution. In his statement, Dulla was bold, fearless and angry. He held that the foundations of the Mughal State had cracked. His enmity was deep, real and unending. His death would not kill his long struggle. He would live in the eyes, hearts and signs of the people of the Bar. He was like air, fire and water. Since he continuously shifted from one form to the other, he would continue to flow and burn. So long as the Mughal throne existed, he would continue to live as Dulla in the Bar. He would be just another name for the perpetual freedom struggle against Mughal oppression. Malik Ali, while conveying these words, included Dulla's expletives against Akbar. For this mistake, he was ordered to be hanged. The sentence could be postponed if he killed another rebel, Prince Khusrau.[20]

Sometime in the 1990s, this writer watched Gursharan Singh's play *Dhamak Nagare Di* (1978) at the Tagore Theatre in Chandigarh.

152   *Situating Medieval India*

The playwright perceived the fight of Dulla as a peasant uprising in the Sandal Bar.[21] Treating theatre as an instrument of social change, he made an old story relevant to the contemporary needs of the late twentieth century. In the Bar, the peasants hard worked to raise crops. Many a times, the crops failed due to droughts and floods. They did not benefit from plentiful harvests, as the Mughals forcefully emptied their stocks. The oppression of the peasants enabled the Mughal ruling class to live in aristocratic luxury. The peasants were not permitted to carry their complaints to the authorities. When the Bhatti chiefs, Sandal and Farid, resisted Akbar's authority and refused to pay the land tax, they were subjected to inhuman treatment. The peasants, learning from their suffering, decided to change the nature of their resistance and even forced Dulla to conform to their understanding. Theirs was not a fight between Dulla and Akbar. It was futile to loot the merchants caravans and military detachments. Theirs was a struggle of the entire populace of the Bar. It was a fight between the oppressors and the oppressed, the exploiters and toilers. The women of the Bar, fighting alongside men, played a vigorous role. In fact, Dulla's mother Ladhi emerged as a pivot around which the story revolved. She filled the vacuum that the tragic deaths of Bhatti elders had left. She inspired Dulla to revive the struggle after a gap of thirty years. During the Mughal attack on Pindi, she brought her grandson Nur Khan into the field. She enabled the rebels to set up clear targets for the anti-Mughal defiance, including a shift in the tactics. Following Dulla's death, she erased demoralization in the ranks of the rebels and reignited the flame of resistance. Her indomitable spirit overcame personal losses with dignity. Gursharan Singh, while exposing the elitist character of education and describing the last words of Dulla, borrowed from Najm Hosain Syed. The drum, which was associated with the movement of the Mughal army, emperor and nobles, became instead a perpetual symbol of peasant resistance. During the dark days of terrorism, communalism and state repression in the Indian Punjab, the play went a long way in delineating the real issues facing the society.

In 1956, a Panjabi film *Dulla Bhatti* was released in Pakistan.[22] According to its narrative, an unnamed Bhatti woman had a son

Revolt of Dulla Bhatti against the Mughal State   153

named Dulla. She also brought up Haidari, the son of the governor of Panjab. On growing up, Haidari went back to his parental home. Dulla, gathering a band of companions, looted the rich. He fell in love with Nooran and their marriage was fixed. The governor's men failed to bring Dulla to book. Haidari, tasked with apprehending Dulla, met his foster brother in an emotional union. Haidari revealed his love for Nooran. Dulla sacrificed his love for Haidari, who married Nooran. In a palace conspiracy, Mirza Khan assumed power and imprisoned the governor and Haidari. Nooran sent a message to Dulla for help. Dulla, arriving with his retinue, killed Mirza Khan and rescued the prisoners. Dulla died fighting for the governor and Haidari, while Nooran died in her attempt to save Dulla. The governor declared that Dulla was never a rebel against political power. The film is silent on the fate of Sandal and Farid. It hesitates to name the Mughal emperor Akbar and his son Salim. It is equally reticent on Dulla's leadership of the peasantry and the Mughal attack on Pindi. Dulla, far from mobilizing the lower classes of the Bar against the contemporary rulers, emerges as an obedient ally of the existing power structure. Since the film had a number of missing links, it created enough room for a longer film which however, remained within the old ideological groove.

On 7 September 1984, the Evernew Pictures released a coloured Punjabi film with the earlier title.[23] The story told us that Ladhi, out of compassion, became the wet nurse of Haidari, the son of the governor of Panjab. She brought up the child along with her own son Dulla. The governor probed the death of Farid at the hands of Fazl Khan, the dismissed administrator of Lahore. Fazl Khan, submitting fake documents, proved the criminality of Farid and secured his own reinstatement. Turning to entertainment, the film portrays the growing love between Dulla and Nooran, while Mehru Posti carried on an affair with the confectioner's wife Guplo. Dulla, in four episodes, came out in support of the distressed. Nooran, ignorant of the underlying cause his chivalry, persuaded him to abjure violence. The complainants met Fazl Khan and demanded action against Dulla. The officer marched to Pindi and, in a duel, lost his life. The governor deputed Haidari to bring Dulla before him. In dramatic circumstances, Haidari was united with his foster

154 — Situating Medieval India

family, besides falling in love with Nooran. From then onwards, Ladhi betrayed an irrational tilt towards Haidari. She organized Nooran's marriage with Haidari and induced others to fall in line. She saved Haidari from capital punishment, as he was held guilty of colluding with Dulla and receiving Nooran in bribe from the culprit. In a palace intrigue, the governor and Haidari were thrown in jail. Nooran sent a message to Dulla through a pigeon to rescue the prisoners. Dulla, heading an armed retinue, climbed his way into the palace. In a fierce fight, he wiped out the conspirators and rescued the prisoners. He was killed in the effort. Nooran, suddenly transformed into a fighter, killed many opponents before dying in a bid to save Dulla's life.

In the narrative of these two films, Dulla sacrificed his life to restore the crumbling Mughal State. While taking his last breath, he received the official certificate of his loyalty to the ruling class. The three leading lights of Pindi—Ladhi, Dulla and Nooran—gained proximity to the highest rung of the Mughal polity, but did not raise a little finger on the plight of the peasantry. Dulla's brave companions, who represented the best youth of the Bar, never questioned their leader's inexplicable support to the Mughal rulers. Ladhi's maternal affection for Haidari urged her to save him from the gallows. This did not allow her to be blind to the long-standing Dulla-Nooran love, besides the class and cultural differences between Nooran and Haidari. Instead of taking pride in Dulla's sympathy for the poor, she held this virtue as a vice against him. Ladhi and Dulla could have easily prevailed upon Haidari to give up his sudden interest in Nooran. They were so slavish that they did not even try. The filmmakers, in their anxiety to please the feudal-military regime of Pakistan, portrayed Dulla as an active collaborator of the Mughal State, not as an anti-Mughal rebel and champion of the tax-paying peasantry. In fact, Akbar, the architect of an anti-peasant power system, is not even mentioned, as he was accepted as a sacred cow. In Pakistan, the deep state is as suspicious of the rebellious Dulla Bhatti as the axe-wielding rustic Maula Jat.

Ashiq Husain Jatt, introducing his musical feature *Dastan Dulla Bhatti* (1982), states that the tale was popular in all parts of Panjab. Apart from enactment in theatres, folk artists (*rasdhari*) narrate it

Revolt of Dulla Bhatti against the Mughal State   155

with folk instruments. Panjabi mothers related the story to little children as soon as they were able to remember events. The Mughals, with the establishment of their rule, often crossed the Ravi and plundered the peasants of the Bar. Sandal and Farid, the Bhatti chiefs of twelve Pindis, mustered a retinue of young men to resist the Mughals. At different points of time, they died fighting against the Mughals, who subjected their bodies to inhuman treatment. Ladhi, fearing for the life of her son, did not let him know anything about a tragic past. Once he learnt of the Mughal cruelty, he began to loot trade caravans and distributed the booty among the poor, earning the wrath of merchants. Ladhi warned Dulla to restrain himself, but to no avail. On the arrival of Mirza Nizamuddin, Dulla took the advice of the Brahmin and left for Chiniot. During his absence, Ladhi asked Mehru Posti to put up a fight, but he was killed in the effort. The Mughals placed the Bhatti women on camels and carried them to Lahore. Roorha Jat rushed to Chiniot with the sad news. Ashiq Jatt, borrowing from Ahmad Salim's compilation, has described the decisive intervention of Lal Khan Bhatti. Dulla succeeded in getting the hostages released, but spared the life of Mirza at the instance of Ladhi. The singer does not go into the question of Dulla's death. Fazal Jatt, the son of Ashiq Jatt, carries on the legacy of his father, though he confines himself to only a few episodes and has introduced some entertaining elements to suit the modern consumerist tastes.

The musical feature (1991), *Dhawan Dilli De Kingre (I Pull Down the Ramparts of Delhi),* of Kuldip Manak comprised the complete story of Dulla Bhatti in three forms—narration, drama and song.[24] On the birth of Dulla, there were festivities in Pindi and fear among the Mughals. Akbar, relying on his artillery, vowed to cut off Dulla's head and destroy the Bhatti tribe. On the other hand, the Bhattis of twelve Pindis resolved to continue their struggle in the face of Mughal might. If one Bhatti died, ten were reborn. They had received chivalry in their inheritance. They would cultivate crops and reap the harvest, but would not pay any land tax to the Mughal State. The Mughals, inflicting oppression in the Bar, pulled down houses and temples. They had killed Farid and his body was hung with that of his father Sandal. Dulla, on growing up, looted traders

156   *Situating Medieval India*

bringing valuables from Kabul. Ignoring Ladhi's advice, he relied on unity among his followers and their spirit of sacrifice. He killed the governor of Kashmir and sent his head to Akbar. The Mughals declared a reward of one lakh rupees on Dulla's head. Remaining undeterred, Dulla vowed to bring down the ramparts of Delhi, uproot the throne of Lahore and turn the Mughal Begums into widows. Since his elders had sacrificed their lives, he had imbibed the Rajput valour in legacy. The singer's narrative has covered familiar ground comprising Dulla's departure for Chiniot, valiant role of Ladhi, bravery of Mehru Posti, destruction of Pindi and the march of hostages to Lahore.

Dulla, inspiring his companions, condemned the Mughals for shedding blood of the toilers. His people must rise up and eradicate oppression from the face of earth. Dulla succeeded in freeing the hostages and, in the effort, quaffed the goblet of martyrdom (*jam-i shahadat*). He laid down his life for provincial autonomy, protecting regional culture and asserting economic independence. Dulla's movement did not end with his death. His son Nur Khan, along with the companions of the deceased, swore at his dead body to carry on the struggle, so that the Mughals were not able to establish their sway in the Bar. Recalling his exploits against the Mughals, they believed that his name had been immortalized. His revolutionary ideology (*inqlabi vichardhara*) percolated to every child of the Bar and every militant young man of the country.

Sharif Ragi has produced two version of the tale.[25] The first is an audio cassette in nine parts, each comprising a prose narrative that formed the context for the following song. At the orders of Akbar, Dulla was brought to Lahore, while the shopkeepers came out to look at the warrior. Chhalla Mirasi, who belonged to Pindi, sought Dulla's help in the marriage of his son. Dulla asked him to escort Ladhi to Lahore, so that she could see her son fighting. Since he could uproot trees, Akbar was nothing for him. He would turn the Mughal women into widows. Shimli, a Rajput in Mughal service, provided hospitality to Dulla in his house. Akbar granted this permission to Shimli, provided he produced Dulla in the court the next day. Shimli, while conversing with Dulla, revealed his plan to kill Akbar and enthrone the Bhatti rebel. He also proposed

Revolt of Dulla Bhatti against the Mughal State   157

that his son be married to Dulla's daughter. Dulla, treating the match as below his dignity, killed the boy and cut his body in four parts. Shaikhu, acting on Akbar's orders, brought Dulla in chains to Lahore. Unmarried girls, standing on terraces, vowed to make offerings to Ghaus Pak (Abdul Qadir Jilani) if Dulla's shackles were unlocked. Ladhi reminded Shaikhu of sucking her milk and exchanging turbans with Dulla. Akbar agreed to loosen Dulla's chains, while Shaikhu went to bring a blacksmith. Dulla declared that he would push a dagger into Akbar to avenge the executions of his father and grandfather. He was shocked to learn from Chhalla Mirasi that the Mughals had destroyed Pindi, forcing Ladhi to hide in the wilderness. Ladhi, while sending Dulla to the battlefield, tied a thread on his right arm and exempted him thirty-two streams of milk. Dulla apologized to Lal Khan Bhatti and his kinsmen for an old crime and, thus, secured their support in the ensuing conflict. The story concludes with the details of the battle in which Dulla emerged victorious.

Sharif Ragi, in his stage performances, deleted references to Shimli and Chhalla Mirasi. He prefers sticking to the conventional narrative of folklore. Stories of warriors and lovers, who sacrificed their lives for a cause, had a great impact on listeners. In pursuit of his research, Sharif Ragi visited the villages and tombs of heroes. He saw an image (*tasvir*) of Dulla in Pindi. The Bhattis of Pindi were not dacoits, thieves or plunderers. Sandal and Farid, the owners of Pindi, refused salutation to Akbar. The Mughal State was transient, while the Bhattis were permanently entrenched in Pindi. Akbar, in the interest of his authority and prestige, hanged the Bhatti chiefs in the Lahore fort. He chose Ladhi to suckle Shaikhu, so that he imbibed the traits of a warrior. Dulla's raids were designed to provoke Akbar into leading punitive expeditions, so that the former could avenge himself. When Mirza Nizamuddin camped outside Pindi, Dulla left for Chiniot at the advice of the astrologer. Ladhi lamented that she had advised Dulla to refrain from violent acts. The Mughals were likely to carry them away as hostages. Dulla's wife Bhulran, pointing to her bad omens, resolved to jump into the battle, as she too was the daughter of a Rajput. If Dulla must go to Chiniot, he must pass under her leg. Sharif Ragi has placed

158   *Situating Medieval India*

Mehru's valour in the context of tributes to Hazrat Ali and principles of Islamic spirituality. Whoever recited the name of Ali earned victory in battle. When Mehru mounted his horse, he raised a slogan in Ali's honour (*nara-i haidari*) and glorified Lal Shahbaz Qalandar. On the fourth day, the Bhatti women, wearing male clothes and donning turbans, gave a tough time to the Mughals. The *qazi*, nurturing an old grudge against Dulla, revealed the internal situation of the Bhattis to the Mughals. At his advice, the Mughals ravaged Pindi and carried the women on elephant howdahs.

Dulla Bhatti, who led a revolt of the toilers of the Sandal Bar (Rachna Doab), did not figure in the official records. A poetic biography (*Haqiqat ul-Fuqara*) of Shah Husain, composed in 1662, refers to the execution of Dulla Bhatti. The traditional bards (Mirasis) nurtured the story of Dulla Bhatti through performances in rural gatherings. Across the centuries, his chivalry is being celebrated in the winter festival of Lohri (Maghi). In the second half of the nineteenth century, the arrival of printing press enabled balladeers (*qissakars*) to carry the story to a larger readership. The spread of Marxist ideology induced intellectuals to perceive the progressive implications of Dulla Bhatti's revolt. Ishaq Muhammad, Najm Hosain Syed and Gursharan Singh laid emphasis on Dulla Bhatti's success in mobilizing the peasants, artisans and menials in an armed challenge to the Mughal State. Famous folk singers like Ashiq Husain Jatt, Sharif Ragi and Kuldip Manak popularized the tale, employing the medium of audio cassettes. Admittedly, the construction of the memory of Dulla Bhatti has been subject to contestation. Two Panjabi films have portrayed Dulla Bhatti as a faithful ally of the contemporary ruling class and, thus, deprived the story of its revolutionary appeal. However, this narrative has remained feeble and receded into the background. On both sides of the Indo-Pakistan border, writers and folksingers have fortified the image of Dulla Bhatti as a fighter for the downtrodden. At the end of this exercise, we pay a warm tribute to the inimitable Idu Sharif, who sang the story to the accompaniment of Sarangi and Dhadd.

Revolt of Dulla Bhatti against the Mughal State   159

NOTES

1. For an earlier version of this paper, see Surinder Singh, 'Mughal Centralization and Local Resistance in North-Western India: An Exploration in the Ballad of Dulla Bhatti', in *Popular Literature and Pre-Modern Societies in South Asia,* ed. Surinder Singh and Ishwar Dayal Gaur, New Delhi: Pearson Longman, 2008, pp. 89-112.

2. A *zamindari* right provided its possessor with income, which varied in name and magnitude. It comprised remuneration for his services in revenue collection, besides exclusive use of local assets (orchards, tanks, wells and trees) and unpaid labour from menials. The right evolved through a long process with a set pattern. A caste or clan drove out the previous one and, in turn, could itself be driven out. At some stage, the dominion of the victorious clan crystallized into the *zamindari* right. Irfan Habib, *The Agrarian System of Mughal India,* New Delhi: Oxford University Press, 2nd rev. edn., 1999, pp. 179-87, 197-8.

3. John F. Richards, *The Mughal Empire,* New Delhi: Cambridge University Press, 1993, p. 79.

4. Abul Fazl Allami, *Ain-i Akbari,* vol. II, Eng. tr. H. S. Jarrett and Jadunath Sarkar, New Delhi: Oriental Books Reprint Corporation, rpt., 1978, pp. 41-2; Hidayatullah Bihari, *Hidayat ul-Qawanin,* Abdul Salam Collection 379/149, Aligarh: Aligarh Muslim University, ff. 16a-17a.

5. Dulla Bhatti and his ancestors appear to have been intermediary *zamindars,* who were classified between the higher autonomous chiefs and lower primary *zamindars.* They collected land revenue from primary *zamindars* and paid it to the imperial treasury or, in certain cases, kept it themselves. Forming backbone of the land revenue administration, they were also responsible for maintaining law and order. In cases of displeasure, the Mughal State reserved the authority to dismiss or transfer them, besides interfering in their succession. S. Nurul Hasan, 'Zamindars under the Mughals', in *Religion, State and Society in Medieval India: Collected Works of S. Nurul Hasan,* ed. Satish Chandra, New Delhi: Oxford University Press, 2005, pp. 143-6.

6. When Akbar searched a wet nurse for Shaikhu, he learnt that Ladhi, the widow of Farid, knew how to transform jackals into tigers. Along with the child Dulla, she was brought to the Lahore fort and, giving up enmity with the Mughals, began to suckle Shaikhu. She saw a deardful dream. Farid, filled with rage and using abusive language, castigated Ladhi for providing her milk to Shaikhu. She was guilty of eating unlawful food of the Mughals, rubbing salt in his wounds, inflicting injustice on Dulla and disgracing the fair name of the Bhatti Rajputs. Only a low caste weaver woman (*julahi*)

160   *Situating Medieval India*

could stoop so low. A terrified Ladhi reversed the sequence of feeding. She gave her right breast to Dulla and left one to Shaikhu. As a result, Dulla grew up stronger than Shaikhu. There was a stark difference between the right breast and the left one. Ladhi's course correction did not ease her position in the society. The people did not forget her undignified act of suckling Shaikhu. Babu Rajab Ali, *Qissa Dulla Bhatti*, in *Ankhila Rajab Ali*, ed. Sukhwinder Singh Suttantar, Samana: Sangam Publications, n.d., pp. 140-4.

7. Kishan Singh Arif, *Qissa Dulla Bhatti*, ed. Gian Chand (*Qissa Dulla Bhatti Ate Us Di Bhav Jugat*), Amritsar: Ravi Sahit Prakashan, 1987, pp. 71-7. (Hereafter cited as Kishan Singh Arif).

8. Ibid., pp. 77-81.

9. Ibid., pp. 81-8.

10. Ahmad Salim, *Tin Lok Vaaran*, Amritsar: Ravi Sahit Prakashan, 2015, pp. 30-9. (Hereafter cited as Ahmad Salim).

11. Kishan Singh Arif, pp. 96-100; Ahmad Salim, pp. 39-41.

12. Kishan Singh Arif, pp. 101-6; Ahmad Salim, pp. 41-9.

13. Kishan Singh Arif, pp. 106-8.

14. Ahmad Salim, pp. 51-3.

15. Babu Rajab Ali, *Qissa Dulla Bhatti*, pp. 150-5, 177-81.

16. Kishan Singh Arif, pp. 109-17.

17. Major Ishaq Muhammad was born at Akhara, a village in district Jalandhar of undivided Panjab. He passed matriculation (1937) from Urmur Tanda and, for the next two years, studied at DAV College, Jalandhar. During his student days, he lived in great poverty. While studying at M.O. College in Lahore, he started writing. In 1952, he was jailed in the Rawalpindi Conspiracy Case along with leading communists such as Faiz Ahmad Faiz and Sajjad Zaheer. After serving his sentence, he adopted legal practice for some time. Associated with labour organizations, he fought for the rights of the oppressed. As a result, he was imprisoned many times and, during his phase of underground activism, suffered confiscation of property. While in jail, he wrote (1971) his famous play 'Mussali'. Jagtar Singh, 'Introduction', to Major Ishaq Muhammad, *Quqnas*, Jalandhar: Deepak Publishers, 1980. (This portion is without any pagination).

18. Najm Hosain Syed was born (1936) at Batala in an influential Qadiri family. Moving to Lahore at partition, he took his M.A. in English from the Forman Christian College. He joined the Pakistan Civil Service and retired in 1995. He has made a multifaceted contribution to Panjabi literature. He founded the Majlis Shah Husain and Panjabi Adabi Sangat. He has retrieved the Panjabi rebellious tradition through his penetrating analysis

Revolt of *Dulla Bhatti against the Mughal State*   161

of Panjabi folklore, ranging from Puran and Rasalu to Ranjha and Mahiwal. Equally critical are his studies on the poetry of Shah Husain and Bulle Shah. Writing on the professions on the way of extinction, he has preserved the richness of Panjabi culture for posterity. His creative writings and critical essays have raised him to the status of a literary giant. Besides his poetry, his brilliance shines in *Recurrent Patterns in Panjabi Poetry* and *Sedhan, Saran Ate Hor Lekh*. For an appreciation of his approach, see Zubair Ahmad, 'Najm Hosain Syed: A Literary Profile', *Journal of Punjab Studies*, vol. 13, nos. 1&2, pp. 255-64.

19. Najm Hosain Syed, *Takht Lahore*, Introduction by Jagbir Singh; transliteration by Man Singh Amrit, Amritsar: Ravi Sahit Prakashan, 2005, pp. 34-65.

20. Ibid., pp. 83-103.

21. Gursharan Singh (1929-2011) was the most famous theatre personality of Panjab. He was a playwright, actor and director. Holding a master's degree in Chemistry, he served the Canal and Irrigation Department for 20 years. He has written 200 plays that were published in 17 books and 7 anthologies. He began working for theatre in 1958 and founded the Amritsar Natak Kala Kendra in 1964. During Sikh militancy, he travelled across rural areas, giving 150 performances in a year. He became a household name by playing the role of Bhai Manna Singh in a serial of Jalandhar Doordarshan. Often the voice of the oppressed and marginalized sections, he did not hesitate to take up cudgels against social evils. He played a stellar role in strengthening the forces of democracy, secularism and progress. His reach went far beyond the shrinking space of the Marxists. He was honoured with the Sangeet Natak Award in 1993 and Kalidas Samman in 2004.

22. Its director was M.S. Dar and producer was Agha G.A. Gul. Ghulam Ahmad Chishti provided the music, while Tufail Hoshiarpuri wrote the lyrics. The leading actors were Sudhir, Sabiha, Alauddin, Zeenat and Neelo. Running into 151 minutes, its copies were produced and sold by Sadaf DVD.

23. Its director was Waheed Dar and producer was S.A. Gul. Master Inayat Husain composed its music. Its leading actors were Anjuman, Yousaf Khan, Mustafa Qureshi, Talish, Nazli, Sabiha, Nanha and Rangila. Its copies were produced by Jadoon Videos, Tooting Video Centre, London.

24. Kuldip Manak (1951-2011) was the most popular folk singer of Panjab in the late 1970s and early 1980s. Born in village Jalal of district Bhatinda, his original name was Latif Muhammad. His ancestors sang devotional hymns (*kirtan*) as Hazoori Ragis for Raja Hari Singh of Nabha. His father Nikka Khan and brother Siddiq were also singers. Though he took to hockey in school, his teachers persuaded him to sing on stage. He learnt music from

162   *Situating Medieval India*

Ustad Khushi Muhammad Qawwal of village Bhuttiwala in Muktsar. His raw rustic voice, coupled with energy and passion, conformed to the rebellious streak of Punjabi folklore. While singing, he played on the Toombi and mastered the genre of *Kaliyan*, wherein episodes of love tales were recast in contemporary lyrical idiom. He climbed the charts of popularity with *Tere Tille Ton, Chheti Kar Sarwan Bachha, Garh Mughlan Diyan Naaran, Maan Hundi Hai Maan* and *Sucha Soorma*. He sang and acted in Panjabi films like *Saidan Jogan, Lambardarni* and *Balbiro Bhabi*. In 1996, he unsuccessfully fought the elections from the Bhatinda parliamentary constituency as an independent candidate. His death at the age of 61 due to bad health left a permanent void in the domain of Panjabi folk singing.

25. A few years before partition, Muhammad Sharif Ragi was born in Phagwara, a town between Ludhiana and Jalandhar. Migrating to Pakistan, his family of cattle traders settled in village Dhoodiwala of district Faislabad. As a young boy, he became a disciple of the famous folk singer Muhammad Sadiq. The Ustad, being childless, adopted Sharif as his son. The boy, having learnt to play on the small drum (*dhadd*), accompanied his Ustad for the next 34 years. Thereafter, he formed his own troupe comprising five musicians, who handled the *alghoza, toomba, dholki, ghara* and *king*. Their distinctive apparel included a white turban with flowing ends, a long white shirt and a colourful waistcloth. He dominated traditional musical arenas (*akharas*) in rural areas, singing about the struggles of lovers, warriors and saints. He has visited the places associated with them and collected stories from the grassroots. This has lent authenticity to his performance, which combined lyrical poetry with prose narration. He has become a living legend due to his prodigious memory, flawless renditions, majestic presence and handsome looks. To his credit, he has nearly 90 volumes of audio cassettes that Rehmat Gramaphone Company produced. In 2007 and 2009, he visited the Indian Panjab and performed before large audiences in the villages of Nakodar, Nurmahal and Phillaur. On one occasion, he was gifted a gold bangle (*karra*) of 3.5 *tolas*, while his colleagues received rings of one *tola* each. During performances, he keeps the microphone in his shirt pocket, while his right hand holds a handkerchief to wipe the sweat on his face and left hand holds currency notes received from the appreciative crowds. Interview with Nasir Kasana, *Ik Pind Panjab Da*, 25 May 2018.

CHAPTER 7

Travelling Across Northwestern India: The State of Rivers, Bridges and Boats during the Mughal Age

The roots of this chapter can be traced to the famous Panjabi folksong *Chhalla*. A number of Panjabi singers[1]—Inayat Ali, Shaukat Ali, Ashiq Husain Jatt, Fazal Jatt, Arif Lohar, Gurdas Maan and Harbhajan Mann—have sung it. The song encapsulates the suffering of a father, who lost his son in tragic circumstances. Jalla, a boatman, plied his boat on the ferry of Harike on the Satluj. He earned his living by transporting passengers to and from the opposite banks of the river. He was blessed with a son, who was named Chhalla. When the boy was young, his mother passed away. Jalla brought up the boy and, in the process, became deeply attached to him. Life went on smoothly until Challa attained the age of twelve years. One day, Jalla was unwell. A group of passengers arrived at the ferry and wished to cross the river on the first trip (*pehle poor*). Jalla declined the request, as he did not have the strength to drive the oars. Since the passengers were committed to an urgent task, Jalla agreed to depute Chhalla in his own place. The passengers sat in the boat, while Chhalla guided it into the river. He never returned. A distraught Jalla, failing to reconcile with this bereavement, kept on searching for his son. Day and night, he walked along the Satluj and raised loud cries for his son. It was believed that his obsession drove him to insanity. In due course, the wailings of Jalla assumed the form of a folksong that established itself in the rich reservoir of Panjabi folklore.

This song was a grim reminder of the times when boats were the only means of crossing the rivers, while there were no bridges.

164   *Situating Medieval India*

To the parents, the sons were a sweet fruit (*mithre meve*) of the conjugal union and, therefore, Allah must bestow sons on every one. The mothers, who nourished their children with their milk of kindness, were as protective as cool shades (*thandiyan chhavan*). Since the daughters were an alien property (*dhan paraya*), the attachment to the sons was deep and abiding. If the son died in young age, the parents were condemned to mourn the loss throughout their lives. A river manifested the might of God and the bounty of nature. The same river, which nourished the soil, could cause havoc in the life of humans due to a sudden twist of fate. A dead person went to reside in an unknown abode, but never returned to his dear ones. Yet, the memory of the deceased was never erased from the hearts of the survivors.

Babur, during a month long stay (winter of 1519) in the undulating tract of Sind Sagar Doab, overcame the barrier of rivers using different devices. At the outset, he decided to travel without excessive baggage and with adequate preparations. In order to identify a suitable ford on the Indus, he deputed Mir Muhammad Jalaban (raftsman) and his brothers to survey the bank up and down. Babur marched to the side of the Swati to hunt rhinoceros and, meanwhile, those who had gone to inspect the crossings came back. On 16 February 1519, horses and camels, loaded with baggage, crossed the Indus through a ford. The camp market, foot soldiers and donkeys were taken across on rafts. By noon, everyone had crossed and, by the evening, camped besides the Kachakot (the Harru). Next morning, they crossed the Kachakot and, moving through the Sangdaki Pass, crossed the Suhan. It was a long march, rendered difficult due to fatigue of horses, many being left behind. Babur reached Kalda Kahar, a flat plain bearing a large lake, which received rainwater from surrounding mountains. Moving away from the Hamtatu Pass, Babur camped on the bank of the Jhelum. Heavy rain flooded the entire plain and a stream, lying between Bhera and the hills, turned into a broad lake. Near Bhera, there was no crossing, so that the horses swam across the rushing waters. The soldiers, leaving their heavy baggage behind, shouldered their weapons and, stripping their horses bare, made them swim across. Next morning, boats were brought in and soldiers used them to

Travelling Across Northwestern India   165

shift their baggage. Two miles upstream, Quj Beg's men discovered a ford, which enabled the remaining troopers to cross over.

For a day, they stayed in the fortress of Bhera and, fearing the flood, shifted to some hills north of Bhera. During the next three days, while political transactions with local elements were afoot, Babur and his companions undertook excursions in boats and enjoyed drinking parties. On one occasion, anchor was dropped in the middle of the river, while the revellers slept for the night. On returning from Bhera, Babur crossed the Suhan and approached a ford on the Indus negotiated on the onward march. A large raft, loaded with grain was stuck in mud. The owners, in spite of best efforts, could not move it. Babur seized the grain and distributed it among his companions. He stopped below the confluence of the Indus and Kabul Rivers. Six boats, brought from Nilab, were distributed among the three wings of the army. During the next three days (22-24 March 1519), they crossed the Indus on these vessels.[2]

In the medieval times, it was impossible to span the major rivers with bridges. Permanent structures were built only on the seasonal streams. The extant architectural remains bear witness to the success of contemporary building techniques. In most cases, these were in use up to the present times. In the early seventeenth century, a bridge was built on the Sirhind torrent. The structure caught the attention of many observers such as William Finch (1611), Fray Sebastien Manrique (1641),[3] the official diarist of the Dutch embassy (1712) and Abdul Qadir Khan (1797). Its three distinct portions—bearing a length of 24.8 m, 27.7 m and 21.3 m—possessed four, five and three arches. A 12.6 m wide passage ran over it. In the central portion, six octagonal towers were made on each side of the passage, while the first part had five of them. A flight of steps on both sides of the central portion led down to the water level, where rounded cutwaters were provided.[4] About 10 kilometres west of Nakodar (Malhian Kalan) and to the east of the Dakhni Sarai, a bridge was constructed on the White Bein. The arch measured 4.6 m, while the pier of 5.5 m width was provided with triangular cutwaters. A 8.25 m wide road was flanked with a 0.75 m wide parapet.[5] Jahangir, stopping at Nakodar on 29 January 1608,

166   *Situating Medieval India*

noted that Akbar had given Abul Fazl a sum of Rs. 20,000 in gold
to construct a bridge with a waterfall between the subdistricts
(*paganahs*) of Nakodar and Sultanpur. As the site was pleasant and
the bridge harmonious, he ordered Muizz ul-Mulk, the assignee
(*jagirdar*) of Nakodar, to erect a building and lay a garden on the
right side of the bridge, so that the travellers were pleased on seeing
the site.[6]

Remains of two arch bridges exist at Sultanpur, where the Black
Bein pierced the Delhi-Lahore highway. Of the first structure,
only four arches on the southern bank, spreading over a length of
37.4 m, have survived. The breadth of each arch and pier was 3.4 m
and 3.1 m respectively. An additional one metre broad arch, sunk
into each pier, provided outlet for the excess overflows of water.
Following the collapse of a major part of the bridge, a more ambitious structure was raised at a small distance. The middle arches of
this 218.5 m bridge gave way, leaving a unspanned gap of 90 m.
At present, seven arches, spanning 85.5 m on the southern bank
and three arches spanning 43.0 m on the opposite side, were extant.
Each pier was reinforced with a wedge shaped buttress to provide
additional strength. The dissimilar dimensions of the arches and
piers, standing on the northern and southern sections, indicated
that one of the two was restored at a later date. Explaining the destruction of the bridges, Alexander Cunningham argued that the
bridges were built on well foundations and, as the piers had the
same thickness as the span of the arches, one half of the waterway
was obstructed, so that the river made way for itself by cutting
away the bank at one end of the bridge. Subhash Parihar, disagreeing
with the explanation, reminds us that the rivers in the northern
hemisphere had a tendency of wearing away their banks on the
right side. It appeared that the river took an inward turn at this
place, giving more thrust along its N bank. When the N section of
the first bridge was washed away, the second structure was erected.
Again, the N section might have met the same fate. It was sub-
stituted with arches and piers of smaller dimensions. Even this
could not hold its own and came down, leaving only three of its
arches.[7] In any case, this long stone bridge was intact when Jahandar
Shah and the Dutch embassy crossed it (17 May 1712).[8]

Travelling Across Northwestern India 167

Two permanent bridges (*pulha-i pukhta*) enabled the travellers to cross the torrents (*nalha*) of Degh and Baghbacha, as they advanced from Lahore to Aminabad on way to Kabul and Kashmir. The structures proved robust enough to withstand the floods of 1652, though they were submerged under a thick layer of water.[9] About the former, Sujan Rai Bhandari states, 'Shah Daula constructed such a strong bridge on the royal highway, five leagues from Aminabad towards Lahore, as could not have been erected even by wealthy aristocrats (*sahib-i daulatan*).'[10] A local tradition has recorded the method and materials used in its construction, besides illuminating the role of various social classes in the task. To begin with, Shahjahan's journey to Kashmir was disrupted due to a flood in the Degh. He ordered Mirza Badiuzzman, the local administrator (*faujdar*), to construct a bridge. This officer failed to carry out the order as he could get only unburnt bricks from the brick burners, all of whom were imprisoned. In response to his request, Shah Daula arrived to break the stalemate. The saint secured the release of the brick burners and initiated the work. When his first attempt failed, allegedly due to the mischief of a jinn, he dug a deep pit and filled it with lime and mortar, forming a well foundation. He raised two embankments (*bunds*) to keep the water back and, in the process, converted the opposition of a *zamindar* into active cooperation. The bridge has continued to exist in a fair condition up to the modern times, including its fresco paintings and turrets.[11] Shah Daula has been credited with the building of a bridge over the Aik near Sialkot, with seven small pointed arches and equally thick piers. The remains of another bridge he raised have been discovered near Pasrur, a halting place between Sialkot and Kalanaur. He laid yet another bridge on a stream near Gujarat, as indicated by the existing arches of a half mile long structure.[12]

In the hilly areas of Panjab and Kashmir, narrow channels permitted the construction of semi-permanent bridges with simple materials. The Mughal army, while marching (1580-81) north from Machhiwara to Kangra, crossed the Satluj and Beas on wooden bridges. Before crossing the Beas, the scouts searched a suitable site for the bridge, where the troops encamped. Our source was silent on the exact nature of the materials. It was certain that boats

168   *Situating Medieval India*

were not used and elephants were made to ford the rivers.[13] Jahangir, entering Kashmir (1619) from Hasan Abdal, travelled through Hazara Qarlugh, Naushehra, Dhantur, Malgalli and Pakli. He reached the Nainsukh, which flowed down from the hills of Dard, lying between Badakhshan and Tibet. As it bifurcated into two branches, two wooden bridges were prepared. In length, one was 18 cubits and the other was 14 cubits. In breadth, both were five cubits. In this area, they made bridges in a specific manner. On the surface of water, they threw pine trees, fastening the two ends strongly to the rocks. Over these, they threw thick wooden planks that were made firm with pegs and ropes. These structures lasted for years with minor repairs. Jahangir, travelling through the pass of Pim Darang, halted on the Kishan Ganga. Over this river, there was a bridge 54 yards long and 3 yards broad. At both the rivers, Nainsukh and Kishan Ganga, the footmen and horses crossed over the bridges. Since the water was deep and swift, the elephants were deprived of their loads and made to ford the streams.[14] Such wooden bridges could not span every channel of flowing water. The Kashmiris used Zampa, which was a contraption of ropes and planks. Taking two strong ropes, they fastened one end to the top of a hill and other end on the other side of water. Between these two ropes, they placed a large number of planks bearing a width of one cubit. A yard higher than the planks, they fixed two ropes running parallel to each other. The foot passenger, holding the upper ropes for support, walked over the planks. By doing so, they were able to descend from the top of a hill to the bottom on the other side. Such a bridge spanned the Chenab at Bhandarkot in Kishtwar. During military conflicts, the rival forces made and unmade such bridges in accordance with their needs.[15] Since the Zampa was likely to be worn out with perpetual exposure to moisture, it might have required periodic repairs like the wooden bridge.

A variety of floating structures, flat and simple, were fabricated to cross the rivers. In the Sind Sagar Doab, grain was transported over streams on large rafts. On 15 March 1519, Babur was a witness to this device.[16] In the Multan region, inflated skins, besides boats, were used to cross the flowing waters. Humayun, during the course

Travelling Across Northwestern India   169

of his flight through southwest Panjab, carried out raids in the villages within 10-12 leagues of Bhakkar. The cows and buffaloes, thus captured and slaughtered, provided leather bags (*khik*) that became handy for crossing over.[17] In 1607, members of Jahangir's family crossed the Indus on a raft fixed on inflated skins. Locally known as Jala or Shal, it was a platform made of bamboos and grass, below which they placed skins full of air. These devices were safer than boats in rivers and streams, where there were rocks.[18] A group of people, travelling from Ayodheya to Surharpur, were required to cross the Tomsa in haste. On the spur of the moment, they managed to get rafts that were tied to pitchers. In the autobiography of Banarsi Das Jain, an artist Ganesh Pyne has developed its sketch with sheer imagination. There were nine long rafts that were placed side by side and secured with beams on the sides and middle. It was placed on six pitchers, three each on the two flanks. Two persons, who looked extremely worried, sat on the raft. A third person stood on the rear end, holding a long pole in his hands. The lower end of the pole went deep into the water and touched the base of the channel. This man applied pressure on the pole in order to steer the raft forward and guide its direction.[19] Sohni, the daughter of a potter of Gujarat, repeatedly crossed the Chenab on a pitcher to meet her lover Mahiwal.

In the early decades of the sixteenth century, the Mughal ruling class felt the need for efficient means of crossing rivers, particularly in view of the Mughal-Afghan military conflict. Khwandamir, the author of *Qanun-i Humayuni*, credits Humayun with the invention of a movable bridge (*jasr rawan*). In this contrivance, several boats were fastened to each other with hooks and chains (*qulab-ha wa zanjeer-ha nazdik ba-yakdigar dar dariya barham me bandand*). Wooden planks were firmly nailed over them, so that a flat and level platform was formed. It did not shake when the horsemen and foot soldiers moved over it. When the Emperor wished to undertake a journey across the river, the parts of the bridge were dismantled and carried on the surface of water with the speed of wind. When the army was required to cross the river, its parts were joined together in a manner that it spread from one bank to the other. Everyone was saved from the trouble of procuring boats at

170   *Situating Medieval India*

the site. There was no need for the camels and horses to ford the river.[20] Though it was claimed that the device was meant for universal use, it was never seen during the actual crossing of rivers and, therefore, it remained one of Humayun's wondrous creations that Khwandamir has described with great enthusiasm. Interestingly, each one of them was associated with skills in carpentry and mobility on the rivers.

Apart from the movable bridge, Humayun was responsible for three other inventions. Ingenious boat builders (*kashti tarashan*) fabricated several large barges. In the middle of each, a spacious hall was created in order to accommodate several shops. People of all professions were invited to set up their crafts and engage in transactions. A complete bazaar flourished on the river, while the merchants looked up to the Emperor for patronage. In 1532-3, Humayun and his nobles travelled on these barges from Firozabad (Delhi) to Agra over the Yamuna. As the market moved like the breeze, all kinds of goods—food, beverages, clothes and ornaments—were put up for sale. The passengers secured the means of convenience and happiness. In the same manner, the royal gardeners (*baghbanan badshahi*) laid out gardens on the barges. Placing flat boards on the floor surface of the barges, these were covered with a layer of soil fit for horticulture. A variety of plants—fruits, flowers, vegetables, tulips and jasmine—were planted in the four corners.[21] On the same lines, Humayun's intelligence manifested in a movable palace. Consisting of three storeys, it was made of superior quality of timber. Ingenious carpenters and skilled craftsmen designed the components in such a manner that they appeared like a single structure. It could be moved easily from one place to the other. A ladder, leading to the uppermost story, could be folded and unfolded at will. Artful painters adorned the palace in different colours. Astute goldsmiths built a golden dome which, placed on the top, shone like the sun. The chamberlains covered it with curtains of seven colours (*parda-ha haft rang*) that were sewn with fabrics of China, Turkey and Europe.[22]

The length of boat bridges varied in accordance with the volume of water, flowing at any given moment. On 4 May 1607, a pontoon was thrown across the Indus with only 18 boats because at this

Travelling Across Northwestern India 171

time the water of the Indus at Nilab was low.[23] However, this was a contrast from the situation in Spetember 1652, when heavy rain in the entire Indus plain had inundated all the rivers and streams. A bridge of 40 boats was constructed over the Indus at Jalala, while 55, 56 and 50 boats were used for the same purpose at Jhelum, Chenab and Ravi respectively. In that season of prolonged monsoon, a bridge of 104 boats was erected at Buh, where the combined waters of the Beas and Satluj posed a formidable barrier.[24] An account of the Dutch embassy, which visited the Mughal court at Lahore, provided a better idea about the dimensions of the pontoons. In May 1712, 38 flat-bottomed boats, each two and a half fathoms (15 feet) wide, were employed in constructing a eighty fathoms (480 feet) pontoon over the Beas. The width of its platform measured two fathoms (12 feet), so that two carts could pass simultaneously, one besides the other, without any major difficulty.[25]

For the Mughal armies, the common practice was to construct temporary bridges. The task was achieved with tolerable skill. At the suitable site, there could be two bridges, depending on the military compulsions at a particular time and availability of the components in the locality. The requisite number of flat-bottomed boats was placed side-by-side. They were tied together with grass ropes in such a manner that the water just had play between them. Over these boats, a roadway was laid with the stacking of branches, bushes, straw and earth. A flat surface was prepared to prevent the animals from slipping. A strict procedure was adopted to ensure smooth passage of the armies. When two bridges were thrown on the same spot, 200 or 300 paces separated them.[26] A small block house was created near the river bank. The officers, who regulated the movement of traffic, occupied it. They made sure that a large number of people did not carelessly crowd the bridge and, thus, sink the boats.[27] In some cases, the traffic was required to pass through a specially erected gate before approaching the pontoon, so as to prevent overcrowding and perhaps detecting overloaded animals.[28] Only one type of troops—cavalry, infantry, camels, carts and oxen—was allowed to pass at a time and that too in a single file. Even if the bridge parted and collapsed, the river would not take much toll of men, animals and materials. As a rule, the

172 *Situating Medieval India*

elephants were not permitted to set their feet on the pontoons, lest they should sink it with sheer weight.[29]

The Emperor generally camped about half-a-league from the bridge. Delaying his departure, he allowed three days and nights for the army to cross over before following the suit. In spite of these precautions, the danger on the two extremities was not eliminated. The loose moving sand, when trodden under the feet of a multitude of animals, was swept away by the current. The resultant cavities in the ground trapped the animals, who were trampled under the feet of those following them. Even the people passed over the struggling animals in utmost disorder. On these occasions, the troopers attached to the nobles exerted themselves to clear the way for their masters and, while doing so, made an active use of their canes.[30]

During a march, Akbar displayed carefulness and foresight regarding the safety of the army. On the one hand, he paid attention to the provision of cheap corn and potable water and, on the other hand, took a keen interest in the quality of roads and the passage over rivers.[31] In spite of the vast number of troop and animals, grain and fodder was cheap in the camp. Akbar, resorting to insightful planning, dispatched diligent agents to the neighbouring cities and towns, with instructions to bring the supplies from all sides. It was announced that the merchants, who brought goods— grain, maize, pulses and other commodities—to the camp and sold them at cheap rates, would be exempted from taxes and imposts. When Akbar advanced beyond the Mughal territories, he sent heralds to inform the inhabitants through public announcements. If they showed submission, they would not be harmed or deported. They were free to sell what they liked and, that too, without paying any levies. On his return after victory, they would receive his gratitude and favour. If they showed any recalcitrance, they would attract punishment. While passing through the domains of local chiefs, he bonded with them through treaties, gifts and promises. The chiefs, initially terrified at the presence of a vast army and unwilling to provide support, changed their attitude due to their own interests and Akbar's magnanimity.[32]

The Mughal army, during its march (1580-1) from Sirhind to

Travelling Across Northwestern India   173

Nilab, abandoned the usual Lahore route. Instead, it proceeded northwards along the Himalayan foothills. Both strategic considerations and technical reasons determined the itinerary. Akbar was able to move men and materials, where the rivers were yet fordable and favourable to the construction of bridges.[33] Owing to the availability of water, it was possible to acquire grain and fodder, besides the habitat for the ruling elite to indulge in hunting. The abundance of rocks, crags and torrents caused the roughness of roads. In order to overcome the difficulty, sappers and labourers were sent in advance to level the way as far as possible. A former commandant of the Agra Fort, who had risen from the humble position of a sapper to high rank, was given the charge of the task. This man channelized his energies to the swampy glens of the mountains, not to the dry gravel of the plains or perhaps the amphitheatre. A lot of planning went into choosing a site for fording a river or laying a bridge. Akbar, while camping on the Indus, sent an officer upstream to a specific spot and assess the possibility of the cavalry fording it. The officer travelled 25 miles and learnt from the inhabitants that there was no ford in the entire region. Thinking it futile to proceed any further, he retraced his steps. He informed Akbar about the absence of the ford and held that a bridge must be built. Akbar found that this officer had not gone as far as the place indicated to him. As a punishment, he was dragged to the place, bound prostrate to an inflated skin and launched upon the river. As the report spread through the camp, almost the whole army flocked to the bank to see the strange sight. The officer, tossed about in the violent current, raised miserable cries and implored for pardon. Rescued from the river, he was entered in the inventories as a royal property and was auctioned as a slave in the bazaar. One of his friends purchased him for 80 gold pieces and, ultimately, Akbar pardoned him. The public spectacle indicated the importance attached to military discipline and obedience. Perhaps, there was no other way of controlling a vast army during a long march.[34]

Passing through Panipat and Karnal, the Mughal army encountered a stream of the Yamuna. The infantry crossed over a stone bridge, without any crowding or tumult, which sometimes occurred in

174   *Situating Medieval India*

narrow places. In accordance with the royal order, the remaining part of the army comprising cavalry, elephants and camels, crossed over a ford. At Shahabad, the army was forced to halt for some time owing to a violent storm, which rendered the road impassable due to mud and sudden torrents. As soon as the weather cleared, the march resumed. When the army turned east, the gleaming white snow on the Himalayas became visible. The Yamuna arose on this side of the mountain, while the Ganga emerged from the opposite side of the slope.[35] From Ambala, the army took two days to reach Sirhind, a large city divided into separate quarters.[36] Since the inhabitants faced a scarcity of water, a deep artificial lake on the southern side of the city met their needs. Care was taken to fill the lake during monsoons through irrigation channels. Akbar, on reaching Pail, went on several pleasure excursions on a two-horse chariot. Beyond Machhiwara, the army camped on this side of the Satluj. A halt was necessary to allow the construction of a wooden bridge. The river contained crocodiles that were called three headed (*sih sir*). Bearing the girth of a barrel, they crawled on six feet. They swallowed men unawares from below while they were swimming. They seized animals—oxen, buffaloes, sheep and others— by the foot and dragged them down under water when they came to quench their thirst. From this point, the army did not advance to Ludhiana and Sultanpur. Instead, it followed the Satluj into the mountains. The camp was pitched in a country that was rough and very cold. Five days after leaving the Satluj, the army moved north towards Doghari. Fording a small river, the army marched for two days along the Beas. During this time, it searched a ford that elephants could cross, besides a narrow place in the river, where a wooden bridge could be erected. When the scouts found a suitable site for these purposes, the camp was set up. Akbar, accompanied by a select cavalry unit, rode to Nagarkot to settle a dispute between rival claimants to chiefship. He rejoined the army and, crossing the Beas over the newly built bridge, approached Paithan. Thereafter, the army marched southwest along the Ravi until it reached Kalanaur. This place, where Akbar's coronation had taken place 25 years ago, stood on a rivulet that flowed into the Ravi.[37]

Travelling Across Northwestern India   175

TABLE 7.1: STAGES AND DISTANCES FROM DELHI TO KABUL

Stage	Place	Kos	Stage	Place	Kos
1.	Sarai Badli	6	38.	Wazirabad	3
2.	Narela	6	39.	Gujarat Shah Daula	7
3.	Sonepat	8	40.	Khwaspura	15
4.	Ganaur	8	41.	Kharian	6
5.	Samalkha	8	42.	Uzbegabad	6
6.	Panipat	5	43.	Jhelam	10
7.	Gharaunda	8	44.	Rohtas	12
8.	Karnal	8	45.	Sarai Kasian	6
9.	Azimabad	8	46.	Pir Jalal	5
10.	Thanesar	12	47.	Sarai Dhaka	6
11.	Shahabad	12	48.	Sarai Kale Khan	6
12.	Ambala	13	49.	Sarai Takia	8
13.	Sarai Raja	12	50.	Rawalpindi	4
14.	Sirhind	12	51.	Sarai Kharbuza	4
15.	Sarai Khanna	6	52.	Hasan Abdal	7
16.	Sarai Lashkar Khan	6	53.	Sarai Veeran	7
17.	Ludhiana	12	54.	Shamsabad	8
18.	Philaur	12	55.	Attock	6
19.	Sarai Nur Mahal	6	56.	Khairabad	5
20.	Sarai Dakhni	7	57.	Sarai Koraskin	8
21.	Sarai Nakodar	12	58.	Shahabad	10
22.	Sarai Tuti Khas	6	59.	Peshawar	8
23.	Sultanpur	6	60.	Jamrud	10
24.	Goindval	6	61.	Ali Masjid	–
25.	Sarai Aurangabad	21	62.	Lalbeg	6
26.	Nuruddin	6	63.	Dhaka	6
27.	Talab Raja	6	64.	Besul	7
28.	Doabah Manjha	4	65.	Jalalabad	16
29.	Sarai Khankhana	6	66.	Charbagh	5
30.	Lahore	8	67.	Fatehabad	5
31.	Shahdara	3	68.	Namalabagh	8
32.	Fazlabad	4	69.	Gandang	7
33.	Pul Shah Daula	5	70.	Surkhab	9
34.	Aminabad	6	71.	Jagadalah	10
35.	Sarai Gujar	4	72 .	Barikab	11
36.	Chima Gakkhar	5	73.	Butkhab	8
37.	Nizamabad	6	74.	Kabul	6

Source: Abdul Qadir Khan, *Halat-i Manazil az Shahjahanabad ta Kabul*, MS no. Farsiya Akhbar 237, Aligarh: Maulana Azad Library, ff. 2a-13a.

176   *Situating Medieval India*

Leaving Kalanaur, the army crossed the Ravi by a bridge, which was built for the purpose. It marched north along a rough and dangerous road, with constant steep ascents and descents among marshy glens and overhanging crags. It reached the town of Samba, which held a strong position on the slope of the Himalayas and belonged to a chief loyal to Akbar. Its fertile soil and abundant population resembled Nagarkot. The climate was European in type, as the region stretched north from the thirtieth to the thirty-second degree of latitude. Advancing from Samba, the army camped on a green and pleasant plain besides the Nanis (Degh), which flowed into the Ravi four miles from Samba. The tract between the Ravi and Chenab, lying between two rivers, excelled all others in the north for beauty and fertility, besides the variety of its gardens and for the number of its villages and hamlets. Next day, the Chenab was crossed with great difficulty. The river did not permit the construction of a bridge. Those who tried to ford it were drowned. Akbar and many others crossed it on a boat. The army, during the crossing, was delayed for three days. There was an acute scarcity of boats. Mirza Hakim, in order to delay Akbar's pursuit, had ordered all the boats, in which his troops had crossed over, to be broken into pieces. During the crossing of this river, 400 men of all ranks who could not swim, were drowned. Akbar issued an order for the collection of boats from the neighbouring villages and towns. It was surprising to find a large volume of water in the Chenab, considering that the point of its emergence from the hills was not far. A number of obstacles divided it into three branches. Two of them were surrounded by an island, which lay in the broad bed of the river. The river, whose current was not rapid, flowed into the Jhelum after numerous meanderings.[38]

Half way between Sodhra and Akhnur, Akbar altered the direction of his march towards the Jhelum. This was not only the shortest and the best route, it also promised the availability of good water. In spite of all precautions, the army suffered from thirst during the first day's march of seven miles. Next day, Akbar extended the march to 15 miles to avoid the recurrence of the difficulty. On the bank of the Jhelum, Akbar ordered a rest of eight days. The time was devoted to the construction of a bridge, while Akbar went out

Travelling Across Northwestern India   177

hunting with his sons. Since the river had a broad channel and deep bed, it was not fordable even to elephants. The cavalry and infantry could not swim across it. There was no choice but to build a strong bridge. The army, crossing over, camped at the foot of Balnath Hill which, moving westward, became gradually more accessible and open.[39] After halting for four days, the army reached Rohtas and camped on a rivulet, which almost surrounded the fort. After Rohtas, the line of the march proceeded along the bank of a stream. A rash movement of some soldiers, who were riding on horses, camels and elephants but did not know the right path, brought them to peril. The sand of the riverbed, having absorbed water, appeared flat, solid and dry. Anyone going to the place sank down and remained stuck. The more he struggled to get up, the more was his danger of being swallowed up. The troops, thinking that there was nothing to fear in a level plain, rushed into a grave pitfall. On the sixth day, the army reached a large plain through rough roads, narrow defiles and numerous rivulets. Before arriving at the Manikiala Tope, it faced a severe thunderstorm and heavy rain. The tract between Rohtas and the Indus was dry and barren, while the climate was harsh and treacherous. Advancing through Ribat, the army reached Gagar, which was situated on a steep and narrow ridge with three peaks. It crossed a branch of the Indus, which joined the river a little lower down, forming a broad island.[40]

The army camped on the bank of the Indus in a valley of district Hazara. The region, though devoid of fine trees and gardens, was milder and fertile. It raised an abundance of corn, pulses and grass. Owing to large herds of cattle, it produced plenty of milk and ghee. The camp was set up in a large open plain, rich in flocks and supplied with wood and provisions. For 50 days, the army halted at Azarana, 9 miles from the Indus, where it could be crossed out of India. Greatest of the Indian rivers, the Indus received a huge volume of water from the melting of the Himalayan snows. It also received the water from the five above mentioned rivers. The force and quantity of water in the river was such that even the elephants could ford it with greatest difficulty. Since it was swollen with water, it was not possible to erect a bridge over it. A large number of boats were prepared, so that Prince Murad was able to cross it at

178   *Situating Medieval India*

the vanguard of his troops.[41] When Akbar and his entourage crossed the river, the passage was rendered so hazardous owing to the lack of boats that even the nobles crossed it with immense exertion.

In the summer of 1712, a bridge on the Beas was constructed with 38 flat-bottomed boats, each of which was 2.5 fathoms in width. Possessing a length of 80 fathoms and a width of 2 fathoms, the bridge allowed 2 carts to pass over to the other side. About these boats, interesting evidence has come to light from Attock. The length of the hold of the boats varied from 6 to 7 *gaz* and breadth from 3.5 to 4 *gaz*. The steep projecting poop was 3 *gaz* and the projecting front was 2.75 *gaz*. Their sides were made of three planks, the top and bottom of *shisham* (*Dalbergia sisoo*) and the middle ones of *deodar* (*Cedras deodara*). The flat bottom was made of six planks, the outer ones of shisham and the four middle ones of deodar. The planks, four inches in thickness, were clamped with iron. The bottom was lined with wattling of deodar twigs, which pressing against the bottom, prevented its being driven in by the rocks, so plentiful and dangerous at Attock.[42]

The Indus was bridged at two places, one below Attock at Prachoo and the other above Hathi Phatoor. Bridged in *Kartik* (November), the upper remained until the end of *Baisakh* (May) and lower until *Jeth* (June), unless there was a sudden swell, as it happened after three or four days of heavy rains in the mountains when the Indus rose to 30 feet. The upper bridge required 34 boats, while the lower one 20. The lower bridge stood longer than the upper, because it was confined in steep banks, while the upper bifurcated into two channels. The balks, made of 3 rafters bound together, were 3 *gaz* long and had both ends perforated to fit on iron pegs in each gunwale. Over these were spread small rafters that were tied to prevent an animal's foot going in. The whole was levelled with straw. As many as 50 rafters were required to floor one boat and its water way. In each boat, the equipment comprised 10 *sers* of Munj for tying the balks. Ninety bundles of Pata grass were made into 4 inch thick cable of 120 *gaz*, so that there were three pieces of 40 *gaz* each. Two of these were spliced together for the upstream anchor (*kothi*), which was a strong wooden cage (3 *gaz* × 3 *gaz*) that encased large stones weighing 150-175 maunds. The stern cable

Travelling Across Northwestern India 179

was 40 *gaz* long and held a strong bag (*bora*) filled with stones. The first boat was moored ashore. When an upstream boat dropped the anchors, the second boat was tracked to its place and then the third. The cable (*langar*) of the latter was fixed on the anchor of the second. To every boat, there was half of the anchor, one bag and 3 pieces of 40 *gaz* long cable. Each boat required 50 bundles (*trangads*) of grass, costing Rs. 2 for binding the anchor and bag. When the bridge had been standing for some time, the cables tended to rot and, in case of a swell, a heavier anchor was dropped and cables let out. Often, the boats were carried away in these swells. Normally, a bridge was ready in 15 days and, in case of urgency, it was formed in 5 days. When the bridge was made, four men were appointed to each boat, two for the day and two for the night. During the construction, the crew numbered 50 men.[43]

Physical resources and technical capabilities were not enough to convey the travellers across the rivers. The cooperation of local chiefs and *zamindars*, particularly those holding sway along the riverbanks, was equally essential. Since they possessed numerous boats as part of their military equipment and exercised a firm control over the boatmen, they played a crucial role in providing a safe passage across the rivers. Conversely, their indifference or opposition could effectively block the movement of traffic at the fords. It was not without reason that Akbar, while marching towards Kabul (1581) in pursuit of Mirza Hakim, conciliated the Dilazak chiefs before crossing the Indus. It was through their efforts that the Emperor secured 40 boats as well as a huge quantity of timber, with which an equal number of fresh boats were fabricated.[44] The role of *zamindars* was pushed to the centre stage when the Mughal forces (1606) pursued the rebellious Khusrau through the plains of Panjab. Acting in compliance with Jahangir's orders, the *zamindars* did not leave any boat for Khusrau at Shahpur, one of the recognized crossings on the Chenab. When the Prince tried to cross the river from the ferry of Sodhra, the *zamindars* used violent means to prevent the boatmen from providing any service to the fugitives, who were consequently stranded.[45] The *zamindars* blocked the movement of the rebels by fortifying the eastern bank and collaborated with the imperial assignees (*jagirdars*) in capturing the

180   *Situating Medieval India*

leading malcontents. Recognizing the invaluable support of the *zamindars*, who were based between the Chenab and Jhelum, Jahangir rewarded some with village headships and others with land grants.[46]

Improvement in communications, through the provision of bridges, went a long way in strengthening the control of the Mughal State over hitherto isolated pockets. This development undermined the position of *zamindars* in the rural society, as their traditional privileges were eroded. In such situations, they obstructed the construction of bridges in their localities. Buta, a *zamindar* who earned his livelihood by ferrying travellers across the Degh, opposed Shah Daula's move to span the stream with a masonry structure. In order to drown the workers, he breached the embankment, which was raised to hold the water back. Shahjahan ordered Buta to be brought to Lahore, where he was hung from a tall Neem tree. On being released through the intercession of Shah Daula, he cooperated with the local community in the completion of the bridge.[47] Our evidence on the boatmen was limited. Akbar was said to have assigned a village in subdistrict (*parganah*) Chach for the maintenance of boatmen at Attock. Yielding an annual income of Rs. 500, the assignment enabled 40 households with 80 boatmen to settle in Malhayi Tola, a village outside the Attock fort. The boats, 15 in number, were treated as the property of the boatmen. However, they were not permitted to remove the boats from Attock. They were required to keep the boats in a state of repair, as the government did not pay them to acquire a new one in place of one that was sunk. When a pontoon was formed, each boat was paid at the rate of four annas per day as long as the structure stood. At other times, the boatmen plied at the ferry between Attock and Khairabad, charging in accordance with the nature of cargo. These practices appear to have been followed since the reign of Akbar.[48]

The boatmen, who plied the boats, were indispensable to the people in terms of their services. Yet, they were accorded a low social status. This became evident from the case of a boatman in the love tale of Hir-Ranjha. Noora Sambhal, who held an estate (*zamindari*) in the neighbourhood of the Chenab, got a magnificent boat built for himself. He employed the experienced Luddan as

Travelling Across Northwestern India   181

his boatman. Luddan fell afoul of his master, as he innocently allowed some strangers to see the interior of the boat, which had evoked general curiosity. An enraged Noora gave Luddan a beating. Luddan, owing to his humiliation, ran away with the boat and took shelter with the Siyals. The Sambhals, in order to retrieve the boat and custody of their boatman, attacked the Siyals. In the ensuing conflict, there were casualties on both sides. The Siyals, emerging victorious, retained the boat and boatman. The happiness of Luddan was short-lived. He permitted a homeless wanderer Ranjha to sleep in the boat. Hir, the fiery daughter of the Siyal chief, thrashed Luddan for this indiscretion. As soon as she fell in love with Ranjha, she conciliated Luddan with a reward of two buffaloes. We find that Luddan suffered humiliation at the hands of his two successive masters, the Sambhals and Siyals. In both cases, he acted out of innocence and kindness. He was unfairly held guilty of serious lapses. He was beaten and insulted, though he was quite old.[49]

Contemporary sources record many incidents of accidents on the rivers. Mirza Hakim, while retreating from Lahore and rushing back to Kabul, was in great haste. He and a part of his troops crossed the Chenab in boats. The remaining forces were constrained to swim across. During this exercise, 400 men of all ranks, who could not swim, were drowned. The Mughal army following in pursuit, faced a lot of difficulty at the Chenab. Many of those who tried to ford the river were drowned, though our source was silent on the exact toll.[50] Jahangir, while camping in Gujarat (1607), averted a catastrophe. A torrential rain and violent hailstorm flooded the Jhelum and broke the specially erected bridge. Jahangir and some members of the royal family crossed the Jhelum in a boat. Since the boats were few, he forbade his men from crossing in these and ordered the rebuilding of the pontoon.[51] During the Mughal expedition (1619) against Kishtwar, Dilawar Khan placed 80 soldiers on rafts (*jhala*) that were launched across the Chenab at night. Since the water was flowing with great momentum, the rafts were carried away with equal force and 68 men were drowned. Ten soldiers, who resorted to swimming, reached the shore of safety and the remaining two fell into the hands of the Kashmiri opponents.[52]

182   *Situating Medieval India*

Sohrab Khan, the son of Rustam Mirza, relying on his expertise in swimming, resolved to bathe in the Jhelum. People tried to dissuade him, as the cold water was violent enough to roll over an elephant. Sohrab Khan, owing to his pride and negligence, jumped into the river along with two servants. Unable to withstand the stormy waves, he was drowned along with one his servants.[53]

Mahabat Khan, during his revolt on the Jhelum (1626), took Jahangir in his custody and destroyed the bridge. The loyalists, confined on the opposite bank, made desperate attempts to rescue the Emeperor and, in the process, many of them drowned.[54] In 1652, unprecedented rains towards the end of monsoon impeded the movement of the Mughal army returning from Qandhar. The bridge, which Saifullah, the *Mir-i Bahr*, had erected on the Indus, was swept away. The army halted for 5 days, so that a new bridge was put together. Though it crossed the Jhelum and Chenab on pontoons, the plain from Aminabad and Jahangirabad to Lahore was submerged in a thick layer of water. The permanent bridges on the Degh and Baghbacha were covered in the overflow from these streams. Halting for four days to allow the flood to subside, the march was resumed. However, many members of the advance party, which moved towards Lahore, were drowned in the two streams. When the royal pavilion approached the Ravi, it was decided to load some tents on camels that would cross the bridge. The remaining baggage would be placed on boats and carried across the river. Afterwards, it would be loaded again and brought to the royal gardens in the city. Unexpected torrential rains swelled the river and swept away the bridge. Since the neighbouring lands were inundated, the tents remained in water for two days. When the water receded, the tents were retrieved and, dried during the next three days, transported on boats across the Ravi to be brought to the gardens of Faiz Bakhsh and Farah Bakhsh.[55]

In the middle of 1711, the nephew of Ghazi Khan Bahadur Rustam Jang collected a number of boats and laid a bridge on the Satluj at Ropar. Owing to a flood in the river at night, the bridge collapsed and the boats were washed away. The superintendent of the ford (*darogha-i guzr*), with the help of some boatmen, collected the boats at a distance of two leagues. Though four or five boats

Travelling Across Northwestern India 183

were not retrieved, it was decided that a new bridge would be built.[56] After two months, a similar mishap occurred on the Beas. Because of a swell at night (14 June 1711), the pontoon was washed away and the boats were damaged. The boatmen, following a search, recovered many boats. Since the river was still in spate, it was not possible to lay another bridge. In fact, water had damaged Prince Azim ush-Shan's camp, which was on the other side of the river. There was no choice but to shift the camp back.[57] In the middle of 1712, Jahandar Shah and the ambassador of the Dutch East India Company crossed the Beas on two pontoons. Owing to the terrible heat, many people died and their bodies lay on the ground along the road. A horseman, who was in the service of the Dutch, tried to cross the Beas on horseback. Due to the rapidity of the stream, he lost his footing. He perished in the waves, though his horse was salvaged. A number of locals were sent to search the body of the deceased. They were not able to find the body among the multitude of the dead, who were floating down the river. One of the ambassador's boats, which was too heavily laden with people who had forced themselves into it, sank into the swollen waters. All the goods were pulled out. Another boat, with numerous soldiers, passengers and women, was overturned by an elephant, so that many people drowned.[58] A worse fate met Nadir Shah's army when it crossed the Chenab at Akhnur (14 June 1739). Though boats had been firmly secured with iron chains, the pontoon collapsed due to a sudden inflow of water, leading to the death of 2,000 Qizilbash soldiers. It was believed that the locals threw tree trunks into the river which, striking the pontoon with great force, snapped the chains and shattered the boats. It took the Persian army a month to be ferried across the river 30 miles downstream from Akhnur.[59]

During the monsoon of 1746, Yahya Khan met an accident on the Beas.[60] Owing to several factors—disturbed political conditions, confusion in his mind and great physical haste—he did not take the necessary precautions. Bereft of troops and equipage, he took an unknown route and arrived at the swollen Beas (*ba-rah ghair mutaaraf bar dariya-i biah keh dar nihayat taghian bud*). He found that the boat was redundant and the boatmen hapless. Though

184 *Situating Medieval India*

his companions were unwilling, he resolved to cross the river in a boat. Owing to the inexperience of the boatmen, a strong gale and turbulence in the river (*na-tajarbakari mallahan wa ashob bad wa baran keh aab ra ba-talatum dasht*) shook the parts of the boat. Yahya Khan, who had taken off his clothes and wrapped them around his waist with a loincloth (*lungi*), sat in comfort and smoked his tobacco pipe (*huqqa*). Seeing the miserable condition of the boat, he jumped into the river. Since he had learnt swimming during childhood, he began to move his hands and feet in the water. Just then, an old man, with a radiant forehead, gave him two gourds (*kaddu*) and asked him to place these under his chest to swim across. Yahya Khan, taking the gourds, did as instructed. With his little endeavour and the grace of God, he reached the bank in safety. As soon as he jumped out of the boat, it sank into the river and 40-50 of his companions drowned in the stormy water.[61]

Two decades later, Ahmad Shah Abdali met a disaster at the end of his seventh invasion (1765) of Panjab. Though heavily laden with booty, the Afghan army had no difficulty in crossing the Beas and Ravi. As it approached the Chenab, the scouts were sent to search a ford. On their return, they informed that it would be easier to ford the river at the foothills, where it fragmented into eight streams. The Afghan army crossed the first six with ease. The remaining two were not only deep and swift, they were also in a violent spate. As soon as the troops and baggage descended into the stream, they were annihilated in the deluge. Thousands of animals—horses, camels, bullocks, buffaloes and donkeys—who were loaded with treasure and equipment, were swept away. Women, falling from their litters on camels, fell into the currents and disappeared from sight. It appeared as if the day of judgement had arrived. No one cared for anyone. The fathers abandoned their sons, while the mothers threw their children in the water. In terms of life and property, the Afghan loss was more than that suffered in the battles against the Sikhs. The Afghan army, having learnt a bitter lesson, crossed the Jhelum on a pontoon.[62]

NOTES

1. An earlier version of this paper appeared as 'River Crossing in North Western India During the Mughal Times', *Proceedings of the Indian History Congress*, 59th session, Patiala, 1998, pp. 434-43.

2. Zahiruddin Muhammad Babur, *Babur Nama*, Eng tr. (*The Babur Nama: Memoirs of Babur, Prince and Emperor*), Wheeler M. Thackston, New York: The Modern Library, rpt., 2000, pp. 270-81. (Hereafter cited as Babur).

3. William Finch, *India as Seen by William Finch*, ed. R. Nath, Jaipur: The Historical Research Documentation Programme, 1990, p. 70; Fray Sebastien Manrique, *Travels of Fray Sebastien Manrique*, vol. II, Eng tr. C.E. Luard and H. Hosten, Nendeln: Kraus Reprint Limited, 1927, p. 183.

4. Alexander Cunningham, *Report on a Tour in the Punjab in 1878-9*, vol. XIV, Varanasi: Indological Book House, rpt., 1970, p. 7.

5. Alexander Cunningham, op. cit., p. 57; John Marshall, *Annual Report, Archaeological Survey of India, 1923-4*, Calcutta: Government of India, Central Publications Branch, 1926, p. 136; *Objects of Antiquarian Interest in Punjab and its Dependencies*, Part IV, Lahore: Public Works Department Press, 1875, pp. 4-5.

6. Nuruddin Jahangir, *Tuzuk-i Jahangiri*, Eng. tr. Alexander Rogers and Henry Beveridge, New Delhi: Low Price Publications, rpt., 1989, vol. I, pp. 135-6. (Hereafter cited as Jahangir).

7. Subhash Parihar, *Islamic Architecture of Punjab (1206-1707)*, New Delhi: Aryan Books International, 2015, p. 104; Subhash Parihar, 'Relics of Agra-Lahore Road at Sultanpur Lodi', *Indologica Jaipurensia*, vol. II, 1988-95, pp. 86-7.

8. D. Kuenen Wickstead and J. Ph. Vogel, 'Embassy of Mr. Johan Josua Katelaar, Ambassador of Dutch East India Company to the Great Mughals—Shah Alam, Bahadur Shah and Jahandar Shah', *Journal of the Punjab Historical Society*, vol. X, part I, 1929, p. 37. (Hereafter cited as The Dutch Embassy).

9. Muhammad Waris, *Badshah Nama*, Persian ms., Sitamau: Shri Natnagar Shodh Samsthan, f. 68a.

10. During Akbar's reign, a few villages were separated from Sialkot and reconstituted into the subdistrict (*parganah*) of Gujarat. The town gained prominence when Shah Daula settled here and constructed a number of mosques, wells, tanks and bridges. In his youth, he was a devotee of Khima Badehra. He had deep faith in saints, particularly Miyan Syedna. He served his mentor for a long time. The mentor, before dying, looked

186   *Situating Medieval India*

at Shah Daula with a blissful gaze (*nazr faiz asr*) in a manner that his interior was illuminated with divine light. At this time, he shifted from Sialkot to Gujarat. Droves of followers came from four directions to pay their respects to him. He received a huge quantity of offerings in cash and kind. He distributed his blessings and gifts in much larger quantity. The sheer volume of his bounty made people forget Hatim. He died in the seventeenth regnal year of Aurangzeb. Sujan Rai Bhandari, *Khulasat ut-Tawarikh*, Persian text, ed. M. Zafar Hasan, Delhi: G. and Sons, 1918, p. 74. (Hereafter cited as Bhandari).

11. A.C. Elliot, *The Chronicles of Gujrat*, Patiala: Languages Department, Punjab, rpt., 1970, pp. 58-9; Abdul Rahman and James L. Wescott Jr., *A Historical Geography of Medieval Gujarat*, Lahore: Dost Associates, 1993, p. 88.

12. Alexander Cunningham, *Archaeological Survey Report, 1878-79*, vol. IV, p. 45; *Imperial Gazetteer of India, Provincial Series: Punjab*, vol. II, Calcutta: Superintendent of Government Printing, 1908, p. 87; A.C. Elliot, op. cit., p. 19; Abdul Rahman and James L. Wescott Jr., op. cit., pp. 90, 96; Irfan Habib, *An Atlas of the Mughal Empire*, Delhi: Oxford University Press, 1982, p. 12.

13. Father Monserrate, *Commentary of Father Monserrate*, ed. S.N. Banerjee and J.S. Hoyland, Jalandhar: Asian Publishers, rpt., 1993, p. 104. (Hereafter cited as Monserrate).

14. Jahangir, vol. II, pp. 127-8.

15. Mutamad Khan, *Iqbalnama-i Jahangiri*, Persian text, ed. Abdul Haii and Ahmad Ali, Calcutta: Royal Asiatic Society of Bengal, 1865, pp. 143-4; Khwaja Kamgar Husaini, *Maasir-i Jahangiri*, Persian text, ed. Azra Alavi, Bombay: Asia Publishing House, 1978, p. 293.

16. Babur, p. 280.

17. Jauhar Aftabchi, *Tazkirat ul-Waqiat*, Persian text, Sajida Sherwani, Rampur: Rampur Raza Library, 2015, p. 68.

18. Jahangir, vol. I, p. 101.

19. Banarsi Das Jain, *Ardhakathanaka*, Eng tr. (*Half A Tale: A Study in the Interrelationship between Autobiography and History*), Mukund Lath, Jaipur: Rajasthan Prakrit Bharati Sansthan, 1981, pp. 68-9.

20. Khwandamir alias Ghiasuddin Muhammad, *Qanun-i Humayuni*, Persian text, ed. M. Hidayat Hosain, Calcutta: Royal Asiatic Society of Bengal, 1940, pp. 63-4.

21. Ibid., pp. 61-3.

22. Ibid., pp. 65-6.

23. Jahangir, vol. I, p. 101.

24. Muhammad Waris, *Badshah Nama*, ff. 67b-68b; Muhammad Saleh

Travelling Across Northwestern India   187

Kamboh, *Amal-i Saleh*, Persian text, ed. Ghulam Yazdani, Calcutta: Royal Asiatic Society of Bengal, 1939, vol. III, pp. 152-3.

25. The Dutch Embassy, p. 36.

26. Francois Bernier, *Travels in the Mogul Empire: AD 1656-1668*, Eng. tr., Archibald Constable, ed. Vincent A. Smith, Delhi: Low Price Publications, rpt., 1994, p. 380.

27. Monserrate, p. 81.

28. The Dutch Embassy, p. 36.

29. Monserrate, p. 81.

30. Francois Bernier, op. cit., pp. 380, 387.

31. Monserrate, pp. 109-10.

32. Ibid., pp. 79-80.

33. Jean Deloche, *Transport and Communication in India Prior to Steam Locomotion, vol. I: Land Transport*, Eng. tr. James Walker, Delhi: Oxford University Press, 1993, p. 140.

34. Monserrate, pp. 79-83.

35. Ibid., pp. 98-100.

36. Sirhind was so named because it was situated on the frontier provinces of India including Lahore. Since the word *sarhad* meant frontier, the name of the city signified the frontier of India. It was great in size. It was divided into separate quarters and, in this respect, resembled Memphis in Egypt. The city had a very famous school of medicine and, from here, doctors were sent all over the empire. It manufactured a variety of goods such as bows, quivers, shoes, greaves and sandals. Traders exported these goods to all cities of the empire. The city, situated on a very broad plain, was beautified by many pleasant gardens and groves of trees. On the southern side, an artificial lake met the urban needs of water. During monsoons, care was taken to fill the lake through irrigation channels. In the middle of the lake stood a tower, which was open to public for enjoyment. From this tower, a pleasant scenario was visible over the lake and surrounding gardens and parks. Monserrate, pp. 101-2.

37. Ibid., pp. 93-105.

38. Ibid., pp. 105-9.

39. Ibid., pp. 109-10; the account of Monserrate largely corroborates the chronicle of Abul Fazl. According to the latter, Akbar crossed the Satluj at Machhiwara by a noble bridge. Between Khokhowal and Kahnuwan, he crossed the Beas by a bridge. He crossed the Ravi at Kalanaur over a freshly laid bridge. He crossed the Chenab at Ramgarh and Jhelum by a bridge between the Jhelum ferry and Rasulpur. On 11 July 1581, he camped on the confluence of the Indus and Kabul. He ordered Qasim Khan to

188   *Situating Medieval India*

construct a bridge on the Indus. Marching through the spring and summer of 1581, Akbar's army crossed every river in Panjab over a newly fabricated bridge. Though Abul Fazl was silent on the materials used, boats were most probably roped in to span the channels. Abul Fazl, *Akbar Nama*, Eng. tr. H. Beveridge, New Delhi: Atlantic Publishers & Distributors, rpt., 2019, vol. III, pp. 508-23.

40. Monserrate, pp. 116-18.
41. Ibid., pp. 121-4.
42. Alexander Burnes et al., ed., 'Political, Geographical and Commercial Reports 1835-1837', *The Panjab Past and Present*, vol. XII, April 1978, p. 67.
43. Ibid., pp. 67-8.
44. Monserrate, p. 122.
45. Husain Beg Badakhshi, a leading partisan of Khusrau, arrived at Sodhra. His men could get only one boat without boatmen and another boat full of firewood and grass. Husain Beg wished to transport his men from the second boat to the first one, so that Khusrau was conveyed across. At this crucial moment, Kilan, the son-in-law of Kamal Chaudhari of Sodhra, reached the spot. On seeing a body of men about to cross the Chenab at night, he cried out to the boatmen that there was an order of Jahangir forbidding unknown men from crossing at night and, therefore, they must be careful. Owing to the uproar, the people of the neighbourhood gathered. Kilan took from the boatmen the pole (*balli*) with which they propelled the boat and, thus, made the boat unmanageable. Though money was offered to the boatmen, no one would ferry the rebels over. Abul Qasim Namkin, then present in Gujarat, learnt of the emergency and rushed to the site with his sons and a small retinue. Husain Beg, out of desperation, shot arrows at the boatmen. Kilan retaliated with arrows from the bank. The boat, which had drifted down the river on its own, grounded at the end of the night. At daybreak, Namkin and his men assembled on the west of the Chenab, while the *zamindars* fortified it on the east. The people, both on elephants and boats, captured Khusrau. Jahangir, vol. I, pp. 66-7.
46. Jahangir, vol. I, pp. 66-9; Mutamad Khan, *Iqbalnama-i Jahangiri*, pp. 15-17; Khwaja Kamgar Husaini, *Maasir-i Jahangiri*, pp. 85-7.
47. A.C. Elliot, op. cit., p. 59.
48. Alexander Burnes, op. cit., p. 66.
49. Damodar Gulati, *Hir Damodar*, Pbi. Text, ed. Jagtar Singh, Patiala: Punjabi University, rpt., 2000, pp. 82-92, 105-8.
50. Monserrate, p. 109.

Travelling Across Northwestern India · 189

51. Jahangir, vol. I, p. 92.
52. Mutamad Khan, *Iqbalnama-i Jahangiri*, p. 144; Khwaja Kamgar Husaini, *Maasir-i Jahangiri*, p. 293.
53. Jahangir, vol. II, pp. 132-3.
54. Beni Prasad, *History of Jahangir*, Allahabad: The Indian Press, 5th edn., 1973, pp. 369-77.
55. Muhammad Waris, *Badshah Nama*, ff. 67b-68b; Muhammad Saleh Kamboh, *Amal-i Saleh*, vol. III, pp. 152-3.
56. *Akhbarat-i Darbar-i Mualla*, 8 Rabi ul-Awwal 1123/15 April 1711, 5-6th RY of Bahadur Shah, Sitamau: Shri Natnagar Shodh Samsthan, vol. I, p. 147.
57. Ibid., 9 Jamadi ul-Awwal 1123/14 June 1711, 5-6th RY of Bahadur Shah, vol. I, p. 187.
58. The Dutch Embassy, pp. 36-7.
59. Khwaja Abdul Karim, *Bayan-i Waqai*, Persian text, ed. K.B. Nasim, Lahore: Idarah-i Tahqiqat-i Pakistan, University of the Punjab, 1970, p. 46; Anand Ram Mukhlis, *Tazkira-i Anand Ram*, Persian ms. no. SHR 94, Amritsar: The Sikh History Research Department, Khalsa College, pp. 65-6.
60. Zakariya Khan, the governor of Panjab, died on 1 July 1745. He left behind three sons, viz., Yahya Khan, Shahnawaz Khan and Mir Baqi. A tussle erupted between the elder two over governorship and patrimonial property. Yahya Khan, being the nephew and son-in-law of the *wazir*, Qamruddin Khan, enjoyed an initial advantage. The Mughal ruler Muhammad Shah assigned the two provinces to the *wazir* who, in turn, appointed Yahya Khan as his deputy over Lahore and Shahnawaz Khan over Multan. As the dispute remained unresolved, the adherents of the two brothers often clashed in Lahore. Shahnawaz Khan extracted a sum of Rs. 6 lakhs as his share of ancestral property. He defeated Yahya Khan and threw him into prison. He established his control over the region and, fearing the *wazir's* wrath, sent an emissary to the Emperor with the aim of legalizing his usurpation. Yahya Khan, suffering confinement of four months, escaped from prison and rushed to Delhi. On the way, he faced a violent storm on the Beas. Hari Ram Gupta, *Later Mughal History of the Punjab (1707-1973)*, Lahore: Sang-e Meel Publications, rpt., 1976, pp. 64-6; Ganda Singh, *Ahmad Shah Durrani: Father of Modern Afghanistan*, New York: Asia Publishing House, 1959, pp. 41-2.
61. Anand Ram Mukhlis, *Tazkira-i Anand Ram*, pp. 108-9.
62. Qazi Nur Muhammad, *Jang Nama*, Persian text, ed. Ganda Singh, Amritsar: The Sikh History Research Department, Khalsa College, 1939, pp. 168-76.

CHAPTER 8

Political Culture in the Mughal Empire: An Idealistic Vision and the Ground Reality

During the second half of the sixteenth century, the Mughal military machine brought large parts of the Indian subcontinent under its sway. A racially heterogeneous nobility—Turanis, Iranis, Afghans, Indian Muslims and local chiefs—served the centralized polity, which was built on numerical military ranks (*mansabs*) and transferrable revenue assignments (*jagirs*). A distinct set of administrators governed the provinces (*subahs*), while hundreds of functionaries, trained in Persian and accounts, managed the collection of the land tax. Abul Fazl, who documented the achievements of the ruling class and compiled the statistics of the agrarian economy, developed a political ideology for the Mughal Empire.[1] Muzaffar Alam has shown that Nasiruddin Tusi's *Akhlaq-i Nasiri* exercised profound influence in the Perso-Islamic world up to the heyday of the Mughals. It was one of the five important books read out to Akbar and a favoured reading among his nobles. This treatise envisaged an ideal polity that ensured the welfare of diverse religious groups through cooperation. This was attained through mutual love and justice. An imprint of these ideas was visible in the *Ain-i Akbari* and *Muizah-i Jahangiri*. For long, the former has resonated in the studies on the Mughal period.[2] The latter, certainly lesser known, deserved a closer look.

Muhammad Baqir descended from the eminent Najm-i Sani family, which had risen to prominence in the Safavid Iran. His ancestor Yar Ahmad served Shah Ismail Safavi as the prime minister (*vakil us-sultanat*) and received the title of Najm-i Sani. He was

Political Culture in the Mughal Empire 191

noted for rectitude, ability and magnificence. At the instance of Shah Ismail he marched to Turan and assisted Babur against the Uzbegs. Taken a prisoner, he was executed at the orders of Abdullah Khan Uzbeg. The father of Baqir served as the *diwan* of Khurasan. Adverse circumstances forced Baqir to migrate to India. Since he was a youth of merit and promise, he was enrolled with the rank of 300. Jahangir, mindful of his distinguished ancestry and recommendation of Khan Jahan Lodi, promoted him to the rank of 900. Following his marriage to the daughter of Khadija Begum (sister of Nurjahan), fortune smiled on him. Favoured with a rank of 2,000, he was appointed the governor of Multan. Owing to hard work, he imposed the Mughal authority on the tribes—Balochis, Dudiyan and Nahars—dominating the vast area from Multan to Qandhar. Jahangir, out of affection, addressed him as son (*farzand*). After a stint as the governor of Awadh, Baqir was transferred to Orissa. In 1631, he undertook military operations in the tract between Orissa and Telangana, occupying the fort of Mansuragarh after a siege. Next year, he was removed from Orissa following reports of his unjust actions against the inhabitants. After serving in Gujarat and Allahabad, he died in 1637. He was known among his peers for his courage and military skills, particularly his accurate aim in archery. He excelled his contemporaries in letter writing, poetry, prose and calligraphy.[3] The Central Asian traveller Mahmud bin Amir Wali Balkhi, who attended Baqir's court in Kattak (Orissa), attested to his mastery in drafting letters, history and calligraphy, besides a love for music. Baqir's extant works demonstrated a sophisticated style of writing and keen interest in philosophy, mathematics, religion and ethics. Maintaining the traditions of the Mughal nobility, he extended patronage to poets and literateurs and, thus, contributed to the enrichment of Mughal culture.[4]

Baqir's short treatise *Muizah-i Jahangiri*, running into 70 printed pages, was divided into two unequal parts. Each part was fragmented into sections. The first part revolved around the Emperor, while the second was devoted to the nobles. At the outset, Baqir discusses the rationale behind the writing of the work. Stressing the need for political authority, he underscored the role of Prophet Muhammad in developing the Shariat to keep the people on the

192   *Situating Medieval India*

correct path. The kings, as successors of the Prophet, dispensed justice with the power to inflict punishments. Besides bearing personal qualities, the king planned his measures in consultation with his advisors. Among the nobles, the civil administrators were superior to military generals. In addition to honesty and competence, the nobles had to possess high birth. The second portion of the work took the reader by surprise. Here, Baqir was relatively bold in speaking from the perspective of the nobles. The life of a noble was exposed to numerous hazards that were traceable to the shortcomings of the king. These difficulties did not distract the noble. He could acknowledge the benefits attained from royal patronage and the opportunities of doing good for the people. The rampant mutual jealousies led to slander which, in turn, could ruin careers and reputations. A noble expected the king to make a personal judgement of the situation and, thus, evaded malicious tales of motivated rivals. A noble could face difficulties with the help of his friends, though true friendship had become rare. It was appropriate to aspire for material gains in life. Nevertheless, it was advisable to suppress worldly ambitions and, with the practice of contentment, submit to the will of God. What is noteworthy, Baqir articulated these thoughts when he was in the early stages of his career (1612) and the Mughal Empire had not witnessed major developments such as the dominance of Nurjahan's family, the military successes in Kangra and Mewar, the setbacks in Deccan and Qandhar, besides the rebellions of Prince Khurram and Mahabat Khan.

Baqir has invoked the authority of God and Prophet Muhammad in the affairs of humankind. To begin with, God, with His penetrating wisdom and without any assistance, created the universe with the utterance of two words. God perfected this macrocosm by firmly placing man in its centre. Man, however, was the source of both good and evil. God ensured that Prophet Muhammad guided the fallible man, who was often lost in deviance, to the right path of the Shariat. The Prophet, owing to his unique position as the seal of messengers and initiate into divine kindness, ably performed this role. Yet, the wise and intelligent knew that good advice (*sakhan niku*) was a beautiful jewel. It possessed transformative power of

Political Culture in the Mughal Empire   193

turning adulterated copper into pure gold. Since speech was not enough, particularly for limited intellect, the pen fulfilled the need. A person, who was imbued with wisdom and learning, devoted the best part of his life to study good advice and meaningful writings. Though it was difficult to remove ignorance and deviance, good advice could reform the arrogant and stubborn minds. Baqir claimed that he had always been inclined to give an ear to and study good advice. Whenever he could avoid the company of casual friends, he devoted himself to reading sublime words on good advice. In fact, he inscribed them on his mind and, thereafter, desired to write them down. His multifarious engagements did not permit him to realize his object. It was essential for him to attain peace of mind as well as physical privacy. While writing, he added his own thoughts to what he had imbibed from other sources. His book, like a bouquet of flowers, strung the jewels of good advice in an ornament of gold. Entitled *Muizah-i Jahangiri*, it was organized into two parts and comprised a total of ten chapters. The first part laid down exhortations of the emperor, while the second embodied admonitions of subordinates and nobles.[5]

The human race had been classified into many types on the basis of their qualities that were both intrinsic and potential. Individuals did not employ these qualities to gain divine knowledge (*maarifat*). Law (*qanun*) was required to maintain order in worldly affairs, ensure social amity and avoid oppression. For this purpose, God had raised prophets from among humans. These exalted figures, being imbued with special characteristics—worldly intimacy, seclusion and divine grace—guided those who had strayed from the goal of salvation and divine bounty. The prophets instituted the law, known as the Shariat, so that the individual, who faithfully adhered to it, remained immune from divine wrath (*qehar ilahi*) and grievous punishment. The continuum of prophecy reached its culmination in Prophet Muhammad. After him, it became essential to have a wise and powerful ruler who, with his high authority, maintained order and strengthened religion. He endeavoured to generate peace and security for the welfare of humankind. Besides possessing the virtues of justice and uprightness, he refrained from extremes of emotion, particularly anger and sensuality. Such a ruler

194 *Situating Medieval India*

ensured that people avoided illegal acts and, thus, led prosperous and peaceful lives. Imbibing the qualities of Prophet Muhammad, he conducted the political affairs in accordance with the Shariat. He promulgated his policies in accordance with the advice of the theologians (*isharat-i hukma wa kashf-i rumuz-i ulama*). As a result, his kingdom became prosperous and his people attained contentment. In this context, Baqir has paid rich tributes to Jahangir, who has been compared to eminent rulers of Iran and Central Asia such as Faridun, Timur and Jamshed. He was hailed as the fountain of Akbar's deepest hopes. With kindness and beneficence, he performed the obligations of the state, implemented the injunctions of the Shariat and strengthened the foundations of the Muslim community. In particular, he dispensed justice in a manner that the weak and strong lived in fraternal amity. A number of feudatory rulers had accepted his suzerainty, while the masses lived in peace and comfort. Baqir prayed to God for sustaining Jahangir's empire and power, besides ensuring the fulfilment of his desires and aspirations.[6]

In the opening section of his political discourse, Baqir linked imperial power to justice and discipline (*adalat wa siyasat*). In his view, the position of the king was unique. It was attained, not through effort, but with divine assistance, resilient power and good fortune. The king, on his part, recognized the importance of his office. He instituted rules and framed procedures in order to dispense justice.[7] Through his compassion and benevolence, people attained peace and security. A just ruler was the sanctuary of the oppressed and protector of the fallen (*padshah-i adil panah-i mazluman wa dastgir-i uftadgan*). A Prophetic tradition held that an hour of justice outweighed sixty years of worship. If the rule was based on justice, both the kingdom and religion were set on a firm basis. If the parameters of justice were violated, the foundations of the empire were shaken. The commands of the king, owing to its potential for resolving problems, had a direct impact on the life and possessions of the people. The king occupied the throne to dispense justice, not to lead a life of pleasure. Justice ensured the sustenance of rule, the permanence of fame and a reward in the hereafter. Therefore, the king was bound to work for the welfare of

Political Culture in the Mughal Empire 195

the people. He must listen to the petitioners, including peasants, old, weak and poor. He must personally investigate the condition of the oppressed (*haqiqat-i ahwal-i mazluman*) and find solution to their problems. If the king was like a physician, the petitioner was like a patient. A physician could diagnose the disease only after the patient fully explained his condition. Justice, which brought peace and security, was intimately connected with the governmental function of imposing discipline. Only with the authority to inflict punishment, the state power was strengthened, injunctions of the Shariat were implemented and roots of rebellion were eradicated. If the state displayed any weakness in this regard, revolts and disturbances spread everywhere. The king was expected to employ kindness towards the virtuous and divine wrath towards the rebellious. Baqir, while underscoring the parallelism between justice and discipline, suggested a judicious mix of punitive authority with benevolent compassion.[8]

Baqir realized that the connection of kingly power with justice and discipline created an impression of fear and cruelty. In order to soften such an image, he held that the king must possess the virtues of generosity, bravery and forbearance (*sakhawat wa shujaat wa hilm*). A king, through his generosity, gained religious and worldly happiness. The Quran (6: 160) promised tenfold reward for a good deed.[9] To the king, it brought fame, prosperity and success. Seeds of kindness yielded happiness in this world and bounty in the hereafter. The high mindedness of the king strengthened the basis of his power. Baqir, giving precedence to bravery over generosity, did not see the convergence of these two qualities. It was not possible to stabilize kingly power without perfect vigilance, firm determination, robust judgement and sharp sword. In the ultimate analysis, the kingly power, which engendered peace and security, sustained only with the success of the sword. As such, the author has attached more importance to military glory and fair reputation than to material wealth. Heroic warriors preferred the pain of a thousand wounds than the misery of sickness on the bed. However, thinkers underscored the interdependence of generosity, bravery and forbearance. The benefits of generosity were limited to a narrow group of people, who enjoyed state patronage. Similarly,

196   *Situating Medieval India*

bravery became useful only on rare occasions. In contrast, the gains of forbearance percolated among a vast social spectrum comprising the small and big, base and dignified, nobles and commoners, soldiers and peasants. The imperial regulations governing life, property and honour, were equally applicable to lowborn and highborn as well as the ordinary and grandees. The forbearance of the king had a direct impact on the formulation of royal orders. In the absence of this quality, the kings fell into rage and jeopardized the life and property of the people, leading to widespread suffering. It was easy for a king to outclass Hatim and Isfandiyar in generosity and bravery, but he could stifle generosity with a single tyrannical act and raise a thousand mortal enemies.[10] Even if he remained far away from generosity and bravery, he could employ his benevolence to benefit peasantry and soldiers, besides bringing the subjects into a relationship of loyalty and goodwill.[11]

Forbearance, as a laudable quality, had a wide scope. It subsumed the ability to suppress the king's anger and forgive the guilty. The ruler must know the proper time for the use of these faculties. By shedding rage, it was possible to reach the level of truthful ones and accumulate the virtues of ethics and character. The strength of a person could be gauged from his capacity to suppress his rage at the moment of its eruption. Since it was human to commit an error, it was unwise to punish every crime. Since a ruler was endowed with intellect, wisdom and eternal bounty, he was entitled to offer clemency as a matter of grace. The ruler, in order to show his gratitude to God for vesting him with sovereignty and power to inflict punishment, preferred clemency over punitive action. Even if the executon of a person was essential, he must exercise patience. If he executed a person in haste, it was impossible to bring him back to life. He must privilege clemency over retribution. He had to realize that every action, good or bad, resulted in corresponding reward and punishment.[12]

Before undertaking any step, a prudent ruler took recourse to consultation and planning (*mashawarat wa tadbir*). By doing so, he could achieve what an army could not. With ease, he could defeat a kingdom and break an army. Following the Quranic verse (3: 159) 'Consult them in affairs', he built his actions on the

Political Culture in the Mughal Empire 197

planning of perfect ministers and wise counsellors (*tadbir-i waziran-i kamil wa mushiran-i aqil*). Good advice strengthened the king's power and consolidated the empire, leading to peace. A ruler, who ignored advice, lacked circumspection and farsightedness. He was like a patient, who did not follow the advice of the physician, resulting in degeneration of his malady. The planning of several minds was more profitable than that of one mind. When he faced an administrative issue, including the dispatch of a military expedition, he discussed its gains and losses with individuals known for their wisdom, experience and foresight. At the very start of an endeavour, he did not hesitate to consider the possibility of a failure in the end. Since he avoided haste and exercised patience, he achieved success in his campaigns. However, he did not discuss matters of state with everyone. Treating them as secret, he shared them with trustworthy advisors, who were tested for their piety, wisdom and uprightness. If the deliberations were kept secret, even a failed project did not damage the prestige of the state. Baqir has identified seven types of people, who could not be taken into confidence. Generaly speaking, these people were inimical to the ruler for their own reasons. Concluding this piece of advice, Baqir advised the ruler to safeguard his secrets even from himself. If he was unable to keep his secrets, he could not expect the others to do so.[13]

The Mughal rulers faced rebellions from diverse quarters such as princes, nobles, chiefs and intermediaries. Baqir, in his discussion of the subject, did not clearly identify the enemy. Nevertheless, he felt that a wise ruler exercised vigilance against his enemies. Like a small fire that blazed into an inferno, even a weak enemy could grow into a formidable challenge. Most problems could be overcome with an antidote, but the flame of rancour could not be suppressed with the water of seven rivers. A temporary antagonism between two persons could be sorted out. If a new animosity was added to an old tiff (*adawat-i qadim*), it was impossible to reverse it. Such an ominous situation could go only with the end of the two. For the ruler, the remedy lay in circumspection and caution (*hizm wa ihtiyat*). At the outset, he made a careful assessment of the strength of the enemy. He should not underestimate an enemy even if he

198 *Situating Medieval India*

was weak. In addition, he should never trust an enemy. The enemy, assuming humility, could show cordiality and even resort to flattery. The ruler, owing to his alertness, was not be fooled by these postures. The enemy always retained a speck of malice that, like a frozen charcoal, could burst into a mighty flame. The enemy, taking advantage of a minor laxity, often made a surprise attack and left no scope for recovery. The king had no alternative but to overpower and destroy the enemy. He should resort to war only if the enemy was strong enough to spread to other territories and threatened the life of the peasantry, vulnerable and poor.

In case of a powerful enemy, the king tried to avoid military conflict and took recourse to a clever artifice tempered with benevolence. A strong tree could be uprooted from its base with water, whereas a fire would burn only its portion above the soil. The king must avoid undue caution, because it impaired the royal prestige, encouraged the enemy and blocked creative thinking (*charah andeshi*). If the enemy was seen determined to take his life, the king must march to the battlefield for an armed confrontation. If he was victorious, his valour was printed on the pages of time (*safah-i ruzgar*). If he was vanquished, he was still able to assert his manliness and honour. The brave secured the protection and assistance of God, while the enemy stood demoralized. As inscribed in the Quran (2: 249), a small force had often defeated a larger one with God's will.[14]

The state recruited four categories of employees. Though all of them were useful, they performed different functions and, as such, differed from one another in the degree of their importance.[15] At the top, the high-ranking nobles, being men of the sword, defended the frontiers of the kingdom and eradicated the evil of enemies. Next to them were ministers and revenue collectors who, as men of the pen, strengthened the foundations of the state and conducted its administration. They were superior to the wielders of the sword for several reasons. The sword was useful against enemies, while the pen was useful both for benefiting friends and warding off enemies. The people of the sword cultivated the ambition of acquiring sovereignty, while the people of the pen never behaved in this manner. The former emptied the treasury, while the latter

Political Culture in the Mughal Empire 199

replenished it. A successful ruler entrusted the administration and military expeditions to a minister (*wazir*), who was wise, sagacious, selfless, honest and magnanimous. If the minister was unfair and evil minded, the peasantry and people did not benefit from his measures. The third category of employees were the administrators (*hakim*) who, representing the king, punished the strong to protect the weak, besides suppressing the adulterers and sinners. The fourth category of employees were the news reporters. They sent truthful and independent reports to the king regarding the conditions of the country, the conduct of revenue collectors and state of the peasantry. If the news was concealed from the king, disturbances arose everywhere and foundations of the empire were shaken. Therefore, the king was advised to train a group of people, who were distinguished for wisdom, knowledge, honesty, integrity, dutifulness, piety and loyalty. He should not assign two offices to one person, as every individual was capable of doing only one job.[16] He must personally investigate the conduct of revenue collectors (*ummal wa aminan*) with reference to their treatment of the peasantry. In the training of the employees, he must employ a judicious mix of kindness and severity. In grooming and supporting the nobility, he must accord a special place to each of them. Avoiding raising one of them as his partner or equal (*sharik wa sahim*), he must encourage harmony among them and discouraged conflict.[17]

An employee was expected to possess a host of qualities that were associated with his professional competence and moral character. The rulers, while selecting an employee, focused on three of them— honest actions, truthful speech and pure lineage. Baqir has discussed the last one in detail. He advised the ruler to refrain from according an equal treatment (*maqam-i barabari*) to the lowborn and highborn employees, as he associated the former with incompetence. As a principle in the laws of the kingdom and rules of governance, he must maintain a difference in their ranks (*tafawat-i maratib*). If the lowborn were placed in equality with the middling and middling with the highborn, it would undermine the prestige of kingship and cause confusion among the nobles. Because of this, the past rulers did not allow the mean and lowborn (*mardam-i faromaya bad asl*) to learn calligraphy, accounts and arithmetic. If

200 *Situating Medieval India*

the trend acquired permanence and artisans entered the ranks of aristocrats (*arbab-i hirfat maarz-i ashab-i daulat*), the economic resources of the select and ordinary were disturbed. Apart from the requirements of the job, the king paid attention to the purity of lineage and high calibre (*asl-i pak wa himmat-i aali*). A lowly person, being miserly, did not recognize the value of favours and rewards.[18] He turned the king away from generosity and prevented him from bestowing favours on others. The one, without claims to high lineage, was not destined for high office. The one, who possessed purity of lineage, was endowed with virtues and was free from mean tendencies. Such a person combined the qualities of righteousness, integrity and loyalty. The king was advised to promote such a person, so that he gradually reached the rank of nearness to the king and authority and, as a result, his dignity was firmly established in the eyes and hearts.[19]

Astute rulers, making keen enquiries, chose employees who were learned, competent and skillful. They did not patronize the wicked and mean, as they could not bring uprightness and integrity to their work.[20] Though it was nearly impossible to reform such people, the rulers did not entirely deprive them of royal favours, lest they should abandon the job and turn towards the enemy. The ruler, resorting to ambiguity, placed them between fear and hope as well as between promises and deception. It was true that the highly placed nobles undertook military campaigns. Yet, an ordinary retainer, who appeared insignificant and powerless, could be of some use to his master. The ruler perpetually tried to increase the sheer number of his employees, ranging from nobles to attendants. Once he patronized a person, he should not humiliate him. In case of any indiscretion, the ruler must have firm evidence before taking any action. The ruler should not pay any attention to what the employees spoke about one another. They must overlook minor faults and offer forgiveness, particularly in case of ordinary people. They must not reverse their decisions and, if it was necessary, they must allow a gap between two orders. If they bestowed undue favours on a noble in terms of rank, wealth and prestige, it had to be rectified at the earliest, lest the noble should resort to sedition. In view of the political uncertainty, a ruler was advised to organize

Political Culture in the Mughal Empire 201

his army, which must always be equipped for war. Since this was an outstanding duty, he must stress its need to the nobles and ministers. He must assign proper rank and corresponding assignment (*mansab wa jagir*) to every noble, so that he was able to maintain the requisite number of soldiers. Every year, he must inspect his own troops and the contingents of nobles. The ruling class could not be obsessed with accumulating wealth at the cost of maintaining a well-provided army.[21]

In the Mughal Empire, the ruler and nobles were associated with ruthless authority, unlimited wealth and dazzling magnificence.[22] However, Baqir has drawn our attention to the seamy side of kingly power and the perils of imperial service. He has gone to the extent of associating royal privileges with evils like wine, women and scoundrels that invariably resulted in disgrace. A person, hoping to benefit from imperial service, was mistaken because, in reality, he was helpless (*bechara*). The position of a noble in relation to the king was vulnerable. This was due to the inherent defects in the king himself. His promises were unreliable, while his goodwill was shaky. His generosity and grace were mixed with spite and deceit. He had no regard for sincerity, friendship and previous service. Associating with the king was like planting seeds in a marshy land in the hope of a harvest (*umid-i mahsul tukhm dar zamin-i shora*). Since an employee remained in fear and doubt, he felt as if he was sleeping with a panther and dwelling with a lion (*ham khwabah palang wa ham khanah sher*). He saw contradictions in the decisions of the king, who rewarded the criminals and harassed the competent. The king was not grateful to individuals, who surrendered their entire wealth to the royal coffers. Once a noble gained proximity to the king, he faced the hostility of his friends and enemies. His friends became jealous of his rise, while his enemies resented his increasing role in the state affairs. He felt depressed at the contrast between the arbitrariness and injustice of the worldly court and the benevolence and grace of the divine court.[23]

Baqir has laid down his advice to the noble on the manner he could cope with a master, whose actions betrayed contradictions. At this point, he appeared to have reversed his stance. In spite of his vulnerability, a noble was not advised to shun imperial service.

He could not overlook the gains he and his relatives had made in terms of favours, fame and honour. In return for these benefits, he was bound to serve the king with sincerity and integrity, even to the extent of putting his life at stake for the fair name of his patron. He must abstain from greed, bribery, lies, flattery and rudeness. He must politely warn the king if he felt that an enterprise would end in failure. He must continue his efforts until the decision was changed. He must identify the gains likely to flow from an administrative measure. He must bring home to the king the damages accruing from tyranny and beneficence emanating from justice. Using all possible means, he must collect information about the state employees and communicate it to the king. On the other hand, the king, becoming familiar with the integrity and wisdom of the employees, could benefit from their services and patronize them in accordance with their abilities. The noble was expected to recommend the case of a person only after testing him several times, besides having absolute trust in him. Since his proximity to the king was transient, he could not be arrogant about his position. He must not be disturbed and angry at the perpetual appeals of the needy at his door. His position gave him an opportunity of doing good to the people and his subordinates. Taking advantage of his access to the imperial court, he could pass on the gains of benevolence to both the high and low. Through his good deeds, he brought acclaim to his master, prosperity to the country and contentment to the masses (*neknami sahib wa abadani mamlikat wa khushnudi khalaiq*). In return, he would find happiness in this world and blessings in the next. The king, impressed with his conduct, would raise his prestige and seek personal intimacy with him. Even after his demise, his name would be commemorated in the pages of time.[24]

Baqir has made it incumbent on the king to hold consultations with his advisors on all important matters. He needed to distinguish between nobles who were to be consulted and those who were to be shunned. The advice of the former, who constituted only a small group, was based on their concern for the welfare of the state. With loyalty and integrity, they endeavoured to earn a good name for their master and his salvation in the hereafter. A majority of

Political Culture in the Mughal Empire 203

employees remained in service for personal ends. Owing to their greed and the difference in their dignity and rank (*kam wa besh-i izzat wa mansab*), they developed jealousy with one another and reported incidents that never occurred. If the king did not investigate the matters, a number of disturbances arose. A vigilant ruler who, wholly or partly investigated the matter, separated truth from false-hood, secured the foundations of his empire and attained salvation in the hereafter. If he failed to probe the facts and listened to the slander of accusers, the king and the nobles lost credibility. In such a situation, the innocent were annihilated, while the offenders remained safe. As a result, those present declined administrative tasks and those absent refused to serve. There could be numerous confusions, while the foundations of the empire were uprooted. Baqir, speaking on the authority of the learned, advised the ruler to avoid five types of people—envious, greedy, traitors, talkative and slanderers—who damaged the political system in different ways. A just ruler, imbued with clear judgement and sharp intellect, subjected all reports to careful scrutiny. In no case should he permit a person to speak ill of others. He should consider what people say only if they were supported with evidence. When a noble gained nearness to the king, his rivals resorted to various tricks to spoil his honour. Displaying a fake concern for the welfare of the state, they did not rest till they had alienated the ruler from that noble. The king was confused, while the country was pushed into violence. At the earliest, the king must eradicate the evil of slander with his sword. In view of the potential loss, there could be no scope for forgiveness.[25]

Baqir has explored the nature of friendship, particularly from the standpoint of the Mughal nobles. The learned thinkers had privileged association (*sohbat*) over solitude (*khilwat*). If one could not find a companion, who was virtuous, affectionate and caring, one could take to isolation, which was difficult to endure. Sincere friends were the most valuable form of wealth. Since their status was higher than all others, their companionship was superior to all pleasures. It was advisable to have as many friends as possible. Wise people had always associated with one another and, with honest intent and pure hearts, tried to bring this relation to fruition.

204   *Situating Medieval India*

Both during prosperity and adversity, the meaning of true friendship became evident. In difficult times, they stood by each other and enabled each other to return to happier existence. They nurtured their friendship with mutual amity. It was advisable to make friends with people who were knowledgeable, virtuous and selfless. Such friends covered up one's mistakes and offered critical advice. It was proper to avoid friendship with people who were immoral, foolish and liars. They circulated false stories about others and their advice turned out to be harmful. According to a famous proverb, a wise enemy was more advantageous than a foolish friend. The former, owing to wisdom, struck his adversary at a time when one could discern his hostility and thus defend oneself against it. Since the latter was bereft of wisdom, his conduct was unhelpful in managing any important matter. Because of the unsound advice of this person, one was likely to be entangled in a perilous situation. In view of the varying impact of different types of people, they had been compared to food, medicine and pain. Baqir has advised his reader to associate with the learned, virtuous and pious, as their company brought innumerable benefits. In contrast, he was advised to shun the illiterate, ignoble and vile, as their company brought nothing but degradation.[26]

Baqir, writing in a tone of disappointment, believed that true friendship had become rare. It was difficult to find a person who was endowed with selflessness, reliability and fidelity. Since most people were unpredictable, the quality of faithfulness was as scarce as the mythical bird (*simurgh*). It was nearly impossible to find a person, who kept his promise and remained true to his words. One who looked for support from such people exposed himself to danger. A person worthy of friendship was known from the nature of his relationships. He identified a shortcoming in a manner that it was eradicated. He repeatedly highlighted the abilities that he found in his friends. When he did a favour to his friends, he did not remember it and, when he received a favour, he did not forget it. If he saw a flaw in his friend, he did not snap the relation, but accepted an apology. His friendship was based on selflessness and truthfulness. The companionship with such a person conferred a number of privileges. It removed the sadness in one's heart. The basic attributes of his friendship were fidelity, sincerity and steadfast-

Political Culture in the Mughal Empire 205

ness. Faithfulness, in terms of excellence, was as charming as the black mole on the cheek of a beauty. In contrast, the marks of hypocrisy and faithlessness were discernible in contemptible people. Same was true of people who broke promises and made excuses. Individuals, possessing manliness and accomplishments, became friends with ease and turned opponents with difficulty. People, associated with meanness, took a long time to be friends, while their friendship was fragile. A wise person distinguished between friendship that was free from a selfish motive and one that was built on momentary opportunism. One must make every effort to strengthen the former type of friendship and, after an extended association, ask about one's flaws. The enumeration of one's drawbacks must be viewed as a favour. The gesture deserved warm reciprocation. It was advisable to be friendly with the friend of a friend and, by the same reason, it was proper to refrain from mingling with the enemy of a friend.[27]

Baqir, while elaborating the difference between wealth and poverty, drew attention to their respective features and consequences. In general, people aspired for plenty of wealth, promotion in rank and salvation in the hereafter. With the help of wealth, one could acquire the means of pleasure and social prestige. Wealth bestowed courage, polished opinions and supported power. In contrast, poverty deprived the poor man of worldly pleasures and salvation in the next world.[28] A Prophetic tradition held that poverty was a disgrace on one's face in both the worlds. A poor man resorted to unlawful means to earn his livelihood and, as a result, received punishment in this world and disgrace in the next. Poverty was the root cause of all afflictions. A poor man did not attract any friend. His desires remained unrealized, while his tasks failed to reach completion. Removing the mask of shame, poverty destroyed grace and accumulated evils. Instead of vigour and happiness, a poor man earned suffering and dejection. Losing his intelligence and wisdom, he became a target of allegations. Every quality, which brought praise for the rich, evoked condemnation for the poor. If a poor man aspired to ameliorate his condition, the rich despised him as greedy. Still, he need not despair, as his remedy lay in struggle (*jad wa jehd ra dakhli azim ast*). Giving up laziness and taking courage in both hands, he fixed high targets for himself.

206 *Situating Medieval India*

Only by toiling hard and facing hardships, he attained the goals of wealth and honour. If it was impossible to achieve his objective in his own country, he must travel to another land. It was agonizing to separate from loved ones. Yet, it was travelling that opened for him the opportunities of advancement, besides making him tough, disciplined and refined. Hard work was the occupation of the brave. When he settled to an orderly life and acquired wealth, the others sought his friendship. Here, Baqir appeared to be drawing on his own struggle, comprising his journey from Persia, teething troubles in the Mughal service, his promotion through the ranks and, finally, proximity to the ruling family.[29]

Baqir, conscious of the mismatch between human aspirations and ultimate frustrations, tried to offer remedies. Since eternity, divine will has determined the course of events on earth. What God inscribes in the destiny of a man, it was manifested in his lifetime. Man, howsoever learned and ingenious, could not undo the decree of destiny. Unless God's will was in his favour, he could not get the reward for his endeavours. For this reason, knowledgeable persons, who deserved wealth, have been forced to starve, while ignorant individuals had attained honourable positions. There was no choice but submitting to the divine ordinances. Owing to man's imperfect capabilities, he could not see the mysterious functioning of the divine power. On deep reflection, he found his welfare in conforming to divine dictates. A wise man, with gratitude and cheerfulness, accepted the divinely ordained afflictions. Discarding the pervasive evil of greed, he was not attracted to the transient worldly riches and grandeur. Real wealth comprised the assets he deposited in the hereafter such as fair speech, praiseworthy actions, pious character and decent manners. He suppressed the demands of his carnal soul and embraced the virtue of contentment. He did not desire more than what God had apportioned in his name. The joys and sorrows were transient. A wise man did not rejoice at the bestowal of an honorific robe. Nor did he grieve at a monetary loss. People who acquired huge amounts of wealth remained sad. They could attain a high stature even with sparse material possessions. If they pursued their carnal soul, they showed evils of bitterness, jealousy, cruelty, deceit, arrogance and hypocrisy. They were advised

Political Culture in the Mughal Empire   207

to seek solace in solitude and seclusion, as they brought greater benefits than associating with people.[30]

Baqir has concluded his political discourse on a mystical note. He compared the world to an inn, which was ephemeral and harsh. Its pleasures were mixed with sorrow. The life of every creature was amenable to death. This pattern conformed to the Quranic verse (28: 88), whereby all living things perished except God's own face. The world was like a wicked old woman, who was dressed like a new bride.[31] With numerous outward adornments, she ensnared the immature and unwise people, who could not fulfil their desires even for one night. People, who were wise and insightful, did not fall into her malicious trap. They understood that their life, passing through youth and old age, culminated in a sudden and inevitable death. In these circumstances, Baqir argued, one must realize the worth of life and value every moment of it. Since the past could not be retrieved and the future was unknown, the present was both relevant and priceless. Discarding negligence and ignorance, one should not waste even a moment in frivolous pursuits. He must suppress carnal desires, besides abandoning the obsession with wealth, power and dignity. Keeping himself busy day and night, he must repent his faulty priorities and compensate himself for the loss of time. He must devote the remaining part of his life to submission, devotion and austerities. He must strive for acquiring a fresh set of virtues—intellectual accomplishments, moral uprightness, purification of the soul and accumulating rewards for the next world (*talb-i fazail wa tahsil-i kamalat wa tahzib-i akhlaq wa tazkia-i nafs wa ihraz-i sawab-i akhirat*). As a traveller on the path of spirituality, he distanced himself from the material world and prefered a journey into the next world. As the Quran insisted, he was no longer misguided like the cattle.[32]

NOTES

1. Abul Fazl, while developing the theme, derived inspiration from within the Islamic tradition—Unity of Existence (*wahdat ul-wujud*) and Perfect Man (*insan-i kamil*) from Ibn Arabi, symbolism of the sun from the Ishraqi

208 *Situating Medieval India*

philosophy of Shihabuddin Suhrawardi Maqtul and the theory of great spiritual souls from the Nuqtawi theoretician Mahmud Pasikhani. Advocating the necessity of political authority, Abul Fazl appealed to a theory of social contract. The human nature, owing to intrinsic failings, generated disturbances and injustice. A just ruler, being the recipient of divine light, employed terror to remedy the situation. For this purpose, he maintained an army, treasury and resources for grandeur. The people paid wages of protection (*dast muzd-i pasbani*) to the king for protecting their property, life, honour and religion. Irfan Habib, 'A Political Theory for the Mughal Empire: A Study of the Ideas of Abul Fazl', *Proceedings of the Indian History Congress*, 59th session, Patiala, 1998, pp. 331-2.

2. Muzaffar Alam, *The Languages of Political Islam in India: c. 1200-1800*, Delhi: Permanent Black, 2004, pp. 54-61.

3. Shaikh Farid Bhakkari, *Zakhirat ul-Khwanin*, vol. II, Persian text, ed. Syed Moinul Haq, Karachi: Pakistan Historical Society, 1970, pp. 354-5; Shah Nawaz Khan and Abdul Hayy, *Maasir ul-Umara*, vol. I, Eng tr., H. Beveridge and Baini Prashad, Kolkata: The Asiatic Society, rpt., 2003, pp. 385-8.

4. Muhammad Baqir Najm-i Sani, *Muizah-i Jahangiri*, Persian text, with Introduction, Translation and Notes, Sajida Sultana Alavi (entitled *Advice on the Art of Governance*), Albany: State University of New York Press, 1989, p. 12. (Hereafter cited as Baqir).

5. Ibid., pp. 139-44.

6. Ibid., pp. 144-5.

7. Abul Fazl has drawn a distinction between a pious ruler and selfish one. Both possessed abundant treasury, army, material resources, servants, workmen and subjects. In case of the former, these possessions were durable and led to beneficial results such as security, health, chastity, justice, polite manners, faith, truth and sincerity. Since the latter was bound to external forms of royal power, there was insecurity, oppression, strife and robbery. The former, having received divine light (*farr-i izadi*), directly from God, possessed qualities of paternal love for his subjects, large heart, increasing trust in God, besides prayer and devotion. Free from sectarianism, his actions were based on reason and wisdom. He was averse to infliction of violence and ensured that there was no injustice in his kingdom. Abul Fazl Allami, *Ain-i Akbari*, vol. I, Eng. tr., H. Blochmann and D.C. Phillot, Kolkata: The Asiatic Society, rpt., 2010, pp. 2-5.

8. Baqir, pp. 147-9.

9. According to this Quranic verse (6:160), 'Whosoever brings a good deed shall have ten times the like thereof; but whosoever brings an evil deed shall

Political Culture in the Mughal Empire 209

be recompensed only with the like thereof, and they shall not be wronged.' It is one of the several verses indicating God's leniency in judging human actions and His great bounty towards them, multiplying the reward for good deeds, while recompensing evil deeds equitably. Similar verses (4:40, 27:89 and 28:84) indicate that multiplication of good deeds is a manifestation of Divine Bounty, while the equitable recompense of evil deeds manifests Divine Justice. Seyyed Hossein Nasr et al., *The Study Quran: A New Translation and Commentary*, New York: Harper One, 2015, pp. 401-2.

10. Baqir, pp. 150-3.
11. Jahangir and Shahjahan, in their conversations with Miyan Mir, received advice on the functions of the monarchical state. The Qadiri exemplar of Lahore refused to enrol Jahangir as a disciple because his rule was necessary for the care of humankind (*pasbani-i khalq allah*) and his justice enabled the saints to engage in spiritual pursuits. Speaking to Shahjahan, he admitted that the king occupied a unique position (*mazhar khas*) in the society, though a mystic was sovereign in the spiritual domain. It was imperative for just rulers (*padshahan adil*) to attend to the welfare of the peasantry (*raiyyat*) and empire (*mamlikat*). If the peasantry was contended and country flourishing, the army remained peaceful and treasury abundant (*sipah asuda wa khazana mamur ast*). When he performed a good deed, which brought happiness to the Muslims, he must pray to God without expecting anything for himself. Dara Shukoh, *Sakinat ul-Auliya*, Persian text, ed. Tara Chand and Syed Razazada Jalali Naini, Tehran: Muassasa-i Matbuat-i Ilmi, 1963, pp. 46-8.
12. Baqir, pp. 153-5.
13. Ibid., pp. 156-60.
14. Ibid., pp. 161-4.
15. Abul Fazl was the first to propose that the body politic comprised four categories of officers. Organized in a hierarchical order, their functions were comparable to fire, wind, water and earth. The nobles fought in the battlefield and headed the departments of paymaster, court ceremonies, correspondence, stables and forests. The second category of officers was expert in accounts and records, thereby handling the financial departments. The third category of officers was known for its learning and wisdom. Apart from being the companions of the Emperor, it served as judges, physicians and astronomers. Lastly, the servants provided domestic services in the royal household. In the eyes of Abul Fazl, this fourfold classification in the body politic was parallel to a fourfold division of the Indian society, wherein he identified the warriors, the artificers and merchants,

210 *Situating Medieval India*

the learned, and the husbandmen and labourers. Abul Fazl, *Ain-i Akbari*, vol. I, pp. 4-7.

16. The problem of governmental appointments was not new. Nizam ul-Mulk Tusi (1018-92), the famous Seljuqid *wazir*, applied his mind to it. According to him, the enlightened kings and astute ministers never gave two posts to one man or one post to two men. In case a man was given two appointments, he performed one task with dedication and neglected the other. The trend also led to unemployment. When two men were assigned a single post, each tended to shift his responsibility on the other. Both shrank from hard work, feeling that the credit could go to the other person. When the two were asked to explain the unsatisfactory results, each tended to excuse himself and put the blame on the other. The confusion could not be attributed to the two employees. Rather, the fault lay with the superior authority, who made the appointments in the first place. Nizam ul-Mulk Tusi, *Siyasatnama*, Eng. tr., Hubert Darke (entitled *The Book of Government or Rules for Kings*), Richmond, Surrey: Curzon Press, rpt., 2002, pp. 158-9.

17. Baqir, pp. 168-70.

18. Baqir, who was endowed with a scholarly mind, could not have been ignorant of Ziauddin Barani's *Tarikh-i Firoz Shahi* and *Fatawa-i Jahandari*. In the first work, Barani approved Iltutmish and Balban for excluding the lowborn from state services, while castigating Muhammad bin Tughluq for giving high posts to men belonging to menial castes. In his second work, Barani was even more categorical on the subject. In his view, God ordained the highborn to adopt noble professions and, consequently, possessed all virtues. The lowborn, being ordained to adopt baser avocations, possessed all vices. If they were appointed to government jobs based on their intelligence and ability, they would fail to perform the tasks and, thus, discredit the ruler in both the worlds. The lowborn must be kept away from education, lest they should become governors, revenue collectors and auditors. The teachers who dared to teach them deserved punishment. Ziauddin Barani, *Fatawa-i Jahandari*, Eng. tr., Mohammad Habib and Afsar Umar Salim Khan, Allahabad: Kitab Mahal, n.d., pp. 49, 98-100.

19. Baqir, pp. 170-1.

20. Under Akbar, the imperial discipleship, comprising the divine faith with four degrees of devotion (*ikhlas-i chahargana*), was employed to create an exceptionally loyal and reliable cadre of nobles, carefully screened and recruited to form a body of life guards. Every week, a substantial body of men was inducted in groups of 12 into an intense relation with the person of the Emperor. Jahangir perpetuated the practice. In his first regnal year, he chose Shaikh Ahmad Lahori, the Mir Adl, to recommend persons worthy

Political Culture in the Mughal Empire   211

of receiving the seal ring (*shast*) and likeness (*shaba*) of the king. Mirza Nathan, who served in Bengal with his father Ihtimam Khan, frequently mentioned Jahangir as his spiritual master and treated the imperial service as greater than the worship of God. In response to Nathan's petition for enlistment as a disciple, Jahangir sent the two symbols through a messenger. John F. Richards, 'The Formation of Imperial Authority under Akbar and Jahangir', in *The Mughal State 1526-1750*, ed. Muzaffar Alam and Sanjay Subrahmanyam, Delhi: Oxford University Press, 1998, pp. 150-7.

21. Baqir, pp. 172-7.

22. The *mansabdars*, forming the ruling class of the Mughal Empire, included entire nobility, bureaucracy and military hierarchy. Between 1596 and 1657, there was a massive increase in numbers of *mansabdars* in all grades. The word noble (*amir*) was applicable to those holding the rank of 1,000 and above. During the later part of Jahangir's reign (1621), the number of those holding medium ranks (500 to 900) was 70, those holding high ranks (1,000 to 4,500) was 148 and those holding the highest ranks (5,000) and above was 24. Under Akbar, all *mansabdars*, i.e. 1671 accounted for 82 per cent of estimated revenue (*jama*). In other words, 487 top ones controlled 66.69 per cent of estimated revenue. Under Akbar, the top 25 claimed 30.29 per cent of estimated revenue, while under Shahjahan this figure was 24.3 per cent. M. Athar Ali, *The Mughal Nobility under Aurangzeb*, Aligarh: Centre of Advanced Study in History, AMU and Bombay: Asia Publishing House, rpt., 1970, pp. 7-9; M. Athar Ali, *The Apparatus of Empire: Awards of Ranks, Offices and Titles to the Mughal Nobility (1574-1658)*, Aligarh: Centre of Advanced Study in History, AMU and Delhi: OUP, 1985, p. xx; Shireen Moosvi, *The Economy of the Mughal Empire c. 1595: A Statistical Study*, Aligarh: Centre of Advanced Study in History, AMU and Delhi: OUP, 1987, pp. 221-3.

23. Baqir, pp. 177-9.

24. Ibid., pp. 179-82.

25. Ibid., pp. 165-7.

26. Ibid., pp. 183-5

27. Ibid., pp. 186-90.

28. Nazir Akbarabadi (1740-1830), the popular poet of Agra, has examined the impact of poverty. A great curse, it did not spare anyone on grounds of profession, religion and gender. A number of professionals—physicians, teachers, painters, musicians, dancing girls and prostitutes—lost their patronage, status and dignity. No one paid any regard to the abilities and birth of a poor man. His house was in a dilapidated state, as its bricks had crumbled and chains sold away. There was no fuel in the hearth and no

water in the pitcher. An atmosphere of mourning prevailed in the house. Being out of job, he faced humiliation at every step. At the public distribution of free food, he was not given enough to eat. At the marriage of his children, he was unable to provide dowry and pay tips to petty servants. When there was a death in his family, he could not provide a decent burial and, therefore, consigned the dead body to the river. In the end, he was forced to adopt beggary, while his son became a thief. Surinder Singh, 'Socio-Religious Ideas in North Western India during the Eighteenth Century: Analysing the Verses of three Major Poets', Sardar Mahan Singh Dhesi Annual Lecture, 2014, *Journal of Regional History*, vol. XX, 2014, pp. 16-17.

29. Baqir, pp. 191-7.
30. Ibid., pp. 198-202.
31. In South Asia, prominent spiritual masters, who were rooted in diverse traditions, condemned materialism. They saw it as the anti-thesis of spirituality. Bu Ali Qalandar perceived the world as an old woman, who trapped the young and old through deceit. Hazrat Ali divorced her and ruled over the Prophet's kingdom. In contrast, Yazid married her and destroyed true religion. Kabir saw the world as a prostitute, who appeared beautiful and displayed seductive charms. A poisonous serpent, her blandishments had conquered the three worlds, won over the trinity of gods, destroyed great kings and colluded with five passions. Only the saints, having received God's grace, recognized her evil ways and remained immune from her influence. Shah Sharfuddin Bu Ali Shah Qalandar, *Masnavi*, ed. Muhammad Muslim Ahmad Nizami, Delhi: Kutubkhana Nazirriyya, 1964, pp. 14-15; Manmohan Singh, *Sri Guru Granth Sahib*, Text with Eng. and Pbi. tr., Amritsar: Shiromani Gurdwara Prabandhak Committee, rpt., 1982, pp. 480, 871-2.
32. Ibid., pp. 203-5.

CHAPTER 9

A Central Asian Visitor at the Mughal Court: Meetings of Mutribi Samarqandi with Emperor Jahangir

Maulana Mutribi al-Asamm Samarqandi, who visited Lahore in 1626, has left a record of his 24 conversations with Jahangir.[1] Born in 1559 in Samarqand, he acquired the knowledge of traditional Islamic subjects in the city. His heart was drawn to poetry and music. He went to Bukhara, where he began learning the craft of composing verses from Khwaja Hasan Nisari. Having developed a keen interest in music, he learnt to play on the flute (*nai*) and harp (*qanun*). With a view to perfect his musical skills, he took lessons from a number of specialists, including Kamaluddin Hafiz Abdul Rahim. Thereafter, he blossomed as a talented poet and, bearing the pseudonym of 'Mutribi', meaning minstrel, he earned a fair reputation in the literary circles and ruling elite of Transoxiana. In 1604, working under the patronage of the ruler Wali Muhammad Khan, he produced an anthology of poets entitled *Tazkirat ul-Shuara*. Following the death of his patron in 1612, he found it difficult to meet the needs of a 20-member family.

Mutribi's search for alternative sources of patronage turned his attention to India, where the Mughal State had been generous in encouraging different forms of art. He resolved to try his luck at the Mughal court. Since he could not embark on this enterprise empty-handed, he prepared a fresh account of poets to be presented to Jahangir. In 1622, he travelled to Balkh, Taliqan, Faizabad and Qunduz. At these places, he met several poets and collected information about their lives and specimens of their poetry. The resultant

214 *Situating Medieval India*

work, *Nuskha Zeba-i Jahangir*, contained notices of 292 poets. A manuscript of this work, wrongly labelled as *Tarikh-i Jahangiri*, has been preserved in the India Office Library and Records, London. Abdul Ghani Mirzoyef, Tajikistan academician, discovered the mistake regarding this large compilation. He also recognized the autonomous character of the smaller appendix comprising a record of Mutribi's 24 meetings with Jahangir and went on to prepare its text under the title of *Khatirat-i Mutribi Samarqandi*. The Institute of Central and West Asian Studies, University of Karachi, Karachi, has published the text along with a short introduction. The distinguished historian Riazul Islam drew my attention to this work and graciously sent a copy to me.

The visit of Mutribi might be placed in the context of the multifarious relations between the Mughal State and Central Asia. The former, in a quest for legitimacy, associated itself with Timur. For the Mughal rulers, Sharfuddin Ali Yazdi's *Zafarnama*, the official history of Timur, was a favourite text. Abul Fazl perceived Timur as the forerunner of Akbar. In several Mughal paintings, the Mughal Emperors were portrayed as receiving their crown from Timur.[2] During the second half of Akbar's reign (1575-95), the Turanis formed the largest ethnic group (39 per cent or 64 out of 184) among the nobles holding ranks from 500 to 5,000 and above.[3] During the later part of Jahangir's reign (1621), this proportion fell to approximately 20 per cent, owing to the relative increase in the proportion of the Iranis and Afghans.[4] During the reign of Akbar, the Mughals and Uzbeks recognized the Hindukush as the border between them. Jahangir, in view of internal strife in Transoxiana following the death (1598) of Abdullah Khan Uzbek, toyed with the idea of conquering that region. In 1621, the rising Safavid power induced the Mughals and Uzbeks to restore diplomatic relations. In 1624-5, the Mughals defeated two Uzbek invasions on Kabul, forcing the adversaries to seek friendship. Nazr Muhammad Khan and Imam Quli Khan sent their envoys, Shah Khwaja and Khwaja Abdur Rahim, to the Mughal court. Jahangir received them with all marks of courtesy.[5] Mutribi, arriving at Lahore in these circumstances, claimed association with Imam Quli Khan, though its exact nature remained unknown.

A Central Asian Visitor at the Mughal Court   215

The India-Central Asia overland highway, passed through Lahore and Kabul. Beyond Kabul, seven different routes led to Samarqand and Bukhara. Trips were made from mid-April to mid-November, avoiding the heavy snows on the Hindukush passes. Indian exports included bulky staples such as sugar, indigo, tobacco and cotton textiles. The imports included horses, silk, fresh and dried fruit.[6] Ruling elite of India and Central Asia shared a common interest in Persian poetry and devotion to the Naqshbandis. Mughal histories often concluded with a list of poets and specimens of their verses. Two Mughal poet laureates, Faizi and Talib Amuli, attained universal repute for their prolific poetry. Faizi produced a *diwan* of 9,000 verses and a *khamsa* of five narrative poems including Nal-Daman and Sulaiman Bilquis. In prose, he wrote a voluminous un-dotted commentary on the Quran and collaborated in translating Sanskrit classics into Persian.[7] Talib Amuli, following a chequered career in Persia, came to India (1607) and earned the patronage of Chin Qulich Khan, Abdullah Khan Firoz Jang and Itimad ud-Daulah. In a ceremony (1619) at Kalanaur, Jahangir nominated him as the poet laureate. His poetry, marked with features of eloquence and elegance, employed musical language and novel imagery.[8] In this ambience, a number of Central Asian poets—Nadiri Samarqandi, Qasim Arsalan, Wasili Marwi, Abdul Karim Qazi, Sahmi Bukhari and Niyazi Samarqandi—flourished under Mughal patronage.[9] Mushfiqi, who received many favours from Akbar during his two sojourns, was seen as a Salman of the age for his panegyrics (*qasidahs*) and noted for the subtle tone of his satires.[10]

The Mughal rulers were devoted to the lineages of Naqshbandi masters, who were identified as Ahrar, Dahbidi and Juebari. The Mughal State gave military ranks and administrative posts to the descendants of these families. Abdul Rahim Juebari, coming to India as the ambassador of Imam Quli Khan, received unprecedented honour from Jahangir. More than once, he figured in the Emperor's conversations with Mutribi, who also arrived in Lahore at precisely the same time. Coincidentally, another Central Asian traveller Mahmud bin Amir Wali Balkhi was already in the midst of his Indian odyssey.[11] However, the Mughal State was not in the best of its political health. Its credibility had eroded due to military

216 *Situating Medieval India*

setbacks in Deccan and Qandhar, besides the rebellion of Khurram. Though Jahangir emerged unscathed from the custody of Mahabat Khan, his health was impaired due to the consumption of alcohol and opium. He died (28 October 1627) shortly after the departure of Mutribi.

We must hasten to note that Mutribi's memoirs were not the first of their kind. Abdul Sattar had already compiled a record of Jahangir's 113 nocturnal assemblies (*shabnamchah*) held from 1608 to 1611. During the late sixteenth and early seventeenth centuries, the compiler assumed the role of a cultural broker. In collaboration with Jeronimo Xavier, he produced a series of Persian works that aimed at familiarizing the Mughal elite of the Greco-Roman and Christian foundations of European culture. In addition, he participated in the initial stages of the composition of *Jawidan-i Khirad* (Eternal Wisdom), the first Persian translation of Ibn Miskawayh's *al-Hikmat al-Khalida*, an anthology of maxims from Greek, Iranian, Indian and Arabic traditions. He had written an abridged version (*Guzidah-i Zafarnama*) of Sharfuddin Ali Yazdi's biography of Timur (*Zafarnama*). Interestingly, Jahangir himself had commissioned these two works. Regarding Abdul Sattar's record of Jahangir's assemblies (*Majalis-i Jahangiri*), it becomes evident that the Emperor presided over the gatherings, comprising nobles, ambassadors, poets and dignitaries recently arrived from Iran and Central Asia, besides religious specialists ranging from Brahmins and Muslim theologians to Jesuit and Jewish scholars. The themes, while excluding major political events, focused on literature, religion, history and science. The discussions were highly codified. No one was supposed to intervene unless requested by Jahangir, who acted as the ultimate arbiter. In the Islamic court culture, the meetings were conceived as a essential attribute of sovereignty and, simultaneously, functioned as instruments for acquisition of knowledge and entertainment, besides providing a stage for royal patronage. The compilation portrayed Jahangir as a spiritual master. It was a record of his spiritual discourses (*malfuzat*) meant for the small circle of his newly enrolled disciples. In form and function, the *Majalis-i Jahangiri*, was a dialogical text, which was built on the literary traditions of disputation (*munazara*) and Sufi teachings (*malfuzat*). Jahangir

A Central Asian Visitor at the Mughal Court 217

treated three countries—Iran, Turan and Hindustan—on different planes. He adopted an attitude of superiority towards the Safavids, but paid little attention to the Astrakhanids. Neutral towards the peculiarities of Hinduism, he took credit for domesticated native martial tribes.[12]

The drafts of Abdul Sattar's compilation were first read out to Mirza Aziz Koka, so that the choicest episodes could be included in Jahangir's memoirs. The Emperor periodically saw the drafts and suggested modifications. A major study draws our attention to the debates between the Jesuits and Muslim notables. Often, the theme was one of the controversial aspects of Christianity. At the outset, they discussed the case of a Jew who, masquerading as a Christian, caused dissensions in the community. They examined the unique relation of Jesus with God and other Apostles. They took up the question of two simultaneous existences of Jesus, earthly and eternal. More important, they went into the circumstances in which Jesus was crucified, with reference to his conduct on the cross. They deliberated on the virginity of Mary and paternity of Jesus. A lot of heat was generated on the miraculous abilities of Jesus to revive the dead and cure the sick. A keen interest was taken in the making of the Gospel, besides the threefold personality of Divine Being (Trinity) comprising Father, Son and the Holy Ghost. They engaged with the failure of Mary Magdalene to recognize Jesus when he came out of his grave. Once, they grappled with the differences between the Christians and Jews on permissible foods. On another occasion, a Jesuit questioned Muhammad's prophethood and attacked tenets of Islam. Abdul Sattar played a central role in the debates, as he was familiar with Christian literature and could read from the Persian translation of Bible (*Mirat ul-Quds*) that he had prepared with Jeronimo Xavier. All debates ended in the embarrassment, if not humiliation, of the Jesuits. Jahangir, conscious of his position as universal manifestation (*mazhar-i kull*), enjoyed the debates and generally remained playful, though he sometimes felt irritated.[13]

With this background, we can turn to the memoirs of Mutribi. In his opening meeting, Jahangir assured him of four presents— expenses for maintenance, clothes for wearing, a saddled horse for

218   *Situating Medieval India*

riding and a slave boy for domestic services. These would not be given to him in one go, but at suitable intervals. At the outset, he was free to choose between one of the four. Mutribi had no hesitation in expressing his preference for cash on account of many reasons. It was not advisable to be without cash. It not only engendered more cash, but it was also better than credit. Instantly, Mutribi was given Rs. 1,000, each of which was equal to two and a half *misqals* of Turan. The servants of Nurjahan added a sum of Rs. 500. Mutribi, mindful of the Mughal descent from Timur, asserted that his meeting with Jahangir was similar to that of Hafiz Shirazi with Timur. According to Khwaja Hasan Nisari, Timur summoned Hafiz after conquering Shiraz. Wielding his sword, he had conquered the world in order to control Samarqand and Bukhara. Hafiz, while exchanging these cities (in a poetic metaphor) for a mere beauty mole of the Turk of Shiraz, had jeopardized the grand conquest. Hafiz retorted that this very exchange had reduced him to penury. Amused at the remark, Timur assured Hafiz of four gifts that would not be granted in one go. Since Hafiz was reputed for his mystical tongue (*lisan ul-ghaib*), he had to correctly guess the gift to get it. He would not get what he did not conjecture. Hafiz requested that his empty bowl, which lay beneath his robe, be filled with a fistful of gold. Timur announced that Hafiz had acquired clothes, but not a horse and saddle. Hafiz remarked that if he were given gold, he would easily purchase the horse and saddle from the bazaar. Timur said that it was not possible to help a person, who was willing to lose because of his own fault.[14]

In the second meeting, Mutribi received a robe of honour, a fine turban and a Kashmiri shawl. His son Muhammd Ali was given a gold embroidered robe, a turban with golden thread and an embellished apparel (*fotah-i minaqsh*).[15] On Jahangir's lunar birthday, Mutribi was showered with a rain of gifts. He received two trays of coins (*tankahs*), a silver almond, numerous miniature paintings and an additional Rs. 100. In all, he received two thousand items that Jahangir poured into his bag with his own hands. Mutribi was asked to choose between an Iraqi horse and Turki one, besides picking a saddle of velvet or broadcloth. Mutribi went in for the Iraqi horse and the velvet saddle. Though Jahangir pointed out

A Central Asian Visitor at the Mughal Court 219

their relative disadvantages, Mutribi insisted on having them as they were more expensive.[16] During the eighth meeting, Mutribi was given a duck (*surkhab*), which Jahangir had hunted with his gun (*tufang*). He received an award of Rs. 100 for composing a quatrain suitable to the occasion.[17] In the next meeting, Jahangir gave him another hunted duck (*murghabi*). When it was stuffed and cooked, its meat tasted delicious (*gosht laziz*).[18] During the tenth meeting, Mutribi was asked to indicate his preference from a fair-skinned slave boy and dark-skinned one. As his gaze shifted back and forth, both captivated him and, therefore, he praised their looks in two different quatrains. Though he showed his inclination towards the green complexion, it was not clear which slave boy he ultimately took.[19] During the thirteenth meeting, Mutribi received a cash reward of Rs. 200 from Jahangir, who was impressed with his poetic skills and invited him to join him for a visit to Kashmir.[20] When Mutribi went to enquire about Maktub Khan's health, he received an offering of superior cloth and Rs. 500.[21]

Jahangir took a keen interest in Mutribi's *Nuskha Zeba-i Jahangir*. Every day, Fasih Khan read out the contents to the Emperor for one watch (*yak pehar*). He discussed the nuances of the freshly read portions with the author. During the twenty-first meeting, he appreciated the sweet language in which the episode of Maulana Nazri Badakhshi was described. Given Mutribi's style of analysis, he was advised to add more depth to his work.[22] Once Fasih Khan completed the reading of the book, Jahangir asked Maktub Khan to preserve it in his personal library with care in accordance with the Quranic verse (55: 58), *As if they were rubies and coral*. At this moment, he suggested that Mutribi's work could be a complement to his own anthology.[23] During his days as a prince, he collected the names of poets living in Akbar's reign. Since it was very short (*basiyar mujuz*), it was fit to be added to Mutribi's compilation, which would then be deemed as complete.[24]

Jahangir has made a specific mention of Muhammad Yusuf Khwaja, the son of Tajuddin Hasan Khwaja Juebari. On reading his ode (*ghazal*), he was convinced of his talent and found that he composed decent poetry. Though Jahangir knew him before Khwaja Zainuddin Naqshbandi introduced him, he hardly knew anything

220 *Situating Medieval India*

TABLE 7.1: LIST OF POETS IN JAHANGIR'S
TAZKIRAT USH-SHUARA

S.No.	Name	S.No.	Name
1.	Ghazzali Mashehadi	42.	Qarari Gilani
2.	Qasim Kahi	43.	Ghairati Shirazi
3.	Husain Marwi	44.	Hayati Gilani
4.	Abul Faiz Faizi	45.	Fahmi Tehrani
5.	Husain Nisari	46.	Sahmi Bokhari
6.	Urfi Shirazi	47.	Niyazi Samarqandi
7.	Sheri Lahori	48.	Mir Juzbi
8.	Qaidi Shirazi	49.	Fazli Bukhari
9.	Yadgar Halti	50.	Mazhari Kashmiri
10.	Qasim Arsalan	51.	Chishti Dehalwi
11.	Momin Lang	52.	Mir Haj Lang
12.	Ulfati	53.	Bahram Saqqa
13.	Malik Gujarati	54.	Haidari
14.	Shaikh Rihayi	55.	Jurmi
15.	Mir Duri	56.	Faraghi
16.	Syed Muhammad	57.	Khatami (1)
17.	Muamayi Rafi	58.	Khatami (2)
18.	Syed Muhammad Najafi	59.	Mulla Kami
19.	Mirza Quli Meli	60.	Hashim Muhatram
20.	Zarifi	61.	Nui Sabukash
21.	Mushfiqi Bokhari	62.	Mulla Baqayi
22.	Sabuhi Kabuli	63.	Mulla Amani
23.	Nasir Sawji	64.	Sarmadi Isfahani
24.	Ahdi Razi	65.	Farsi
25.	Mir Muhammad Mahwi	66.	Taqi Shustari
26.	Mir Masum Nami	67.	Tarkhan
27.	Baba Talib Isfahani	68.	Aseeri
28.	Maulana Ubahi	69.	Halati
29.	Hashim Qandhari	70.	Dayi
30.	Khwaja Sahri	71.	Shadi
31.	Lutfi	72.	Naziri
32.	Mir Raughani	73.	Baqayi
33.	Lawandi Nishapuri	74.	Masum
34.	Shakibi Isfahani	75.	Wafai
35.	Mir Farghi	76.	Shauharti
36.	Yulquli Anisi	77.	Fanai
37.	Mahzuni	78.	Azizi
38.	Judai	79.	Waqafi
39.	Qadiri Shirazi	80.	Imani
40.	Tashbihi Kashi	81.	Ghurbati Bukhari
41.	Sharif Waqui		

A Central Asian Visitor at the Mughal Court   221

of his poetry. Since he had understood the magnitude of his artistic competence, he believed that he was more talented than all the Khwajas of Juebar.[25] In 1615, Khwaja Zainuddin, who was one of the Naqshabandi Khwajas, arrived from Mawara ul-Nahr and, meeting Jahangir, gave an offering of 18 horses.[26]

Jahangir, impressed with the verses of Miram Siyah, heard them a second time. However, Mutribi had a slightly different opinion. Miram Siyah, a native of Khurasan, had gained wide notoriety for speaking nonsense (*haziyan gui*). On account of this, hardly anything was written about him. Some people believed that he was inclined towards God and, owing to this element of spiritual absorption, it was not possible for everyone to unveil the secrets of his poetry. On a festive gathering, Abdul Rahman Jami asked him to recite an ode.[27] Following the presentation, Jami could not understand that Miram Siyah, who composed such sublime poetry, could be guilty of producing absurdities. A merchant requested Jami to write an ode, which he would take back to Samarqand for the benefit of scholars. In Jami's view, no ode could surpass that of Miram Siyah and wrote it out for him. This particular ode attained a high reputation in the Persian knowing elite circles. One of the rulers of Turan directed Mutribi to convert this ode into stanzas of five lines (*mukhammas*). Mutribi, besides noting his response to the piece, has also added the response from Jahangir and Maktub Khan. Following was a gist of Mutribi's modified version.[28]

Before embarking on the path of love, it was proper to listen to some advice. In the garden on the riverbank, the companionship of a beautiful idol is a boon. No one can assure the continuance of life. One should not look for sustenance in every corner, as greed has brought respectable persons to ruin. One who exercises authority for a short time must heed to the wise. Do not underestimate a weak enemy, as the tiny mosquito deprives the mighty elephant of sleep. The beloved has no mercy on my miserable state. Even a good person can be disloyal to his tribe, as hardhearted people are found everywhere. Once Mutribi attained sobriety, he lost the desire for gardens and meadows. Miram, discarding the gossip, takes the cup of wine from the hands of one with tulip cheeks.

Miram Siyah's ode, along with Mutribi's addition to it, generated a lot of interest in the Mughal court. Jahangir recited two couplets in praise of purple wine (*sharab arghwani*), which one should drink

222   *Situating Medieval India*

in old age, as it ignited the desire for youth. A number of nobles, following in the footsteps of the Emperor, composed their responses (*jawab*) to the theme. Later on, Mutribi learnt that Maktub Khan also prepared his response to Miram Siyah's ode. The day he intended to present it to the Emperor, he fell down and fractured his arm. When Mutribi went to enquire about his condition, he received these verses with a gift of fine cloth and Rs. 500 in cash. In these pieces, Maktub Khan spoke of his broken hand, which was put into a wooden splint. Besides expecting generosity of the Emperor, he reiterated the merit of drinking purple wine, which revived the joyful memories of youth in old age. Maktub Khan, bound by the ties of protocol, could not conceal his submissiveness even in his composition written under the pseudonym of Farsi.[29]

Mutribi has drawn an interesting character sketch of Maktub Khan. He was one of the most trustworthy servants of the Mughal court (*bandgan sadiq ul-ikhlas*). For a long time, he served as the superintendent of the imperial library and atelier (*daroghgi-i kitab-khana wa naqashkhana mualla*). He possessed numerous qualities of head and heart. The roots of his family were traceable to Shiraz and, for this reason, he used Farsi as his pen name. By nature, he was eloquent, humble and polite. He stood out among the Indian poets for his camaraderie, pure heartedness and warmth. Though seventy years of age, his poetry was imbued with freshness of monsoon clouds and richness of articulation. Jahangir, on his accession, ordered the poets to prepare chronograms of the event. He adjudged Maktub Khan's chronogram as the best and included it in his autobiographical account.[30] In this composition, he hailed Jahangir as the second (Timur) lord of conjunction (*sahib-i qiran sani*), whose enthronement was marked with sweetness, fortune, authority, grandeur and victory (*iqbal wa bakht wa daulat wa fateh wa shukoh wa nusrat*). Mutribi, having praised Maktub Khan for his skill in producing rhyming couplets, has included specimens of his poetry in his memoirs.[31]

Owing to weakness, I fell from the thread of my shirt.
From head to toe, the wind of speech pulls me down.
To begin with, my shadow fell from me to the earth.
Now, I have fallen to the earth from my shadow.

A Central Asian Visitor at the Mughal Court   223

An eyelash had slashed my heart.
Such an art cannot be learnt.
You must not waste a teardrop.
These invaluable jewels must be preserved.
The turbulence of love forms the kernel of heart.
Every breath is akin to a flame.
I asked about the person who loves you.
It is Farsi, who has burnt himself alive.

A few European merchants (*tujjar firang*), then present in Lahore, laid out their goods in the Mughal court. One of them was a booklet with dimension of four fingers. Comprising twelve yellow folios, it was closed with a lock and key. Jahangir, unlocking it, showed it to Mutribi and explained its characteristics. Anything written on it with a pencil appeared black. When it was erased, the page became white again. This exercise could be repeated any number of times. If all the books in the world were written in this way, they could all be erased clean. Jahangir made a demonstration with his own hands. Mutribi was amazed, as he could not imagine a book of this kind. He refused to purchase it for one rupee and, taking it as a talisman (*tilism*), feared that it would bring some harm. Following Jahangir's assurance about its harmlessness, Mutribi accepted it as a gift out of respect. If it brought him good luck during his journey to Turan, he would present it to the ruler Imam Quli Khan.[32] On another occasion, Muhammad Husain Khalf brought a huge lump of sugar all the way from Lucknow to Lahore. Weighing half-a-maund according to the weights in Bukhara, it was placed on a silver stool, so that the nobles could watch it. Mutribi, receiving it as a gift from the Emperor, decided against consuming it at Lahore, as he did not wish to be sick. He decided to take it back to Samarqand, where it might be gifted to Imam Quli Khan or Khwaja Hashim Muhammad Dahbidi.[33] On still another occasion, Mutribi's son purchased from Jahangir a slave boy for Rs. 120. It turned out that the boy, being deaf, could not respond to ordinary commands. Jahangir, realizing his oversight, waived the payment and instead gave a sum of Rs. 100. Later on, the boy, showing signs of saintliness, performed services such as bringing the ablution water and carrying the prayer carpet.[34]

224 *Situating Medieval India*

One evening, Mutribi attended a function in the royal palace. The venue appeared to have been a roofless courtyard, as the moonlight illuminated it. All the walls appeared white, while white silken sheets were spread on the floor. Jahangir, clad in white apparel, sat on a throne of white marble (*takht-i az sang safed marmar*). The nobles, who stood around him, were also dressed in white. Mutribi, unaware of the occasion, found himself in a somewhat embarrassing position. The officers, who blocked his way, informed him of the royal order, stipulating a white dress. One who was not dressed in white clothes was denied entry. Mutribi conveyed his problem to Jahangir through a quatrain, which was sent through Fasih Khan. In accordance with a quick royal order, Mutribi was provided with a white turban and a white robe, so that he was able to join the gathering.[35] Not long after, Mutribi observed animal fights in an arena, which had been lit up with 1,500 lanterns. Jahangir was seen enjoying himself. A fight (*nazara-i jang*) between deer was followed by that between camels. Mutribi felt thrilled. Replying to a question from Jahangir, he stated that he had seen camel fights in Mawara ul-Nahr, but not the deer fights. Jahangir revealed that he had arranged the spectacle only for the benefit of Mutribi. On his part, Mutribi composed a quatrain to mark the occasion.[36]

If a person is sad due to tyranny of the world.
Even if his heart is blacker than tar,
The mirror of his dark heart is brightened,
Owing to the camel fight of Emperor Jahangir.

Jahangir, while listening to a poetic recitation in the sweet voice of Fasih Khan, initiated a discussion on music. Mutribi spoke about Jahangir's uncle Mirza Hakim, who was a master of musical arts. It emerged that Mutribi too possessed this knowledge, particularly because he bore the pseudonym of Mutribi, which denoted a minstrel. In the fifteenth meeting, Jahangir asked Mutribi to demonstrate his musical skills, so that the courtiers profited from it. Initially, Mutribi expressed his inability to sing, as age had impaired his voice. Jahangir assured him that perfection in singing would compensate for any deficiency in voice. In family gatherings, he had heard plenty of songs in the old style. However, he preferred

A Central Asian Visitor at the Mughal Court   225

to hear the compositions of Ustad Ali Dost, the pipe player, who was associated with the reign of Abdullah Khan Uzbek. A tambourine (*daira*) was handed over to Mutribi, who made two presentations. First, he sang the Saut ul-Amali, which had been set in the mode of Ahang Iraqi and rhythmic cycle Nim Saqil. Second, he sang a *naqsh* in the mode Ahang Sih Gah and rhythmic cycle Dur Shahi. Jahangir was all praise for the melodies, as the beat and renditions (*zarb wa natq*) were in line with each other. In response to a question on the sources of twelve musical modes, Mutribi pointed to a difference of opinion. The works of Maulana Hasan Kokabi and Khwaja Kalan Majroohi traced the twelve modes to twelve zodiac signs. The planets, while passing through different houses, produced a sound corresponding to a specific mode. Mir Ataullah al-Husaini, relying on Fariduddin Attar's *Mantiq ul-Tair*, traced the sources to holes in the beak of the mythical bird Phoenix. However, Mutribi was favourably inclined to the interpretation of Khwaja Hasan Nizari, who delved into the life of Hazrat Musa.[37] This prophet wandered in the (Egyptian) deserts for 40 days with the tribe of Bani Israil. Since they suffered from thirst, God commanded Musa to strike the stone with his staff. When Musa did so, twelve springs burst out from the stone. Each of the twelve tribes of Bani Israil were assigned a spring, each flowing with a specific strain. As God commanded Musa to memorize this song (*ya musa qeyi*), a combination of two words became the name of an art form (*mausiqi*).[38]

While discussing the elegance (*latafat*) of Samarqand, the topic turned to the spelling of Samarqand, i.e. the use of 'K' and 'Q' in the middle of the name. In several books, including *Tarikh-i Tabari*, the city was referred to as Samarkand. In popular usage, the name was spelt as Samarqand. Some people believed that Samar and Qamar, two slaves of Alexander, had built the city and, therefore, it was named after them. Their graves were found in the market square (*chahar suq*) of the city. Jahangir, relying on his study of literature, agreed that the word was spelt in both ways. He wished to know the name of scholars of Samarqand, who were capable of his company. They had to be learned, articulate, decent and companionable (*fazil wa sukhangoi wa khush taba wa nadim bashad keh*

226 *Situating Medieval India*

laiq sohbat wa majilast ma dashta bashad). Jahangir was willing to send money so that they could travel to India. Mutribi's son Muhammad Ali mentioned the name of Akhund Maulana Sabiri, the son of Hafiz Tashkandi, showering him with lavish praise. Jahangir appeared to approve the name, as he was reminded of his own childhood when he saw Akbar conversing with Hafiz Tashkandi,[39] who was a fine person.[40] Jahangir acknowledged the merit and ambition of Shaikh ul-Islam Khwaja Faulad. It was regretful that this man had not come to India and that this country had not benefited from this erudite scholar from Samarqand. Jahangir hoped that Mutribi would convey his complaint to the distinguished Khwaja.[41]

In two meetings, Samarqand figured with respect to the mausoleum of Timur.[42] Jahangir was keen to know the condition of the tomb. Mutribi, in a rather curt reply, stated that he had described the condition in his book *Nuskha-i Zeba-i Jahangir* and, therefore, hoped that the Emperor would learn everything about it. Jahangir, displaying a black stone, wished to know if Timur's tomb was made of similar stone. Mutribi submitted that the actual material was brighter (*raushan tar wa baraq tar*), as it was possible to see one's face in it. Muhammad Ali felt that the material was not stone but black gold (*talai siyah*). Mutribi, who never believed in the existence of black gold, ultimately came around to the view that such a material did exist.[43] Jahangir appeared to have been dissatisfied with the maintenance of Timur's tomb.[44] He wished to know the amount of money required for its repair. Mutribi felt that a sum of Rs. 10,000 was needed to do the work with thoroughness. Otherwise, Rs. 5,000 was sufficient. Jahangir, relying on this information, agreed to send a sum of Rs. 10,000 for the purpose.[45]

Jahangir's concern for the upkeep of Timur's tomb might be placed in the larger context of the state of public buildings in Samarqand. The shrine of Qusam bin Abbas (a cousin of Prophet Muhammad, who came to the city with an Arab expedition in the late seventh century) had suffered defacement). A seven-sided stone had been fixed at its entrance with an inscription, which promised the fulfilment of desires, provided a Fatiha was recited for the master craftsman Ali Tabrezi. During the reign of Baqi Muhammad

A Central Asian Visitor at the Mughal Court   227

Khan (r. 1601-4) in Transoxiana, a man named Mirak, the son of Shamsuddin Muhammad, misinterpreted the inscription. He believed that one's wishes could be obtained from the stone. One night, he brought a ladder and, removing the stone, carried it away. The custodians of the shrine, on noticing the theft, informed Baqi Muhammad Khan. The state action led to the arrest of Mirak and recovery of the stone. On examination (*mulahiza*), it was found to be black gold stone (*sang tilai siyah*). Jawanmard Ali Khan pronounced the punishment. Mirak, carried to the top of the seminary of Ulugh Beg Khan Gurgan (a grandson of Timur), was thrown down to his death. In 1626, the visitors discovered that the place was still bereft of the stone.[46] The episode indicated that the state did not tolerate any damage to the public building. Yet for unknown reasons, it did not restore the stone to its rightful place in the shrine.

Mutribi has strengthened the fact of Jahangir's interest in various forms of creative art, particularly painting.[47] He made earnest endeavours to ensure that the portraits of the Central Asian elites were perfected to the minutest detail. When minor blemishes were brought to his notice, he did not rest until these were removed. During the eighteenth meeting with Mutribi, Jahangir studied the portraits of two individuals. Mutribi correctly identified them as Abdullah Khan Uzbek and Abdul Momin Khan. Jahangir desired to know if his painters had rendered accurate likenesses of the Transoxianian rulers. Mutribi pointed out that Abdullah Khan Uzbek was not so fleshy, but he was rather slim. His chin was not straight, but rather deflected towards the left. Regarding Abdul Momin Khan's portrait, Mutribi felt that he had been painted somewhat greenish, whereas he possessed a fair complexion. His turban, tied neatly, was pointed towards the front. Jahangir asked Mutribi to take off his turban and show the exact manner in which Abdul Momin Khan wrapped it. Once this was done, Jahangir did not hesitate a moment in accepting Mutribi's judgement. He summoned the painters and directed them to carry out the changes Mutribi suggested. Jahangir was pleased at the modifications. Abul Bey Uzbek, known as Bahadur Khan, held that Abdul Momin Khan did not wear his turban in that manner. Jahangir, making a

228   *Situating Medieval India*

decisive intervention, argued that Mutribi was speaking of times when Abdul Momin Khan was a prince, which was 50 years ago. At Jahangir's wish, Mutribi recited a verse of Abdul Momin Khan, who also composed poetry. One of the attendants declared the verse to be flat. Jahangir upbraided him for his stupid remark. In the view of Mutribi, it was inappropriate to find fault with the words of kings, as these were majestic in character. In the presence of kings, one had to be cautious about one's eyes, hands and speech.[48]

In the medieval times, there could be no conversation without paying due regard to Islamic spirituality. All individuals, ranging from kings to commoners, held the Sufis in awe and remembered them for their supernatural abilities. Shaikh Nuruddin Baseer was known as the fourteenth axis of the world (*qutb chahar deham*). Owing to his spiritual eminence, he was regarded as one of the forty bodies (*chehal tan*) on which the world stood. Like Mutribi's maternal grandfather, he was totally blind. Though his face was bereft of any feature, he was able to do everything that people with eyesight could do. His tomb was located inside the fort of Samarqand. The building and the dome was covered with white tiles (*kashi safed*). However, the dome had fallen into disrepair. Aaq Khanum, the wife of Sultan Saeed Khan, had it repaired during the governorship of Jawanmard Ali Khan. A majority of the forty saints were buried in the azure mosque. There was a popular tale about the mosque. When a group of mystics was engaged in the recollection of God's name (*zikr*), the roof of the mosque flew up to the sky and settled down again in its place. Shaikh Nuruddin's hospice (*khanqah*) nurtured the practice of vigil. Every Thursday night, Sufis and devotees remained awake and chanted God's name. The Shaikh had desired the practice to continue until the day of judgement. People believed that such a day would occur on a Friday and at a time when none was awake. The Shaikh held that God would send his angels to ensure that the vigil was duly undertaken. Mutribi, on one occasion, participated in the exercise. The Shaikh's sons stood up to lead the chant. The devotees, while whirling around and clapping rhythmically, stamped their feet on the ground. At dawn, they cooked sweets (*halwa*) and, after the morning prayer, they ate a dish of bruised wheat, meat and herbs (*harisa*). A man,

A Central Asian Visitor at the Mughal Court 229

who tried to test Shaikh Nuruddin, threw a needle on the ground and started looking for it. The Shaikh, in spite of his blindness, placed his staff on the needle. He also composed verses on mystical themes. In one of his quatrains, he chided his contemporaries for their lack of piety. They did not obey God even for a moment. Nor, did they repent for their sins. They tried to become Sufis, censors of morality and scholars. They could become all these, but still could not become Muslims.[49]

A slave, living near the market of basket sellers (*bazaar sabd faroshan*) and displaying eccentric behaviour, was believed to possess mystical qualities. Day and night, he walked through the streets crying *Haq Haq* in a loud voice. He did not sleep even after returning to his house, but remained committed to the duty of his soul. Sometimes, he came to the house of Saqi Ramini, the chief judge, who treated him with respect. One day, the slave passed in front of a school. A child was reciting verses from the poetic compendium of Amir Qasim Anwar. The slave quietly kept on listening until the child reached the couplet, 'Those who look at anything other than your face were short-sighted. How short-sighted they were?' The slave let out a sigh and, falling to the ground, died instantly. In this connection, Maktub Khan, the librarian of Jahangir, narrated a similar episode. Once Jahangir visited one of the provinces of India. Some Qawwals, endowed with melodious voices, sang mystical songs. They presented two rhyming hemistiches, the first one of Shaikh Nizamuddin Auliya and the second of Amir Khusrau. Ahmad Ali, the seal maker who was in the service of Jahangir, heard this couplet and, letting out a sigh, passed away. Before they could provide any medical aid, he was no more.[50] Mutribi knew that Jahangir had narrated this incident in his memoirs.[51] The two hemistiches were as follows:

har qaum rast rahe deeni wa qibla gahi
ma qibla rast kardim ba tarf kaj kulahi

Every race was directed to the right road of faith and its altar.
I have found true altar towards the one with a turban awry.

In an amusing anecdote, Mutribi had described the celebration of Nauroz in Samarqand. It was a period of festivities (*aish wa*

230 *Situating Medieval India*

nishat). Young libertines collected at three places—Pushta Rasd, Juwaz Kaghaz and Khwaja Choban—for drinking liquor. On one such occasion, Abdul Latif Khan, who appeared to have been the police chief, forbade the transportation of liquor out of the city. Anyone guilty of the act was to be treated as a criminal. Owing to the strict vigil of the inspectors and sentries (*muhtasiban wa gumashtgan*) at the city gates, it was impossible for anyone to take the liquor out. However, Mulla Shama Yak Pulli was not deterred. This man had visited India during the reign of Humayun. After spending some time there, he returned to Transoxiana and became a boon companion (*nadim majlis*) of Abdul Latif Khan. Since he was extremely fond of duck meat (*gosht murghabi*) and could not remain an hour without wine, he conspired with his friends to deceive the municipal authorities. He sent his associates including some students and a few wicked characters to Juwaz Kaghaz in advance, assuring them that he would bring wine by any means. He filled a leather flask (*khik*) with wine and placed it in a coffin. Tearing his shirt, he wrapped a black cloth around his head and kept his turban on the coffin. He and his companions assumed the form of a funeral procession. Carrying the coffin on their shoulders, they began to mourn for an imaginary Mulla Khiki. The inconsolable Mulla Shama ran besides the coffin and, tearing his shirt, lamented, 'O my dear brother Mulla Khiki. Why did you die? It is regretful that you have to be buried on this day. Your loss can not be told. If I could meet Abdul Latif Khan, I would complain about the angel of death.' In the midst of this noise, the mourners hoodwinked the guards and passed through the city gates. At the appointed site, the cups of wine were circulated and the drinking party became hot. A strange clamour rose up. Abdul Latif Khan, who was celebrating Nauroz along with the nobles in the midst of cannon fire at Pushta Rasd, heard the drunken songs. He learnt that Mulla Shama was drinking wine with his friends. When the inebriated culprits were hauled up, he asked them to reveal how they had smuggled wine out of the city. Amused at the confession, he rewarded the defaulters with prizes and robes.[52]

Mutribi has drawn our attention to the strange pursuits of Maulana Jalali, who lived in Ku-i Ghaziyan of Bukhara during the

A Central Asian Visitor at the Mughal Court   231

reign of Abdullah Khan Uzbek. An expert physician and credible poet, he was proficient in the art of magic and talismans (*ilm shubda wa tilismat*). He had constructed a large box (*sanduq*), which was as tall as a man and contained many rarities. Installed in the centre of his house, one could walk around it and examine its exterior. Like Mutribi, a number of people came to see it and felt engrossed in it. Closed from all sides, it had a hidden opening (*daricha poshida*) through which a lion's head stuck out. Opposite to the lion's head was a wooden horse. Below the opening, there was an iron rod bearing a monkey. In its left hand, the monkey had a bronze cup and, in its right hand, it had an iron hammer. When an hour of the day or night passed, the hammer pushed the monkey's right hand and, making it drink from the cup, sounded the bell indicating the hour. Maulana Jalali had invented another device, which enabled him to predict the future of visitors. He gave a bead (*mohra*) of seven metals to an individual, who was required to wish for something. The man threw the bead into the mouth of the horse, so that it fell to the bottom of the box. The bead, with a hissing sound, climbed up and, emerging from a lion's mouth, fell into the cup. Instantly, a window opened to expose a man, who held folded papers in his hands. The writing indicated the individual's wish, besides advice on ordinary problems such as health, business and travel. As Jalali finished reading the paper, the window closed and the box returned to its original form.[53]

Khawaja Abdur Rahim Juebari figured thrice in the conversations. Jahangir held him in high regard.[54] He felt so close to Juebari that he treated him as an elder brother. Jahangir had been waiting for the arrival of Juebari, so that he could join the royal entourage on a visit to Kashmir. When Juebari arrived, Jahangir felt that he was honoured.[55] Mutribi, at the request of Jahangir, composed a eulogy in Arabic (*qasidah-i arabi*). This piece praised the spiritual eminence of Juebari in superlative terms. God, speaking with a perfect voice and noble heart, gave a call to the Khwaja. God had endowed him with the virtues of authority, glory and honour. A person, on meeting him, secured the fulfilment of his desires. His breath, imbued with messianic powers, gave a new life to decayed bones. His grace transformed poisonous winds into a

232 *Situating Medieval India*

pleasant breeze. A person like him was never born in any age. A large number of people, who were devoted to him, looked forward to his blessings. Numerous tribes, including those of Salim and Tamim, were covered under his beneficence. Mutribi, in relation to the Khwaja, saw himself as a humble servant, who was no better than a poor orphan. He hoped that the Khwaja's grace would erase the burden of his sins. His words would serve as the decisive voice in the prayer of the sufferers. The shadow of his kindness would always protect his devotees until resurrection. Jahangir applauded Mutribi for reciting the eulogy.[56]

The royal physician Masih ul-Zaman was a man of good nature. He was very close to Jahangir, who had implicit faith in his words. Mutribi saw him receiving an award of Rs. 10,000 from Jahangir. However, he could not figure out if it was given for his couplet relating to Khwaja Abu Hashim Dahbidi or it was a remuneration for some medical treatment. Mutribi, in view of Jahangir's favourable reference to Masih ul-Zaman in his memoirs, has quoted it in full. According to the Emperor, Khwaja Abu Hashim Dahbidi, the axis of the age (*qutb zaman*), had warmed the market of saintliness (*bazaar darveshi*) in Mawara ul-Nahr. In response to Dahbidi's gifts that his disciples had brought, Jahangir sent him a verse that Babur had written for the Khwaja's grandfather Makhdum-i Azam.[57] It stated as follows:

Following a misguided lower self, we wasted our life.
Before the people of God, we are ashamed of our way.
Take a glance towards us, so that with our confused heads,
We had been bereft of mastership, while we are slaves of the Khwaja.

Jahangir sent another poetic piece along with 1,000 Jahangiri *mohars* through the Khwaja's disciples. In this verse, he acknowledged the boundless kindness of the Khwaja towards him and, in return, he was willing to renounce all worldly possessions. His heart had been filled with joy on account of his news as well as his limitless favours. Jahangir asked his courtiers with a poetic temperament to respond to his quatrains. Of the several responses, he adjudged that of Masih ul-Zaman as the best and, therefore, gave the said prize.[58]

A Central Asian Visitor at the Mughal Court   233

Though we have the business of kingship before us.
Every moment, we remember the former dervishes.
If the heart of a dervish was pleased with us
We count it as a profit of our kingship.

In the account of his last meeting, Mutribi has narrated the circumstances in which he secured Jahangir's permission to return to Samarqand. At this time, the Emperor, along with his nobles and functionaries, was preparing for a visit to Kashmir. The official transactions dealt with the grant of positions and distribution of gifts. Mutribi would have preferred to devote his remaining years to imperial service. A number of factors induced him to adopt another course. In accordance with the Hadis, 'Love of one's land was integral to one's faith,' (*hub al-watn min al-iman*), he had begun to feel homesick. Old age and physical weakness had ruled out service of the Mughal State. Common ailments—cold, cough, sneezing and yawning—did not allow him to attend the royal gatherings. A reference to Fariduddin Attar's book urged him to maintain a distance from the kings. Royal service, even if gainful in material terms, could endanger one's life. A Quranic verse (2: 195) 'Do not, with your own hands, cast yourself into ruin,' advocated goodwill towards rulers from a distance. Of course, there were people who threw their lives into peril on account of proximity to kings. Mutribi, caught between these unenviable positions, had received divine insight to seek the permission to return home. He could no longer keep his children and relatives wait in uncertainty. In the presence of nobles and courtiers, Mutribi recited an ode (*ghazal*) asking Jahangir's permission to return to his native land. The gathering, including Asaf Khan, was stunned into silence. Jahangir, though upset, controlled his feelings. He recited a couplet which equated the state of a broken heart to a hundred deaths. Since it was composed on a theme and meter similar to Mutribi's, he desired it to be added to the ode. Mutribi assured Jahangir that he would convey his gifts to the spiritual masters in Samarqand. He was committed to care for a family of 20 dependents. Jahangir offered to send a sum of Rs. 2,000 to Samarqand, so that the members of his family joined him in Kashmir. Seeing the insistence of Mutribi, Jahangir placed his hand on his chest and granted the permission, provided he promised to return within one year.[59]

234 *Situating Medieval India*

NOTES

1. An earlier version of this paper appeared as 'The Indian Memoirs of Mutribi Samarqandi', *Proceedings of the Indian History Congress*, 55th session, Aligarh, 1994, pp. 344-54.
2. Richard C. Foltz, *Mughal India and Central Asia*, Karachi: Oxford University Press, 1998, pp. 21-4.
3. Iqtidar Alam Khan, 'The Nobility under Akbar and the Development of His Religious Policy, 1560-1580', in *India's Polity in the Age of Akbar*, Ranikhet: Permanent Black and Ashoka University, 2016, p. 132.
4. M. Athar Ali, *The Apparatus of Empire: Awards of Ranks, Offices and Titles to the Mughal Nobility (1574-1658)*, Aligarh: Centre of Advanced Study in History and Delhi: Oxford University Press, 1985, pp. xx-xxi.
5. Shah Khwaja, on behalf of his master, presented to Jahangir a gift of Rs. 50,000. In return, Jahangir gave Rs. 30,000 to Shah Khwaja. Soon after, Jahangir received Khwaja Abdur Rahim and his deputy Khwaja Hasan with great honour. He ordered the leading nobles to escort the ambassadors. At the time of audience, Jahangir asked Rahim to sit near the imperial throne, which was a very rare honour. The emissary was conferred Rs. 50,000 in cash and a jewelled dagger. Imam Quli Khan, in his letter to Jahangir, recalled the Mughal-Uzbek ties since Akbar's reign and proposed an anti-Persia alliance to clear the route to Mecca. He also advised Jahangir to forgive Khurram and advised the Prince to desist from rebellion. M. Athar Ali, 'Jahangir and the Uzbeks', in *Studies in Polity, Ideas, Society and Culture*, New Delhi: Oxford University Press, 2006, pp. 323-4.
6. Stephen Frederic Dale, *Indian Merchants and Eurasian Trade, 1600-1750*, New Delhi: Cambridge University Press and Foundation Books, 1994, pp. 21-6, 54.
7. Z.A. Desai, 'Life and Works of Faizi', *Indo-Iranica*, vol. XVI, no. 3, rpt., Calcutta: Iran Society, 1964, pp. 19-35.
8. S. Nabi Hadi, *Talib-i Amuli (The Poet Laureate of Jahangir): His Life and Times*, Aligarh: Aligarh Muslim University, 1962, pp. 90-112.
9. Richard C. Foltz, op. cit., pp. 117-18.
10. Abdul Qadir Badauni, *Muntakhab ut-Tawarikh*, vol. III, Eng. tr. Wolseley Haig and B.P. Ambashthya, Patna: Academic Asiatica, rpt., 1973, pp. 452-3.
11. Mahmud bin Amir Wali Balkhi spent over six years (1625-31) in India. Starting from Balkh in northern Afghanistan, he reached Cape Camorin on the southern tip of the peninsula. He visited a number of places such as Peshawar, Lahore, Sirhind, Delhi, Mathura, Allahabad, Benares, Patna, Rajmahal, Midnapore, Jagannath Puri, Hyderabad and Mangalgiri. On his

A Central Asian Visitor at the Mughal Court 235

return, he travelled through Agra, Jaisalmer, Bhakkar and Bust. He took a keen interest in Hindu temples and religious practices. He became familiar with the Jogis, Sannyasis and Bairagis. He noted the large presence of women in popular festivals. He also observed the participation of Muslims. Iqbal Husain, 'Hindu Shrines and Practices as Described by a Central Asian Traveller in the First Half of the Seventeenth Century', in *Studies in Polity, Economy and Society of the Trans-Gangetic Valley: Fifteenth-Nineteenth Centuries*, Delhi: Primus Books, 2013, pp. 19-30.

12. Corinne Lefevre, 'The *Majalis-i Jahangiri* (1608-11): Dialogue and Asiatic Otherness at the Mughal Court', *Journal of the Economic and Social History of the Orient*, vol. 55, 2012, pp. 255-86.

13. Muzaffar Alam and Sanjay Subrahmanyam, 'Catholics and Muslims in the Court of Jahangir (1608-1611) ' in *Writing the Mughal World: Studies in Political Culture*, Ranikhet Cantt.: Permanent Black, 2011, pp. 286-310.

14. Mutribi al-Asamm Samarqandi, *Khatirat-i Mutribi Samarqandi*, Persian text, ed. Abdul Ghani Mirzoyef, Karachi: Institute of Central & West Asian Studies, University of Karachi, 1977, Meeting 1, pp. 21. (Hereafter cited as Mutribi).

15. Ibid., Meeting 2, p. 21.

16. Ibid., Meeting 6, pp. 22-3.

17. Ibid., Meeting 8, p. 35.

18. Ibid., Meeting 9, pp. 35-6.

19. Ibid., Meeting 10, pp. 39-40.

20. Ibid., Meeting 13, p. 45.

21. Ibid., Meeting 17, p. 60.

22. Ibid., Meeting 21, pp. 65-6.

23. Ibid., Meeting 23, p. 70.

24. The text of Jahangir's *Tazkirat ush-Shuara* was verbatim identical with Nizamuddin Ahmad's account of the poets of Akbar's reign. The two works were similar with regard to the identity of poets, sequence of their reference, facts of their lives, comments on their styles and specimens of heir verses. Ahmad's chronicle was published in 1592, i.e. 34 years before Mutribi's visit. If the work was the product of Jahangir's effort, Ahmad would not have dared to include it in his history and that too without acknowledgements. Since Ahmad's work was already in the hands of readers for over three decades, it is not clear why Jahangir should have claimed it as his. There was another possibility. Mutribi, on his own, might have included the short tract in his larger book. By so doing, he proved to his Central Asian contemporaries that his Indian visit was a success and his meetings with Jahangir were effective. Syed Husamuddin Rashidi, 'Introduction,'

236   *Situating Medieval India*

Jahangir ibn Jalaluddin Akbar, *Tazkirat ush-Shuara*, Persian text, ed. Abdul Ghani Mirzoyef, Karachi: Institute of Central & West Asian Studies, Universiy of Karachi, 1976, pp. 80-6.

25. Mutribi, Meeting 20, p. 64.

26. Nuruddin Jahangir, *Tuzuk-i Jahangiri*, Eng. tr., Alexander Rogers and Henry Beveridge, Delhi: Low Price Publications, rpt., 1989, vol. I, p. 289. (Hereafter cited as Jahangir).

27. Abdul Rahman Jami (1414-92), being attached to the Naqshbandi order, trained in the disciplines of Saiduddin Kashghari and Ubaidullah Ahrar. His chief contribution lay in presenting Ibn Arabi's thought in intelligible terms. In him, Sufi traditions of Ibn Arabi and Rumi united. A prolific writer, he produced numerous works in prose and poetry. In *Lawaih* (Gleaming Lights), he summarized the doctrines of Ibn Arabi. In *Nafhat ul-Uns* (Breath of Familiarity), he provided an account of the Sufis of Central Asia and Persia. His long poetic work *Haft Aurang* (Seven Thrones) comprised seven odes (*masnavis*) including Yusuf-Zulaikha and Laila-Majnu. His *Baharistan* (Spring Land) was composed on the lines of Saadi's *Gulistan*. He translated 40 traditions (*hadis*) of the Prophet into Persian quatrains. He has earned the title of the Seal of Poets (*khatam ul-shuara*). Seyyed Hossein Nasr, ed., *Islamic Spirituality: Manifestations*, New York: The Crossword Publishing Company, 2012, pp. 174, 344.

28. Mutribi, Meeting 17, pp. 56-8.

29. Ibid., Meeting 17, pp. 60-1.

30. Jahangir, vol. I, p. 12.

31. Mutribi, Meeting 4, pp. 26-8.

32. Ibid., Meeting 3, pp. 22-3.

33. Ibid., Meeting 7, p. 33.

34. Ibid., Meeting 16, pp. 53-4.

35. Ibid., Meeting 11, pp. 41-2.

36. Ibid., Meeting 12, pp. 42-3.

37. According to the Quran (7: 159-60), among the people of Moses (there was) a community which guided by the truth, and by means of it acted fairly. We divided them (into) twelve tribes as communities, and We inspired Moses, when his people asked him for water: 'Strike the rock with your staff,' and (there) gushed forth from it twelve springs—each tribe knew its drinking place—and We overshadowed them (with) the cloud, and We sent down on them the manna and the quails: 'Eat from the good things which We have provided you.' They did not do Us evil, but they did themselves evil. A.J. Droge, *The Quran: A New Annotated Translation*, New Delhi: Oxford University Press, 2015, p. 102.

A Central Asian Visitor at the Mughal Court   237

38. Mutribi, Meeting 15, pp. 50-2.

39. Hafiz Tashkandi, also called Hafiz Kumaki, was regarded in Mawra ul-Nahr as a most learned man. In 1569, he came to India from Tashkand. Abul Fazl listed him among the scholars, who possessed the knowledge of philosophy and theology. He had something of a soldier in him and, like all Turks, used to travel about with the quiver tied to his waist. He was exalted with many favours. He received a sum of Rs. 30,000-Rs. 40,000 from the Emperor and his nobles, besides some gold from Abdur Rahim Khan-i Khanan. He went to Hijaz and from there to Constantinople, where he refused the office of *wazir*. Thereafter, he returned to his country, where he died. Abul Fazl Allami, *Ain-i Akbari*, vol. I, Eng. tr. H. Blochmann and D.C. Phillot, Calcutta: The Asiatic Society, rpt., 2010, p. 609; Khwaja Nizamuddin Ahmad, *Tabaqat-i Akbari*, vol. II, Eng. tr. Brajendranath De, Calcutta: The Asiatic Society, p. 686; Abdul Qadir Badauni, *Muntakhab ut-Tawarikh*, vol. II, Eng. tr., W.H. Lowe and B.P. Ambashthya, Patna: Academica Asiatica, 1973, rpt., pp. 190-1.

40. Mutribi, Meeting 22, pp. 68-9.

41. Ibid., Meeting 20, pp. 64-5.

42. The 'Grave of the King' (*gur-i amir*), situated on the southwest corner of Samarqand, evolved as a part of the ensemble which Timur's grandson Muhammad Sultan had built. Timur, on returning (1404) from a campaign in the west, ordered the construction of a mausoleum for this grandson. A year later, Timur was buried in it. During the next half a century, direct descendants of Timur—Miran Shah, Shah Rukh, Pir Muhammad, Ulugh Beg and Timur's spiritual guide Syed Barakah—received a final resting place here. The monument stood behind the south facade of a square court, which lay between a seminary (*madrasah*) and a hospice (*khanqah*). An entrance portal stood in the middle of the north side of the court, while four minarets were raised from its four corners. On the exterior, the mausoleum was a modified octagon with five sides exposed. On the interior, a square chamber was provided with four rectangular bays. From the southeast corner of the dome chamber, a stairway led to a crypt containing tombs of the Timurids. The dome and the drum stood out for intricate tile work in geometric patterns and inscriptions. Lisa Golombek and Donald Wilber, *The Timurid Architecture of Iran and Turan*, vol. I, Princeton: Princeton University Press, 1988, pp. 260-2.

43. Mutribi, Meeting 2, pp. 19-20.

44. Jahangir, while permitting (1620) Mir Baraka Bukhari to leave for Transoxiana, entrusted Rs. 10,000 to him. Of this amount Rs. 5,000 was to be conveyed to Khwaja Saleh Dahbidi, who from his ancestors was one

238   *Situating Medieval India*

of the well wishers of the Mughal State. The remaining Rs. 5,000 was to be distributed among the custodians (*mujawirs*) of the tomb of Timur. Jahangir also ordered Mir Baraka to make every effort to procure mottled fish teeth from any quarter and at any price. Jahangir, vol. II, p. 196.

45. Mutribi, Meeting 22, p. 69.

46. Ibid., Meeting 2, pp. 20-1.

47. The roots of the Mughal painting were traceable to Persia and Central Asia. During the reign of Akbar, the genres of painting included book illustrations, sumptuous albums and portraiture. Jahangir, carrying this art to its highest point, built on the artistic heritage from Akbar. Apart from rare animals and flowers, Jahangir was attracted to political events, court ceremonies, popular festivals and hunting scenes. Jahangir sent his leading portraitist Bishandas along with Shah Alam, the ambassador to Persia, so that he could prepare portraits of Shah Abbas, his family members and nobles. Asok Kumar Das, 'Mughul Painting', in *The Mughul Empire: The History and Culture of the Indian People, vol. VII*, Bombay: Bhartiya Vidya Bhawan, 1974, pp. 807-17.

48. Mutribi, Meeting 18, pp. 61-3.

49. Ibid., Meeting 13, pp. 46-8.

50. Ibid., Meeting 16, pp. 54-5.

51. In the presence of Jahangir, some Qawwals from Delhi were singing, while Syedi Shah performed an ecstatic dance. Jahangir wished to know the meaning of the second hemistich. Mulla Ali Ahmad, the seal engraver, who was the leading expert in his craft and bore the title of Khalifa, replied on the authority of his father. One day, Shaikh Nizamuddin Auliya, putting his cap on one side of his head, sat on a terraced roof on the bank of the Yamuna and watched the devotions of the Hindus. Drawing the attention of Amir Khusrau to the crowd, he uttered the first hemistich. Amir Khusrau responded with the second one. Mulla Ali Ahmad, while uttering these words, became senseless and fell down. The physicians exerted themselves to revive him, but did not succeed. Jahangir had never seen a death of this kind. Jahangir, vol. I, pp. 169-70.

52. Mutribi, Meeting 9, pp. 36-8.

53. Ibid., Meeting 3, pp. 23-5.

54. Jahangir took action against two Ahrari Naqshbandis, but exchanged gifts with the Dahbidi family. He maintained a close contact with the Juebari Naqshbandis of Bukhara, who rose to prominence during the rule of Abdullah Khan Uzbek. Khwaja Saad, a leading Juebari exemplar, acquired a vast landed estate and received gifts from India, Turkey and elsewhere. Two of his sons, Abdul Karim and Abdur Rahim, left Bukhara for political

A Central Asian Visitor at the Mughal Court 239

reasons and migrated to India. The first one entered Akbar's service and, reaching the rank of 1,000 under Jahangir, died in 1607. Imam Quli Khan sent Abdur Rahim to India with an important diplomatic proposal. He sent a gift of one lakh *tankahs* to Jahangir, while Rahim brought the best novelties of Central Asia including horses, camels, mules, furs, books, calligraphies and three lakh *tankahs* in cash. The Mughal subjects were amazed at the lavish hospitality to Rahim. Jahangir delayed his departure for Kashmir, enabling Rahim to spend the summer of 1627 with him. He secured the pardon and restoration of a disgraced Ahrari noble, Abdullah Khan. Jahangir was said to have died of overindulgence in feasts hosted for the emissary. Rahim went to Agra and presented himself before Shahjahan, who seated him near the throne along with the princes. Rahim died in 1629. His son Muhammad Sadiq carried his body to Bukhara for burial. Richard C. Foltz, op. cit., pp. 97-102.

55. Mutribi, Meeting 13, p. 45; Meeting 19, p. 63.

56. Ibid., Meeting 14, pp. 48-9.

57. Jahangir's account of the episode (at least in the English version) was slightly different. Khwaja Hashim Dahbidi was a prominent dervish of Transoxiana and people of that country had immense faith in him. One of his disciples came (1615) to India and brought his mentor's letter for Jahangir along with a coat (*farji*) and bow. Khwaja Hashim wrote about the friendly connection between his ancestors and the Mughal ruling family. As a proof of the relation, he sent a couplet of Babur. In the last hemistich, Babur registered an intimate bond with a Dahbidi exemplar (Khwajagi) and treated himself as a servant of the saint. After this reference, Jahangir quoted his own impromptu quatrain and followed it up with another one by Hakim Masih ul-Zaman, besides the royal cash award to him. Jahangir, vo. I, pp. 303-4.

58. Mutribi, Meeting 17, pp. 59-60.

59. Ibid., Meeting 24, pp. 71-3.

CHAPTER 10

Pictures of Amazement in Medieval India: Looking into the Works of Mushtaqi, Jahangir and Bhandari

In the medieval times, the Persian chronicles have revolved around the fortunes of the ruling classes.[1] The major writings have been enthusiastic in narrating conquests and rebellions, besides the promotion of literature and construction of buildings. However, some works were not averse to the description of strange phenomena. Amir Khusrau, while asserting the uniqueness of India, pointed to the peculiarities among living creatures. Shams Siraj Afif, in his attempt to show the ideal character of Firoz Shah Tughluq's reign, noted some curious facts.[2] He has devoted the fifth chapter of the fifth part of his history to record congenital deformities in humans, animals and birds. Two prominent Sufi works, coming down from Shaikh Nasiruddin Mahmud Chiragh-i Delhi and Fazlullah Jamali, have attributed miraculous powers to the Chishti and Suhrawardi saints. Similarly, the hagiographies of Bhakti saints were heavily loaded with incredible feats of the protagonists. Simon Digby, in his anthology of wonder tales, has detailed the romance of Madhumalati-Madhukar, the story of the Flower of Bakawali, the life of Gorakhnath and the Sufi tales of the Jogis.[3] This chapter is confined to three chronicles that were produced in a century extending from the late sixteenth to the late seventeenth century. In subject and approach, there was little in common among them. While reconstructing the political developments of their times and the earlier periods, they took a keen interest in what appeared as strange, incredible and amazing. However, they differed from one

Pictures of Amazement in Medieval India 241

another regarding the rationale of their interest in the strange elements as well as the nature of their descriptions of the same.

The ancestors of Shaikh Rizqullah Mushtaqi migrated from Bukhara and served the Khalji and Tughluq governments. His grandfather Malik Firoz, a renowned warrior, rose to prominence during the reign of Bahlol Lodi (r. 1451-89). His father Shaikh Saadullah, a disciple of Shaikh Muhammad Mangan, was associated with nobles like Khan Jahan and Zainuddin. Mushtaqi was brought up in an atmosphere imbued with scholarship and Sufism. A disciple of Shaikh Budhan Shattari, he worked as an Imam and composed poetry in Persian and Hindi. In his *Waqiat-i Mushtaqi*, he set for himself the task of writing the history of a century, extending from the rise of Bahlol Lodi to the accession of Akbar, besides the kingdoms of Malwa and Gujarat. His thrust was confined to the reign of Sikandar Lodi (r. 1489-1517) and leading nobles of the Lodi period. Finding it difficult to restrict himself to political and military matters, he gave a free rein to his natural passion for narrating anecdotes (*hikayat*). As the frequent insertion of stories into a weak political narrative did not satiate his hunger, he devoted the last chapter of 60 pages entirely to telling wondrous anecdotes.[4] His tales were both miraculous and non-miraculous. Even where the miracles were absent, the stories were incredible enough to ignite a strong sense of amazement. Averse to overt sermonizing, he did not fail to convey subtle ethical messages. His stories constituted a vast stock of evidence for reconstructing the socio-cultural history of medieval India. They also enable us to dig into the human mentalities and moral fabric of the times.

In the first love story, a man from Jaunpur got married and took his bride to Zafarabad in a palanquin. As they rested under a tree, a recluse, captivated by her beauty, gazed at her. The wife, returning after four days, found that the recluse had died. She offered a prayer at his grave and left. When the people opened the grave, they saw the recluse in a bridal dress and henna on his hands and feet. In a similar story, a Nuhani Afghan escorted his newly wedded wife to his house. They crossed a river by placing her palanquin in a boat. A recluse, travelling in the same boat, was enraptured at her looks and kept staring at her. As her shoe fell into the river, the recluse

242   *Situating Medieval India*

plunged into the water to retrieve it, but did not appear again. The bride, overpowered by a spontaneous love for the recluse, also jumped in. When nets were thrown in, the two were found in an embrace, while the recluse held the shoe. The people wished to bury them in the same grave. At the orders of the governor of Ghazipur, they were buried side-by-side in separate graves. In the third episode, a Muslim student was travelling through Bhongaon. He stopped at a well and, seeing a beautiful girl, insisted on drinking water from her hands. As the girl poured water, the student kept looking at her, allowing the water to flow down. The irritated girl threw a challenge to the boy, who jumped into the well. The girl, whom the friends chided, followed the suit. When they were taken out, they were found holding hands. Though the girl was a Hindu, she was buried besides the boy. The girl's relatives, wishing to cremate her, opened the grave but did not find her body. When they opened the other grave, they found the two sitting together and closed it. In the fourth anecdote, a traveller stayed with a gardener in a village of Bhander, near Jhansi. He was captivated by the gardener's wife, who served him. After three days, the traveller left. Following a long gap, he returned to the village and found that the woman had died. He saw a vessel containing her remains and died due to the shock of permanent separation from his beloved.[5] In these stories of love at first sight, the boundaries of matrimony and religion were crossed. The society, after the deaths of the protagonists, accepted their love as pure and, thus, allowed them to be buried close to each other.

Early during the reign of Bahlol Lodi, the Afghans raided a village in the subdistrict of Nimkhar, which fell in the jurisdiction of Qanauj. An Afghan noble Khwaja Khan Mewati became curious about the loving relationship between a man and his wife. The man, who was a shepherd and milkman, invited Mewati to stay with him, so that he could narrate his experience. Many years back, the shepherd was in love with the daughter of a grocer. In a raid, a Afghan soldier carried her away and married her. The shepherd wandered from place to place in her search. When he reached Sirhind, he saw her in the house of the Afghan. Assuming the garb of a Jogi, he appeared before her and begged for alms. Though she

Pictures of Amazement in Medieval India 243

recognized him, she complained against him out of modesty. The servants beat him up. He managed to win the confidence of the Afghan, who employed him in his stable. This gave him an opportunity to be near his beloved. She kept on complaining against the intruder, but her husband took no action. After two years, the Afghan joined a military expedition to the east. He wrote to the shepherd to escort his wife to the camp. Since there was some delay during the journey, the Afghan got him whipped and tied to a tree. Before he could attack the shepherd with a sword, he died of drinking sherbet, which a snake had contaminated. The widow accepted the tragedy as God's will and, marrying the shepherd, lived happily thereafter.[6] Since the lovers were patient in their love and did not transgress the boundaries of social relationships, they were rewarded with a joyful union and enviable reputation in the locality.

Another story established that physical lust, in contrast to true love, ended in crime and punishment. The incident was reported from Jaunpur during the reign of Sultan Ibrahim Sharqi.[7] A student saw a beautiful woman on the roof of a house and desired to develop physical intimacy with her. He took the help of a friend, who was the son of a merchant. The two contacted a woman cheat, who in order to conceal her avocation, carried religious symbols of a Muslim saint. In return for a number of gold coins, she formulated an elaborate plan. She won over the confidence of the woman's husband, who, according to her, resembled her son. The man began to treat her as his mother and invited her to stay in his house. She managed to impress the wife with her wondrous tales. She agreed to accompany the wife to a holy man, who would grant her the boon of a son. The two women reached a venue, where the boys had organized a feast with wine, betel rolls and a bed. The cheat, receiving a purse of gold coins, slipped out. The nervous wife, having consumed wine, fell on a knife and died on the spot. The boys placed the body in a earthen vessel and threw it in a river. The *kotwal* retrieved the body and, following the order of the Sultan, investigated the case. With the help of local vintners, he arrested the merchant's son, who had purchased the wine. The Sultan ordered the boy to be executed. A large number of people gathered at the site, where the

244 *Situating Medieval India*

student also appeared. Each of them confessed to have committed the murder alone. Since the Shariat ordained execution of only one person for a murder, the *qazi* sent the boys to prison, so that the culprit could be found in due course. The truth could not be ascertained and the boys could not be detained beyond a stipulated period. On their release, the boys revealed the entire conspiracy to the authorities. The Sultan hauled up the deceitful woman and, through her, summoned all the cheats of Jaunpur. At first, 1,300 cheats were employed with salaries and rewards. Invited to a royal banquet, they were carried in boats to a river, where they were drowned. In this manner, the Sultan cleansed Jaunpur of its criminals.[8]

Mushtaqi has developed three stories around graves. Once, Malik Adil Qanauji reported that a vast area was inundated due to an overflowing Ganga. Many old graves on the bank were washed away. Some Bukhari Syeds collected the bones, so that they were buried at safer places. In one of the graves, the body appeared to be buried on the same day, as it was wrapped in a white sheet and covered with flowers. In another grave, the body was found covered with scorpions. According to the second story, a cook of Qanauj constructed for himself a beautiful grave with a terrace and garden. A jealous Syed remarked that the cook was not worthy of being buried there. One day, the Syed died and he was buried in the family graveyard. The cook, after his death, was taken to the grave he had built. When it was opened, the Syed's body was found there, as he was fond of the place. Consequently, the cook was buried by his side. During the reign of Sher Shah (r. 1540-5), a prominent noble Khawas Khan stayed in Ludhiana. He was informed that two coffins had been found in a flooded area. On opening them, it was found that one body was wrapped in a white sheet and the other was covered in a faded sheet. No one had ever seen a grave there. A local person, enlightened through his dream, revealed that the deceased were brothers. They were memorizers of the Quran and did not wish to be buried elsewhere. The sheet was white in case of the brother, who recited the Quran after ablutions, while the colour was faded in case of the brother who was not particular about the ritual. Khawas Khan, informed of the dream, had the coffins buried there.[9]

Pictures of Amazement in Medieval India 245

In Mushtaqi's reportage on crime, the women figured as perpetrators, accomplices and victims. A villager had two wives. He loved one of them and neglected the other. The latter killed her own son and accused her rival of murder, so that she could be expelled. A carpenter, who was divinely gifted for settling disputes, was summoned. Since there was no witness to the murder, he devised a novel way to reach the truth. Of the two, the one who was quicker in taking off her clothes would be innocent. The murderer took off her clothes, while the other did not. The former was declared guilty. The second case revolved around a soldier of Samana. When he left for military duty, he asked his neighbour to keep an eye on his wife. In the husband's absence, the wife began an illicit affair. To carry it on, she killed her infant son and, to cover up the murder, killed her paramour. The soldier, on returning, learnt the truth from his neighbour, only to be burnt to death. The witness reported the crime to the local officer of Samana, so that the woman was tried and put to death. During the reign of Islam Shah (r. 1545-54), the city of Lahore witnessed two similar crimes. A cheat trapped innocent people on the pretext of marrying his daughter. Following the ceremony, he killed the guests with poisoned food. When caught, 60 corpses were discovered in the well of his house. Another cheat gave amulets to needy women, provided they came alone. If they were rich, he killed them and took away their jewellery. He was caught when he failed to dispose the body of a Khatri woman. The citizens were shocked to know that he had filled four wells with skeletons. Sometimes, women operated as members of criminal gangs. During the reign of Sikandar Lodi, a charming woman trapped Husain Khan Sarwani with a fake story of distress and a spiked betel leaf. Her accomplices took away his weapons. When he recovered, the robbers fled away. He dragged the woman for some distance and, as she was beautiful (*sahib husn*), kept her in his household. During the reign of Ibrahim Lodi, an old woman trapped a young man in Chandausi. The unconscious victim was brought to a forest. As soon as he became alert, her accomplices ran away. The man handed the woman over to the local officer.[10]

Mushtaqi's anecdotes, with or without miracles, stood on the border between fact and fiction. During the reign of Sikandar Lodi,

246 *Situating Medieval India*

a horsekeeper (*saturban*) came under the grip of a jinn. Magicians failed to exorcise the jinn, while Quranic recitations and prayers, proved futile. Ultimately, the jinn agreed to leave after listening to *Surah-i Rahman* in the melodious voice of Hafiz Bukhari. Pleased at the recitation, the jinn revealed that he merely used the horse-keeper as a means to reach the gifted reciter.[11] In the camp of Malik Allahdin Jilwani, Mushtaqi saw a man who had not answered the call of nature for 16 years. People, keeping a close watch, saw him consuming milk, gram and lentils without any effect. The man revealed that he had learnt the technique from a saint, who had been free from excrement for 24 years.[12] Shaikh Ghuran, returning from the camp of Humayun, stated that the Mughal army would march to Gujarat the next day. A Brahmin (*zunnardar*) asserted that Humayun would leave for Agra. A bet of 1,000 *tankahs* was laid. Next morning, Shaikh Ghuran brought the news that the kitchen and royal tent (*matbakh wa peshkhana*) was leaving for Gujarat. Humayun, covering a short distance, turned towards Agra. The Shaikh handed over the promised sum to the Brahmin.[13] The life of Miyan Walid was a combination of piety and aristocracy. Devoted to religious pursuits, he was generous towards servants and guests. He oversaw the production of perfumes and glass items that were sold for profit. His secret addiction to wine was revealed through his barber. Feeling ashamed, he abandoned the habit and, enrolling as a disciple of Shaikh Budhan Shattari,[14] engaged in perpetual austerities.[15] During the reign of Sikandar Lodi, a man acquired a bunch of peacock feathers at Mahavan and hoped to sell it to a buyer. He joined a caravan of merchants bound for Iran. Some dacoits looted all the goods, except the peacock feathers. Accidently, a single peacock feather reached the hands of an Iranian, who purchased more of them. Since peacock feathers commanded a high price, the man acquired a number of horses and returned to India much richer.[16]

Jahangir's memoirs comprised an account of 17 years of his reign. He penned the events of first twelve years, while Mutamad Khan (the author of *Iqbalnama-i Jahangiri*) accounted for the next seven years. The work reads like a diary, wherein the major and minor events were recorded in a strict chronological sequence. Besides

Pictures of Amazement in Medieval India   247

describing military engagements of the Mughal army and celebration of festivals in the royal court, Jahangir noted the appointment and promotion of officers. Travelling through different regions—Panjab, Kashmir, Kabul, Rajasthan, Gujarat and Central India—he has described the topographical features, the local tribes and products. His hunting expeditions enabled him to examine the characteristics of the flora and fauna. He was fond of conversing with saints like Miyan Mir of Lahore and Gosain Jadrup of Ujjain. He was candid about his addiction to alcohol and treatment of ailments. Though his approach to the world around him was rational and objective, he did not hesitate to describe strange occurrences. Such descriptions, appearing at fair intervals in his work, have not been forcibly inserted in the narrative. Instead, these have been properly contextualized and skillfully interwoven into the text, providing a literary charm that he might have cherished in his great grandfather Babur's autobiography. Jahangir was quite scrupulous in stating that an event had been recorded for its sheer strangeness, not due to any belief in irrational mysteries and miraculous events.

Jahangir recorded the following incident because it was not devoid of strangeness. While hunting during last two years, he shot a particular blue bull (*nilgau*) with his gun. Since it was not hit at a fatal place, it escaped with its life. In 1611, he came across the same onager. Though he shot at it thrice and pursued it on foot for three leagues, he failed to hit the target. He vowed that if the onager fell, he would distribute its cooked food among the poor in the name of Khwaja Muinuddin Chishti.[17] He also vowed a gold coin and rupee in the name of his father Akbar. Soon after, the onager, worn out with fatigue, appeared on its own. The target was hit and Jahangir fulfilled his promise. As the meat was being cooked, a gold coin and rupee were spent on sweets. All eatables were distributed among the poor and hungry. Two or three days later, Jahangir encountered another onager. Since it did not stand still at one spot, he could not take a shot at it. With the gun slung across his shoulder, he chased it until sunset. When he had despaired of killing it, it escaped from his tongue, 'Khawaja, this *nilgau* also is vowed to you.' Jahangir's remark and its sitting happened at the same moment. He found the target and, as on the previous occasion,

248 *Situating Medieval India*

distributed the cooked food among the poor.[18] It appeared that Jahangir was not an efficient hunter and, exposed for his tardiness and poor aim with the gun, he invoked the help of the prominent Chishti saint. No doubt, he had inherited his faith from Akbar.

Jahangir has described the circumstances in which Mulla Ali Ahmad died, as he found the episode strange. Once Jahangir was attending a musical session, where some Qawwals of Delhi performed and Syedi Shah mimicked a religious dance as a buffoon. The following verse of Amir Khusrau was the refrain of the song:

Each race has its right road of faith and its shrine.
I have set up my shrine in the path of one with the cocked cap.

Jahangir sought the meaning of the verse. Ali Ahmad, who was unsurpassed in the craft of engraving seals, replied on the authority of his father. Jahangir, during his childhood, had studied under Ali Ahmad's father. According to the answer, Shaikh Nizamuddin Auliya,[19] having put his cap on the side of his head, sat one day on a terraced roof besides the Yamuna and watched the devotions of the Hindus. When Amir Khusrau appeared on the scene, the Shaikh recited the first hemistich. The poet, without hesitation and with respect, recited the second hemistich. As soon as the words escaped Ali Ahmad's tongue, he lost his senses and fell down. Jahangir, fearful of his state, rushed to his head. Those who were assembled suspected that it was an epileptic fit. The physicians made enquiries, felt his pulse and brought medicines. Since his body was still warm, they believed that some life was still left in him. In spite of their exertions, they could not revive him. It became certain that he was dead. As his body was carried to his house, Jahangir sent money to his sons for his shroud and burial. He had never seen a death of this kind.[20]

That Jahangir had some belief in the miraculous power of Sufis was indicated in his account of Shah Alam (d. 1485). He paid homage at his shrine, which was located between Cambay and Ahmedabad. He was a descendant of Syed Jalaluddin Bukhari, the famous Suhrawardi saint of Uch. The local inhabitants, high and low, had strong faith in his spiritual eminence. In particular, it was believed that he could revive the dead. After he had brought back

Pictures of Amazement in Medieval India   249

several dead persons to life, his father forbade him from interference in the workshop of God, as the act was contrary to obedience. Shah Alam did not follow the advice. Owing to his prayer, a female attendant was blessed with a son. As this boy died at the age of 27, she requested Shah Alam to revive her only son. She also asked Shah Alam's son, who greatly loved her, to intercede on her behalf. Though the boy was tender in years, he beseeched his father to do the needful. Shah Alam declared that he could live if the boy gave up his life for him. The boy accepted the wish of his father and the desire of God. Shah Alam, lifting up his son from the ground, turned his face towards heaven and said, 'O God, take this kid in place of that one.' Instantly, the boy surrendered his soul, while the attendant found her son alive. Jahangir observed that many stories of this kind had gained currency in Gujarat. He tried to know the truth from Syed Muhammad, who held the spiritual seat of Shah Alam. The saint replied that he had heard such things from his father and grandfather, but only God knew the truth. Jahangir wrote, 'Although this affair is beyond the laws of understanding, yet, as it has attained great notoriety among men, it has been recorded as a strange occurrence.'[21]

Jahangir believed that the Sufis, owing to their superhuman powers, could predict their death and accordingly planned it. In this context, he has described the end of two Sufis, Mulla Gadai of Kashmir and Shaikh Salim Chishti of Fatehpur Sikri. The former was a disciplined dervish, who lived in a monastery of Srinagar for the last forty years. Two years before his demise, he selected a corner in the monastery for his burial and secured the approval of the heirs of the institution for his choice. He announced the time of his final departure on the basis of divine order. Everyone was filled with wonder, as even the prophets did not have such information. Mulla Gadai, sticking to his words, gave instructions about the disposal of his humble possessions. He directed a confidant to sell his copy of the Quran, which was worth 700 *tankahs* and spend the money on carrying his coffin to the grave. Declaring that he would breathe his last at the call for Friday's prayer, he distributed his goods among his disciples and acquaintances. He took his bath and retired to his cell. When the door was opened at the stipulated

250   *Situating Medieval India*

time, he was found sitting on his knees with his face turned towards Makka. In this posture, he had given up his soul to God.[22]

Jahangir, as a rational thinker, held that the saints disapproved the display of miracles due to their humility. Such wonders, though entirely unintentional and designed for the sake of teaching, occasionally appeared in the excitement of ecstasy. For example, Shaikh Salim Chishti had conveyed to Akbar the good news of the birth of Prince Salim and his brothers.[23] One day, Akbar asked the Shaikh about his age and the time of his departure from the world. The Shaikh replied that only God knew such matters. On being pressed, he observed that he would meet his end when Salim, through instruction of a teacher or in any other way, memorized something and recited it. Akbar, in order to avoid this eventuality, forbade the attendants from teaching the Prince anything in prose or verse. Two years and seven months passed under this precaution. A woman, who had access to Salim, dramatically changed the situation. She used to burn a particular shrub to avert the evil eye on Salim and, in return, received alms and charities. One day, she found him alone and, unmindful of the instruction, taught him the opening verse of Jami's *Yusuf Zulaikha*, 'O God, open the rosebud of hope. Display a flower from the everlasting garden.' Salim went to the Shaikh and repeated the couplet. The Shaikh informed Akbar of the incident. In accordance with fate, the same night the Shaikh had traces of fever. Next day, he requested Akbar to send Tansen Kalawant. While he listened to the master vocalist, he sent someone to call Akbar. He told Akbar that the promised time of union had come and he must take leave of him. He took off his turban and, placing it on Salim's head, said, 'We have made Sultan Salim our successor and have made him over to God, the protector and preserver.' Gradually, his weakness intensified and signs of his end became increasingly evident until he attained union with God.[24]

During a three-month hunting expedition (1606) to Nandanah and Girjhak (Salt Range), Jahangir witnessed a strange phenomenon. At Chandwalah, he shot an antelope in the belly. When wounded, it emitted a sound, which he had not heard, except in the rutting season. His companions and old hunters, astonished at it, did not remember any such thing. Nor had they heard it from their fathers.[25]

Pictures of Amazement in Medieval India 251

Once, a female antelope, which was in milk, was brought before Jahangir. It allowed itself to be milked with ease, yielding four seers of milk every day. He had never seen or heard anything of this kind. Not differing from the milk of cows and buffaloes, it was beneficial in the malady of asthma.[26] On another occasion (1609), one of the goatherds, who constituted a particular tribe, brought a gelded goat before Jahangir. It had teats like a female and every day gave milk sufficient for a cup of coffee. Since milk was one of the favours of God and a source that nourished numerous animals, Jahangir looked upon this strange affair as an omen for good.[27]

Jahangir, owing to an interest in the breeding habits of big cats, recorded some incidents as strange.[28] Akbar, who had collected 1,000 cheetahs, tried to pair them without success. He made male and female cheetahs copulate in gardens, but it did not come off. However, in Jahangir's reign, a male cheetah, having slipped out of its collar, went to a female and paired with it. After two and a half months, three cubs were born and grew up. During his reign, claimed Jahangir, the wild beasts had abandoned their savagery. Tigers became so tamed that a large herd, without any chains and shackles, moved among people without any harness. By chance, a tigress became pregnant and, after three months, bore three cubs. In the past, a wild tiger never paired in captivity (*na shudah bud keh baad az griftari juft shudah bashad*). It was heard from physicians that the milk of tigress was useful in improving the eyesight. They made every effort to extract moisture of milk in her breasts, but did not succeed. Jahangir reasoned that milk appeared in a mother's breasts on account of her affection for their young, for whom its blood turned into milk. When a tigress, which was ferocious by nature, found itself forcibly restrained, its rage increased to the extent of drying the milk in its breasts.[29]

Apart from the milk producing mammals, Jahangir noted the strange behaviour in birds and reptiles. During hunting (1623), a black partridge was captured. He ordered its gullet to be opened in his presence. Though its gullet was narrow, he was astonished on finding an entire undigested mouse, which it had swallowed. In his words, 'Without exaggeration, if anyone had told me that tale, I should not have believed it. As I saw this myself, I have

252   *Situating Medieval India*

recorded it on account of its strangeness.'[30] A year later, a similar incident was recorded. A large black hooded snake, which had swallowed another snake, was dug out of its hole. When they opened its belly, the hood of a snake it swallowed came out whole. Though the victim was of another kind, it was similar to the predator in length and girth.[31]

Jahangir did not ignore the exceptional elements among humans. During a visit (1607) to Kabul, he heard that a man named Khwaja Tabut (Yaqut) had died near Zuhak and Bamiyan centuries back. Though he had been buried in a cave, his limbs had not decomposed. Since the case appeared strange to Jahangir, he sent a confidential record writer along with a surgeon to the cave. They were instructed to examine the state of affairs and prepare a special report. It was discovered that half of the body touching the ground had dismembered. The other half, which did not touch the ground, remained in its own condition. The nails of hands and feet, besides the hair of the head, had not been shed. The hair of the beard and moustache, as far as one side of the nose, had been shed. According to an engraving at the door of the cave. the death occurred before the time of Sultan Mahmud (r. 998-1030), but nothing could be said for certain.[32] In 1619, Jahangir encountered another uncommon phenomenon. At Daulatabad, on the route from Lahore to the Jhelum, the daughter of a gardener was brought before him. Her physical appearance was like that of a man. She had a moustache and thick beard as big as the hilt of a sword. She had hair in the middle of her chest, but did not have any breasts. It was felt that she would not bear any children. Since she could be a hermaphrodite, Jahangir asked some women to take her aside for examination. They found that she was not different from other women. Jahangir recorded the episode on account of its strangeness.[33] During the reign of Firoz Shah Tughluq, two married women with breasts and beards were noted.

Sujan Rai Bhandari, a Panjabi Khatri who served the Mughal State as a clerk, completed his *Khulasat ut-Tawarikh* in 1695. This work provides a survey of the Indian history from the battle of Mahabharat to the defeat of Dara Shukoh at the hands of Aurangzeb. He relied on a large corpus of historical literature, including *Singhasan*

Battisi, Rajawali, Rajatarangini and *Padmawat*. He also studied the writings of Ziauddin Barani, Husain Khan Afghan, Abul Fazl, Jahangir, Mutamad Khan, Muhammad Waris and Muhammad Kazim. At the outset, he identified the benefits of studying history, the characteristics of the Indian subcontinent and various religious sects. He has given an account of the provinces of the Mughal State, laying emphasis on their geography, products and holy places. His account of the Hindu rulers, extending from Yudhishtra to Prithvi Raj Chauhan, was replete with supernatural elements. However, this streak rapidly declined in his history of the Muslim rulers. Yet, he could not sanitize his chronicle from strange happenings. For the reigns of Akbar and Jahangir, he has devoted entire sections to describe exceptional events. More interesting was the incredible feats that a group of acrobats and magicians performed in front of Jahangir, royal princes and nobles. Bhandari was aware of the Muslim saints, who earned popular adulation cutting across religious communities. In his view, their spiritual eminence had been built on collective memory of their miracles.

Since Bhandari belonged to Batala, he was emotionally attached to the landmarks of the town and its suburbs. The mausoleum of Shah Shamsuddin Dariayi was situated at village Dipaliwal in the subdistrict of Kalanaur. People narrated strange tales (*naqalha-i hairat afza*) of his miracles. Once, Dipali, a close disciple, expressed a desire to bathe in the Ganga along with his relatives. Dariayi persuaded Dipali to abandon his intention. Instead, he urged Dipali to remind him of it when the day arrived. Dipali did so. Dariayi asked him to close his eyes. When Dipali closed his eyes, he found himself at the bank of the Ganga. He joined his relatives in taking the bath. When he opened his eyes, he saw himself standing before Dariayi. When his relatives returned, they admitted that Dipali bathed along with them, but did not travel in their company. Nor did he return with them. They could not figure out his presence before their return. When Dipali revealed the truth, they were amazed at the miracle of Dariayi. A more incredible story emerged many years after the demise of Dariayi. A local administrator of Kalanaur targeted the Albizia (*siris*) tree near the shrine of Dariayi. He intended to acquire its timber for building purposes. The

254 *Situating Medieval India*

carpenters cut the trunk, which was converted into planks and boards. Suddenly, a loud sound arose and the earth trembled. The carpenters, out of fright, fled from the site. The trunk assumed its original shape, while the branches and leaves became green. As the story spread in all directions, the faith of the people became more intense. The place became a centre of pilgrimage (*ziyaratgah*) for one and all. Every Thursday evening, particularly the new moon, thousands of men and women converged here with offerings of milk, rice, sugar, ghee and flour. Every one succeeded in attaining his or her desire. The custodianship of the shrine has been in the hands of Hindus, who were the descendants of Dipali. Muslims had made vigorous efforts to remove them. Nevertheless, they had remained firmly entrenched in their position, owing to the blessings (*nazr khas*) of Dariayi on Dipali.[34]

Bhandari, in a chapter of his work, put together the uncommon happenings of Akbar's reign. We are told that Rawat Tika, the headman of Buxar, died of injuries on his waist and temple. His grandson, who was born after sometime, had scars on the same spots on his body. A blind man came to the Mughal court and recited poetry from his armpits, not his mouth. He had acquired this ability through practice and not through the impact of any *jinn*. A woman, whose husband appeared in the Mughal court, had given birth to 21 sons, all of whom were alive. A man, since his birth, was bereft of ears or substitute holes, but he could listen to what others said. A comet, owing to its evil disposition, caused a commotion in Khurasan and Iraq. Akbar wished to confirm if the human speech was attributable to social environment. A number of infants were segregated along with nurses who were dumb. After four years, Akbar found that they could only utter meaningless sounds and, thus, confirmed his initial thinking. The seventh occurrence was most interesting. A Mughal expedition was sent to punish rebels near Agra. Two Khatri brothers, who were twins, took part in the action. One of them was killed and his body was sent to his house in Agra. Since the brothers resembled each other in every respect, both wives claimed the body to be that of her husband and prepared to commit *sati*. The *kotwal*, in his predicament, transferred the dispute to the Mughal court. The two women appeared before Akbar. The wife of the elder brother, who was born an hour

Pictures of Amazement in Medieval India 255

earlier than his twin, offered a proof. She stated that her husband had on his heart a scar, which was formed following the death of her 10-year old son a year ago. Akbar ordered his experienced surgeons to cut the chest. The discovery of the scar caused amazement. The sudden arrival of the younger brother confirmed the discovery of the surgeons and claim of the woman. Akbar, praising her intelligence, allowed her to commit *sati*.[35]

Bhandari has devoted a chapter of his chronicle to the strange occurrences of Jahangir's reign. In Agra, a woman, who had borne three twin daughters, gave birth to a boy and two girls, all of whom were alive. The wife of a goldsmith underwent three long pregnancies of one year, 18 months and two years. In accordance with the practice in poor families, she performed all household chores with ease. Once, Jahangir came across a gardener's daughter, who had thick moustache and beard like any male. She had hair on her chest, but no breasts. A woman, who checked if she was a eunuch, found that she was a female. On another occasion, Jahangir organized a fight between a lion and a bull. The large gathering included some naked Jogis. Suddenly, the lion clasped the Jogi and, appearing as if engaged in coitus, separated only after the act. According to a royal order, the lion was deprived of his chain and collar, so that he could mix with 15 other male and female lions, who freely moved under the royal balcony. It was learnt that Hakim Ali had constructed a room underneath a tank in his house. A number of books and clothes were placed in it. The workmanship had employed air to block the entry of water into the room. A person, desirous of watching the spectacle, wore a loincloth and descended through the water. On reaching the room, he removed the loincloth and put on fresh clothes kept there. Ten to twelve persons could sit there for conversation. Jahangir, who had gone into the room, felt so pleased that he granted the rank of 2,000 to Hakim Ali. On another occasion, a ball of lightning fell in a village near Jalandhar, so that an area of 12 yards in length and breadth was burnt.[36] At the orders of the local administrator Muhammad Saeed, a 5-6 yards deep pit was dug and a piece of hot iron weighing 160 *tolas* was extracted. Jahangir sent it to Daud Lohar who, mixing it with a third of ordinary iron, fashioned two swords, one dagger and a knife.[37]

Jahangir, during a visit to Mathura, called on a dervish. Some

256　　　　　　　　*Situating Medieval India*

people swore by his saintliness due to his miracles, while others felt that he was a magician. After he had offered his prayer, five mendicants joined him in making a supplication with raised hands. Suddenly, 700 gold coins rained down. The dervish distributed half of them to the mendicants. He gave the other half to Jahangir, assuring him that his treasury would never be empty. When Jahangir walked away from the place, he realized that he had not kissed the dervish's hands. Instantly, the dervish's servant rushed to Jahangir and informed him that his desire had fulfilled. The Emperor, in his amazement, attributed the phenomenon to miraculous power, divine knowledge or the act of *jinn*. In the ultimate analysis, it was the result of devotion and austerities. Lovers of God, with their touch, could turn earth into gold and stones into diamonds.[38]

A troupe of acrobats and magicians arrived from Bengal and performed in the palace of Jahangir. The show continued for two days and nights. In the end, they received a remuneration of Rs. 50,000 along with robes. Nobles and princes, including Khurram (Shahjahan), gave the performers a reward of one lakh rupees. The following was a selection out of a total of nearly 30 items. At the outset, they created a garden. Planting kernels in the ground, they walked around in circles and recited incantations. A number of fruit trees—mulberry, apple, mango, coconut, guava, pineapple, apricot and date—grew to their full length. The fruits were served to Jahangir and the nobles. A number of birds, singing melodies, appeared on the trees. Soon after, the trees sank into the ground and disappeared from sight. They dug out a tank, which was filled with water and covered with a sheet. When it was uncovered, the water had turned into hard ice. They fixed a fountain, which emitted ten yard high spouts of water. The colour of water changed without making the ground wet. When the fountain was pulled out, it did not reveal any source of water. Fixed again, the fountain emitted boiling water and sparks. They showed an empty bag and, taking out different kinds of birds, made them fight. Similarly, they raised two tents on the corners of an empty space. On the wishes of the gathering, they brought out different species of animals that fought against each other. Twenty snakes, pulled out of the mouth of an acrobat, were engaged in a fight. Jahangir was given a notebook

Pictures of Amazement in Medieval India   257

comprising plain papers. When the pages were turned one by one, a colourful picture appeared on it. Equally amazing was a bag of books. They put a particular book in it and, when they took it out, it had turned into another title. For example, they put *Diwan-i Hafiz* into the bag and, taking it out, found it to be *Diwan-i Sulaiman* and so on.

An acrobat stood on the shoulders of another. In this manner, 60 acrobats built up a formation, standing on the shoulders of one another. A fresh acrobat, carrying all of them on his shoulders, walked away. A man stood behind another, putting his arms around his waist. Forty men formed a chain, which the first man pulled around in circles. The body of one of them was dismembered, so that the parts lay there for an hour. When the curtain was raised, the man appeared intact. A roll of yarn was thrown up into the sky, forming a straight line. An armed acrobat climbed up and, soon after, his parts fell down one by one. His wailing wife committed *sati* on the funeral pyre. The man reappeared on the scene and revealed that the parts belonged to the enemy. He cried on seeing the state of his wife, who also came back to life. A fifty yard long iron chain was thrown up into the sky, so that it stood straight like a pole. A number of animals, one after the other, climbed up. When the chain was pulled down, the animals did not return. Forty-nine arrows were shot up and, joining one another, formed a long chain. When the fiftieth arrow was released, all the arrows fell down. A large number of swords, with their points facing up, were fixed in the ground. An acrobat rolled over them, though his body remained free from any scratch. Two empty earthen pots were shown and, owing to a trick, were filled with sweets that kept on changing. A huge cauldron was filled with 20 maunds of meat along with rice, spices and water. The food was cooked without any fire and it was served among the people. They brought a huge tray with a delicious dish of meat. First, it was covered and, when the cover was removed, it had a variety of dry fruits. Uncovered many times, the tray showed a different eatable. In a similar exercise, a tray displayed different types of living creatures, such as fish, snakes and ducks. A four-sided cage, on being rotated, revealed different species of birds.[39]

258 *Situating Medieval India*

The cognizance of wondrous phenomena was not confined to hagiographical literature. During the thirteenth and fourteenth centuries, Amir Khusrau took pride in the supernatural abilities of ancient spiritual masters, while Shams Siraj Afif referred to physical abnormalities in humans and animals. The Mughal period witnessed a more profound engagement with what was essentially uncommon. Abul Fazl, describing the provinces of the Mughal Empire, noted the exceptional practices in Kangra, Malwa and Kamrup. The continuity of this trend, with attendant variations and diversities, was attributable to a number of impulses. In the first instance, the writer wished to deviate from the beaten track and leave a creative precedent for the posterity. In some cases, the intention was to break the monotony of linear political narrative, which was often tedious, insipid and repetitive. In other cases, the aim was to make reading a pleasurable exercise through interludes of thrill and excitement. The writers employed different means to attain these aims. Mushtaqi knew that he was weak in recording political developments and, in order to compensate for this weakness, inserted a disproportionately large measure of sensational stuff. He was admittedly courageous in exploring the unchartered domain of love and crime. Bhandari satisfied himself with brief accounts of extraordinary events pertaining to the reigns of Akbar and Jahangir. He made every effort to insulate his reconstruction of the past from diversionary intrusions. In contrast to Mushtaqi and Bhandari, Jahangir has skillfully interwoven the references to strange occurrences in his chronological record of an expanding polity. Almost invariably, he has discussed the inexplicable events in a proper context and, thus, did not trouble his reader with shocks and jerks. Scientific in approach and partial towards the Sufis, his memoirs maintained a constant thread of charm in a recollection of experiences in life.

NOTES

1. An earlier version of this paper entitled 'Strange, Amazing and Miraculous: Understanding the Patterns of Narration in Some Persian Histories' was presented at the National Seminar on *Exploring Medieval India Through*

Pictures of Amazement in Medieval India   259

Persian Sources, Centre of Advanced Study, Department of History, Aligarh Muslim University, Aligarh, 20-22 February 2017.

2. A very short man, bearing the height of a yard, was kept at Delhi and Firozabad. Two very tall men, brought from Lal Pahar to Delhi, were known as Mansukh. When they walked, they looked like moving minarets. A number of curious people came to see both types of men. Two dark women, who were married, had breasts as well as beards. They were brought from Hindustan to Delhi. The strange creatures included a three-legged goat, a five-legged cow, a black crow with red beak and feet, a parrot with black beak and feet, besides a fish with a head as large as that of an elephant. All these uncommon creatures were presented at the court, where Afif saw them with his own eyes. Shams Siraj Afif, *Tarikh-i Firoz Shahi*, Persian text, ed. Maulavi Wilayat Husain, Calcutta: Asiatic Society of Bengal, 1890, pp. 384-8.

3. Simon Digby, *Wonder Tales of South Asia: Translated from Hindi, Urdu, Nepali and Persian*, New Delhi: Oxford University Press, 2000.

4. Shaikh Rizqulah Mushtaqi, *Waqiat-i Mushtaqi*, Persian text, ed. Iqtidar Husain Siddiqui and Waqar ul-Hasan Siddiqi, Rampur: Rampur Raza Library, 2002, pp. 196-256. (Hereafter cited as Mushtaqi).

5. Ibid., pp. 47-53.

6. Ibid., pp. 234-8.

7. Malik Sarwar, the *wazir* of the Delhi Sultanate who enjoyed the title of Malik ush-Sharq, founded the Sharqi kingdom of Jaunpur towards the close of the fourteenth century. Its territory extended from Kol in the west to Tirhut in the east, while it touched the border of Nepal in the north and Malwa in the south. The kingdom attained its glory under Ibrahim Shah Sharqi (r. 1401-40). Imposing his authority on the chiefs of north Bihar, he snatched Qanauj from Delhi. At the instance of Shaikh Nur Qutb-i Alam, the famous Chishti saint of Pandua, he attacked Bengal in order to protect the Muslims from the repression of Raja Ganesh. His intervention in the internal affairs of Kalpi brought him into conflict with Malwa. Towards the end of his rule, he forced the Syed ruler of Delhi to form a matrimonial alliance with him. Mian Muhammad Saeed, *The Sharqi Sultanate of Jaunpur: A Political and Cultural History*, Karachi: University of Karachi, 1972, pp. 41-63; Mohammad Habib and Khaliq Ahmad Nizami, ed., *A Comprehensive History of India, vol. V: The Delhi Sultanate (AD 1206-1526)*, New Delhi: People's Publishing House, rpt., 1982, pp. 714-19.

8. Mushtaqi, pp. 214-20.

9. Ibid., pp. 251-3.

260   *Situating Medieval India*

10. Ibid., pp. 220-7.
11. Ibid., p. 58.
12. Ibid., p. 55.
13. Ibid., p. 232.
14. Shaikh Buddhan (d. 1488) was the mentor of Mushtaqi. Nothing was known about him except that he was a disciple of Shaikh Hafiz, who was a pupil of the founder of the Shattari order Shah Abdullah (d. 1485). The lineage flourished in central and west Asia under different names. Shah Abdullah, migrating to India, travelled across Jaunpur, Bengal, Rajasthan, Gujarat and Malwa. He wore the apparel of a Sultan, while his followers dressed as soldiers. Ghaus Gwaliari (d. 1563), who wrote many books including the biographical encyclopaedia *Gulzar-i Abrar,* attained great prestige. Humayun had close ties with the family of this leading Shattari. Adopting puritan ways, the Shattaris stressed the validity of Unity of Existence (*wahdat ul-wujud*), exorcism through a mysterious invocation of the names of Allah, assimilation of Indic cults like Tantra and a liberal approach to religion. As a result, they faced strong opposition from orthodox elements, including the Naqshbandis. Saiyid Athar Abbas Rizvi, *A History of Sufism in India,* vol. II, New Delhi: Munshiram Manoharlal, 1983, pp. 151-73; Qazi Moinuddin Ahmad, *History of the Shattari Silsilah,* Delhi: Idarah-i Adabiyat-i Delli, 2012, pp. 130-1, 169-70.
15. Mushtaqi, pp. 241-3.
16. Ibid., pp. 254-5.
17. In 1570, Akbar twice visited the shrine of Khwaja Muinuddin Chishti as thanksgiving for the birth of Salim and his second son. He also paid such visits after the conquests of Chittor, Bihar and Bengal. In all, he visited it 14 times. Owing to his patronage and endowments, its fortunes dramatically improved. Following disputes among the Khwaja's descendants, Akbar appointed a Mughal officer to manage the shrine. In 1582, Salim visited the place. A year later, he symbolized his devotion and gratitude by boring his ear lobes. His friends, soldiers and servants followed the suit. To these people, he presented pearls worth Rs. 36,000. In three years he was in Ajmer, he visited the shrine nine times. He believed that he owed his life and throne to the Khwaja. A miniature painting of Bachittar showed Jahangir receiving the orb and crown of imperial office from the Khwaja. P.M. Currie, *The Shrine and Cult of Muin al-Din Chishti of Ajmer,* New Delhi: Oxford University Press, 1989, pp. 101-7; John F. Richards, 'The Formulation of Imperial Authority under Akbar and Jahangir', in *The Mughal State, 1526-1750,* ed. Muzaffar Alam and Sanjay Subrahmanyam, New Delhi: Oxford University Press, 1998, p. 134.

Pictures of Amazement in Medieval India   261

18. Nuruddin Jahangir, *Tuzuk-i Jahangiri*, vol. I, Eng tr. Alexander Rogers and Henry Beveridge, Delhi: Low Price Publications, rpt., pp. 189-90. (Hereafter cited as Jahangir).

19. Amir Khusrau, as an intimate disciple of Shaikh Nizamuddin Auliya, often attended his assemblies. The Shaikh had deep affection for Khusrau. When Khusrau embarked on his literary career, the Shaikh conferred on him the boon of sweet language and advised him to compose love poetry on the beauty of tresses and moles. Khusrau wrote several panegyrics (*qasidahs*) on the Shaikh and prefaced his narrative poems (*masnavis*) with eulogies of the Shaikh. Whenever he completed a work, he took it to the Shaikh who, holding it in his hands, recited the Fatiha. The Shaikh wrote a number of letters to Khusrau, addressing him as the Turk of God. In fact, he desired that the poet be buried besides his grave and this wish was fulfilled. Khusrau, on returning from Lakhnauti, learnt of the Shaikh's demise. He blackened his face, tore his shirt and rolled on the ground. He died after six months. Amir Khurd, *Siyar ul-Auliya*, Persian text, Delhi: Matbah-i Muhhib-i Hind, 1885, pp. 301-5; Mohammad Wahid Mirza, *The Life and Works of Amir Khusrau*, Delhi: Idarah-i Adabiyat-i Delli, rpt., 1974, pp. 177-203.

20. Jahangir, I, pp. 169-70.

21. Ibid., I, pp. 421-2.

22. Ibid., I, pp. 290-1.

23. Shaikh Salim Chishti (1480-1572) was a descendant of Baba Farid. In 1524, he went to Makka for Haj and spent 13 years visiting Iraq, Syria, Turkey and Iran. In 1554, he again left for Haj and returned after many years. Setting up a hospice at Sikri, he attracted large crowds, including nobles and stonecutters quarrying stone for the Agra fort. The birth of Salim, owing to the Shaikh's prayers, inspired Akbar to develop the capital complex of Fatehpur Sikri. Under the Shaikh's supervision, a mosque and hospice were built. Akbar, emplacing the Shaikh's tomb within the walls of the grand mosque, drew upon its sanctity and assimilated it into his own authority. He did not permit the descendants to manage the shrine, but enlisted them into the Mughal bureaucratic (*mansab*) system. Islam Khan Chishti, a descendant of the Shaikh, served as the governor and conqueror of Bengal in the early seventeenth century. Saiyid Athar Abbas Rizvi, *A History of Sufism in India*, vol. II, New Delhi: Munshiram Manoharlal, 1983, pp. 279-83; John F. Richards, op. cit., pp. 132-4.

24. Jahangiri, II, pp. 70-1.

25. Ibid., I, p. 83.

26. Ibid., I, p. 148.

27. Ibid., I, p. 155.

262 *Situating Medieval India*

28. Jahangir has described 33 species of animals and 11 species of plants, while his incidental references numbered respectively 37 and 57. He noted their local names, geographical distribution, structural characteristics and behaviour. His descriptions were marked with originality, accuracy and meticulous observation. His establishment contained all kinds of carnivorous beasts, hunting birds and domesticated species. These were maintained to carry out observations, tests and experiments. Nobles and visitors brought animals for him from far and wide. His painters, particularly Ustad Mansur, excelled in portraiture of animals and flowers. His spirit of inquiry was reflected in measuring the depth of a pond near Ajmer, the healing power of bitumen and comparing the air quality in Ahmedabad and Mahmudabad. M.A. Alavi and A. Rahman, *Jahangir: The Naturalist*, New Delhi: Indian National Science Academy, rpt., 1989, pp. 1-9.

29. Jahangir, I, pp. 240-1.

30. Ibid., II, p. 287.

31. Ibid., II, p. 297.

32. Ibid., I, pp. 117-18.

33. Ibid., II, pp. 119-20.

34. Sujan Rai Bhandari, *Khulasat ut-Tawarikh*, Persian text, ed. M. Zafar Hasan, Delhi: G. and Sons, 1918, p. 68.

35. Sujan Rai Bhandari, *Khulasat ut-Tawarikh*, Urdu tr. Nazir Hasan Zaidi, Lahore: Urdu Science Board, 2002, pp. 376-8.

36. On 10 April 1621, a meteorite fell in a village of the subdistrict of Jalandhar. Jahangir and two contemporary historians have described the incident in detail. These writers have concentrated on the reaction of the inhabitants and the role of the local collector (*amil*) Muhammad Saeed. Interestingly, the matter was regarded as important enough for the attention of the Emperor. Jahangir, owing to his scientific bent of mind, got the object examined and handed it over to the master craftsman for conversion into a sword, dagger and knife after mixing with a third of fresh iron. The episode, particularly the response of Jahangir, became the theme of a quatrain from Bebadal Khan. Jahangir, II, pp. 204-5; Motamad Khan, *Iqbalnama-i Jahangiri*, Persian text, ed. Maulavis Abdul Haii and Ahmad Ali, Calcutta: Asiatic Society of Bengal, 1865, pp. 179-80; Khwaja Kamgar Husaini, *Maasir-i Jahangiri*, Persian text, ed. Azra Alavi, Bombay: Asia Publishing House, 1978, pp. 327-8.

37. Sujan Rai Bhandari, *Khulasat ut-Tawarikh*, Persian text, pp. 456-7.

38. Ibid., pp. 457-8.

39. Ibid., pp. 458-64.

CHAPTER 11

Historical Dimensions of Islam in South Asia: Modern Writings on Polity, Religion and Culture

Late nineteenth century witnessed the emergence of historiography on medieval South Asia in the English language.[1] British bureaucrats, keen to seek legitimacy for the colonial state, reconstructed the history of medieval centuries identified as Muslim rule. Elliot and Dowson's eight volumes, comprising English translations of excerpts from Persian chronicles, generated an abiding interest in the subject. The technology of printing and lithography enabled the Asiatic Society of Bengal (Calcutta) and Munshi Nawal Kishore (Lucknow) to publish texts of numerous Persian works. In major cities of British India, the newly established universities and colleges nurtured historians, who were conversant with the theoretical underpinnings of the historian's craft as well as the knowledge of classical languages. At the outset, they traced the fortunes of ruling dynasties and individual rulers. Besides administrative institutions and economic activities, attention was given to religious movements, social structure and art forms. In the post-independence period, the impact of Marxism manifested in the study of social classes, particularly the oppressed peasantry and powerful intermediaries. In contrast, the Cambridge School proposed a more complex analysis of medieval realities. In recent times, the saffronization of educational institutions and funding bodies has breathed fresh life into the communalist approach to Indian history. The role of Islam in pre-modern times has penetrated the public discourse owing to four decades of sectarian politics and the increasing anti-Muslim intolerance in ordinary life. In these circumstances, it is appropriate to take a stock of the writings on South Asian Islam.

264 *Situating Medieval India*

The history of the Delhi Sultanate was no longer confined to the narratives of military conquests, dynastic revolutions and court intrigues. Its consolidation brought about a slow change in the agrarian relations. In the early thirteenth century, it allowed the continuance of the existing political structure, so that a tribute was imposed on the rural aristocracy (*rais* and *ranas*) who, in turn, collected land revenue from the peasantry as before. In the early fourteenth century, the polity was strong enough to subvert the rural aristocracy and deprive the village headmen (*khuts* and *muqaddams*) of the customary privileges. A new class of intermediaries, necessary to collect the land tax, was created out of the elements from the rural aristocracy and village headmen. The *chaudhari*, a foremost representative of this emerging class, headed a collection of several villages. From the middle of the fourteenth century, the *zamindar* became a blanket term for the entire superior class.[2] The increasing burden of the land tax resulted in a widespread peasant uprising in the Doab. A scheme of promoting agriculture through loans ended in a failure. As a result, the Delhi Sultanate shifted its focus to the cis-Satluj tract and Multan region. Forming alliances with the *zamindars* and Sufis, the state attained agrarian expansion through canal networks. The exercise involved the introduction of winter crops (*rabi*), settlement of villages and development of urban centres.[3] Following Timur's invasion, these positive trends crumbled and encouraged a revival of the old rural aristocracy. The Afghan State (1450-1550), owing to internal dissensions and lack of political sagacity, entangled itself in bloody conflicts with the tribes such as Gakkhars, Niazis, Langahs, Balochis and Jats. For south India, we find that Burton Stein has applied the concept of 'segmentary state' to the kingdoms of the Cholas and Vijaynagar, generating a lively debate.[4]

A landmark in historiography was achieved (1963) with a study of the agrarian system prevailing in the Mughal times. The complexity of the historical experience, owing to variations in topographical features, complicated our understanding of agricultural production, means of cultivation and marketing of crops. The state of widely scattered peasantry was uncovered with reference to the ownership of land and composition of the village community.

Historical Dimensions of Islam in South Asia 265

Equally crucial was the internal stratification in the class of intermediaries which, relying on customary incomes and military resources, shared the agricultural surplus with the Mughal State. The administrative machinery employed different methods of assessing the land tax, besides paying the bureaucracy through revenue assignments and maintaining religious classes through land grants. An agrarian crisis, traced to the transferability of revenue assignments, manifested in defiance of intermediaries. Popular uprisings of several groups—Marathas, Jats, Satnamis and Sikhs—were seen as expressions of agrarian distress.[5] Nevertheless, Akbar's success in creating a large and stable empire was attributed to centralization and systematization of administration. This underlying principle was manifest in the classification of nobles into military ranks (*mansabs*) and corresponding evolution of revenue assignments (*jagirs*). The estimated revenue (*jama dami*) equalled the sanctioned pay (*talb*), while restrictions were placed on assignment holders (*jagirdars*) through the constant transfer of assignments. The powerful intermediaries (*zamindars*), who dominated the countryside, largely accommodated themselves to the new system. The administrative structure of one province became an exact replica of the other. The chain of officers at various levels, controlled by the ministers at the centre, gave identity to the Mughal administrative institutions irrespective of the regions they functioned.[6]

According to a critique of literature on the Mughal State, the Aligarh School, designated as ostensibly 'nationalist-Marxist', often appeared closer to the colonialist positions than the school of 'constitutionalist' nationalist historians associated with the Allahabad University in the 1940s and 1950s, but whose legacy had often been neglected.[7] Engaged with the systematic and systemic features of the Mughal State, it focused mainly on the state as a revenue sponge or fiscal mechanism. What was sometimes termed as the Mughal agrarian system meant only the fiscal system. Irfan Habib, receiving Moreland's work as a model, shared many of the analytical preoccupations and methodological preconceptions of his British predecessor. What appeared to Moreland as Oriental Despotism resurfaced in Habib as class-based exploitation. A close reading of Abul Fazl's *Ain-i Akbari* points to the severe limitations to the

266 *Situating Medieval India*

application of the regulation (*zabt*) territories and, thus, militates against the picture of unremitting centralization and a uniform bureaucracy penetrating the countryside.[8] Tracing the Mughal decline to systemic contradictions, the Aligarh School emphasized the tensions between the numerically calibrated elite and amorphous mass of peasantry, besides the tension between the Mughal State and the rural gentry (*zamindars*). Instead of attaining perfection by 1600, the Mughal State perpetually underwent evolution from 1530 to 1750. Since the incorporation of new regions into the Mughal domain necessitated adjustment to local conditions, the state eventually resembled a patchwork quilt rather than a wall-to-wall carpet. Many of the post-Mughal states were based on ethnic or sectarian groupings—Marathas, Jats and Sikhs—without bearing any real precedent in the medieval past.[9]

Aligarh scholarship, under the stewardship of Mohammad Habib, took up the study of the Chishti order, which had developed a vast network in northwestern India during the Sultanate period. A distinction was drawn between the genuine and spurious sources. Only three works—*Fawaid ul-Fuad*, *Khair ul-Majalis* and *Siyar ul-Auliya*—were adjudged as authentic. A number of mystical discourses (*malfuzat*), associated with Chishti exemplars from Usman Haruni to Nasiruddin Mahmud Chiragh-i Delhi, were found to be fabrications. These findings of Mohammad Habib influenced Khaliq Ahmad Nizami, who explored the contributions of first five major Chishti masters. The discussions revolved around the development of spiritual territories (*wilayat*), cultivation of extreme poverty, dependence on unasked charity (*futuh*), organization of hospices (*khanqahs*), service of humanity, training of disciples and aloofness from the state.[10] The popularity of the Chishtis among the people has been attributed to their understanding of Indian conditions and willingness to assimilate indigenous customs. In contrast, the Suhrawardis stood marked for their close association with the contemporary rulers and accumulation of wealth. In an attempt to explain the limited sway of the Suhrawardis, Nizami argues that unlike the Chishtis, who believed in the control of emotional life as prerequisite to the control of external behaviour, the Suhrawardis tackled the problem from the other end and

Historical Dimensions of Islam in South Asia 267

emphasized the necessity of regulating actions prior to the control of emotions.[11]

The Chishtis held musical sessions (*sama*) as integral to their mystical practice. Of the modern writers, Nizami entirely ignores it, while Rizvi was sparse in his discussions. Ernst and Lawrence regarded it as indispensable along with the recollection of God (*zikr*). Amir Khurd has devoted the ninth chapter of his voluminous *Siyar ul-Auliya* to a comprehensive treatment of the theme. He has quoted from the *Fawaid ul-Fuad*, the notes of Shaikh Nizamuddin Auliya and his disciple Fakhruddin Zarradi's *Usul us-Sama*. His numerous references to the Prophet's interest in poetry indirectly approved the practice. The Chishtis, though fond of it, laid stress on the essential conditions. A series of instructions revolved around the singers, listeners, venue, clothes, outward behaviour and inner state. The mystical verses, normally in Persian and sometimes in Hindi, were understood in their context. Attractive parts of the human body figured as metaphors for divine creativity. The impact of a performance, appearing in various forms (*anwar, ahwal* and *asaar*) were linked to the spiritual planes (*jabrut* and *malkut*). If the listener lost control over his senses, he was permitted physical movement—hand clapping, foot tapping, raising cries, falling in ecstasy, weeping, dancing with raised hands and tearing clothes–in accordance with strict protocols. The use of musical instruments harp (*chang*) and rebeck (*rabab*) was disfavoured, though they were rarely discarded in practice. In Delhi, Hamiduddin Nagauri established musical sessions on a firm footing. Though the clerics issued legal opinions (*fatwas*) against him, no action was taken owing to the support from Minhaj-i Siraj Juzjani, an ardent practitioner of audition. The mystical verses and musical modes, known to have moved the listeners to heights of spiritual arousal, attained great fame in Delhi. Poets and Qawwals vied with one another to compose fresh couplets and create novel melodies. Owing to the spiritual authority of Shaikh Nizamuddin Auliya, who often stood up to weep and drench his handkerchief with tears, the audition acquired unprecedented acceptability.[12]

Amir Khurd, relying on the testimony of his father, has described six musical gatherings of Shaikh Nizamuddin, besides the distinct

268 *Situating Medieval India*

abilities of his Qawwals. More importantly, he has provided a vivid account of the Shaikh's appearance in the court of Sultan Ghiasuddin Tughluq (r. 1320-5). Husamuddin Farjam and the deputy judge Qazi Jalaluddin Lawanji, garnering the support of some orthodox elements, prepared a complaint against the Shaikh's audition along with the legal opinions regarding Hamiduddin Nagauri. The Sultan, ignorant of the law and traditions, summoned the Shaikh to face the charges. The Shaikh, remaining unperturbed, did not allow his disciples Fakhruddin Zarradi and Wajihuddin Paili to prepare any formal defence. In the court, the nobles and theologians were present in full strength. While all eyes were fixed on the Shaikh, the Sultan repeatedly urged the audience to keep quiet. The Shaikh displayed remarkable patience when Lawanji, while giving his satirical sermon, threatened to pronounce a punishment. The Shaikh did not refute the allegations of Farjam, as the latter did not even know the meaning of audition. The Sultan asked Maulana Ilmuddin, a grandson of Shaikh Bahauddin Zakariya who had penned a monograph on audition, to adjudicate the matter. Ilmuddin stated that audition was permissible to those who listened with their hearts, not to those who listened for sensual pleasure. The Sufis in the lands of West Asia—Baghdad, Sham and Rum—held auditions with musical instruments. No attempt had ever been made to stop the practice, which had been prevalent since the times of Shaikh Junaid and Shaikh Shibli. The Sultan, at the request of Shaikh Nizamuddin, refrained from issuing any verdict. Later on, Shaikh Nizamuddin, while conversing with Amir Khusrau and Mohiuddin Kashani, berated the clerics of Delhi, who had failed to give due weightage to the Hadis in their arguments. Expressing his resentment, the Shaikh foretold calamities for the city in the form of famine, plague and outmigration.[13]

That the people of Delhi were strongly attached to Sufi music manifested in a spontaneous protest, which was staged after the interrogation of Shaikh Nizamuddin. Ghiasuddin Tughluq had imposed a strict ban on musical assemblies, including recitation of the Quran in a melodious voice. In these dismal circumstances, Shaikh Wajihuddin Usman Siyah Sunami invited Hasan Qawwal (the chief Qawwal in attendance at the hospice of Shaikh Nizamud-

Historical Dimensions of Islam in South Asia 269

din) to sing in his characteristic style. As a precaution, the door was chained and Hasan kept his pitch low. On hearing the mystical verses, Sunami became ecstatic and Hasan abandoned all inhibition. A large number of people, including 200 Qawwals and several Sufis, joined the assembly. This gathering of thousands comprised two categories of people—those who were swayed by spiritual emotion and those who were interested in merriment. Sunami led the procession to the royal palace at Daulatabad, while singing and dancing reached a passionate fervour. The Sultan refrained from punishing the protesters in view of their large numbers. He wished to punish Sunami for receiving money from the deposed ruler Khusrau Khan. The allegation could not be proved, as Sunami had actually rejected such an offer. The Sultan, forced to change his mind, invited Sunami and his companions to stay in the palace for three days. At the end of this sojourn, the Sultan offered a big cash amount to Sunami in gratitude. Sunami declined the gift and, instead left for Ghiaspur, where he called on Shaikh Nizamuddin.[14] The people of Delhi, through this protest, expressed their solidarity with the distinguished Chishti master.

Shaikh Nizamuddin was not the first Sufi to face a trial at the Sultan's court. Hamiduddin Nagauri was found in a perpetual state of ecstasy, which was generated in his musical assemblies (*sama*). If ever he was sober, he attended the court of Iltutmish (r. 1210-36), who held him in reverence. Two orthodox jurists (*muftis*) Saad and Imad, deeming Nagauri's pursuits as heretical, persuaded Iltutmish to summon Nagauri for a dose of humiliation. However, the Sultan received Nagauri with all marks of honour and made him sit near him. The jurists, having planned to overwhelm Nagauri in debate, asked the ruling of the Shariat on singing. Nagauri replied that it was forbidden if the listener was an ordinary scholar and permissible if the listener was a man of the (spiritual) path. Nagauri reminded Iltutmish of a musical assembly in Baghdad, where he and the Sultan (then a boy) were present. In that nightlong performance, the boy, without being asked, kept on cutting the burnt wicks of the candles. As a recompense for this service, the Sufis conferred the kingdom of Hindustan on the boy. Since then, Nagauri had been following the Sufis of Baghdad in his ecstasy

270   *Situating Medieval India*

and dance. The Sultan recalled the incident and fell at Nagauri's feet with a hundred apologies. Nagauri's detractors, stunned and astonished, asked for forgiveness and gave up their demands.[15]

Besides this incident, some other stories of Nagauri's attachment to Sufi music were current in Delhi. He kept a Qawwal named Mahmud in his permanent service. In regular musical gatherings, Mahmud's performances induced Nagauri to break into impassioned dance. In order to test Nagauri, sharp thorns and burning charcoals were scattered on the floor. Nagauri, oblivious of the injuries and pain, kept on dancing for one hour. He recovered from his trance only when Mahmud stopped singing. On another occasion, Nagauri invited Saad and Imad to a feast at his hospice. When the guests had enjoyed the dinner, Mahmud started singing a melody in the Iraqi mode. From the beginning, the music melted the hearts of the listeners, ranging from pious devotees to uninitiated lay men. The entire assembly, thrown into a trance, kept on dancing for a long time. It recovered its consciousness when the muezzin gave the call for prayer. The participants prepared to offer the *Isha* (night) prayer. As the door of the hospice was opened, they were astonished to find that the night had passed in the twinkling of an eye and the day had dawned. The melody worked like an enchanting magic and inflamed the feelings of lovers. In Hindustan, the hunters sang a song to immobilize a deer, which was effortlessly captured or became an easy target for arrows. If melody produced such a powerful impact on animals, one could only wonder at an unaffected human being.[16]

A recent work on the Chishtis distances itself from the oft-repeated model of classicism, decline and revival. Instead, it proposed a five-stage periodization based on faithfulness to Chishti ideals and norms. The first two cycles pertained to an early phase outside India, while the last three were confined to India. Of the Indian cycles, the first ended in the heyday of the Tughluqs. The second covered fourteenth-eighteenth century and the third encompassed eighteenth-twenty-first century. Since identity and legitimacy were important for Sufi orders, the Chishtis expressed the authority of the past through genealogies. Equally important was attention to historical beginnings and transnational origins, though the

Historical Dimensions of Islam in South Asia   271

prominent hagiographies—*Akhbar ul-Akhyar, Safinat ul-Auliya* and *Mirat ul-Asrar*—adopted different strategies. Two core Chishti practices were the recollection of God (*zikr*) with breath control and listening to music (*sama*) with attendant conditions and impact. The former involved the treatise of Nizamuddin Aurangabadi (d. 1729) and the latter a series of writings from Ali Bin Usman Hujweri (d. 1072) to Ashraf Jahangir Simnani (d. 1425). Next to the core practices, the Chishtis stressed the merit of pilgrimage to Sufi shrines. In the early eighteenth century, Muhammad Najib Qadiri wrote the *Makhzan ul-Aras*, laying down a calendar of death anniversaries and guidelines for correct behaviour at visitations. During the colonial period, the development of the Chishti order was seen through the work of two branches, Nizamis and Sabiris. The former grew under the leadership of Kalimullah Jahanabadi (Delhi) and Sulaiman Taunsavi (Panjab), while the latter was associated with Haji Imdadullah (d. 1899) and Zauki Shah (d. 1951). In view of the challenges from Muslim reformers and secular modernists, the Chishti exemplars employed vernacular journalism and printing press as the new means of communication. The prolific writings of Hasan Nizami (Nizami branch) and Ashraf Ali Thanvi (Sabiri branch) threw ample light on the Chishti response to the changing socio-political context. In modern times, Hazrat Inayat Khan (Nizami branch) and Captain Wahid Bakhsh Sial (Sabiri branch) carried the Chishti message to the west. In our days, the expansion of cyberspace has enabled the Chishtis to communicate with a growing following across the globe, cutting across racial and cultural barriers.[17]

The role of Shaikh Ahmad Sirhindi (1563-1624) has been the subject of a contentious debate among historians, who have differed on his attitude to the Mughal State, Islamic revival and mystical path. Qureshi, who believed in a unique and separate identity of the Muslim community in the Indian subcontinent, held that Sirhindi strengthened orthodoxy to the extent of bringing both the Mughal rulers and Islamic mysticism within its fold. In contrast, Rizvi asserts that Sirhindi, in spite of his tirade against the Hindus and Shias, failed to change the liberal character of the Mughal State. He argues that Sirhindi's sectarian revivalism failed to gain ground

272   *Situating Medieval India*

in the face of the ongoing trend of cultural assimilation, which was based on pantheism and articulated through Muhibullah Allahabadi, Miyan Mir, Mulla Shah Badakhshi, Dara Shukoh and Sarmad. Friedmann complains that modern historians of the Indian subcontinent, owing to the influence of contemporary politics, had focused on Sirhindi's attitude to state and religion, which was peripheral to his thought. Therefore, he urges that Sirhindi be treated essentially as a Sufi, who had to be assessed within the Sufi framework of reference. Sharply disagreeing with this approach, Shuja Alhaq insists that it was not possible to examine Sirhindi's discourse on mysticism in isolation from his ideas on state, religion, Islam and non-Muslims. He not only invalidates the mystical experiences of Sirhindi, but also demolishes his contribution to the development of mystical thought. In his view, Sirhindi identified Islam with political domination and checked the evolution of a pluralistic spiritual culture, leaving no room for Sufism to survive.[18]

Since Rizvi has performed the herculean task of writing the history of South Asian Islam, his contributions deserved a distinct notice. He initiated a lifelong pursuit with a study on the two revivalist movements, the Mahdawis and Naqshbandis. In a parallel volume, he reconstructed the intellectual currents prevailing in the reign of Akbar. The life and work of Abul Fazl, the celebrated historian, has been contextualized in a ideological tussle between the orthodox and liberal elements. His religious and political thinking, which became an essential ingredient of Mughal kingship, was traced to diverse sources such as ancient Indian legal texts, Mongol histories and works of Firdausi, Ghazzali, Avicenna, Nizam ul-Mulk Tusi, Nasiruddin Tusi and Jalaluddin Dawwani.[19] Rizvi, in his works on Shah Waliullah and Shah Abdul Aziz, delved into the intellectual dynamism in the city of Delhi. Shah Waliullah, a prolific writer in Persian and Arabic, drew his authority from visionary contacts with the Prophet and his descendants, besides his varied claims of being the wise, righteous one, pivot among saints and renewer (*mujaddid*). This enabled him to clear difficulties in understanding the Quran, Prophetic traditions, Islamic jurisprudence, Shariat and mysticism. Though he refused to see any substantive difference between Unity of Being and Unity of Appearance,

Historical Dimensions of Islam in South Asia   273

he became an ardent Sunni partisan in the Shia-Sunni polemics. In view of the decline of the Mughal State, he visualized an efficient state (caliphate). In addition to the virtues of the caliph, he focused on the management of the army, taxation, supporters and rebels. He urged the Mughal emperor and Nizam ul-Mulk Asaf Jah to reform the administrative institutions. In his letter to Ahmad Shah Abdali, he exposed the weakness of the Mughal State and called for action against the Marathas and Jats. He asked the Rohilla chief to suppress the Jats and Sikhs. Upset at the social chaos in Delhi, he advocated the hereditary principle and demographic balance among various professional classes such as the soldiers, traders, artisans and farmers. Blaming the failure of the Sufis and clerics, he condemned immoral pursuits and un-Islamic practices like visiting tombs, Ashura mourning and Shab-i Barat.[20] Shah Abdul Aziz (1746-1824), the son of Shah Waliullah, headed his father's seminary and, as a prolific writer, confined himself to his intellectual inheritance. He was required to deal with differences between the Shariat and customary law, besides the questions of land grants and usury. Bulk of Rizvi's study comprised an analysis of Aziz's major work on the Shias, entitled *Tuhfa-i Isna Ashariyya*, and resultant responses from both the sects.[21] For a more realistic picture of Islam in Delhi, Rizvi took on board the contribution of Tariqah-i Muhammadiyya under Khwaja Mir Dard and Chishti lineage of Shah Kalimullah Jahanabadi and his spiritual successors.

Rizvi's voluminous study on the Twelver Shias (Isna Asharis) revolves around the role of Shia bureaucrats in the medieval states and Shia scholars in polemical debates. In the early medieval times, the Ismailis were found in Sind and Multan, while they figured in a violent revolt in Delhi during the reign of Raziya. Firoz Shah Tughluq claimed to have unleashed severe persecution of the Isna Asharis. In different parts of India, the disciples of Ala ul-Daula Simnani and Shah Niamatullah Wali propagated the Shia creed. In Kashmir, Syed Ali Hamdani (d. 1385) and Nur Bakhsh (d. 1465) promoted adulation of the Prophet and his family. During the sixteenth century, Kashmir witnessed intense Sunni-Shia tensions. As for the Mughal State, Iranis formed a fourth of the nobles (1575-95) holding ranks above 500, while Sunni-Shia

274   *Situating Medieval India*

controversies erupted in the Ibadat Khana. The Bahmani kingdom employed many Irani officers and, later on, Sunni-Shia strife appeared in Bijapur and Golconda. Nurullah Shustari, who served as the Qazi of Lahore, emerged as the leading Shia scholar. His *Majalis ul-Mominin* and *Ihqaq ul-Haq* ushered in a new era of Shia awakening. The former discussed Isna Ashari beliefs, holy places and notables, while the latter was a response to the Sunni treatise of Fazlullah bin Ruzbihan. His death at the hands of Jahangir was treated as martyrdom. Nurjahan's marriage with Jahangir brought her family to prominence. The Mughal patronage of Shia nobles was reflected in the careers of Mahabat Khan, Ali Mardan Khan and Mir Jumla. The Nawabi state of Awadh encouraged the growth of Shia institutions, though the position of the Sunnis remained intact. The Shia intellect, facing a onslaught from Shah Waliullah and Shah Abdul Aziz, stood on its own with the writings of Rahman Ali Sonepati, Shaikh Ali Hazin and Ghufran Maab. In the non-political domain, Shah Fatehullah Shirazi stood out for his inventions. Besides his water works and Ilahi calendar, he invented a number of devices such as a machine for cleaning gun barrels, a multi-barrelled cannon and a portable cannon. The Persian poets from Husain Sanai to Mirza Ghalib and Aurangzeb's leading historians—Muhammad Kazim Shirazi, Saqi Mustaid Khan, Aqil Khan and Khafi Khan—were Shia. The celebration of Muharram, which commemorated the tragedy of Karbala, became integral to the Shia creed. The devout attended the recital of the Karbala narratives and joined mourning processions of the replicas of the tombs of martyrs. In spite of the persistent opposition of the Sunnis, the observance spread to all parts of South Asia, owing to official support in Delhi, Awadh and Hyderabad.[22]

A study of Richard M. Eaton, choosing the region of Bijapur, analysed the social role of different types of Sufis (warrior, reformist, literati, landed and dervish) in relation to rulers, clerics, Islam and non-Muslims. He suggested that after the disintegration of the Sufi networks in the eighteenth century, Sufi shrines continued to function as 'dynamic catalysts' in deepening Islamic acculturation among several convert communities. His application of this insight to the evolution of the shrine of Baba Farid (1175-1265) at

Historical Dimensions of Islam in South Asia 275

Pakpattan opened a new field of research. This Sufi master trained disciples in Chishti mysticism and distributed amulets in return for offerings. After his demise, his spiritual charisma (*barakah*) was believed to reside in his tomb and descendants. A series of rituals—death anniversary (*urs*), community kitchen (*langar*), musical sessions (Qawwali), succession to the spiritual seat (*dastarbandi*) and passage through the southern door (*bihishti darwaza*) of the tomb—were institutionalized to form what has been designated as theatre-oriented Islam. The shrine, receiving land grants from the Tughluq rulers, began to play a new socio-political role. The spiritual head (*sajjadah nishin*), who managed the endowments, came to be known as Diwan. Since he received the state share from crops that were charged revenue in kind, he began to promote cultivation of foodgrains. A number of pastoral clans, who had been shifting between the central uplands and riverine tracts, were settling as sedentary cultivators with the help of the Persian wheels. At the same time, they underwent a slow process of Islamization owing to their participation in theatre-oriented Islam rooted in the shrine. The relationship of the clans was further cemented, as the clan chiefs offered their daughters in marriage to the Diwan and his kinsmen. As an intermediary institution, the shrine played a dual role, political and social. On the one hand, it stood as a link between the clans and Delhi Sultanate through the instrument of land grants and, on the other, between the clans and Islam through a series of rituals.[23]

The shrine of Khwaja Muinuddin Chishti attained popularity within a century of his demise, as it attracted the attention of Muhammad bin Tughluq and the rulers of Malwa and Gujarat. In early sixteenth century, Jamali noted its numerous attendants, massive offerings and droves of Muslim and Hindu pilgrims. During a century of the Mughal rule (1560-1660), the cult made impressive gains with state patronage. Around the tomb, numerous structures—gateways, mosques, cells, offices, tanks and cauldrons—served the needs of pilgrims and staff. During the Mughal decline, change of political masters in Ajmer did not erode the popular appeal of the shrine.[24] The number of pilgrims, numbering 20,000 in 1879, rose to 1.5 lakhs in 1920. The daily schedule of ceremonies was

276   *Situating Medieval India*

modified during the annual death anniversary when the Diwan presided over the musical sessions. A peculiar spectacle was witnessed during the looting of hot rice dessert from the cauldrons. The motives of the pilgrims were material, ritual and spiritual. The pilgrimage enabled them to escape the social hierarchy of their native places and bask in the gentle equality (communitas) prevailing at the site.[25] The attendants (*khuddam*), numbering 1,400 in 1976, regulated the ceremonies and assisted the pilgrims through clientship. Sadly, the offices of the spiritual head (*sajjadah nishin*) and manager (*mutawwali*) were mired in disputes.[26] The shrine received endowments and cash donations from the Mughals and Nizams of Hyderabad, besides offerings from pilgrims. The income was spent on ceremonies, annual festivities, salaries of servitors, maintenance of mosques and charitable institutions.[27] During the colonial period, protracted litigation yielded authentic evidence on administrative changes and financial matters.

Salar Masud Ghazi was not a Sufi. He was a warrior saint, who sacrificed his life to protect his following of cowherds and their cows. His cult, anchored on his shrine at Bahraich, has evolved during 700 years in large parts of north India, extending from Panjab to Bihar and spilling into Nepal. Amir Khusrau (d. 1325) noted that the fragrance of the tomb had scented entire Hindustan. A few decades later, the Tughluq rulers and Ibn Battuta visited it. A search for its past presented two opposing images of Ghazi Miyan. Abdur Rahman Chishti, in a hagiography *Mirat-i Masudi*, portrayed Ghazi Miyan (the son of Sultan Mahmud's sister) as a pious Muslim who died (15 June 1033) fighting Hindu rulers of northern Awadh. This story elaborated the motif of 'Sword of Islam'. In contrast, Muslim balladeers (Dafalis) remember Ghazi Miyan as the cow saving Muslim saint in the model of folk heroes like Pabuji, Ramdev and Guga. The cowherds, out of devotion, made offerings (*shagun*) of milk to Ghazi Miyan every eighth day. The local ruler Sohal Dev imposed a ban on the practice. Enraged at open defiance, he killed many cowherds and took away cows. Jasso Rani, the wife of cowherd chief Nand, rushed to Ghazi Miyan and raised a cry for saving the cows (*gau guhar*). Ghazi Miyan interrupted his marriage ceremony and, fighting against Sohal Dev, died a unwed virgin.

Historical Dimensions of Islam in South Asia   277

He had restored the eyesight of the young Zohra Bibi, who was believed to be spiritually married to him. Her family, based in Rudauli, annually visited Bahraich to complete the nuptials with a dowry. The custom overlapped with Muharram and the wedding of Hasan's son Qasim with Husain's daughter Sakina. Every year, lakhs of pilgrims organized themselves into marriage processions and, reaching Bahraich, solemnized Ghazi Miyan's wedding with Zohra Bibi. Apart from Ahirs, the following of Ghazi Miyan comprised low-caste Lalbegis, Julahas, Doms, Mirasis and Nats.[28]

Shared cultural space also evolved in parts of south India, where the Shia traditions of Muharram were organically entwined with the local culture. The village of Gugudu (Ananta Pura district in Andhra Pradesh) has been the site of a 13-day celebration of Muharram. In a total population of 2,620, only 182 were Muslims. A large majority of pilgrims were non-Muslims, who travelled hundreds of miles from Andhra Pradesh, Tamil Nadu and Karnataka. In 2007, nearly three lakh pilgrims attended the festival. The Muslims saw the saint Kullayappa as the eldest grandson of Prophet Muhammad, while the non-Muslims regarded him as the eleventh incarnation of Vishnu. It was believed that Kondanna, a cow herder, met a Muslim saint wearing a cap (*kullah*) and, thus, founded Gugudu. Kullayappa and other descendants of the Prophet, as installed in the main shrine Pir House, were metallic battle standards of the Karbala martyrs. This place was connected with many other sacred sites such as the fire pit, local Karbala, Anjneya (Hanuman) temple, Peddamma (mother goddess) temple, Veer Brahmam (Jogi) temple, the graveyard of custodians (*mujawirs*) and local mosque. During the annual Muharram festivities, the custodian Husenappa played a key role as he often recited the *fatiha* and Quranic verses, besides offering the prayer. Only he received the offerings, comprising largely of sugar packets and, consecrating them to the Pirs, returned them to the pilgrims for distribution. Tirupatayya, the descendant of Kondana, played an equally crucial role in the rituals. Before every Muharram, the village was cleaned and whitewashed. The festival opened with the sighting of moon and a glimpse of the Pirs. As the fire pit was dug, the Pirs were installed. After a rest of five days, the Pirs were carried through the village in a big

278 *Situating Medieval India*

procession, culminating in the walk over fire. There were performances of music, dance and drumming. On the final day, goods and
animals were sacrificed at the fire pit. The Pirs, deprived of their
clothes, were brought to Karbala for a final bath. The procession
returned to the Pir House amidst sorrow. For the participants, the
period of asceticism (*faqiri*) was linked with pure intention (*niyattu*)
and divine blessings (*barakattu*).[29]

During the medieval centuries, large groups of Muslims were
noticed in parts of south Asia. The scholars, in order to explain the
phenomena, advanced several theories such as religion of the sword,
political patronage and social liberation. Eaton examined these
theories and showed that none of them could stand the scrutiny of
historical facts. It was found that western Panjab and eastern Bengal
came to have large concentrations of Muslim population. Both
these areas were far from the centre of political power. Instead of
urban enclaves, Islam had spread among the rural populace, particularly pastoral groups that had remained unaffected from the
Hindu religion as well as the caste structure. These people underwent the slow process of Islamization in conjunction with their
settlement as sedentary cultivators. The process of Islamization
manifested in the two stages of accretion and reform. In the former,
new deities were added to the existing cosmological stock, while
the latter saw the replacement of pre-existing cosmological structure
with Islamic supernatural agencies. It was noteworthy that the
Muslim judges (*qazis*) and Sufi shrines, not the Sufis themselves,
played a crucial role in the change.[30] Since we have already discussed
the case of western Panjab with reference to the shrine of Baba
Farid, we would consider the cases of Bengal and Kashmir.

In undivided Bengal, the Muslim population of 26 million
constituted a third of the total for the province and 40 per cent of
total Muslim population of India. Predominantly rural in character,
their lower class origin was traced to local tribes such as Namasudras,
Rajbansis, Pods, Kochs and Chandals. Their conversion, invariably
collective in form, occurred in a geographical context where the
fertile soil had been shifting from the moribund west of the delta
to the active eastern and southern parts. In order to meet the
hostility of nature, they resorted to a large pantheon of Pirs, who

Historical Dimensions of Islam in South Asia 279

could tame the adversities. The shrines of Pirs became the nerve centre of the Bengali Muslim society. Bengali Muslim cultural mediators, including many Pirs, produced a large corpus of literature on Islam in Bengali, assimilating the regional idioms, folklore and practices. In contrast, the folk writers, with little interest in theology and mysticism, glorified the numerous Pirs, who assisted the supplicants in the trials of ordinary life. In fact, they Islamized old popular beliefs and practices through the protean process of Pirification.[31] Roy's analysis finds validation and elaboration in the work of Eaton, who also traces the process of agrarian expansion and Islamization to the long term movement of Bengal's major river systems and pioneering efforts of Muslim religious notables. From the sixteenth to the twentieth century, the Pirs institutionalized Islam through subjugating the dangerous forest, dominating the supernatural world and building mosques. The economic development coincided with the consolidation of the Mughal power in the region, besides the growth in overland and maritime trade linking Bengal more strongly with the world economy. The eastward movement, which the land grants to the Muslim religious figures brought about, saw the construction of mosques and shrines. In Eaton's view, the historical process appeared in three aspects—inclusion, identification and displacement—each corresponding to a different relationship between Islamic and Indian superhuman agencies.[32]

In Kashmir, Islam became a religion of the majority of rural folk between the fifteenth and eighteenth centuries. Islamization was not a process of mass conversion at the hands of Sufis through miracles. Instead, it was a gradual transmutation of society, wherein a considerable part of population became Muslim on its contact with immigrant Muslim settlers, including Sufis. The Rishis, playing a major role in the change, allowed the pre-existing Kashmiri popular religion to adapt to the wider Islamic framework. Yet, Islamization needed to be studied at three levels—individual conversion, group conversion and acculturation.[33] The process of acculturation began much earlier with the creation of Islamic ambience in the form of hospices and mosques. It gained momentum with Nuruddin Rishi's efforts comprising his travels

280 *Situating Medieval India*

across villages, his mystical verses, his conversion of Hindu notables including women, besides stressing celibacy and vegetarianism. In the development of the Kashmiri Muslim society, social identity was defined in Islamic terms, not caste.[34] Another writer was unwilling to attribute Islamization in Kashmir solely to the efforts of the Rishi order. For him, it was a complex process that, occurring from the fourteenth to the sixteenth century, revolved around mass conversions. Since the eighth century, Muslims had been migrating from the neighbouring regions and, after two centuries, they attained high positions from the Hindu rulers. Wani has identified a series of landmarks in the history of Kashmiri Islam. A Buddhist ruler Rinchan (r. 1320-3) converted to Islam at the hands of Syed Sharfuddin. In the fourteenth century, hundreds of Muslim migrants arrived with Syed Ali Hamdani and his son, resulting in the rooting of Muslim institutions in the countryside. As this migration continued during the reign of Zain ul-Abidin (r. 1420-70), Nuruddin Rishi's amalgamation of Rishi ideas with Sufism and non-conformist verses of Lal Ded found a fertile ground in the discontent of low castes. Islam attained cultural ascendancy due to its emphasis on monotheism, justice and austerity as reflected in Sufi miracles.[35] Wani, unhappy at the character of Kashmiri Islam, laments the resilience of pre-Islamic customs, veneration of Sufis and visits to their shrines.

Early scholarship did not explore the relation between the Sufis and rulers. It was felt that the Chishti masters, in order to maintain the sanctity of the spiritual discipline, kept aloof from the political power. However, Simon Digby noted the intervention of the Sufis, though sporadic, in the affairs of the state. Sunil Kumar discovered an intense competition between Alauddin Khalji and Shaikh Nizamuddin Auliya with regard to their respective claims to authority. The Sultan, in his inscriptions at the Jami Masjid and an official chronicle (*Khazain ul-Futuh*), claimed a divine dispensation to enforce the Holy Law according to the Hanafi School. The saint, in his discourses, elaborated an alternative universe of Islam and undermined the structures supporting the Sultan. Barani not only berated the Sultan for lacking in commitment to Islam, but also attributed major achievements of his

Historical Dimensions of Islam in South Asia   281

reign to the Shaikh's grace.[36] Tanvir Anjum traces a dynamic relationship between the Chishtis and Sultans. The attitude of the former ranged from tolerance and (or) polite refusal of stately demands to calculated defiance. The attitude of the Sultans ranged from according personal respect to forcing submission and compliance to stately demands.[37] Muzaffar Alam shows that Akbar could not remain immune from the influence of Sufis. Up to 1570, he patronized the Naqshbandis like Khwaja Abdul Shahid and Sharfuddin Husain Ahrari (a grandson of Khwaja Khwand Mahmud). Akbar's alienation from the Naqshbandis has been attributed to the increasing power of the Chaghtais, the adoption of universal kingship and ethnic diversity of the nobility. In these circumstances, Akbar made a decisive shift towards the Chishtis of the Sabiri branch.[38] This fits into the understanding of John F. Richards on the formulation of imperial authority under Akbar and Jahangir. This writer has stressed the assimilation of two major Chishti shrines (Fatehpur Sikri and Ajmer) into the Mughal polity and enrolment of the members of the two Chishti families into the Mughal bureaucracy. It was likely that Akbar's control over the two Chishti shrines and influence over members of the Chishti order enabled him to contend with the orthodox theologians in an ideological struggle.[39]

The initial understanding of Muzaffar Alam on Akbar's engagement with Sufism has expanded into an interesting book, which is a major statement on South Asia's multicultural legacy. The author has presented a nuanced picture of the contestation among Sufi orders during the heyday of the Mughals. He shows that Abdur Rahman Chishti (d. 1683), a prolific writer in the Chishti-Sabiri mould, underscored the close connection between the Chishti masters and Mughal rulers. Chishti, unlike the Naqshbandis, was favourable towards the Shia traditions and refused to privilege any one of the legal schools (*mazhabs*).[40] Chishti traced the spiritual genealogy of Shah Madar (a controversial Malamati) to early Islam and assimilated him into the Chishti discourse.[41] Dara Shukoh, a staunch Qadiri aspiring for the Mughal throne, in his Persian translation of *Yogavashishtha*, imagined himself as a genuine spiritual seeker in the exalted company of Vashishtha and Rama. He brought

282 *Situating Medieval India*

an ancient Indic text into the Muslim imagination and, in the process, saw a model in Rama, who was both a spiritual master and ideal king.[42] Jahanara and Roshanara, the two daughters of Shahjahan, had a passionate attachment to Sufism. Jahanara, retaining her Chishti affiliation, enrolled herself under the prominent Qadiri saint Mulla Shah Badakhshi. She studied the literature on mysticism and went on to write two books on the subject. Roshanara, receiving instructions from Shaikh Saifuddin (d. 1685) through letters, progressed in the Naqshbandi discipline and went on to tutor the women of the palace.[43]

Jahangir and Shahjahan had admitted the Central Asian Naqshbandis in the Mughal bureaucracy. However, the Sirhindi Naqshbandis, extending from Muhammad Masum (d. 1669) to Abdul Ahad Wahdat (d. 1714), gained unprecedented proximity to the Mughal emperors. Shaikh Saifuddin, a permanent representative of the Sirhindi Naqshbandis at the Mughal court, initiated the Mughal ruling elite—Aurangzeb, princes and nobles—in the Naqshbandi order. In their letters and treatises, the Sirhindi exemplars advocated a strict implementation of Sunni orthodoxy and censured Dara Shukoh's engagement with Hindu religious traditions. Defending the controversial spiritual claims of Shaikh Ahmad Sirhindi, they opposed the appointment of non-Muslims to governmental positions and predicted a Mughal victory against the Shia kingdom of Golconda. During the political conflicts of the post-Aurangzeb period, they sided with the victorious regimes. Following the Sikh raids on Sirhind, they shifted to Delhi and contributed to the literary life of the metropolis.[44] The Chishtis, at least those based in Delhi, thought it prudent to accept the growing Naqshbandi influence in the Mughal polity.

In recent times, the subject of South Asian Islam has been explored through aspects of sacred kingship and charismatic sainthood. In 1582, the Mughal State celebrated the arrival of the second millennium. At this time, an important conjunction of the Saturn and Jupiter had reoccurred in the same celestial position as it had near the birth of Islam and the end of the Sassanian-Zoroastrian dispensation. Besides the issue of coins stamped with the word thousand (*alf*), a history of the first millennium (*Tarikh-*

Historical Dimensions of Islam in South Asia   283

i Alfi), extending from the Prophet's death to Akbar's reign, was commissioned. Akbar, while fulfilling the expectations of the previous millennium, was declared as the renewer of the second millennium (*mujaddid alf-i sani*). Nearly three years earlier, a royal decree (*mahzar*) had declared Akbar as the supreme interpreter (*mujtahid*) of the holy law. Two decades later, Akbar claimed to be the supreme spiritual guide of the realm. Not only did he experience divine raptures and claimed the spiritual allegiance (*iradat guzinan*) of nobles through Din-i Ilahi, he favoured the multitudes with guidance, blessings and miraculous cures.[45] Jahangir was the first to inherit a fully functioning system of sacred kingship, whereby the sovereign was both the political leader and spiritual chief of the realm. Unlike *Akbarnama*, his memoirs were restrained and modest in narrating contemporary events. Instead, he employed paintings to construct his image as a saint of the age, who was imbued with all the spiritual and thaumaturgic power that his position entailed.[46] Shahjahan, in view of the grand success of the Mughal State and dominance of the principle of hereditary familial service, asserted the sacrality of his kingship in architecture and painting. In Delhi, the covered throne platform (*jharokah-i khas wa amm*), denoting the centre of the empire, was oriented eastwards to the rising sun and was replete with figural imagery. In a third of the *Padshahnama* paintings, comprising this throne and the space below it, the king was surrounded by messianic symbols and, owing to his association with supernatural beings, portrayed as a millennial sovereign.[47] During the reign of Aurangzeb and rise of the colonial state, the body of the Muslim sovereign, which had been the master symbol of authority, gradually waned. As a result, the Muslim scholars turned inward toward reform of the Muslim self.[48]

The foregoing discussion identifies the prominent strands in the historiography of South Asian Islam. The ruling classes, though ethnically diverse and predominantly Muslim, exercised power through building alliances with diverse local elements. The early studies on dynastic history acquired complexity with an increasing interest in the modes of assessing land tax and stratification of agrarian society. In the pre-independence period, historical scholar-

284 *Situating Medieval India*

ship discerned the profound impact of Islam on religious reform and art forms, besides delving into social structure and living standards. In the post-independence phase, pioneering efforts were made to trace the growth of Sufi lineages. Apart from the biographies of leading Chishti masters, we come across vigorous debates on the revival of Muslim orthodoxy and Shia-Sunni polemics. The emergence of Islamic spirituality in the Deccan has been reconstructed through explorations on Bijapur, Khuldabad and Aurangabad. The researches on Sufi shrines, employing inter-disciplinary tools of analysis, have complicated our knowledge of the social reality, with particular reference to the shared cultural spaces. The conventional theories of religious conversion have lost ground owing to investigations into the processes of Islamic acculturation in Panjab, Bengal and Kashmir. In recent times, efforts have been made to uncover the relation between the medieval states and Sufis lineages. What Sunil Kumar and Tanvir Anjum had begun finds fruition in the admirable work of Muzaffar Alam and A. Azfar Moin.

NOTES

1. An earlier version of this paper, entitled 'Locating Islam in the Historical Experience of South Asia: Reflections on Politics, Society and Culture' was presented at the International Seminar on *Indological Studies and Research: Languages, Literature, History and Culture*, Charles University, Prague, Czech Republic,17-19 June 2010; it was published in *Understanding India: Indology and Beyond*, (*Orientalia Pragensia*, vol. XVIII), ed. Jaroslav Vacek and Harbans Mukhia, Prague: Charles University, 2012, pp. 99-110.
2. Tapan Raychaudhuri and Irfan Habib, eds., *The Cambridge Economic History of India, vol. I: c. 1200–c. 1750*, New Delhi: Orient Longman, rpt., 2004, pp. 56-66.
3. Surinder Singh, *The Making of Medieval Panjab: Politics, Society and Culture, c. 1000–c. 1500*, New Delhi: Manohar, 2020, pp. 245-73.
4. For different strands of the debate, see, Burton Stein, 'The Segmentary State: Interim Reflections', in *The State in India 1000-1700*, New Delhi: Oxford University Press, 1997, pp. 134-61; R.S. Sharma, 'The Segmentary State and the Indian Experience', *The Indian Historical Review*, vol. XVI, 1993, pp. 81-110; R. Champakalakshmi, 'The Peasant State and Society in

Historical Dimensions of Islam in South Asia   285

Medieval South India: A Review Article', *Indian Economic and Social History Review*, vol. VIII, 1981, pp. 411-27; Vijaya Ramaswamy, 'Peasant State and Society in Medieval South India: A Review Article', *Studies in History*, vol. IV, 1982, pp. 307-19; Y Subbarayalu, 'The Cola State', *Studies in History*, vol. IV, 1982, pp. 269-306.

5. Irfan Habib, *The Agrarian System of the Mughal India 1556-1707*, new edn., Delhi: Oxford University Press, 2nd rev. edn., 1999. This author, during the last half century, has done extensive research on political, social and economic aspects of medieval India. Taking up the Delhi Sultanate, he explored its economy and technology. He has brought out two atlases of historical maps. Besides editing a volume of *The Cambridge Economic History of India*, he has contributed to the UNESCO history of humanity. He is bringing out the successive volumes in a series on *A People's History of India*. On the basis of the Vrindavan documents, he has written a regional history of the Braj Bhum, with reference to its peasants, temples and Chaitanya Gosains.

6. M. Athar Ali, 'Towards an Interpretation of the Mughal Empire,' in *The State in India: 1000-1700*, ed. Hermann Kulke, Delhi: Oxford University Press, 1997, pp. 266-7.

7. During the pre-independence period, the Allahabad School produced stalwarts in the field of medieval India. Ishwari Prasad, receiving inspiration and support from L.F. Rushbrook Williams, wrote the history of the Qaraunah Turks (Tughluqs) and the second Mughal ruler Humayun. R.P. Tripathi, covering both the Sultanate and Mughal eras, explored the administrative institutions, with reference to kingship, Wizarat and land revenue. Beni Prasad produced a treatise on the reign of Jahangir, while B.P. Saksena examined the reign of Shahjahan. Tara Chand investigated the impact of Islam on Bhakti reformers and art forms. Allahabad School earned the honour of grooming two leading historians, Syed Nurul Hasan and Satish Chandra, who went on to adopt the Marxist approach to their researches. For the contribution of early exponents of the Allahabad School, see Satish Chandra, 'Some Modern Historians: Ishwari Prasad, R.P. Tripathi, Syed Nurul Hasan', in *State, Pluralism and the Indian Historical Tradition*, New Delhi: Oxford University Press, 2008, pp. 131-47.

8. 'Introduction', in *The Mughal State 1526-1750*, ed. Muzaffar Alam and Sanjay Subrahmanyam, New Delhi: Oxford University Press, 1998, pp. 12-15.

9. Ibid., pp. 56-9.

10. Khaliq Ahmad Nizami, *The Life and Times of Shaikh Fariduddin Ganj-i Shakar*, Delhi: Idarah-i Adabiyat-i Delli, rpt. 1973; *The Life and Times of Shaikh Nizamuddin Auliya*, New Delhi: Oxford University Press, 2007;

286   *Situating Medieval India*

The Life and Times of Shaikh Nasiruddin Chiragh-i Delhi, Delhi: Idarah-i Adabiyat-i Delli, 1991; *Tarikh-i Mashaikh-i Chisht*, vols. I&V, Delhi: Idarah-i Adabiyat-i Delli, 1980 & 1984; *Tarikh-i Mashaikh-i Chisht*, vols. I&V, rpt., Karachi: Oxford University Press, 2007.

11. Khaliq Ahmad Nizami, *Religion and Politics in India during the Thirteenth Century*, New Delhi: Oxford University Press, new edn., 2002, pp. 191-2.

12. Amir Khurd, *Siyar ul-Auliya*, Persian text, Delhi: Matba-i Muhibb-i Hind, 1885, pp. 491-510.

13. Ibid., pp. 526-32.

14. Hamid bin Fazlullah Jamali, *Siyar ul-Arifin*, Persian text, Delhi: Rizvi Press, 1893, pp. 144-6.

15. Abdul Malik Isami, *Futuh us-Salatin*, vol. II, Eng. tr. Agha Mahdi Husain, Aligarh: Centre of Advanced Study, Department of History, Aligarh Muslim University and Bombay: Asia Publishing House, 1976, pp. 229-32.

16. Ibid., pp. 232-4.

17. Carl W. Ernst and Bruce B. Lawrence, *Sufi Martyrs of Love: The Chishti Order in South Asia and Beyond*, New York: Palgrave Macmillan, 2002.

18. Ishtiaq Husain Qureshi, *The Muslim Community of the Indo-Pakistan Subcontinent 610-1947*, New Delhi: Renaissance Publishing House, rpt., 1985, pp. 177-81; Saiyid Athar Abbas Rizvi, *Muslim Revivalist Movements in Northern India in the Sixteenth and Seventeenth Century*, Agra: Agra University, 1965, pp. 334-75; Yohanan Friedmann, *Shaykh Ahmad Sirhindi: An Outline of His Thought and Study of His Image in the Eyes of the Posterity*, Delhi: Oxford University Press, rpt., 2000, p. 111; Shuja Alhaq, *A Forgotten Vision: A Study of Human Spirituality in the Light of the Islamic Tradition*, vol. II, New Delhi: Vikas Publishing House, 1997, pp. 323-4.

19. Saiyid Athar Abbas Rizvi, *Religious and Intellectual History of the Muslims in Akbar's Reign: With Special Reference to Abul Fazl (1556-1605)*, New Delhi: Munshiram Manoharlal, 1976, pp. 352-73.

20. Saiyid Athar Abbas Rizvi, *Shah Wali Allah and His Times: A Study of Eighteenth Century Islam, Politics and Society in India*, Canberra: Marifat Publishing House, 1980, pp. 287-316.

21. Saiyid Athar Abbas Rizvi, *Shah Abdul Aziz: Puritanism, Sectarian Polemics and Jihad*, Canberra: Marifat Publishing House, 1982, pp. 245-470.

22. Saiyid Athar Abbas Rizvi, *A Socio-Intellectual History of the Isna Ashari Shiis in India*, 2 vols., New Delhi: Munshiram Manoharlal, 1986.

23. Richard M. Eaton, 'The Political and Religious Authority of the Shrine of Baba Farid', in *Essays on Islam and Indian History*, New Delhi: Oxford University Press, 2000, pp. 203-24.

Historical Dimensions of Islam in South Asia 287

24. P.M. Currie, *The Shrine and Cult of Muin al-Din Chishti of Ajmer*, New Delhi: Oxford University Press, 1989, pp. 97-116.
25. Ibid., pp. 119-40.
26. Ibid., pp. 141-73.
27. Ibid., pp. 174-84.
28. Shahid Amin, 'On Retelling the Muslim Conquest of North India', in *History and the Present*, ed. Partha Chatterjee and Anjan Ghosh, Delhi: Permanent Black, 2002, pp. 24-43; Kerrin Grafin Schwerin, 'The Cow-Saving Muslim Saint: Elite and Folk Representations of a Tomb Cult in Oudh', in *Living Together Separately: Cultural India in History and Politics*, ed. Mushirul Hasan and Asim Roy, New Delhi: Oxford University Press, 2005, pp. 172-93; Tahir Mahmood, 'The Dargah of Salar Masud Ghazi of Bahraich: Legend, Tradition and Reality', in *Muslim Shrines in India: Their Character, History and Significance*, ed. Christian W. Troll, New Delhi: Oxford University Press, 1989, pp. 24-43; Marc Gaborieau, 'The Ghazi Miyan Cult in Western Nepal and Northern India', in *On Becoming an Indian Muslim: French Essays on Aspects of Syncretism*, ed. M. Waseem, New Delhi: Oxford University Press, 2003, pp. 238-63.
29. In recent times, Muharram has become a site of contestation between local Islam and localized Islam. The former reenacted the entire history of the village. Open and malleable, Muharram offered possibilities of shared devotion. In contrast, young reformist Muslims, speaking for localized Islam, forcefully rejected the Muharram tradition. Relying on increasing accessibility of texts on the Quran and Hadis in Telugu, the preachers criticized the local Muharram festivities and advocated removal of impure practices that were attributed to the exposure to Hindu ways. However, they insisted that their efforts had nothing to do with fundamentalism. The erosion of a shared religious culture has strengthened the local Muslims' sense of belonging to a global religious community. Afsar Mohammad, *The Festival of Pirs: Popular Islam and Shared Devotion in South India*, New York: Oxford University Press, 2013, p. 159.
30. Richard M. Eaton, 'Approaches to the Study of Conversion to Islam in India', in *Religious Movements in South Asia 600-1800*, ed. David N. Lorenzen, New Delhi: Oxford University Press, 2004, pp. 105-27.
31. Asim Roy, *The Islamic Syncretistic Tradition in Bengal*, Princeton: Princeton University Press, 1983, pp. 207-48.
32. Richard M. Eaton, *The Rise of Islam and the Bengal Frontier 1204-1760*, New Delhi: Oxford University Press, rpt., 1997, pp. 269-85.
33. M. Ishaq Khan, *Kashmir's Transition to Islam: The Role of Muslim Rishis*

288   *Situating Medieval India*

(Fifteenth to Eighteenth Century), New Delhi: Manohar, rpt., 2002, pp. 177-9.

34. Ibid., pp. 194-5.

35. Muhammad Ashraf Wani, *Islam in Kashmir (Fourteenth to Sixteenth Century)*, Srinagar: Oriental Publishing House, 2005.

36. Sunil Kumar, 'Assertions of Authority: A Study of the Discursive Statements of Two Sultans of Delhi', in *The Making of Indo-Persian Culture: Indian and French Studies*, ed. Muzaffar Alam, Nalini Delvoye and Marc Gaborieau, New Delhi: Manohar, 2000, pp. 37-62.

37. Tanvir Anjum, *Chishti Sufis in the Sultanate of Delhi 1190-1400: From Restrained Indifference to Calculated Defiance*, Karachi: Oxford University Press, 2011, pp. 358-67.

38. Muzaffar Alam, 'The Mughals, Sufi Shaikhs and the Formation of the Akbari Dispensation', in *Expanding Frontiers in South Asian and World History: Essays in Honour of John F. Richards*, ed. Richard M. Eaton et al., New York: Cambridge University Press, 2013, pp. 143-55.

39. John F. Richards, 'The Formulation of Imperial Authority under Akbar and Jahangir', in *The Mughal State 1526-1750*, ed. Muzaffar Alam and Sanjay Subrahmanyam, Delhi: Oxford University Press, 1998, pp. 130-9.

40. Muzaffar Alam, *The Mughals and the Sufis: Islam and Political Imagination in India 1500-1750*, Ranikhet: Permanent Black and Ashoka University, 2021, pp. 116-22.

41. Ibid., pp. 158-63.

42. Ibid., pp. 239-58.

43. Ibid., pp. 262-301.

44. Ibid., pp. 334-88.

45. M. Azfar Moin, *The Millennial Sovereign: Sacred Kingship and Sainthood in Islam*, Delhi: Primus Books, rpt., 2017, pp. 133-42.

46. Ibid., pp. 177-9.

47. Ibid., pp. 219-29.

48. Ibid., pp. 234-40.

CHAPTER 12

Cultural Ethos of Medieval Panjab: The Pathways of Resistance to the Structures of Dominance

Khushwant Singh (1915-2014) was a famous writer.[1] Besides writing history and fiction, he translated excerpts from the Sikh scripture and poetry of Allama Iqbal. One of his books bears the attractive title of *Punjab, Punjabis & Punjabiyat: Reflections on a Land and its People.* In spite of the vast promised scope of the title, the book is confined to some historical aspects of the Sikhism. A complex evolutionary process, which was visible in diversity, has been restricted to the Sikh past.[2] The reader does not find a single word on the numerous non-Sikh phenomena that dominate the contemporary evidence. This Sikh-centric approach has determined much of modern historiography on the region. Aitzaz Ahsan, a distinguished lawyer and leading politician of Pakistan, has written a book, entitled, *The Indus Saga and the Making of Pakistan.* Fortunately, he speaks of heroes like Porus, Rasalu, Jasrath Khokhar, Dulla Bhatti, Chakar Khan Rind and Ahmad Khan Kharral. The struggles of these heroes, operating in tandem with the developments since the Harappan civilization, accorded a distinct individuality to the Indus region, so that it culminated in the formation of Pakistan. In other words, Pakistan had been perpetually existing since the primordial times.[3] Throughout his narrative, the author uses the word Indus for Panjab and even for (West) Pakistan. What is equally surprising, the inhabitants of this region had been labelled as the Indus persons. The present essay distances itself from these narrow propositions. Instead, it adopts a holistic and inclusive approach to uncover the cultural strands of medieval Panjab. Wading

290 *Situating Medieval India*

through a wide range of evidence—Persian chronicles, mystical discourses, scriptural doctrines and Panjabi folklore—it identifies resistance as the dominant ingredient of the Panjabi culture. It was boldly manifest in the anti-state opposition of the warlike tribes, autonomous chiefdoms and rural intermediaries. Apart from the female voice in the Sufi poetry and the struggles of legendry lovers, it was also seen in the Sikh quest for social equality.

The Turkish warlords of Afghanistan, while carving out their kingdoms in Panjab, encountered stiff opposition from the local tribes. In the early eleventh century, the Ghaznavid intervention in Panjab brought the Jats to prominence.[4] They had looted the Ghaznavid army returning from Somnath with a rich booty. Since many rivers intersected the Multan region, the Jats had developed expertise in river warfare. In a fierce battle on the Indus, the Jats employed 4,000 armoured boats against a large Ghaznavid force comprising 1,400 boats, two cavalry units and numerous elephants. Failing to escape through land, they were pushed back to the river, where a majority of them were killed, while the remaining were captured or managed to escape.[5] A little later, they assisted the Ghaznavid general Tilak in defeating the rebel governor Ahmad Niyaltigin and, in lieu of this service, received a sum of 10,000 dinars along with ample booty.[6] After a gap of nearly 150 years, the Jats opposed the Ghorid occupation of cis-Satluj area. Sultan Muizzuddin, following his victory (1192) over Prithviraj Chauhan, assigned Kuhram and Samana to Quitbuddin Aibak, besides posting Nusratuddin in the fort of Hansi. The Jats, mobilized under an unnamed chief, besieged this place and engaged in a fierce fight at the foot of the citadel. Aibak, rushing from Kuhram, arrived at Hansi to relieve the Turkish garrison. The Jats raised the siege and, fleeing south to the dry tract of Bagar, suffered a defeat. The account of Aibak's victory pointed to the stiff resistance of the Jats. It was claimed that Aibak perpetrated so much carnage that the blood-tinged hoofs of his horse became red like the rubies of Badakhshan and he scattered the heads of the Jat commanders like balls in a game of horse-polo. He forced the Jat chief to surrender and put him to death. He regarded this success as an embroidery on his previous conquests, an ornament on the body of the bride and a

Cultural Ethos of Medieval Panjab

gift of divine grace. In view of the significance of the event for the Ghorids, letters of victory were dispatched to Ghazni as well as the cities of Hind and Sind.[7]

The Khokhars, strongly placed in northwestern Panjab,[8] opposed the emergence of the Ghorid kingdom. At one time, they supported the last Ghaznavid ruler Khusrau Malik in recovering Sialkot from Ghurid control. As soon as Sultan Muizzuddin extended his sway up to the Yamuna with a decisive victory at Tarain (1192), the Khokhars were galvanized into action. Occupying the tract between the Jhelum and Chenab, the Khokhars planned to annex Lahore. They pushed back the Ghorid fief-holders of Sehwan and Multan.[9] A large number of Khokhars, mounted on swift horses, fought a pitched battle at the ferry of the Jhelum against three Ghurid commanders—Sultan Muizzuddin, Qutbuddin Aibak and Shamsuddin Iltutmish. The Khokhars, suffering heavy casualties, crossed the Jhelum and took shelter in the impregnable fort of Nandanah. In spite of their recent defeat, the Khokhars prepared to defend the citadel even at the cost of their lives. When the Ghorids pulled down the ramparts, the Khokhar chief sought a peaceful settlement and accepted the position of a vassal. Apart from surrendering the fort, he paid an enormous booty comprising horses, slaves and arms.[10] The defeat dealt a severe blow to the Khokhar pride. Refusing to accept the humiliation, they hatched a plan to kill Sultan Muizzuddin. One night, a group of Khokhars entered the royal tent, killed a few guards and murdered the Sultan in his sleep.[11] Tajuddin Hasan Nizami, in spite of his association with Qutbuddin Aibak, has showered fulsome praise on the Khokhars for their valour.[12]

The Khokhars did not accept the authority of the Delhi Sultanate. They acted as guides to the Mongols who, having entrenched themselves in the upper Sind Sagar Doab, often invaded the lands up to the Jhelum. Ulugh Khan (Ghiasuddin Balban), marching out from Delhi, entered the Jud mountains, plundered the Khokhars and scattered their families. The position of the Khokhars weakened as the Delhi army pierced the hills, cut the jungles and occupied forts.[13] The warlike tribes of Panjab—Khokhars, Jats and Mandahars—were forced to surrender superior breeds of horses to the

292   *Situating Medieval India*

Delhi government.[14] Balban, during the early years of his reign, acquired so many horses from the Koh-i Jud that their prices fell to 30-40 *tankahs* in the army.[15] The tribes—Khokhars, Jats, Bhattis, Minas, Mandahars and others—faced a considerable pressure from Sher Khan during his military expeditions against the Mongols.[16] During the early decades of the fourteenth century, the Khokhars abandoned their association with the Mongols and, instead, tilted towards the Delhi Sultanate. They joined hands with Ghazi Malik, the governor of Dipalpur, and played a major role in his bid for sovereign power at Delhi.[17] Amir Khusrau notes the substantial Khokhar presence in the Dipalpur retinue, while Isami describes their decisive role in the battles at Sarsuti and Delhi. The Khokhar chiefs Gul Chand and Sahij Rai, leading the vanguard of the Dipalpur troops, gave ample proof of their bravery. At both places, Gul Chandra killed the rival parasol bearer and, snatching the parasol, raised it over the head of Ghazi Malik. The Khokhars not only earned military success for Ghazi Malik, but also conferred the first symbol of royalty on him.[18] Though the Khokhar-Tughluq alliance was short lived, it became a precedent for the local elements in Panjab. A number of rural elites (Rana Mal Bhatti of Abohar, the Tak *zamindars* of Thanesar and Mote Rai Chauhan of Hissar) and the Shaikhs heading Sufi shrines between Uch and Delhi were incorporated in the polity of the Delhi Sultanate.

Timur's invasion, hastening the collapse of the Tughluq regime, encouraged the local chiefs to seek autonomy and fief-holders (*muqtis*) to revolt. In the first half of the fifteenth century, the Khokhar uprising erupted with great fury. Jasrath Khokhar dominated the political stage of Panjab for two decades (1421-42). Many times, he descended from his mountainous stronghold beyond Sialkot and ravaged the plains of Panjab, including Lahore, Jammu, Kangra, Jalandhar, Ludhiana, Ropar and Bajwara. During his predatory raids, he attacked senior officers holding revenue assignments (*iqtas*) and their allies among local chiefs. At different points of time, he had prominent nobles like Zirak Khan and Sikandar Tohfa in his custody. He abandoned the siege of Sirhind only when facing the combined forces of the Sultan, leading Panjab officers and local elites. He not only killed Rai Bhim, the chief of Jammu, but also

Cultural Ethos of Medieval Panjab   293

plundered the domains of Rai Kamal Muin from Ropar to Ludhiana. In his sustained opposition to the Syed regime, he collaborated with Shaikh Ali of Kabul and Faulad Turkbacha of Bhatinda. After his victory (1432) over Allahdad Kaka Lodi, the governor of Lahore and Dipalpur, a Delhi army marched into his territories and carried out widespread depredations. Fortunately for him, the attention of Delhi was diverted to the rise of the Afghans under Bahlol Lodi at Sirhind. Jasrath Khokhar joined hands with Sikandar Tohfa in military operations against one of the Afghan warlords.[19] In 1441, the Syed ruler confirmed Lahore and Dipalpur on Bahlol Lodi in return for punitive measures against Jasrath Khokhar. The latter made peace with Bahlol Lodi and promised to support his bid for the throne of Delhi. The Lodi contender promised not to interfere in his territories. The neutrality of Jasrath Khokhar contributed, to some extent, in the establishment of the Lodi dynasty in Delhi. As might be recalled, more than a century back, the Khokhar chiefs had played a crucial role in bringing the Tughluqs to power in Delhi.

Koh-i Jud (Salt Range), the land of the Khokhars sheltered the famous monastery of the Jogis at Tilla Balnath. They figured in a variety of evidence such as official chronicles, Sufi literature, Sikh scripture and Panjabi folklore. The Jogis were mendicants who renounced the world and withdrew from the caste-ridden society.[20] As followers of Gorakhnath, they sought to control their physiological and mental processes to unite with the Absolute. They perceived Gorakhnath as the preceptor of Prophet Muhammad as well as the Hindu trinity of Brahma, Vishnu and Mahesh. Their religious practices were traceable to both Islam and Hinduism. As staunch monotheists, they conceived God as sovereign and changeless. In contrast, they held His creation as subject to subordination and decay. A practitioner freed himself from the material world through the path of Jog, which meant union with the eternal domain. The human heart, as the abode of God (*bait allah*), engaged in His remembrance with the help of Jog. Of their numerous austerities (*jalsat*), the most important was *Pranayama* involving control of breath (*habs-i nafs*). They sat in a specific posture and, gazing between the two eyes, inhaled and exhaled through different nostrils to activate a particular part of the pubis. From the tip of the pubis

294   *Situating Medieval India*

to the top of the head, there were seven levels, each of which was associated with a particular part of the human body. These levels threw up numerous veins, including the crucial three indentified with sun, earth and moon (*ida, pankhla* and *sukhumna*). Perfection in this exercise conferred superhuman abilities and extraordinary long lives. During his research, Kaikhusrau Isfandiyar came across numerous Jogis and books on the subject in Hindi and Persian.[21] He saw the *Amritkunda*, which had been translated into Persian under the title of *Hauz ul-Hayat.*[22]

Tilla Balnath, situated 40 kilometres northeast of the Jhelum, formed the highest point (3,242 feet) on an isolated hill in the Salt Range. The monastery, enclosed within a wall, had temples dedicated to Shiva, Bhairava, Lakshman and Hanuman. On a lower level, there were storerooms and residences of the Jogis. Attached to the main enclosure were a cowshed, a tank and Samadhis. A cave was named after Bharthari, while a stone slab marked the spot where Ranjha was initiated.[23] In 1581, a community of 300 Jogis inhabited the monastery. The novices were required to undergo an apprenticeship of two years. They performed a variety of onerous tasks such as cutting wood, fetching water, grazing cattle, cooking food and serving meals. On the occasion of enrolment as full members of the order, they vowed to keep themselves pure and chaste. They were permitted to wear a new set of garments including a cloak, a turban and a long robe. Since the clothes were dyed in a kind of red chalk, they appeared to have been painted in this colour. Invested with this apparel, they were allowed to go anywhere and beg to live. If they violated the rules, they were expelled from the order. A spiritual head, who never left the summit, presided over the affairs with the advice of a group of old men. On his death, these men elected a successor. At sunrise and sunset, the Jogis offered a prayer to the accompaniment of flutes and conches. Devoted to a frugal life, the Jogis did not follow any restriction regarding food and social interaction. Akbar, who stayed at the summit for four days, showed a keen interest in the teachings and observances of the Jogis. With bare feet and loosened hair, he paid homage at the sacred site. The chief Jogi conducted him around the complex.[24] Another monastery of the Jogis, situated in the village Jakhbar Jogian

Cultural Ethos of Medieval Panjab

(District Gurdaspur), flourished under the Mughal patronage and received land grants that were confirmed in a series of documents.[25]

The large space of the Jogis has been reflected in the Panjabi folklore. The timeless legend of Puran Bhagat revealed the resistance of the Jogis to the dominant political and social structures. The Jogis came out in support of those whom the society maltreated and discarded. To such marginalized individuals, they provided asylum, dignity and identity. They showed great courage in fighting against oppression, discrimination and cruelty. The authority of the ruling classes failed to overawe them. Employing their miraculous powers, they cured the victims of serious ailments. The path of Jog, which was based on renunciation of the world, was extremely difficult. It required complete resistance to the temptations of wealth and sex. The Jogis obeyed the orders of their mentor (*guru*) without raising any doubt. In outward appearance, they deliberately looked different from the ordinary members of the society. They wore saffron robes, bored their ears, carried a begging bowl and blew the conch. They begged to survive and accepted only cooked food, but not any valuables. They accepted alms only from the hands of the owner or mistress of the house, but not from servants. Generally, the society showed reverence towards the Jogis, particularly those who were reputed for their spiritual excellence and miraculous powers. When a charismatic Jogi arrived in a town or village, the people flocked in large numbers to make their obeisance and seek blessings for the fulfilment of their desires.[26]

Najm Hosain Syed has decoded the life of Puran as a perpetual symbol of resistance. During his childhood, Puran was pitted against two types of egotisms—one operating through the blind power of Salvahan and the other operating through the deceit of Luna. Salvahan represented a regime that was cruel, insensitive and self-righteous. It punished Puran in a manner that his very existence was erased. Once Puran joined the fraternity of the Jogis, he attained new life. Gorakhnath guided his journey on the path of humanization. As a result, Puran was not insulated from the society. Aware of the malaise afflicting the old order, he assumed the task of pulling it down and ushering in a new one. At the outset, Sundran tried to wean him away from Jog and mould him into an instrument of

296   *Situating Medieval India*

her sexual gratification. When Puran received a rousing reception in Sialkot, he exposed the enormities of the system that Salvahan presided over. He rejected the throne offered to him on a platter. As Jogi, Puran not only resisted the material temptations, but also employed his transformative power for the benefit of people. He revived a deserted garden and restored the eyesight of his long-suffering mother. Overcoming the natural instinct of revengeful bitterness, he conferred the boon of a son on Salvahan and Luna.

By now, Puran had realized that his role as a Jogi had come to an end, but his resistance had to assume a new form. He needed to do something fundamentally radical. When Rasalu was born, Puran predicted that the parents would not see the child for 12 years and, after this period, would spend the rest of his life in wanderings. Rasalu denoted at once a constructive and destructive force. Puran, a Jogi of uncompromising integrity, was a man of knowledge who went on to be a teacher, visionary and martyr. In Rasalu, Puran reappeared in the incarnation of a fighter. Rasalu, like Puran, saw the injustice of Salvahan. As a growing lad, he displayed his defiant spirit by breaking the pitchers of women fetching water from the well. Salvahan, failing to restrain Rasalu, banished him from the kingdom. Rasalu merged into the wilderness and, befriending animals and birds, emerged as a warrior. On the one hand, he defeated the tyrant Raja Sirkap and, on the other, deposed Salvahan. The old king had denoted power-for-possession and possession-for-power. In contrast, the Jogis were engaged in the pursuit of strength-through-dispossession and dispossession-for-strength. In Puran, the society looked inward to attain concentrated integrity that resisted evil. In Rasalu, the society expanded to discover, experiment and create.[27] The two images, as manifest in the experiences of Puran and Rasalu, appeared to have percolated into Shah Husain and Dulla Bhatti. Further, both images dissolved in the Sikh struggle of social equality and political power.

The fate of Ranjha, the male protagonist in the famous legend of Hir-Ranjha, was no different from that of Puran. The former, having suffered at the hands of a combination of orthodoxy and patriarchy, assumed the garb of a Jogi to acquire justice in the form of his beloved Hir. The philosophy of Jog revolved around

Cultural Ethos of Medieval Panjab

the Infinite (*alakh*), which was recognized as the fundamental characteristic of God. The Jogis performed hard spiritual penance (including breath control), which led them to a state of trance. Trained to suppress human feelings, they were unaffected by joy and sorrow. They lived in a void, where there was no scope for expressing their emotions. They neither washed their body nor rubbed perfume on it. They were perpetually on the move, travelling from one sacred centre to the other—Ganga, Godavari and Jagannath Puri—and attending religious festivals. To be able to survive, they ate what was available in the jungle such as lotus, herbs and roots. To this simple fare, they added intoxicants (hemp and poppy) in order to generate a sense of ecstasy. They were required to suppress the natural cravings of lust, anger, greed, attachment and ego. After severing all connections with worldly life, a seeker joined a hermitage under the tutelage of a spiritual master (*guru*). His formal enrolment involved an elaborate ceremony of initiation, which the mentor presided over and the disciples attended. His head and eyebrows were shaved, while his ears were bored and inserted with large wooden rings. He wore an ochre robe and smeared ash on his body. His most prominent possessions were a staff, horn and bowl. Every morning, he entered a human settlement and, going from door-to-door, begged for alms. He was required to be an absolute celibate and avoided any contact with a woman. In case, he encountered a woman, he was instructed to treat her as a mother or sister. Bulleh Shah (d. 1758) in one of his mystical poems, enabled Hir to reveal her feelings for the Jogi. Hir, addressing her friends and relatives, declared her resolve to go with the Jogi and, in the process, disowned her marriage with Saida Khera. Hir's portrait of the Jogi was, in fact, her battle cry against patriarchy. Following is the gist of the lyrics, as Nusrat Fateh Ali Khan sang in a masterpiece (*ni mein jana jogi de naal / kanni mundran pa ke mathe tilak laga ke*).

I am going with the Jogi, wearing rings in my ears and applying a sacred mark on my forehead. Ever since I belonged to the Jogi, no ego remained in me. He is not really a Jogi, but a form of God. Yet, the identity of a Jogi suits him. This Jogi has pulled out my heart and now he abides in it. I am speaking the truth, which I swear by the Quran. This Jogi is my religion and faith. As

298   *Situating Medieval India*

I belong to him, I am not fit for anyone else. The Kheras are telling lies. I sacrifice my head for the Jogi. I know only the Jogi, not anyone else. No one has assessed his limits, as he has cast his shadow over the entire world. His fame has spread all around the earth. Even the sky kisses his shoes. This Jogi is intoxicated. In his hand, he carries a rosary of God's oneness. His name is the blanket-wearer (*kamli wala*). If he comes to my house, all disputes will come to an end. I will clasp him to my chest after celebrating lakhs of happy omens. Bulle Shah! The Jogi has come. He has raised commotion in our house. He has looted Hir Siyal, appearing in a disguise.

Parallel to Jog, Islamic spirituality evolved as an important ingredient of Punjabi culture. In particular, it played a crucial role in the growth of medieval urban centres. Baba Haji Rattan, traditionally associated with Prophet Muhammad, appears to have left the earliest Sufi shrine at Bhatinda. Ali bin Usman Hujweri (d. 1072), the author of a major treatise on Sufism (*Kashf ul-Mahjub*), became the patron saint of Lahore. During the early thirteenth century, the Chishtis were established in Pakpattan, while the Suhrawardis were rooted in Multan and Uch. Bu Ali Qalandar, developing the Chishti-Qalandari mysticism, was identified with Panipat. The Chisht-Sabiris, extending from Shamsuddin Turk to Usman Zinda Pir, worked from Panipat, though Abdul Quddus Gangohi spent nearly 30 years in Shahabad near Ambala. During the fifteenth century, the Qadiri order emerged in Uch and Shergarh. Lahore became a leading Sufi centre during the presence of Shah Husain, Miyan Mir and Pir Hassu Teli. The suburbs of Batala preserved the tombs of numerous saints such as Shihabuddin Bokhari, Shah Kharab, Shah Ismail, Shah Niamatullah and Shaikh Allahdad. In the cis-Satluj tract, the shrine of Haidar Shaikh attracted droves of devotees to Malerkotla. In the neighbouring town of Sirhind, Shaikh Ahmad Sirhindi displayed great energy in shaping the Naqshbandi tenets. Shah Daula, a contemporary of Shahjahn, attained an enviable reputation for his miraculous powers, charitable works and public buildings. During the eighteenth and first half of the nineteenth centuries, a Chishti resurgence was witnessed in western Panjab owing to the dynamism of Nur Muhammad Muharawi and Muhammad Sulaiman Taunsawi.

Baba Farid,[28] invoking sexual imagery, perceived the seeker as

Cultural Ethos of Medieval Panjab

wife and God as her husband. When she failed to enjoy sexual union with her husband (*kant*), her bodily organs were twisted. Only a deserted wife (*duhagan*) understood the misery of spending the night in loneliness. She was blessed if she was married (*suhagan*) in the true sense. If she was unable to experience the marital bliss in her youth, she lamented this inability even in her grave.[29] If the search for her Beloved turned futile, her body smouldered like a slow fire. Owing to the ever-present demands of her body, she was forced to suppress her senses. Though delicious foods like dates and honey were available, the deprivation had reduced the span of her life.[30] In order to control her husband, she wore the dress of three parts—the word of humility, the quality of tolerance and the charm of sweet tongue.[31] While separated from her husband, she was unable to know her fault. She had become desperate as her youth was leaving. If she knew that her divine groom was innocent like a child, she would have shed her ego. If she had anticipated separation from her Beloved, she would have tied the bridal knot tightly.[32] In the absence of sexual union with her husband, there would be no milk in her breasts.[33] Her condition was like that of a black cuckoo, which was burnt in the fire of separation. Owing to the intensity of her passion, she would not be deterred by physical obstacles like heavy rain, a muddy street and a wet blanket.[34] A wife, yearning to meet her husband, took a bath and put on fresh clothes. If he failed to turn up, her body lost the fragrance of musk and acquired the pungent smell of asafoetida. She would not fear the departure of youth, provided the love of her husband remained firm. Her experience of painful longing had convinced her that love was inseparable from separation (*birha*). A body that did not nurture the affliction of separation was as dead as the cremation pit (*masan*).[35]

Guru Nanak, chronologically placed between Baba Farid and Shah Husain, took up the cudgels on behalf of women. He rejected the stigma attached to female biological functions, particularly menstruation. A child was conceived in a woman's womb. After its birth, it was naturally attracted to the milk of its mother's breasts.[36] On growing up, a man sought companionship (*dosti*) with a woman. Human life was reproduced through women. They could not be

300 *Situating Medieval India*

held inferior, as they gave birth even to kings. Throughout this hymn, the Guru referred to women as a vessel (*bhandu*), as he saw her as a cornucopia from which the entire creation poured forth. Thus, the woman was validated through the imagery of conception, gestation, giving birth and lactation.[37] The Guru, in a composition entitled 'Twelve Months' (*barah mah*), articulated the mental state of a bride during the change of seasons and, in the process, endorsed the natural concerns of female sexuality. The spring (*chet*) saw the growth of vegetation and singing of cuckoo, but the bride suffered from pangs of separation as her husband was away. During the hot summer (*jeth* and *asarh*), she hoped to dissolve in her Beloved and attain true virtue through His grace. With the onset of monsoon (*savan*), she found herself in love with her spouse to the core of her body and soul. Since he had gone to foreign lands, she was distressed to find a lonely bridal bed (*sej*). The rain set the stage for merriment, but she remained restless in the absence of her Spouse. Between summer and winter (*assu*), the appearance of greenery filled her with hopes of meeting Him. In early winter (*maghar*), the virtuous bride (*gunwanti*) recited the praise of her Lord in song, music and poetry. During the peak of winter (*poh*), the presence of the Lord's light in the procreation of living beings enabled her to feel His presence in her body and soul. As winter receded (*phalgun*), she adorned herself with silks, garlands, pearls and perfumes. Her union with the Spouse enhanced the beauty of her embellishments. In her house, the bridal bed attained splendour because He enjoyed her. She became jubilant as her destiny awakened and perpetual union ensured. Also, her marital life was placed on an even keel.[38]

Shah Husain felt that a bride tried to cherish every moment of love with her husband.[39] She understood the meaning of wearing the set of bridal bangles (*lal choora*) and putting on the ceremonial head covering (*saloo*), the two symbols of her conjugal life.[40] Conscious of the transience of her physical beauty, she employed every means to attract the attention of her husband. A woman, dyeing herself in the colour of her husband, was regarded as truly married (*suhagan*). In her account of good deeds, only the nights spent in the company of her husband were listed.[41] Unable to conceal her happiness at the arrival of her husband, she asked her companions

Cultural Ethos of Medieval Panjab   301

to congratulate her. The light emitted from his forehead illuminated the entire courtyard.[42] During the spans of her separation, her body was shattered. As she burst into bouts of crying, tears of blood flowed from her eyes like rain. Her heart burnt like an oven (*tanur*) and her sighs shot up like flames. While she lay tossing on her bridal bed (*sej*), her entire physique was roasted. Since her flesh eroded and bones cracked, she was reduced to a skeleton.[43] Separation acted like a butcher (*kasai*), who used a large knife to probe her entrails. Still, she was keen to please her beloved. She filtered the blood of her heart and, slashing her liver into pieces, offered them to her beloved.[44] It was impossible for her to withdraw from the loving bond, as the divine pen (*qalam rabbani*) had willed the choice. Since she had wasted her childhood in games and youth in swaggering, she failed to learn the art of winning the love of her beloved.[45] The woman who slept in the arms of her husband was hailed as a chaste wife (*suhagani*). A wife who slept without her husband was mightily cursed (*kulakhani*). The one who remained awake was immensely fortunate (*vad bhagi*).[46]

In the eyes of Bulleh Shah (1680-1758),[47] physical love (*ishq majazi*) was the essential preliminary step on the path of divine love. Imagining himself as a woman, he felt that love was a great benefactor, who yielded the wealth of ecstatic bliss. As it was absorbed in the lover's bone marrow, each pore of her body became intoxicated, though she kept on withering.[48] On the night of meeting her beloved, she experienced great joy. For this union, she resorted to numerous charms at the advice of reputed magicians. Forgetting prayer and fasting, she planned to extend the night and prevent the onset of day. She urged the watchman (*ghariali*) to throw away the gong and leave the place. She did not want the recurrent sound to disturb the meeting with her beloved. She prepared a suitable environment for the tryst. As the unstruck melody (*anhad*) took over, the expert musicians presented sweet songs and distillers offered overflowing cups of wine. The bridal bed was dear to her, as her turn had come after a long wait. It was impossible for her to separate from her beloved. She hoped to live with him for a million years.[49] She was unable to fulfil her desire. Her playful beloved resorted to tricks like a clever sorcerer. He resided in her

302 *Situating Medieval India*

house and spent joyful hours with her. Without a warning, he flew away like a hawk, leaving her to grieve.[50] In preparation for a union, she took a bath and adorned herself. She hoped to clasp him to her chest in order to imbibe his fragrance. In view of the wasteful effort, she felt like burning her jewellery and adornments.[51] Love, implanted in her at the beginning of life (*azal*), led to terrifying consequences. It pierced her heart like an arrow, which could not be pulled out. It fried her body in a pan of boiling oil, thus crushing her to death. Like a spark in fire, love had set her on fire.[52] Unable to sleep, she spent the night in ceaseless crying.[53] She strained the blood of her body and, extracting her heart, cut it into pieces as an offering to her beloved.[54] She did not get solace from any quarter. She received rebukes from her father, mother and brother.[55] Outside the house, the people jeered at her. In her misery, she feared meeting the fate of Sabir, Zakariya, Mansur and Sulaiman.[56]

In most societies, love tales constituted essential ingredients of the collective memory. These stories were orally transmitted from one generation to the other. Fluid and malleable, they underwent modifications at each transmission. Yet, the plot retained the basic kernel of events. In Panjab, three sets of lovers—Hir-Ranjha, Mirza-Sahiban and Sohni-Mahiwal—appeared to have lived in the fifteenth, sixteenth and seventeenth centuries respectively. In their efforts to unite with each other, they were pitted against patriarchy and orthodoxy. On the one hand, they displayed unprecedented commitment to each other. On the other hand, they suffered untold miseries and laid down their lives at the altar of their love. Prominent Sufi poets like Shah Husain, Bulleh Shah and Shah Abdul Latif assimilated love tales in their spiritual discourses. Largely following the same goal, the balladeers (*qissakars*) produced impressive accounts of their struggles. Bhai Gurdas, the distinguished Sikh scholar, has paid a rich tribute to lovers such as Laila-Majnu, Hir-Ranjha, Sohni-Mahiwal and Sassi-Punnu.[57] Guru Gobind Singh, while approving the sacrifices of Hir-Ranjha, saw living among the Kheras as hell. Before proceeding further, it would be appropriate to take a close look at the three love tales in brief outline.

The first story reveals that Ranjha, the son of a *zamindar* of Takht Hazara, left his joint household in protest against injustice of his

Cultural Ethos of Medieval Panjab

303

brothers. During his wanderings, he fell in love with Hir, the daughter of the Siyal chief. He served the Siyals as a herdsman. As the affair became public, Hir's parents married her to Sahiba, the Khera boy. Hir, offering tenacious resistance to patriarchy, refused to consummate the marriage. Ranjha enrolled as a Jogi at Tilla Balnath and, following an elaborate plan, eloped with Hir. The Siyals caught up with the fugitives, who received shelter from the Nahars. In the ensuing Siyal-Nahar conflict, many lives were lost. In a trial at Kot Qabula, the *qazi* restored Hir to the Kheras and punished Ranjha with lashes. The supernatural powers of the lovers, coupled with the support of the local people, forced the authorities to reverse the verdict, leading to a reunion of the victims.[58] In the second story, Mirza, the son of a Kharal *zamindar*, lived with the Siyals, his maternal grandparents at Khiva. He fell in love with his cousin Sahiban while studying in the school. The Siyals, disturbed at the affair, fixed Sahiban's marriage among the Chanddars. Mirza, failing to get the support of the Kharals, decided to rescue Sahiban. Proud of his valour, he rejected the advice of his mother and sister. On the wedding day, he eloped with Sahiban.[59] A joint Siyal-Chanddar retinue killed the fugitives. The Kharals, in retaliation, inflicted a big defeat on the Siyals and retrieved their honour. The third story occurred in the town of Gujarat on the Chenab. Sohni, the daughter of a potter Tulla, fell in love with Mirza Izzat Beg, a merchant from Bukhara. This man lost his wealth in the pursuit of love. Since he began to work for Tulla as a herdsman, he came to be known as Mahiwal. Sohni's parents, upset at the relation, dismissed Mahiwal and married Sohni in the family of a fellow potter. Sohni rejected the marriage and continued to meet Mahiwal, who had settled on the Chenab as a mendicant. Every night, she crossed the Chenab on a pitcher for her trysts. Her sister-in-law, discovering the truth, placed an unbaked pitcher in place of the baked one. Sohni was drowned in the stormy Chenab, while Mahiwal joined her in the watery grave.[60]

As a coincidence, the three love tales were associated with the Chenab. The lovers fell in love under unexpected and dramatic circumstances. When they exchanged vows of fidelity, they felt that their relation with the society was snapped. The clan of the

304 *Situating Medieval India*

women disapproved the relation. Love was intolerable, as it threatened to subvert the clan based social order and deprived the clan of an important privilege. A young woman could not choose her partner. The decision fell in the domain of the clan. In order to retrieve its position and honour, the clan made a careful analysis of the local politics and forcibly married the woman in a clan of its choice. The woman, refusing to consummate the marriage, delivered a severe blow to patriarchy. In Damodar Guilati's narrative, Hir-Ranjha defeated the patriarchal forces and lived happily thereafter. The lives of Mirza-Sahiban and Sohni-Mahiwal were cut short through violent means. The lovers, after their supreme sacrifices, became immortal in both the mystical discourse and folklore. In reconstructing their memory, their struggles were seen in spiritual terms. Perceived as saints and martyrs, their tombs have evolved as sacred sites. In our times, they were a recurrent theme in literature, films and paintings. They have been a perpetual source of nourishment to the Punjabi tradition of resistance. The story of Mirza-Sahiban did not find space in the mystical discourse, as their love was looked upon as flawed. The efforts of the legendry folksinger Alam Lohar, having covered the tragic aspects of this story, have assigned a rightful place to the lovers in the Punjabi cultural ethos.

During the first half of the sixteenth century, Panjab witnessed sustained resistance of the tribes to the state. As early as 1519, Babur examined the relative position of the various tribes (Jud, Janjuha and Gakhhar) in the Sind Sagar Doab. After an initial attack against Hati Gakhhar, he refrained from disturbing the existing political equations and remained satisfied with a nominal allegiance from the tribes. The Mandahars, inhabiting parts of the cis-Satluj tract, refused to accept the Mughal aurthority. A localized tussle between the chief Mohan Mandahar and a land grantee paved the way for Mughal military intervention. The Mandahars routed the Mughal army of 3,000 horsemen under Ali Quli Hamdani. The Mughals, in order to salvage their prestige, fitted out a second expedition. Drawing the Mandahars out of their village through stratagem, the Mughals destroyed the entire village. They killed 1,000 men, captured women and children, besides inflicting a cruel death on Mohan Mandahar. The Afghan State, having supplanted the

Cultural Ethos of Medieval Panjab

305

Mughals, failed to establish its control over the tribes.[61] In the Sind Sagar Doab, a few Baloch chiefs expressed their subordination to Sher Shah (r. 1540-5). The Gakhhars, confident of their numbers and long understanding with the Mughals, asserted their autonomy. Sher Shah ravaged the Gakhhar country and, killing Sarang Khan Gakhhar, constructed the fort of Rohtas as a symbol of Afghan power. However, the chiefs of Multan continued to oppose the Afghan State. Haibat Khan Niazi, winning over Chakar Khan Rind and Bakhshu Langah, overpowered Fateh Khan Jat and Mindu Baloch, both of whom were put to death. The Balochis killed their own women, so that they did not fall into the hands of the Afghans. In spite of their victory, the Afghans were forced to continue the Langah system of assessing the land revenue.[62] The Sumbals, a branch of the Niazis, who were settled along the Indus, killed an oppressive governor and suffered a genocide at the hands of Haibat Khan Niazi.[63] Islam Shah (r. 1545-55), singularly lacking in political acumen, alienated the tribes. The disaffected Niazi nobles returned to Panjab and, mobilizing fellow tribesmen, joined hands with the restive Gakhhars. The Afghan State, in order the crush the tribal resistance, carried out punitive measures that involved cruel bloodshed and construction of a new fort complex at Mankot.[64]

The revival of the Mughal State (1555-6) exposed the hill chiefdoms to attack. The Mughal victory at Mankot and the execution of Raja Takht Mal of Mau intensified the pressure on the hills. The Mughal aggression was revealed in the occupation of the fort of Kangra (1572) and destruction of the temple of Mahamai. The chiefdoms remained undeterred at the growing Mughal power in the area. In 1590, sixteen principalities from the Satluj to Beas challenged the Mughal State with a combined mobilization of 10,000 horsemen and one lakh footmen.[65] Two years later, the rebellion spread to the hills between the Ravi and Chenab. The chiefdoms paid a heavy price for resisting the Mughal State. The Mughal armies, in order to transport their soldiers and haul heavy equipment, cut the jungles to make paths. In some cases, the forts were destroyed and, in other cases, they were burnt to ashes. Slices of their territories were granted to the Mughal officers

306 *Situating Medieval India*

as revenue assignments (*jagirs*).[66] However, they did not allow the Mughals to measure the agricultural lands and, thus, managed to retain internal administrative autonomy. The Mughals succeeded in annexing (1618) the fort of Kangra only after they had suppressed the rebellion of Mau. The Mughals, learning from their experience and aiming to consolidate their gains, divided the entire mountainous belt into two divisions (*faujdaris*) of Kangra and Jammu. The Mughal officers (*faujdars*), holding these charges, employed their military resources to keep the chiefdom under a tight leash. Three successive chiefs of Mau (Raja Basu, Suraj Mal and Jagat Singh), who were assimilated into the Mughal polity with the grant of military ranks (*mansabs*), rose in revolt and invited punitive actions against themselves. Jagat Singh, the most powerful chief in the Panjab hills, posed a formidable challenge to the Mughal State. Shahjahan was forced to undertake the most elaborate military campaign in the area.[67] Though Jagat Singh was obliged to surrender, he has been lionized in the local folklore as a heroic warrior. During a century (1550-1650), the hill principalities often challenged the Mughal authority and, shattering the myth of Mughal military superiority, left important precedents for the Sikh rebellion that also emerged in the hills.

In the plains of Panjab, the spirit of resistance percolated to the peasantry. Dulla Bhatti, a landholder (*zamindar*) of 12 villages in the Rachna Doab, emerged as the greatest hero of medieval Panjab. His father and grandfather had raised the standard of revolt against Akbar.[68] Since they refused to pay the land tax and carried out predatory raids, they were put to death. Their straw filled bodies were hung at the entrance gate of Lahore. Dulla, mobilizing a retinue of 500 young men, threw a challenge to Akbar. He looted trade caravans passing through Pindi. He distributed the booty among his companions and artisans of the village. He deprived Ali of his horses and Medha Sahukar of his goods. He took away the valuables of Akbar's wife, who was travelling to Mecca for Haj. He severed the head of a senior Mughal noble and sent it to Akbar. At the instance of his friend Shaikhu (Prince Salim), he appeared at the Mughal court and gave an audacious proof of his rebellious spirit. Before returning, he wrought havoc in the bazaars of Lahore.

Cultural Ethos of Medieval Panjab 307

Akbar deputed Mirza Nizamuddin to attack Pindi and produce Dulla in chains. Dulla rode to Chiniot to bring his maternal uncles and their men. In his absence, his brother Mehru Posti and son Nur Khan put up a spirited fight. Nizamuddin, having ravaged Pindi, tied the Bhatti women in ropes and dragged them to Lahore. Dulla caught up with the Mughals and, after a fierce battle, got the hostages released. At the persuasion of Nizamuddin, Dulla came to Lahore for an audience with Akbar. However, he was poisoned to death at night.[69]

Dulla Bhatti, through the memory of his anti-Mughal resistance, has carved a permanent place for himself in the cultural landscape of Panjab. Though he belonged to the class of rural elite (*zamindars*), he mobilized the rural toilers to fight against the oppression of the Mughal State. Displaying unprecedented bravery and humanism, he defended the honour of two daughters of a hapless Brahmin. This chivalrous act was commemorated in the annual festival of Lohri, which has been celebrated for centuries. The folk singers— Ashiq Husain Jatt, Kuldip Manak and Sharif Ragi—have prepared musical operas on the life of Dulla Bhatti. Apart from presentations at rural fairs, these have been widely circulated through audio cassettes, CDs and MP3s. The struggle of Dulla Bhatti has been kept alive in the creative works of playwrights, novelists and filmmakers. Najm Hosain Syed, in a seminal contribution, argued that two rebels, Dulla Bhatti and Shah Husain, saw a common enemy in the Mughal State. The ruling class, entrenched in the city of Lahore, constructed a polity that reduced the peasants and artisans to dependence. The inhabitants of the central uplands (*bar*), for seven generations, did not bow to a kingship born in Delhi and grown in Lahore. The Mughal State captured Dulla Bhatti through deceit and hanged him in public to terrify petty functionaries and traders and, thus erase the story of his resistance (*nabri*). Refusing to bend even on the gallows, he added a new dimension to his resistance. Shah Husain, who was present among the multitude, represented a dangerously subversive ideology. Making a bold display of his love for Madho, he demolished the patriarchal norms (*kherashahi*), which had destroyed the natural sexual instincts and deprived women of their agency. The Mughal State, unable to tame Dulla

308 *Situating Medieval India*

Bhatti and assimilate Shah Husain in the system of patronage, was caught in a double siege. From outside, Dulla Bhatti mobilized an army of deprived sections to pull down its ramparts and, from within, the verses and dance (*dhamal*) of Shah Husain pierced through its walls.[70]

For centuries, the Panjabis had been hearing a miraculous story from the life of Guru Nanak. During the course of his preaching, he visited Syedpur that Babur had destroyed. The Guru resettled it and, renaming it as Aminabad, stayed in the house of a carpenter Lalo. Malik Bhago, the Khatri revenue officer (*karori*), was holding a ceremonial feast in the memory of his ancestors, where a large number of Brahmins and Khatris were invited. The Guru, receiving an invitation, refused to attend it. However, he was persuaded to visit the venue. Malik Bhago asked him the reason of refusing to eat with the upper castes and, instead, dining at the house of a menial. The Guru, appearing before the vast gathering, took breads (*roti*) from the house of Malik Bhago and Lalo. When he squeezed, blood oozed from the former and milk from the latter.[71] This was a defining moment in the evolution of Sikhism. While rejecting the ancient caste-based discrimination, it drew a distinction between two modes of income. The upper castes derived their income from oppressive means and, therefore, they could not finance the oblations for ancestors in the hereafter. In contrast, the people belonging to low castes earned their livelihood through honest labour and, therefore, deserved a higher rank in the social structure and divine estimation. We must hasten to point out that the incident was not exceptional. Guru Nanak, both in precept and practice, upheld the principle of social equality. He had intimate relations with individuals, who were treated as socially inferior due to their caste. Bhai Mardana, a Mirasi who sang devotional verses to the accompaniment of rebeck (*rabab*), remained an inseparable companion of Guru Nanak for 47 years.[72] Bhai Buddha, a Jat of the Randhawa clan, became a devoted follower of Guru Nanak and became the most trusted member of the fraternity at Kartarpur. With his sincerity and wisdom, he attained unprecedented honour during the pontificate of five succeeding Gurus.

Guru Nanak designated himself as a bard of low caste. He sought

Cultural Ethos of Medieval Panjab 309

the company of the lowliest and had no desire to equal the status of high castes. No one could be styled as low owing to his birth, as the term was applicable to those who forgot God. People of high castes took pride in their social antecedents, as they could wear a clean loin cloth, anointed their forehead with a sacrificial mark and put a rosary around their neck. He alone was a Brahmin who understood the transcendence of God, performed devotions and observed humility. He alone was a Khatri who performed good deeds, spent his body in charity and planted the seed of beneficence after ascertaining quality of the soil. Since the same Lord manifested in every heart, He did not seek to know anyone's caste. Before the creation, there was no caste and, after death, caste had no meaning. Pride in one's caste was as deadly as poison. Guru Angad held that the four castes performed different functions, but their common creed was reciting God's name. Guru Amar Das believed that the four castes had originated from the same divine source (*brahm binde*). The world was made out of the same clay, but the potter had crafted vessels of numerous kinds, each comprising the same five elements. Guru Ram Das asserted that the most distinguished of four castes was the one who meditated on the Lord. He asked his followers to learn from the example of Krishna, who had immense affection for Bidur and Sudama, who belonged to low castes. Guru Arjan praised a number of saints (Namdev, Kabir, Ravidas, Sain and Dhanna) who, in spite of their depressed social condition, rose up in the spiritual hierarchy owing to their sincere devotion to God. The Supreme Being provided equal nourishment to all human beings irrespective of their social rank.[73]

The Sikh scripture has accorded a prominent place to the verses of three saints, who rejected the caste-based social order in categorical terms. Sant Namdev condemned the priests for denigrating him, beating him and turning him out of the temple. He was forced to perform his devotions outside the temple. He raised his voice against a Sultan, who asked him to revive a dead cow. When he refused to do the bidding, the Sultan tried to trample him under an elephant. He raised doubts about the piety of Brahmanical deities and the merit of Brahmanical beliefs. He exposed a Brahmin for damaging the crop of a peasant and murdering the son of a

310   *Situating Medieval India*

host. He envisioned God as a protector of the oppressed. He saw God as a carpenter, who had made the entire universe.[74] Sant Kabir had strong reasons to delegitimize the Brahmins. He raised serious doubts about the knowledge of Brahmins on creation, death and salvation. Their recitation of the *Vedas* and *Puranas* was similar to loading a donkey with sandalwood. Begging at the door of kings, the Brahmins sold their knowledge in lieu of wealth. Their stance on impurity had subjected the low castes to brutal segregation. He imagined God as a weaver, who treated the earth and sky as His loom and moved the heavenly bodies like bobbins. The divine craftsman, using the same clay, had designed vessels of different shapes. Therefore, no one could be termed as inferior.[75] The hereditary occupation of Sant Ravidas was removing dead cattle out of Benares and, owing to the stigma attached to the work, he faced the slander of upper castes. In his view, one's conduct determined one's purity, not one's birth. Since he had become a merchant of God and adopted the trade of divine knowledge, even the Brahmins prostrated themselves before him. He offered the vision of an alternative social structure, which would be obtained in the city of Begampura. Populous and prosperous, its inhabitants would enjoy freedom of movement and exemption from taxes. He claimed to follow in the footsteps of low caste saints such as Maharishi Balmiki, Sant Namdev and Sant Kabir.[76]

By the early decades of the seventeenth century, the results of the anti-caste plank became visible. The pious congregations (*sadhsangat*), where the Sikhs gathered to receive instructions, abrogated the caste rules. Open to all without discrimination, they welded the four castes into one. The members (*gurmukhs*), having shed their caste associations, acquired a new identity. On meeting, they touched the feet of one another and equally shared the physical labour. Instead of the Hindu deities, they regarded low caste saints— Namdev, Kabir, Ravidas, Dhanna, Beni and Sain—as role models.[77] By Guru Arjan's time, the community had undergone a substantive expansion, as every town came to have a sizeable number of Sikhs. The Khatris were made subordinate to the Jats, who were hitherto regarded as the lowest caste of the Vaishyas. A majority of the Guru's deputies (*masands*) were Jats, while the Brahmins and

Cultural Ethos of Medieval Panjab 311

Khatris were only disciples and followers.[78] Guru Gobind Singh, with the creation of the Khalsa and institution of a new religious code, wiped out the remnants of caste. Persian chroniclers, who observed the Panjab scenario in the eighteenth century, were surprised at the preponderance of low castes among the Sikh warrior bands. During the ascendancy of Banda Bahadur, even sweepers and cobblers were appointed as administrators of their towns. In the mid-eighteenth century, an Afghan writer was impressed with the martial abilities and moral qualities of the Sikhs. Towards the end of the eighteenth century, it was noted that a majority of the Sikhs were Jats, carpenters, shoemakers, barbers, washermen, confectioners, grain sellers and fodder vendors.[79] The Sikhs, by opening their doors to the low castes acquired three characteristics—rapidly increasing numbers, enviable martial skills and an indomitable spirit of sacrifice.

Since the times of Ali bin Usman Hujweri (d. 1072), Sufi shrines had been evolving in different parts of Panjab such as Lahore, Multan, Uch, Pakpattan, Gujarat, Batala, Jalandhar, Malerkotla, Sirhind, Hansi, Shahabad and Panipat. Though every shrine developed in a specific set of circumstances and cultivated a distinct set of rituals, most such sites transformed as shared cultural spaces and attracted devotees cutting across religion, sect, class, caste and gender. By way of illustration, we may consider the shrine of Sarwar Sultan at Bangah near Multan.[80] There were two stories about the origin of this cult. Sarwar, originally a thief, was nominated as the Qutb of Multan by Khwaja Maudud Chishti. The attendants of the shrine of Shaikh Bahauddin Zakariya, jealous of the huge offerings received at Bangah, gave currency to the story that a Chamar, not a Qutb, was buried at the place. Lowly placed Muslims and upper-caste Hindus played a crucial role in popularization of the cult. The former, as represented by the Parahis, were reputed for a dance form (*luddi*), which they performed along with singing and drumming. When a Hindu boy married, two Parahis went to his house and, during a performance, made the newly-wedded couple dance with them. The ritual was regarded as an auspicious beginning of married life. The cult spread to all parts of Panjab up to Delhi. The Hindus, in addition to their deities, believed that their prosperity was due to the blessings of Sarwar. Every Thursday, they lighted an earthen lamp in a cell of their house to the saint. Every year, Sarwar was commemorated in a colourful festival. In the outskirts of every town, spear-like banners were raised and Parahis sang the praises of Sarwar. Droves of Hindus and Muslims gathered to see the spectacle. Traders set up stall under tents, selling sweets and other eatables. Festivities continued throughout the night. Next morning, the spectators returned to their houses. A big procession—comprising devotees, Parahis and shopkeepers—left for Bangah from every town. At this place, the gathering was a thousand times the population of a town or an army. The participants, particularly the poor, spent their entire annual income at the festival.[81] Mirza Hasan Qatil has placed this shrine in the category of sacred places associated with Shah Madar, Salar Masud Ghazi and Shaikh Saddu.

Panjab, comprising the vast plain between the Indus and Yamuna, witnessed momentous developments during the medieval times. The Delhi Sultanate, with an eye on rich tributes, tried to subjugate the local tribes. In the process, it met stiff resistance from the Jats and Khokhars. In the post-Timur phase, the rural magnates gained a considerable autonomy in their hereditary domains at the cost of the Delhi-based regimes. The Jogis, while living in their monasteries and enjoying land grants, distanced themselves from socially dominant elements and came out in support of the marginalized. Islamic spirituality, acting through a network of lodges (*khanqahs*) and shrines (*dargahs*), deepened its roots in all nooks and corners. Panjabi Sufi poetry popularized a loving relation with God, employing a bold sexual imagery. The legendary lovers, flourishing on the banks of the Chenab, laid down their lives in struggles against patriarchal forces. During the first half of the sixteenth century, the Afghan State could not strengthen its authority in the northwestern tracts and the Multan region owing to sustained opposition from the Gakkhars, Niazis, Balochis, Langahs and Jats. In the northeastern mountainous belt, the hill principalities offered frequent resistance to the Mughal State, which could not establish a firm control in the area. Dulla Bhatti, mobilizing the peasant-artisan populace of the Sandal Bar, led a powerful anti-Mughal movement and, ultimately, emerged as a perennial symbol of resistance. The Sikh leadership,

Cultural Ethos of Medieval Panjab 313

having demolished the impregnable bastion of caste, opened the doors of the nascent community to depressed castes and enabled them to wrest political power from the Mughal hands. In sum, the multifarious resistance, often inseparably intertwined with spirituality, constituted the Punjabi culture.

NOTES

1. An earlier version of this paper, 'Evolution of the Punjabi Culture: Exploring the Human Experience of the Pre-modern Times', was presented at the International Conference on 'Socio-Economic and Cultural Relations Between India and Pakistan', Department of History, University of the Punjab, Lahore, Pakistan, 25-27 November 2013.
2. Khushwant Singh, *Punjab, Punjabis & Punjabiyat: Reflections on a Land and Its People*, ed. Mala Dayal, New Delhi: Aleph Book Company, 2018.
3. Aitzaz Ahsan, *The Indus Saga and the Making of Pakistan*, New Delhi: Roli Books, rpt., 2007, p. 25.
4. According to the earliest evidence from Hsuan Tsang and the author of *Chachnama*, a large number of Jats were settled in the marshy lowlands on both sides of the Indus. A large primitive community, they derived livelihood from tending cattle, though they also served as soldiers and boatmen. Owing allegiance to Buddhist *shramans*, they had an egalitarian or semi-egalitarian social structure. Under the Brahmana dynasty, they suffered hard constraints that the Arab conquerors confirmed. In the early ninth century, the Arab governor summoned them to pay *jiziya*, each to be accompanied by a dog as a mark of humiliation. By the early eleventh century, the Jats migrated north from Sind and appeared in southern Panjab (Multan and Bhatiya besides the Indus), where they clashed with the forces of Sultan Mahmud of Ghazni. Irfan Habib, 'Jatts of Punjab and Sind', in *Essays in Honour of Dr. Ganda Singh*, ed. Harbans Singh and N. Gerald Barrier, Patiala: Punjabi University, 1976, pp. 94-5.
5. Muhammad Nazim, *The Life and Times of Sultan Mahmud of Ghazna*, New Delhi: Munshiram Manoharlal, rpt., 1971, pp. 121-2.
6. Abul Fazl Baihaqi, *Tarikh-i Subuktgin*, Eng. tr., *The History of India as Told by its Own Historians*, ed. H.M. Elliot and John Dowson, vol. I, Allahabad: Kitab Mahal, n.d., p. 133.
7. Tajuddin Hasan Nizami, *Taj ul-Maasir*, Eng. tr. Bhagwat Saroop, Delhi: Ibn Saud Dehlavi, 1998, pp. 97-100.

314 *Situating Medieval India*

8. The late nineteenth century sources noted that the Khokhars, a tribe of varying Rajput and Jat status, were numerous along the valleys of the Jhelum and Chenab. In smaller numbers, they were found in the lower Indus and Satluj, besides the foothills from the Jhelum to Satluj. The origin of the Khokhars was as obscure as any Panjab tribe. According to tradition, the Khokhars were connected to the Awans, as both owed their conversion to Islam to the saint Qutb Shah of Ghazni. Their varying status was reflected in their custom of marrying among diverse groups such as Rajputs, Jats, Awans, Janjuhas, Bhattis and Chibbs. According to another tradition, Timur's invasion forced the Khokhars to concentrate on the plains of the Jhelum and Chenab, besides spreading out in the submontane tract including Jammu. Denzil Ibbetson, *Panjab Castes*, Patiala: Languages Department, Punjab, rpt., 1970, pp. 172-3; H.A. Rose, *A Glossary of the Tribes and Castes of the Punjab and North-West Frontier Province*, vol. II, Patiala: Languages Department, Punjab, rpt., 1970, pp. 539-40.

9. Tajuddin Hasan Nizami, *Taj ul-Maasir*, pp. 253-4.

10. Ibid., pp. 262-6.

11. Ibid., pp. 273-5.

12. Tajuddin Hasan Nizami, a native of Nishapur, was caught in the political turmoil cause by the Ghorid occupation of Khurasan. Sometime before 1206, he migrated to Delhi and, in order to gain the patronage of Qutbuddin Aibak, wrote the history of the Muslim conquest of northern India. With a gap of 1202-6, he focused on the military achievements of Aibak and carried the story upto 1217. More of a poet than a historian, his prose was ornate and verbose. It was difficult to sift sober facts from a plethora of unhistorical matter, fantastic metaphors and complex rhetoric. Iqtidar Husain Siddiqui, *Indo-Persian Historiography upto the Thirteenth Century*, Delhi: Primus Books, 2010, pp. 40-4.

13. Minhajus Siraj Juzjani, *Tabaqat-i Nasiri*, Persian text, ed. Nassau Lees, Khadim Husain and Abdul Hayy, Calcutta: Royal Asiatic Society of Bengal, 1864, p. 290.

14. Ziauddin Barani, *Tarikh-i Firoz Shahi*, Persian text, ed. Sir Syed Ahmad, Aligarh: Sir Syed Academy, Aligarh Muslim University, 2005, rpt., p. 53.

15. Ibid., p. 59.

16. Ibid., p. 65.

17. According to Amir Khusrau, the troops of Ghazi Malik, hailing from the upper country of Khurasan and Transoxiana, included Ghuzz, Turks, Mongols of Rum and Rus, besides Khurasani Taziks. Mohammad Habib observed that these warrior races often fought with Ghazi Malik against the

Cultural Ethos of Medieval Panjab 315

Mongols; they were an official disguise for two Hindu Groups (Khokhars and Mewatis) that really joined Ghazi Malik in the move against Khusrau Khan. A recent study has examined each ethnic group, with reference to their habitats, conflicts, migrations and presence on the northwest frontier of India. Mohammad Habib and Khaliq Ahmad Nizami, eds., *A Comprehensive History of India, vol V: The Delhi Sultanate,* AD *1206-1526*, New Delhi: People's Publishing House, rpt., 1982, p. 452; Sunil Kumar, 'The Ignored Elites: Turks, Mongols and a Persian Secretarial Class in the Early Delhi Sultanate', in *Expanding Frontiers in South Asian and World History: Essays in Honour of John F. Richards*, ed. Richard M. Eaton et al., New York: Cambridge University Press, 2013, p. 48.

18. Abdul Malik Isami, *Futuh us-Salatin*, Persian text, ed. A.S. Usha, Madras; Madras University, 1948, pp. 380-7.

19. Yahya bin Ahmad bin Abdullah Sirhindi, *Tarikh-i Mubarak Shahi*, Persian text, ed. M. Hidayat Hosain, Calcutta: Asiatic Society of Bengal, 1931, pp. 194-226; Khwaja Nizamuddin Ahmad, *Tabaqat-i Akbari*, Eng. tr., B. De, Calcutta: The Asiatic Society, rpt., 1973, pp. 300-17.

20. Jog, traced to the canon of Patanjali, placed eternal existence in the domain of annihilation and, in many respects, acted contrary to customs. Patanjali followed the Sankhya philosophy, but acknowledged the Supreme Being as absolute existence and intelligence. A union with intellect engendered five mental states with varying implications for liberation. The cycle of births could be terminated with Jog, which was obtained through twelve principles aimed at overcoming human weaknesses. Its practice comprised meditation on eight parts of the body (*ashtang jog*), eighty-four postures for subjugating the senses and a complex method of breath control. Abul Fazl, *Akbar Nama*, vol. III, Eng. tr., H. Beveridge, New Delhi: Atlantic Publishers & Distributors, rpt., 2019, pp. 513-14; Abul Fazl, *Ain-i Akbari*, vol. III, Eng. tr., H.S. Jarrett and Jadunath Sarkar, Kolkata: The Asiatic Society, 2010, pp. 187-98.

21. Mobad Kaikhusrau Isfandiyar, *Dabistan-i Mazahab*, vol. I, Persian text, ed. Rahim Razazada Malik, Tehran: Kitabkhana Tahuri, 1362 AH/ 1983 AD, pp. 158-61.

22. Ruqnuddin Samarqandi translated *Amritkunda* into Persian with the help of a Jogi. The text dealt with themes such as knowledge of God, man's state as microcosm of universe, preservation of seminal fluids, creation of illusions and controlling the spirits. Some practices were neither distinctively Indian nor restricted to Jog. Most prominent was breath control, which was amenable to spatial measurements. For purification of human body, it refers to 84 postures, providing details of only five. Yusuf Husain, 'Haud

316   *Situating Medieval India*

ul-Hayat: The Arabic Version of Amritkunda', in *On Becoming an Indian Muslim: French Essays on Aspects of Syncretism*, ed. M. Waseem, New Delhi: Oxford University Press, 2003, pp. 63-74; Carl W. Ernst, '*The Islamization of Yoga in Amritkunda Translations*', *Journal of the Royal Asiatic Society*, third series, vol. 13, no. 2, July 2003, pp. 217-20.

23. George Weston Briggs, *Gorakhnath and the Kanphata Jogis*, Delhi: Motilal Banarsidas, rpt, 1982, pp. 101-3.

24. Father Monserrate, *Commentary of Father Monserrate*, ed. S.N. Banerjee and J.S. Hoyland, Jalandhar: Asian Publishers, rpt., 1993, pp. 113-15.

25. B.N. Goswamy and J.S. Grewal, *The Mughals and the Jogis of Jakhbar: Some Madad-i Maash and Other Documents*, Simla: Indian Institute of Advanced Study, 1967, pp. 1-39.

26. Qadiryar, *Puran Bhagat*, ed. Bikram Singh Ghuman, Amritsar: Waris Shah Foundation, 2003, pp. 78-104.

27. Najm Hosain Syed, 'Puran of Sialkot', and 'Revolt of the Sons of Salvahan', in *Recurrent Patterns in Punjabi Poetry*, Karachi: City Press, rpt., pp. 87-128, 159-66.

28. Baba Farid (1175-1265) played a major role in the growth of the Chishti order in northwestern India. Educated at Kahtwal and Multan, he excelled in hard spiritual exercises. He received formal training under Qutbuddin Bakhtiar Kaki at Delhi. After spending 12 years at Hansi, he settled in Ajodhan (Pakpattan). An erudite scholar, he institutionalized the Chishti discipline from his lodge (*jamaatkhana*). He groomed eminent mystics like Nizamuddin Auliya, Jamaluddin Hansavi, Badruddin Ishaq and Alauddin Ali Ahmad Sabir. His fame attracted the attention of the ruling class of the Delhi Sultanate, though he declined a land grant of four villages. He developed a system of helping the needy through the distribution of amulets. Evidence on his life was preserved in *Fawaid ul-Fuad*, *Khair ul-Majalis* and *Siyal ul-Auliya*. His Panjabi mystical verses have been included in the Sikh scripture.

29. Brij Mohan Sagar, *Hymns of Sheikh Farid*, Amritsar: Guru Nanak Dev University, 1999, Shalok nos. 30-1, 54, pp. 26, 28.

30. Ibid., Shalok nos. 87-9, p. 31.

31. Ibid., Shalok no. 127, p. 35.

32. Ibid., Shalok nos. 4-5, p. 24.

33. Ibid., Suhi Lalit, Shalok no. 2.2, p. 38.

34. Ibid., Shalok nos. 24, 26, p. 25.

35. Ibid., Shalok nos. 33-6, p. 26.

36. *Sri Guru Granth Sahib*, pp. 74-5, 137-9, 989.

37. Nikky Guninder Kaur Singh, *The Feminine Principle in the Sikh Vision of*

Cultural Ethos of Medieval Panjab   317

the Transcendent, Cambridge: Cambridge University Press, 1993, pp, 30, 58-9.

38. *Sri Guru Granth Sahib,* pp. 1108-9.

39. Shah Husain (1539-99) was born in a family of weavers at Lahore. Mahmud bin Muhammad Pir has composed his biography in verse. During his adulthood and youth, Shah Husain trained in the Qadiri discipline and undertook severe austerities. When he was 36, a Quranic verse brought about a dramatic change in his life. Adopting the ways of a Malamati, he fell in love with Madho and, roaming the streets with a rowdy band of companions, sang and danced in gay abandon. He clashed with Kotwal Malik Ali on the occasion of Dulla Bhatti's execution. A large number of people, ranging from toiling peasants to the Mughal ruling elite, came under his influence. He attained wide popularity for his Panjabi poetry, which explored the intricacies of spirituality, employing metaphors from ordinary life. In particular, he imagined the seeker as a wayward maiden, who was urged to learn spinning under the watchful eyes of her mother. Mahmud bin Muhammad Pir, *Haqiqat ul-Fuqara: Poetic Biography of Madho Lal Hussayn,* Eng. tr. Scott Kugle, in *Same Sex Love in India: A Literary History,* ed. Ruth Vanita and Saleem Kidwai, New Delhi: Penguin Books, 2008, pp. 165-77.

40. Kala Singh Bedi, *Shah Husain Lahori: Jeevan te Rachna,* Chandigarh: SSB Publishing Company, 1978, Kafi nos. 27-9, 136, pp. 349-50, 388.

41. Ibid., Kafi no. 149, p. 393.

42. Ibid., Kafi no. 122, p. 383.

43. Ibid., Kafi no. 93, p. 373.

44. Ibid., Kafi no. 43, p. 355.

45. Ibid., Kafi no. 17, p. 345.

46. Ibid., Kafi no. 68, p. 364.

47. The mystic thought of Bulleh Shah revolved around God's unity and oneness of all being. Truth had to be expressed even if it faced resistance due to its opposition to the given human condition. The realization of man's separation from God induced a struggle within the seeker's self. There was a basic contradiction between divine love (*ishq*) and canonical law (*shariat*). The former created a vigour and enthusiasm on the path of spiritual realization, while the latter thwarted individual initiative and denied the possibility of transcending the human condition. Love, owing to identification with God, had the potential to transform human nature. Bulleh Shah was strongly opposed to formalist and dualist world outlook. He condemned religious bigotry, hypocrisy and ritualism. Shuja Alhaq,

318 *Situating Medieval India*

A Forgotten Vision: A Study of Human Spirituality in the Light of the Islamic Tradition, vol. II, New Delhi: Vikas Publishing House, 1997, pp. 377-8.

48. Sutinder Singh Noor, *Punjabi Sufi Kaav*, New Delhi: Sahitya Academi, 1997, Kafi no. 120, p. 268.

49. Ibid., Kafi no. 84, pp. 249-50.

50. Ibid., Kafi no. 19, pp. 201-2.

51. Ibid., Kafi no. 31, p. 210; Kafi no. 60, p. 232.

52. Ibid., Kafi no. 45, p. 219.

53. Ibid., Kafi no. 111, p. 263.

54. Ibid., Kafi no. 70, pp. 237-8.

55. Ibid., Kafi no. 50, p. 221.

56. Ibid., Kafi no. 7, pp. 194-5.

57. Jodh Singh, *Varan Bhai Gurdas*, Text, Transliteration and Translation, Patiala: Vision & Venture, 1998, vol. II, Var 11, Pauri 1.

58. Damodar Gulati, *Hir Damodar*, Punjabi text, ed. Jagtar Singh, Patiala: Punjabi University, 2000.

59. Pilu, *Mirza Sahiban*, Punjabi text, ed. Gurmukh Singh, Chandigarh: Lokgeet Prakashan, 2003.

60. Fazl Shah, *Sohni*, Punjabi text, ed. Gurdev Singh, Ludhiana: Lahore Book Shop, 1974.

61. Ahmad Yadgar, *Tarikh-i Shahi*, Persian text, ed. M. Hidayat Hosain, Calcutta: Royal Asiatic Society of Bengal, 1939, pp. 87-9.

62. Abbas Khan Sarwani, *Tarikh-i Sher Shahi*, Persian text, ed. S.M. Imamuddin, Dacca: University of Dacca, 1964, pp. 183-6.

63. Ibid., pp. 232-7.

64. Abdul Qadir Badauni, *Muntakhab ut-Tawarikh*, vol. I, Eng. tr., George S.A. Ranking and B.P. Ambashthya, Patna: Academica Asiatica, rpt., 1973, pp. 498-500; Khwaja Nizamuddin Ahmad, *Tabaqat-i Akbari*, vol. II, Eng. tr., B. De, Calcutta: The Asiatic Society, rpt., 1973, pp. 185-8; Khwaja Niamatullah Haravi, *Tarikh-i Khan Jahani wa Makhzan Afghani*, vol. II, Persian text, ed. S.M. Imamuddin, Dacca: Asiatic Society of Pakistan, 1960, pp. 364-9.

65. Abul Fazl, *Akbar Nama*, vol. III, Eng. tr., H. Beveridge, New Delhi: Atlantic Publishers & Distributors, rpt., 2019, pp. 884-5.

66. Ibid., pp. 1004-6; Allahdad Faizi Sirhindi, *Akbar Nama*, Eng. tr., H.M. Elliot and John Dowson, *History of India as Told by Its Own Historians*, vol. VI, Allahabad: Kitab Mahal, rpt., 1981, pp. 125-9.

67. Abdul Hamid Lahori, *Badshah Nama*, Persian text, ed. Kabiruddin Ahmad and Abdul Rahim, Calcutta: Royal Asiatic Society of Bengal, 1867-8, vol. II, pp. 261-78; Muhammad Saleh Kamboh, *Amal-i Saleh*, Persian

Cultural Ethos of Medieval Panjab 319

text, ed. Ghulam Yazdani, Calcutta: Royal Asiatic Society of Bengal, 1927-9, vol. II, pp. 349-58; Shaikh Farid Bhakkari, *Zakhirat ul-Khawanin*, ed. Syed Moinul Haq, Karachi: Pakistan Historical Society, 1970-71, vol. II, pp. 119-22.

68. Akbar, during the first decade of his reign, allowed Sher Shah's land revenue system to continue. From 1567 onwards, the system was gradually reformed in accordance with the local conditions. Numerous functionaries, trained in Persian and accounts, fanned out into the countryside to collect statistics on cultivated area, estimated revenue, land grants and agricultural prices. Since the land tax was collected through the intermediacy of *zamindars*, information was also collected about their military resources. The most important function of the commandants (*faujdars*) was to ensure the obedient cooperation of *zamindars*, who were chastised in cases of defiance. The penetration of the Mughal State deep into the rural society struck hard at the autonomy of the *zamindars*, who were forced to accept a reduced share in the agricultural surplus. Deprived of their traditional privileges, they were threatened with outright extinction. Surinder Singh, 'Mughal Centralization and Local Resistance in North-Western India: An Exploration in the Ballad of Dulla Bhatti', in *Popular Literature and Pre-Modern Societies in South Asia*, ed. Surinder Singh and Ishwar Dayal Gaur, Delhi: Pearson Longman, 2008, pp. 94-9.

69. Kishan Singh Arif, *Qissa Dulla Bhatti*, Punjabi text, ed. Gian Chand, (*Qissa Dulla Bhatti te Us Di Bhav Jugat*), Amritsar: Ravi Sahit Prakashan, 1987, pp. 71-121; Ghulam Muhammad Ruliya (folksinger, village Bholewal, District Lyallpur)], 'Var Dulla Bhatti', in *Tin Lok Varan*, ed. Ahmed Salim, Amritsar: Ravi Sahit Prakashan, 2015, pp. 30-54.

70. Najm Hosain Syed, *Sedhan, Saran Ate Hor Lekh*, Transliteration in Gurmukhi, Purdaman Singh Bedi, Ludhiana: Jaswant Printers, 2005, pp. 127-33.

71. W.H. McLeod, *Early Sikh Tradition: A Study of the Janamsakhis*, Oxford: Clarendon Press, 1980, pp. 86-7.

72. Harbans Singh, *Guru Nanak and the Origin of the Sikh Faith*, Bombay: Asia Publishing House, 1969, pp. 179-80.

73. Manmohan Singh, *Sri Guru Granth Sahib*, Text with Eng. and Pbi. tr., Amritsar: Shiromani Gurdwara Prabandhak Committee, rpt., 1988, pp. 487-8.

74. Ibid., pp. 675, 875, 1163-6, 1193, 1292.

75. Ibid., pp. 328-9, 331, 482, 484, 654, 659, 858, 875, 1103, 1105, 1349-50.

76. Ibid., pp. 345-6, 659, 858, 875, 1124, 1293.

77. Bhai Gurdas, *Varan: Bhai Gurdas*, Text, Transliteration and Translation,

320   *Situating Medieval India*

2 vols., Jodh Singh, Patiala: Vision & Venture, 1998, Var 12, Pauri, 7-15; Var 14, Pauri 20; Var 23, Pauri 20; Var 25, Pauri 5; Var 27, Pauri 19.

78. Mobad Kaikhusrau Isfandiyar, *Dabistan-i Mazahab*, Persian text, ed. Rahim Razazada Malik, Tehran: Kitabkhana Tahuri, 1362 AH /1983 AD, vol. I, p. 206.

79. Muhammad Hashim Khafi Khan, *Muntakhab ul-Lubab*, Persian text, ed. Kabiruddin Ahmad and Wolseley Haig, Calcutta: Royal Asiatic Society of Bengal, 1874, vol. II, pp. 669-74; Muhammad Hadi Kamwar Khan, *Tazkirat us-Salatin-i Chaghta*, Persian text, ed. Muzaffar Alam, Bombay: Asia Publishing House, 1980, p. 93; Muhammad Shafi Warid, *Mirat-i Waridat*, Persain Ms, Maulana Abul Kalam Azad Arabic and Persian Research Institute, Tonk, Rajasthan, pp. 133a-4a; Qazi Nur Muhammad, *Jang Nama*, Persian text, ed. Ganda Singh, Amritsar: Sikh History Research Department, Khalsa College, 1939, pp. 156-9; Ghulam Ali Khan, *Imad us-Saadat*, Eng. tr., Irfan Habib, in *Sikh History from Persian Sources*, ed. J.S. Grewal and Irfan Habib, New Delhi: Tulika, 2001, pp. 214-15.

80. Colonial officers took a keen interest in the cult of Sakhi Sarwar, also known as Lakhdata and Lalanwala. Their studies focused on the saint's legendry life, sojourn in Baghdad, association with Shihabuddin Suhrawardi and Khwaja Maudud Chishti, besides connection with a ruler of Delhi. The main shrine was located at Nigaha (Dera Ghazi Khan) on the edge of Sulaiman mountains and a stream. Apart from the tombs of Sarwar along with his kin and companions, there were shrines of Guru Nanak and Bhairon. The offerings were shared among 1650 attendants, who were descendants of the three servants of Gannu. Every village in central Panjab has a shrine of Sarwar. These were also found at Moga, Ludhiana, Chamba and Nahan. The Bharais conducted processions from the towns along fixed routes. The pilgrims comprised Hindus, Muslims and Sikhs. H.A. Rose, *A Glossary of the Tribes and Castes of the Punjab and Northwest Frontier Province*, vol. I, Patiala: Languages Department, Punjab, rpt., 1970, pp. 566-72; also see, R.C. Temple, *The Legends of the Punjab*, Islamabad: Institute of Folk Heritage, rpt., 1981, vol. I, pp. 66-81, 91-7; vol. II, pp. 104-132; vol. III, 98-125, 301-21.

81. Mirza Muhammad Hasan Qatil, *Haft Tamasha*, Urdu tr., Muhammad Umar, Delhi: Maktaba Burhan, 1968, pp. 101-4.

CHAPTER 13

Caste, Creed and Custom: North Indian Society Towards the Close of the Eighteenth Century

The students of medieval India are indebted to the historian Muhammad Umar for introducing them to Mirza Muhammad Hasan Qatil and his work, entitled *Haft Tamasha* (Seven Spectacles).[1] Qatil had an interesting background and career. He belonged to the Khatri clan of Bhandaris, which was based in Batala, a town in the upper Bari Doab. One of his ancestors Surat Singh migrated to Baghpat on the Yamuna, seventeen leagues north of Delhi. His grandfather Rai Lalji Mal and father Dargahi Mal were born here.[2] Dargahi Mal was associated with Hidayat Ali Khan, who held the province of Shahjahanabad in revenue contract. Following his retirement, Dargahi Mal received an annual pension of one thousand rupees. In 1757, Diwani Singh was born in Delhi. In addition to Persian and Arabic, he studied a number of subjects such as grammar, arithmetic, philosophy, logic and prosody. He turned to poetry under the guidance of Mirza Muhammad Baqir 'Shahid'. Owing to the influence of his tutor, he embraced Shia Islam at the age of fourteen and acquired a new name. After three years, he revealed the change and separated from his family. During his service (1776-82) under Najaf Khan, he recited his verses in the poetry sessions at the house of Ghulam Hamdani Mushafi. In 1783, he shifted to Lucknow and lived here, with a brief interlude at Kalpi, until his death in 1817. Remaining unmarried, he lived a life of ideological independence like a Qalandar.[3]

In due course, Qatil acquired an enviable reputation in poetry, prose and letter writing. In addition to a compendium of poetry

322   *Situating Medieval India*

in 5,000 verses, he produced nine books on the subjects of his mastery.[4] In the closing years of his life, he wrote the *Haft Tamasha*, which turned out to be the most important of his works. He undertook this task at the request of an Iranian visitor Mirza Muhammad Husain of Karbala. It appears that Nawab Saadat Ali Khan had recommended his name to the visitor.[5] The text of *Haft Tamasha*, running into 194 pages, comprised seven chapters of unequal length. The opening chapter was devoted to orthodox Hinduism (*samaratkan*). Apart from the creation of human life and the unique role of the great serpent (*sesh nag*), it discussed the four Hindu eras (*satyug, tretayug, duaparyug* and *kalyug*) as well as the Hindu trinity of Brahma, Bishan (Vishnu) and Mahadev. It explores the concept of metempsychosis and narrates the tales of Mahabharta. Chapter two sought to clear the confusion between the Rajputs and Khatris. It also revealed the differences between the Panjabi Khatris and Purabi Khatris. Chapter three describes more than a score of sects that fell outside of the pale of Hinduism. Apart from Sufis and Sikhs, it included the Jains, Bairagis, Sannyasis, Madaris, Kabir Panthis and Lal Begis. Chamars and Bhands, both recognized as depressed castes, were also counted in this category. Chapter four was assigned to the Hindu festivals, ranging from Dussehra and Diwali to Holi and Janmashtami. It unveils the nature of Muslim participation in the festivities. Chapter five describes the popular cults associated with saintly figures of Shah Madar, Sakhi Sarwar, Salar Masud and Shaikh Saddu. Chapter six revolves around the four groupings among the Muslims—Mughals, Syeds, Shaikhs and Afghans—with reference to their fluid internal compositions and marital customs. Chapter seven, digressing from the central theme of social structure, recorded some strange practices that generated a sense of amazement. For example, the acrobats and mimics earned their livelihood through their performance of incredible feats.

Qatil has made an ardent attempt to show that the Khatris were not Rajputs. In doing so, he checked their relative proximity to the Brahmins. First, the Brahmins did not accept the food cooked by the Rajputs and, second, the Rajputs did not wear the sacred thread (*zunnar*). As opposed to this, the Saraswat Brahmins took food and smoking pipe from the Khatris. Moreover, the Khatris

Caste, Creed and Custom

always wore the sacred thread, which was a badge of high status among the Hindus. Some Rajputs and other affluent people gave a lot of money to the Brahmins for this permission. Qatil claims to have studied a number of books on the origin of the Rajputs. According to the details, the only surviving heir of a Raja was the son of a concubine. Following his enthronement, he humiliated his uncles and cousins, as they did not share the smoking pipe with him. These relatives, fearing for their lives, migrated to other places. Some of them took up service, while some others learnt crafts and became artisans. The king assumed the title of Rajput to camouflage his lowly birth. If he was really highborn, he would not have to depend on a high sounding epithet. In spite of his best efforts, the Brahmins neither shared his food nor permitted him to put on the sacred thread. Qatil suggested that, if any one was interested in deeper reflection, he could discuss the matter with a knowledgeable Brahmin.[6] In matters of food, the Khatris were both meat eaters and vegetarians. The former ate all types of meat except that of the cows. During the Muslim rule, they kept away from pork. What was more probable, they followed the practice of the local administrator in this regard.[7]

Qatil has drawn a distinction between the Khatris of Panjab and those of the Purab (the Gangetic plain). For long, Panjab, the land of the five rivers, had been the original home of the Khatris, though they were also found in the other parts of the Indian subcontinent. Since the Khatri clans of Panjab shared food and smoking pipe, they contracted marriages among themselves. This was in conformity with the general Hindu practice, whereby they gave their daughters in marriage to a person with whom they ate in the same utensils. In the same manner, they took the daughters of their counterparts into their families. However, they did not maintain such relations with the Khatri migrants from Panjab, who had settled in the Purab and, therefore, designated as the Purbiyas. Interestingly, the Panjabi Khatris, who had been living in Purab for a hundred years, developed social relations with Khatris, who had spent the same span of time in the region. The only condition was that they shared food and matrimony with one another. The case of Panjabi Khatris, who had arrived in the Purab in more recent

324 *Situating Medieval India*

times, was different. Such Khatris, attaining prosperity in the towns of Purab, decided to settle here on a permanent basis. When their son became a youth, he was sent back to Panjab for marriage. They did the same in case of their daughter, who reached the marriageable age. After marriage, they brought the son-in-law along with them. Alternatively, they allowed her to settle there, so that she was not labelled as a Purabi. The two categories of Khatris, the Panjabi and Purabi, did not maintain social relations with each other, precluding the sharing of food and matrimony. Qatil, uncovering this geographical and cultural chasm, asserted that the Khatris were next only to the Brahmins in social respectability, because they were associated with the political authority (*takht wa taj*) in the past and continued to wear the sacred thread.[8] Evidently, what was originally a geographical distance, transformed with the passage of time and amplified into social and cultural difference.

Ganesh Das Wadhera, who wrote a few decades after Qatil, took great pains to distinguish between the Rajputs and Khatris. The ancient ruler Raja Bharat, owing to his benevolence and competence, attained the title of protector (Chhatri). Since *chha* and *kha* were interchangeable, Chhatri and Khatri carried the same meaning. All Khatris were the descendants of Bharat. At this time, four castes were created and every person was ordered to pursue the work assigned to his caste. After Bharat's demise, the number of his descendants increased and, ruling over different parts of the country, inflicted oppression on the people. Manu, whom God authorized to restore order, created the lineages of Surajbansis and Chanderbansis. Wielding power like Bharat, they called themselves Chhatris. With the passage of time, they discarded the tradition of social superiority and married women from inferior groups such as barbers, distillers, peasants and dancers. The offspring from these unions, designated as Rajputs, continued as rulers. Some Chhatris joined them and came to be known as Rajputs.[9] Several Chhatris neither shared food with the Rajputs, nor established matrimonial ties with them. The Chhatris, distancing themselves from the Rajputs, gave up soldiering and took to other professions. Since Rajput dominance was detrimental to the life and property of the Chhatris, the latter migrated from Hindustan and settled in Panjab. Calling

Caste, Creed and Custom 325

themselves Khatris, they had nothing to do with the Rajputs and Chhatris of Hind. Though they had descended from the Surajbansis and Chanderbansis, they abandoned the pursuit of rulership. Instead, they earned their livelihood through service, clerkship, commerce, moneylending and other occupations. During the time of the Ghurids, Lodis and Chaghtais (Mughals), the Khatris settled in cities and large villages, but did not seek government service. Gradually the (Muslim) rulers realized the competence of the Khatris and offered them several inducements to accept official positions. In particular, they were encouraged to learn Persian. In Panjab, none except the Khatris and Brahmins were permitted to learn Persian and keeping accounts. Many Khatris were appointed as *qanungos, chaudharis, amins, faujdars, girdawars, tehsildars, bakhshis, sardaftars* and *munshis*. As the reputation of the Khatris continued to increase, many of them reached the exalted offices of *wazir* and *diwan*. The Khatris were divided into four major branches of Bari, Bawanjahi, Khokhar and Sarin. They were further fragmented into nearly 700 subcastes that were found in Panjab, Multan, Sirhind and other places.[10]

Among the lowermost caste of the Shudras, Qatil included peasant groups like the Jats, Kunbis and Ahirs. Some people also counted the Kayaths among them. However, they claimed to be Kayasthas and contended that they had emerged from the entire body of Brahma. This assertion made them different from the four castes (Brahmins, Khatris, Vaishyas and Shudras), who claimed their origin from Brahma's head, arms, navel and feet, respectively. Qatil was inclined to accept this claim of the Kayasthas and placed them higher than the Shudras. Unlike the Shudras, they did not accept food from other upper castes. Instead, they accepted food only from the members of their own community, besides the Qanauji and Gaur Brahmins. The Kayasthas were divided into fourteen branches, each of which shared food and smoking pipe within its own limited sphere, besides the two Brahmin clans. Generally, they claimed to have descended from Brahma's son Dharamraj, while their earliest ancestor was Chitragupta. One of their offshoots, tracing its origin to the Kayaths, was called Ananya. A majority of people, who worked as clerks (*mutasaddis*) in the offices of the

326 *Situating Medieval India*

royal palace, were Ananyas. Qatil was deeply impressed with their abilities and character. They were unmatched in arithmetic. They trained the Khatris in Persian and accounts. In terms of government service, there was an overlap between the Kayasthas and Khatris. The former served as *mutassadis, qanungos* and *zamindars*. In rare cases, they took to soldiering and revenue collection. Serving as soldiers, they left behind glorious stories of their bravery. They maintained clean floors in their houses. Unless vegetarians, their men and women consumed meat and alcohol. Both in sobriety and inebriation, they were dignified in their manner and treated the others with respect. They often outclassed the Brahmins in the acquisition of knowledge (*ulum-i hindi*), devotion and renunciation. If they abjured meat, they excelled in rotating the rosary of beads. Like the Vaishyas, they succeeded in commerce, though such people were few.[11]

In Hindustan, the Muslims were divided into two broad categories, noble (*ashraf*) and plebeian (*ajlaf*). The former comprised four races of Mughals, Syeds, Shaikhs and Afghans.[12] The term Mughal was applied to the offspring of the natives of Iran and Turan, irrespective of the town they hailed from. If they were decent (*sharif ul-nafs*), they were known as Mughal and, if they were dissolute and troublesome, they were called Mughal Bachha. Any Iranian, who had migrated to India and adopted one of the many professions (service, army, trade or craft), was known as Aqa. The term Mirza was applied to the descendants of Syeds, clerics and office functionaries. The designation might have originated from Amirzada, which stood for a chief. Over a period, it might have been abbreviated to a shorter form. Among the Syeds, the nobles and theologians, who earned distinction in their calling, called themselves Mir or Mirza. Some people, who had descended from a Qizilbash mother, were known as Agha. In Hindustan, the people, out of their simplicity, treated every foreigner (*vilaiti*) as a Mughal. Other than the Syeds, many people displayed talent and valour in the service of kings. In Iran, such people were famous with the title of Mirza even if they were Shaikhs in reality. On migrating to India, they and their descendants became Mirza.

The migrants arriving from Turan were called Khwajazadas. They

Caste, Creed and Custom

could be Syeds as well as Shaikhs. If they were the offspring of Khwaja Ubaidullah Ahrar and, thus, belonged to the pedigree of Khwaja Muhammad Parsa of Mawra ul-Nahr, they were definitely Shaikhs and not Syeds. If they were the offspring of Makhdum-i Azam and, therefore a Naqshbandi, they would be Syeds, because the genealogy of Makhdum-i Azam was traced back to Imam Ali Reza. The claim of a genuine Syed to this exalted status could not be rejected even if a group rejected the assertion. If he was a fake Syed, even lakhs of people could not validate his claim. Khwaja Bahauddin Naqshband,[13] the eldest Turani patriarch, did not have a male heir. His two daughters were married to Syeds. He nominated his grandson as his successor, whose offspring became Naqshbandis. Khwaja Naqshband was a Shaikh Siddiqui and not a Syed. Some Turanis and Hindustanis, owing to their religious orthodoxy, treated him as Syed. However, all Naqshbandis were called Khwajazadas, as they had descended from the Syed son-in-law of Khwaja Naqshband. In Turan, Khwajazadas were known as Mir, Khwaja, Khoja, Khojaji and Khojam. In Hindustan, they retained the same title.[14]

The roots of the Syeds were traced to eight sources. There were original Syeds, whose forefathers had migrated to Hindustan from Arabia, Iran and Turan. Dunbala Syeds were accorded the status in accordance with the social norms of Turan, where descent was traced from the maternal side. A person, who was the son of an Uzbeg father and a Syed mother, was accepted as a Syed, though such a phenomenon was ruled out in Arabia and Iran. Some people, who belonged to the tribe of Tun, enjoyed the title of Mir and prefixed it to their names. On migrating to Hindustan, they married the daughter of a Syed due to the respectability of profession (*sharafat-i hasbi*). Their offspring became Syed due to general ignorance. The Kashmiris attached the suffix Mir to their names. Their offspring, on migrating to Hindustan, shifted Mir as prefix to their names and, thus, became Syeds. Poor people, in order to earn money for their survival, started reciting elegies (*marsiya khwani*) in Hindi and became Syeds. Their claim to this status was supplemented with the nobility of descent and acquisition of knowledge or wealth. The majority of servants and slaves of the

328 *Situating Medieval India*

Syeds claimed the *Siyadat* and even outclassed others in this race. Perfume sellers (*ittar farosh*), who sold their product in bazaars and streets, were known as Mir Sahib. If they abandoned this avocation, they developed an association with books or, acquiring a horse and weapons, enrolled as soldiers, they declared the Syeds as their brothers. In small towns, the Doms, who offered prayers on behalf of the Syeds and other Muslims, were known as Mir Sahib. If they did not know music, they recited elegies and, earning their livelihood, settled in towns other than their native places. They could enrol themselves as soldiers and join the establishment of a noble. Since the Doms did not command respect in the society, they protected their dignity by showing themselves as Syeds among their friends and others.[15]

The Shaikhs, like the Mughals and Syeds, hailed from diverse backgrounds. This was applicable to both types of Shaikhs, the old and new. The former included Siddiquis, Farooquis and Usmanis, besides the descendants of the companions of Prophet Muhammad. The latter comprised of Kambohs, Prachas, Khojas, Bohras, Bahris and Siddiquis of Multan. They also included people, who had converted to Islam in recent times. The case of the Afghans was somewhat different.[16] Their descent was traced to two brothers of Talut named Barkhiya and Armiya. Afghan was the son of Armiya. Qais bin Abdul Rashid, a descendant of Afghan, availed the opportunity of associating with Prophet Muhammad. During the second pious Caliph, a descendant of Qais was appointed to administer the area between Peshawar and Herat, besides promoting Islam. As his offspring flourished, many of them migrated to different parts of Hindustan. Since the mountainous country between Kabul and Peshawar was known as Roh, the Afghans of the area came to be known as Rohillas. The tribe of Straban was regarded as superior to the Kalantaris. A man of the former tribe discovered an abandoned child in a pit and, bringing it up as his own, named it as Kalantari, meaning a pit in Pashto. The Kalantaris (or Kilanis), who were the offspring of the child, gave rise to many tribes such as Bangash, Afridi, Dilazak, Khattak and Orakzai. Besides the Straban and Kalantaris, there were the Ghargasht and Bateen. In the main, there were two types of Afghans in Hindustan. First, there were the

Caste, Creed and Custom

offspring of the above four tribes and, second, there were the slaves and servants of the Afghans who, during the Afghan rule, converted to Islam on their own volition.[17] Qatil, owing to his long domicile in Lucknow, must have been familiar with the rise and fall of the Rohilla kingdom. However, he was silent on the political upheavals in the area.

Qatil, placing the mercantile groups in a separate category, identified them on the basis of the region in which they operated or the goods they traded in.[18] Bohras, who stood at the apex of the list, carried out commercial activities in western India including Multan, Thatta and Surat. Khojas were engaged in selling textiles, perfumes and tents. Parachas rented out articles for marriage functions such as tents, ropes, furniture and ceremonial dress of the bridegroom. Kaliris were found in the business of selling grain, ghee and fuel oil, besides transporting cattle from one place to the other. Qatil was clear on the characteristics of these groups. They had converted to Islam in recent times. They could not be placed among the *Ashraf* and *Arzal*. Rather, they were in the middle of the two. They contracted marriages only among themselves. From the angle of social status, they were not equal to one another. Bohras, divided among Sunnis and Shias, enjoyed superiority over the others.[19] Qatil has spoken highly of the Kambohs. In and around Multan, they were seen as Shudras and according to others as Vaishyas. Some of them embraced Islam and, owing to the patronage of rulers and nobles, attained high dignity. They were noted for their virtues.[20] Learned and dignified, they were loyal to their masters and affectionate towards friends and well wishers. Many of them gained exalted status as theologians and judges, while others excelled in their devotion to God. In their firm adherence to Islam, they outclassed the Mughals. They treated the Syeds as their spiritual mentors. They were strict in marrying their children within their own community. They were equally firm in avoiding such relations with Syeds, Mughals and Afghans.[21] Since they maintained the purity of descent (*hifz-i nasb*), they were regarded superior to other mercantile groups and almost equalled the Syeds and Mughals in social estimation.[22]

The four races (Mughal, Syed, Shaikh and Afghan) were recognized

330 *Situating Medieval India*

as superior, provided they preserved the purity of their profession (*hasb*). Birth was only one of the criteria of this position. They had to follow one of the noble professions that were commensurate with their exalted social rank. If, owing to one reason or the other, they were forced to adopt a calling regarded as low, they were expelled from their own community as well as the larger category of the *Ashraf*. Two examples illustrated this phenomenon. If a Mughal became a water carrier (*saqqa*) or an Afghan started selling milk, they would not find a suitable match for their children in their own communities. They were induced to marry them only among water carriers and milk sellers. This was equally true of the Syeds even if their *Siyadat* was spurious. This was also applicable to the Shaikhs even if they had descended from one of the three pious Caliphs. The Muslims, who followed lowly professions, could never enter the ranks of the *Ashraf*. Many elephant drivers (*mahawats*) claimed membership of the four races, but they could marry only among themselves. When a person changed his profession, he was constrained to form a marriage alliance (*qarabat*) only among fellow workers.[23]

Sometimes, the social norms were broken under special circumstances. In Delhi and other urban centres, the Mughals and Syeds, even if fake, formed marriage alliances between themselves, as both were associated with the Mughal State. They served in the household of nobles and soldiers, but kept away from running shops. The growing importance of wealth undermined the traditional restrictions. However, the Mughals and Syeds did not form such relations with the Shaikhs and Afghans. If the Syeds accepted the daughter of a Shaikh as their daughter-in-law, she did not get the respect that a girl from a higher rank received. It was possible for a Muslim, hailing from the *Ashraf*, to give his daughter in marriage to a boy, who was the son of a slave (*ghulamzada*) belonging to a noble. The boy, owing to a favourable environment and acquisition of education, managed to get a government job. With the passage of time, he was accepted as a Mirza. Other people gave their daughter in marriage to him because they were impressed with the prefix of Mirza in his name, his suitable physical bearing and his position of authority. Apparently, the girl's parents did not adequately

Caste, Creed and Custom 331

investigate the social antecedents of the bridegroom and, at the same time, his parents succeeded in concealing their lowly origin. Qatil argued that the social status of the master played a crucial role in the life of a slave. During famines, poor parents sold their children to escape starvation. If the master was poor, the slave performed menial tasks and remained stuck in his inferior status. If the master was rich, the slave acquired some status and lost traces of inferiority. People began to respect him, but they were alert enough to avoid any matrimonial ties with him. Some Muslims, while looking for a match, considered the respectability of both the parents, while others confined themselves to the father. People associated with the army regarded the scholars and physicians as inferior to themselves.[24]

Qatil has criticized the Hindus for counting the Muslims among the Shudras. This was entirely because of their animosity. In practice, the Muslims were more scrupulous than the Hindus in adhering to the boundaries of social purity (*qaid-i sharafat*). The Muslim elite—kings, nobles and respectable persons—did not allow their women and daughters to dance. Even the lower class Muslims such as servants, water carriers, shopkeepers, pharmacists and perfume sellers followed this restraint. If ever they found any such woman, they became inclined to kill her. In contrast, the Hindu Rajas placed their daughters under the training of dancers, musicians, Doms and Dhadis. No doubt, some Hindu women observed *Pardah*, avoided appearing before males and abjured dancing. They did so because of their association with the Muslims. Accordingly, a Hindu was outraged at the idea of sending his wife to the house of another person. The laxity of the Hindus regarding social purity was reflected in their marriage alliances. High-ranking Khatris, who rode on elephants and travelled in palanquins, gave their daughters in marriage to their caste brethren in lowly occupations such as brokers, grocers and confectioners. In Shahjahanabad (Delhi), a rich and noble Khatri, while riding an elephant in the streets, employed his brother's son-in-law as an escort to carry his water pot.

Among Muslims, the people in lowly professions—servant, water carrier, elephant driver, carpet spreader, perfume seller, confectioner

332   *Situating Medieval India*

and broker—were treated as pariahs. An upper class Muslim, earning five rupees a month, would never establish a matrimonial relation with an elephant driver even if he earned five hundred rupees. If a Syed adopted tailoring or a Mughal took to shop keeping, they would be excluded from the assemblies of upper class Muslims, including their own relatives. Muslim nobles did not permit the reciters of elegies (*marsiya khwan*) to sit in their gatherings, except on Muharram. In contrast, the Hindus did not hold any avocation in contempt. Among them, an elder brother served in the establishment of a high-ranking noble, while his younger brother was a hawker selling ice in the streets. In this context, Qatil came down heavily against lower class Muslims, who propagated that class based social segregation was not prevalent in Iran. Contesting this understanding of the Iranian society, he asserted that a considerable social distance existed between the upper (*sharif*) and lower (*razil*) classes in that country. No doubt, Qatil supported this chasm among the Muslims, whether they lived in Hindustan or Iran.[25]

While speaking of Hindu customs, Qatil unfairly stated that the customs of lower castes were not authentic. Yet, he was quite fair in admitting the internal stratification among the five upper castes such as the Brahmins, Khatris, Rajputs, Vaishyas and Kayasthas. For example, the Kashmiri Brahmins stood out for their elegance, intelligence, writing and speech. They held jobs in offices and army, besides serving in the establishment of nobles. Non-Kashmiri Brahmins were engaged in lowly professions like conducting prayers, cooking, begging or carrying water pots. After saving money, they set up shops and, making further progress, started giving loans on interest. In social respectability, they were seen inferior to the Kashmiri Brahmins. Similarly, the Panjabi Khatris were recognized as superior to the Purbiya Khatris. The former, having learnt Persian, served in government jobs, army and revenue department of the subdistricts. The latter, being ignorant of Persian, earned their livelihood through shopkeeping and artisanal work. On acquiring prosperity, they became moneylenders to rich aristocrats. Of them, few served in offices and fewer still in the army. From the prevailing situation, Qatil has inferred that social respectability (*sharafat*)

Caste, Creed and Custom

333

was of two types, lineage based (*nasbi*) and profession based (*hasbi*). He had no doubt that the Hindus, unlike the Muslims, privileged the former over the latter. Accordingly, it was possible for a Hindu to find a son-in-law, who was a broker. His father rode on an elephant, his wife's brother was a noble and sister's husband was a cloth retailer or sold sweets in the streets. In contrast, the Muslims gave precedence to profession in measuring respectability. A Syed noble would never give his daughter in marriage to a Syed, who ran a shop selling perfumes.[26]

To lineage and profession, Qatil has added the third factor of cultural etiquettes. In Hindustan, a majority of the population were Hindus who, owing to the dominance of Islam, were subordinate to the Muslims. The Hindus, who were close to the Muslims in terms of food, drinks, earning livelihood and beauty of speech, were regarded as more respectable than the others. It boiled down to admitting that respectability was determined by what the Muslims adhered to. For example, the respectability of Kashmiri Brahmins, Khatris and Kayasthas was superior to that of the Rajputs and Vaishyas. The Rajputs were not familiar with Persian and, in their speech and attire, differed from the people living in Delhi and other centrally located cities. In case of the high castes, (Khatris, Kayasthas, Rajputs and Vaishyas), the respectability of lineage matched with that of the Brahmins and government functionaries. In terms of respectability of profession, they were inferior. If the son of a Khatri shopkeeper was married in the family of an elephant riding Khatri, he acquired respectability of lineage from his father-in-law and, as a result, became more respectable among the members of his community. Ironically, this young man did not receive the same amount of respect from the Muslim colleagues of his father-in-law. The Muslim aristocrats did not allow a shopkeeper to sit in their assembly, not to speak of showing respect to him. Hindus, who had lived in the company of cultured Muslims, had adopted Muslim customs in their lives. Their sons became respectful to their fathers. They put amulets of Shaikh Abdul Qadir Jilani around the necks of their children. When inclined towards the Shias, they carried funeral biers in the name of their children from the houses of Muslims. They financed the celebration of death

334 *Situating Medieval India*

anniversaries of Sufis, concealing the charity from their own brothers. Some of them placed their women in seclusion, making them travel only in closed litters.[27]

At another place in his work, Qatil has again noted the factors that induced the Hindus to incline towards Muslims. First, they developed a liking for Muslim ways in term of dress, food and conversation. Second, they stood in awe of the prestige of the Muslim rulers. Third, they came under the influence of the Sufis. Fourth, they tilted towards the Shia sect, because it was the faith of the Nawabs of Awadh. Qatil felt that this entire inclination did not amount to anything. Again, Qatil noted the reasons for this attitude. In his understanding, Hindus avoided Muslim food, took bath every day and persisted with Hindu customs. On their death, they were cremated like their heirs. Outwardly they appeared Muslim, but in reality they were Hindu.[28]

Nearly 150 years before Qatil, the author of *Dabistan-i Mazahab* paid a close attention to a score of heterodox cults. Qatil, in the third chapter of his work, has described a large number of religious sects that were outside the pale of Hinduism. These have been listed in the table that follows. Each had its distinct origin, beliefs, myths, practices, food and dress. One of their features was association with Islam. Qatil, adopting different devices, has uncovered this aspect. The Jogis traced the origin of all religions to Gorakhnath. According to their belief, when Gorakhnath desired to bring the Prophet to this world, he assumed the form of his nurse and

Name of Sect/Cult	Name of Sect/Cult
Aghori	Sannyasi
Charvak	Nanga
Saravagi	Madari
Sevra	Kabir Panthi
Husaini Brahmin	Vedanti
Agarwal	Sufi
Shanvi	Tarak
Bhand	Sarbhangi
Sikh	Chamar
Suthra Shahi	Lal Beg
Bairagi	Zahir Pir

Caste, Creed and Custom

335

brought him up in his lap. This belief enabled the Jogis to eat the flesh of cows.[29] Guru Nanak was not only conversant with Arabic and Persian, but he also travelled across Arabia and Ajam (non-Arab lands). In his verses, he noted the virtues of Muslim elders and admitted receiving grace from the spirit of Prophet Muhammad.[30] Lal Beg, the deity of scavengers (*halalkhor*), was said to be the son of Khwaja Safa, who had been assigned the task of cleaning *Arsh-i Azam* and accepted Islam at the hands of the Prophet. The incident happened during the latter's ascension (*miraj*) to the abode of God. The Husaini Brahmins traced their origin to a Brahmin of Damascus, who sacrificed his eighteen sons to save the severed head of Iman Husain from the soldiers of Yazid. Though the Hindus and other Brahmins rejected the story, Isna Ashari Shias, particularly the Amirzadas, accepted it and treated Husaini Brahmins with great respect. At Kalpi, Qatil met a Husaini Brahmin, whose name was Nur Muhammad Pandey. Qatil found a considerable similarity between the Vedantis and Sufis, though they employed different terms for the same phenomena. Vedantis learnt ecstasy (*wajd*) and dance (*raqs*) from the Bairagis, though these were common among the Chishtis.[31] Qatil read a story of an encounter between Sukhdev and Raja Janak in a book associated with Shaikh Ibrahim Adham.[32] In another tale, a Sufi, who kept away from women, acquired the miraculous power of drying up a canal. Qatil, who had heard the tale in relation to Krishna, wondered at the movement of stories among diverse religious traditions. According to Qatil, the Hindus regarded the Sufis as more eminent than all Hindu sects and, in this sense, they did not have faith in the trinity of Brahma, Vishnu and Mahadev.[33]

Qatil, describing the heterodox sects, identified cultural fusion as their dominant feature. This was most prominent in the case of the Shanvis. They observed the religious practices of Islam and Hinduism with equal fervour. During the month of Ramzan, they kept fasts and recited the Quran. They offered five obligatory prayers (*namaz*) like the Sunnis of the Hanafi School. During nightlong vigils, they performed supererogatory devotions. On Muharram, they participated in the Shia mourning procession, distributing food and sherbet among the poor. On the other hand, they

336   *Situating Medieval India*

undertook all prayers and fasts prescribed for the Hindus, including dancing in front of the image of Kalika Devi, who was a form of Mansa Devi. They visited the Hindu centres of pilgrimage at Mathura and Vrindavan, where they sang couplets (*shalokas*) and listened to the prayers (*aarti*) comprising adulatory verses in honour of Ram and Krishna, the two incarnations of Vishnu. When they were free from their necessary chores by night, they sang devotional hymns in chorus and played on brass utensils as musical instruments. Like Hindus, they abstained from beef and, following the Muslims, they avoided pork. It was difficult to trace their origin. Their names were similar to those of the Muslims. Qatil believed that they converted to Islam due to the oppression of the Muslim rulers. As a result, they were barred from the dining area (*majlis-i tuam*) of the Hindus. Since they had left no space for themselves in Hinduism, they were forced to continue as Muslims. Perhaps, they did not adopt Islam from the core of their hearts. Owing to their lack of understanding, they remained entangled in doubt. They were unable to figure out any path for their salvation and wished to escape interrogation on the day of judgement. Therefore, they followed the apostles of both religions. Their attitude was similar to that of the Bhands, who embraced Islam only to extract money from Muslim clients. The Bhands failed to bring even the *kalima* on their tongues, while remaining far from the five obligatory prayers and yearly fasts.[34]

Qatil had partial knowledge of the Sikhs. He relied on what he heard from others, but did not check it from authentic sources. For him, the adherents of Guru Nanak were called Nanakshahis, though they were also known as Sikhs and Singhs. Guru Nanak, a Khatri of the Bedi clan, renounced the world and travelled to Arabia and Ajam. Endowed with the knowledge of Persian and Arabic, he acquired vast learning and divine intuition. In this way, he brought a wealth of glory to the Khatris. Free from religious fanaticism, he interacted with dervishes of various creeds and picked up the good points in them. Weighing Hinduism and Islam in the balance of reason, he created a new religion distinct from both. He attained fame as Nanak Shah. His followers were of two types. Some renounced the world inwardly and outwardly. Others, owing to

Caste, Creed and Custom 337

compulsions of their profession, subordinated themselves outwardly to the rich, but inwardly inclined to piety. Those known as the Khalsa kept long hair and beards. Following Guru Nanak's example, they had a liking for semolina dessert (*halwa/karah*). After his demise, they cooked it as an offering in his name, hoping to realize their wishes. Even in Qatil's time, the Sikhs demanded cash for this purpose while making peace after a battle. They ate all types of meat except beef, but forbade the use of tobacco. Among them, the Khatris and Brahmins ate bread, which Jats and Khatris had baked. A Panjabi Khatri (a follower of Guru Nanak and relative of Qatil) had seen an Afghan of Qasur, who mixed dough in their army. Three years back, he had placed himself in the hands of the Guru. Evidently, the Sikhs did not observe the rules of caste in their troops.[35]

Guru Nanak was followed by a lineage of nine successors, so that Guru Gobind Singh was the last of them. Qatil has mentioned a Sikh leader named Bhagat Bhagwan, who commanded the devotion of Hindus and Muslims. It was said that his followers— Khatris, Jats, Ahirs, Kahars and even Brahmins—ate the leftovers of his food. Guru Gobind Singh ruled over his followers like a king and aimed at occupying territories. During the reign of Bahadur Shah, the Guru's followers spread out in the towns of Panjab and expelled the Mughal officers from many places. Banda Bairagi, who had performed severe penance as a recluse, brought Guru Gobind Singh under his influence through deceptive speech. Because of an agreement between the two, Banda would teach the mysticism of Bairagis to the Guru and, on his part, the Guru would hand over his political power (*takht wa taj*) to him and leave for pilgrimage. From a beggar, Banda became the master of a kingdom that included Bhakkar, Multan and suburbs of Lahore. He was defeated at the hands of Abdul Samad Khan, who sent him to the Mughal Emperor in a cage. Qatil has indentified a few characteristics of the Sikh code of chivalry. He has revealed their spirit of sacrifice for their leaders and their kindness towards a vanquished foe.[36] When Qatil was reconstructing the history of the Sikhs, their guerrilla bands had not only occupied large parts of Panjab, but they had also led frequent raids into Delhi and Ganga-Yamuna

338   *Situating Medieval India*

Doab. Qatil might not have seen them, but had been hearing their stories that were in circulation. No doubt, some of his observations were incredible. Yet they underscored the manner in which the Sikhs were different from other warring groups that operated in the plains of northern India following the collapse of the Mughal State.

Qatil has placed four major cults associated with Shah Madar, Sarwar Sultan, Salar Masud Ghazi and Shaikh Saddu in a separate category. Their principal shrines were situated respectively in Makanpur, Bangah near Multan, Bahraich and Amroha.[37] Commanding massive following among Hindu and Muslim lower classes, they accumulated large stock of traditions that have fed into distinct sets of rituals. An annual fair, preceded by long processions, became an essential feature. Shah Madar, believed to be a Jew of Aleppo, was independent of the Shariat and learnt mysticism from the Jogis.[38] Thousands of his devotees—weavers, dyers, innkeepers and green grocers—walked to Makanpur carrying black flags. To ensure longevity of their children, they kept tufts on their heads that were shaved on reaching Makanpur. Small shrines of Shah Madar dotted the countryside, where the attendants guided Hindu and Muslim pilgrims.[39] The followers of Shah Madar numbered more than those of Guru Nanak.[40] In Panjab, the cult of Sarwar Sultan was popular among upper-class Hindus and lower-class Muslims. Its shrine, located at Bangah, received large offerings. Every year, processions of devotees left every town on a march to Bangah. Parahis, the low ranked Muslims, who sang songs and performed the Luddi dance, played a vital role in sustaining the devotional practices. The attendants of the mausoleum of Shaikh Bahauddin Zakariya, circulated false rumours about the saint.[41] Salar Masud Ghazi, a nephew of Sultan Mahmud of Ghazni, was remembered as a martyr who died fighting a local ruler. His shrine was found at Bahraich, though he was also connected to Rudauli and Sitrak. Like the Madaris, the lower class Hindus and Muslims, kept tufts on the heads of their children in the name of the saint. Shaikh Saddu's followers, who partook of sacred food at the annual fair, were bound to sacrifice a goat in the following year. Women, wearing fine clothes, engaged in music. One of them, breaking into a trance, imbibed the spirit

Caste, Creed and Custom 339

(*hulul*) of Shaikh Saddu and, as a result, predicted the future of others. Some of these women were believed to possess loose morals, while Shaikh Saddu was portrayed as a sexual predator.[42]

Though Qatil adopted an inclusive approach towards the shrine-centric cults and described them with enthusiasm, he was acutely conscious of their inbuilt exploitative character. In support of his nuanced stance, he has quoted a popular proverb. It was said that if the Pirs did not swallow the offerings of the lower classes, the latter would start looking at the elite with contempt. In other words, the heads of the shrines, keen on maintaining their dominant position, were rather greedy in extracting offerings from their poor followers. Qatil argued that whatever the plebeians earned with the hard toil of a year was spent on the annual festivities at places like Makanpur, Bahraich and Bangah.[43] In his view, the intense faith of the depressed sections merely ended up keeping them financially deprived as well as socially inferior.

Qatil did not limit Dussehra to the burning of Ravana's effigy. He has added the processions of Tisu Rai, the search for Nilkanth and participation of the Muslim ruling elite. Ten days before Dussehra, the Hindus and Muslims made clay statues of Tisu Rai that were mounted on sticks. Carrying it from door to door, the boys sang songs and collected offerings of one paisa or more. On Dussehra, they purchased sweets from this common fund and shared it among themselves. Groups of girls did the same, carrying porous earthen pots. When the boys and girls encountered each other, there was a mild contest in which the boys broke the pots. If two parties of boys encountered each other, there was an actual fight. The victorious Tisu Rai broke the statue of the vanquished, who wished to kill themselves out of frustration. On Dussehra, magnificent processions, headed by respective Tisu Rais and followed by flags and drums, were taken out. The processions included the Mughal Bachas as soldiers and women belonging to artisanal and mercantile groups. The processions returned after immersing the Tisu Rais in the river. Meanwhile, lakhs of people congregated in a vast plain, where a battle between Ram and Ravana was enacted. In the turmoil, where stones and bricks were used, the elephants ran amuck and caused a stampede, resulting in broken limbs. In

340 *Situating Medieval India*

the evening, a sea of humanity, particularly the Khatris, went to the neighbouring jungle in order to behold the bird Nilkanth. Some Muslims, including the local administrator along with leading nobles and armed contingents, felt forced to join. Horses and elephants, decorated with henna and ornamented seats, were an integral part of the spectacle. The nobles, passing through the bazaars, showered coins among the multitudes of every sect. Returning after beholding the Nilkanth, they fired shots from cannon and guns. In the evening, they watched performances of beautiful dancers and melodious singers.[44]

During the festival of Basant, processions of Hindus and Muslims, led by singers and dancers, paid homage at the tombs of local saints. Dancing girls, wearing provocative dresses, danced at the site in gratitude for the blessings of the previous year. In every town of Panjab, Hindus and Muslims, irrespective of gender and profession, put on yellow dresses and assembled in the outskirts to fly kites.[45] Janamashtami, commemorating the birth of Krishna, was observed with a procession in which boys dressed as Krishna, Radha and Sakhis. Scenes from the life of Krishna, particularly his victory over Kansa, were enacted. Muslims celebrated Janamashtami in a distinct way. They made effigies of Kansa and filled its stomach with honey. They tore the stomach and, drinking the honey, showed that they had drunk the blood of a king, who epitomized cruelty. Muslims also watched the performances of music, dance and drama.[46] The festivities of Holi, spread across two months, comprised bonfires and colours. The revellers poked fun at others, using vulgar language and wearing different guises. All classes of Muslims, except the Afghans and orthodox, played Holi with the Hindus—rich with rich, poor with poor and young with young. It was nearly impossible to throw colours on high-ranking officers, because they came out only with their retinues of soldiers and servants. If a horde of impassioned revellers reached their bungalows, the nobles escaped only by paying money. The members of aristocracy, who felt offended at the display of vulgarity, remained inside their bungalows. British rule forbade the throwing of colours on the Muslims. In the house of every Muslim, dancing girls and mimics performed

Caste, Creed and Custom

every evening. During the early years of Nawab Saadat Ali Khan, Lucknow celebrated Holi with great enthusiasm, as lavish gifts were bestowed on courtiers and performers. All Hindus and Muslims, including the educated and dignified but barring the puritans, took part in the celebrations. In the compulsive display of vanity, the Muslim elite faced tough competition from the Kayasthas who, owing to their boldness and generosity, spent a lot of money on the occasion. Qatil did not object to the flow of wealth because ordinary people, including artists and artisans, gained some material benefits.[47]

During the festival of Salona, which fell five days after Dussehra, sisters tied Rakhis of colourful silken threads and artificial pearls on the wrists of their brothers. Brahmins purchased Rakhis from the market and tied them on wrists of non-Brahmins. The one who tied the Rakhi received a cash gift. During the day, the Hindus entertained themselves with music and dance. In the evening, they went out of the city and, choosing a pleasant site, watched the performance of dancing boys. Brahmins had trained their young relatives as dancers, so that they could earn money from the rich. In such assemblies, every participant tried to outclass others in showering cash on the performers. Upper class Muslims avoided these gathering as they regarded them disgraceful. In contrast, lower class Muslims and inhabitants of towns and villages were extremely fond of watching dancing boys.[48] The blessings of Diwali were spread across one month. Houses were painted, confectioners displayed sweetmeats and potters made clay toys. The most passionate pursuit was gambling (*qimarbazi*), which was hailed as a pious act. The losers, deprived of cash, put their wives and daughters at stake. At midnight, some fled from the city and others committed suicide. The winner gave a fourth of his windfall to the house owner and one twentieth to those who prayed for his win.[49] The Muslims, taking part in illuminations and gambling, celebrated Diwali in a distinct way. Muslim women purchased sweets and toys in the name of their children and illuminated the place where they kept these. The practice was believed to ensure the wellness of children during the following year.[50]

342 *Situating Medieval India*

NOTES

1. An preliminary version of this paper entitled 'Understanding the Ethnography of Northern India: The Seven Theatrical Representations of Mirza Muhammad Hasan Qatil' was presented at the UGC National Seminar on 'History, Literature and Punjabi Society', Department of History, Guru Nanak Dev University, Amritsar, 19-20 September 2012.

2. The middle classes comprised groups like merchants, bankers, revenue officers, clerks, accountants, physicians and teachers. The expanding Mughal Empire employed a large number of revenue functionaries, who belonged to castes such as Brahmins, Kayasthas, Khatris and Baniyas. Their important feature was geographical and professional mobility. Akbar's reforms in educational curriculum and revenue administration facilitated the rise of Munshis, who learnt history, poetry, accountancy, epistolography and fiscal management. The role of the Munshis has been examined through the careers and works of Harakaran Das Kamboh, Chanderbhan Brahman, Nek Rai, Nawal Rai, Sujan Rai Bhandari, Rai Chaturman, Prem Kishor Firaqi and Anand Ram Mukhlis. The career of Qatil has rightly been placed in this context. Iqtidar Alam Khan, 'The Middle Classes in the Mughal Empire', *Social Scientist*, vol. V, no. 1, 1976, pp. 28-49; Muzaffar Alam and Sanjay Subrahmanyam, *Writing the Mughal World: Studies in Political Culture*, Ranikhet Cantt: Permanent Black, 2011, pp. 311-428.

3. Mirza Muhammad Hasan Qatil, *Haft Tamasha*, Urdu tr., Mohammad Umar, Delhi: Maktaba Burhan, 1968, pp. 12-20. (Hereafter cited as Qatil).

4. In two works, entitled *Shajarat ul-Amani* and *Nahr ul-Fasahat*, Qatil has examined the characteristics of Persian in India, Iran and Turan. He has discussed linguistic subjects like language, grammar, rhetoric and letter writing. Providing examples of correct and incorrect usage, he proposed a hierarchy of merit in descending order focusing on Isfahan, Shiraz, Khurasan, Azerbaijan and Turan. He noted nuances derived from diverse social classes and chronological phases. Stefano Pello, 'A Linguistic Conversion: Mirza Muhammad Hasan Qatil and Varieties of Persian (ca. 1790)', in *Borders: Itineraries on the Edges of Iran*, ed. Stefano Pello, Ebook, ISBN 978-88-6869-100-3, 2016, pp. 203-40.

5. Qatil, pp. 21-8.

6. Ibid., pp. 30-1.

7. Ibid., pp. 28-9.

8. Ibid., pp. 29-30.

9. The Rajputs shared many common traits with the Mughals. They shared the centrality of horse, sword, bow and arrow. Both opted for heavy cavalry

Caste, Creed and Custom   343

and preferred plains battles. Neither laid emphasis on artillery and infantry. Both disdained cultivators. Bearing loose rules of succession, both understood implications of succession wars, returning from exile and need for outside help. Both knew marriage as a primary form of alliance, with Rajputs expecting to send women to the leader they served. By early Mughal period, there was a consensus on terms of military service and reward in the form of revenue assignment. Stewart Gordon, 'Zones of Military Entrepreneurship in India 1500-1700', in *Marathas, Marauders and State Formation in Eighteenth Century India*, New Delhi: Oxford University Press, 1994, pp. 189-90.

10. Ganesh Das Wadhera, *Char Bagh-i Panjab*, Persian text, ed. Kirpal Singh, Amritsar: Sikh History Research Department, Khalsa College, 1965, pp. 291-3.

11. Qatil, pp. 33-4.

12. The members of four races, owing perhaps to social competition, nurtured rivalry towards one another. Each was believed to possess peculiar traits that led to the construction of stereotypes. The Mughals were treated as boorish and uncultured. The Syeds of Barha remained wedded to their native dialect, being indifferent to correct pronunciation in speech. The Afghans were looked upon as boastful and quarrelsome. Indian Muslims (except Syeds), designated as Shaikhzadas, were known as intelligent but litigious. The Bohras, keen on maintaining a separate identity in appearance and worship, followed Gujarati commercial practices. The Kambohs were noted for their courage, wisdom and decency. Muhammad Umar, *Muslim Society in Norhern India during the Eighteenth Century*, New Delhi: Munshiram Manoharlal, 1998, pp. 5-26.

13. The Naqshbandi order, also called Tariqah-i Khwajgan, received its name from Bahauddin Naqshband (d. 1390). As patron saint of Bukhara, he established ties with Timurid court, trade guilds and merchants. The order attained dominance in Central Asia under Khwaja Ubaidullah Ahrar (d. 1491). The order astutely combined the practice of Islamic orthodoxy, with deep involvement in politics and acquisition of vast land grants. Babur was closely associated with Ahrar's sons. During early decades of Akbar's reign, Central Asian Naqshbandis held high ranks and posts. In the times of Aurangzeb, all Turanis were found attached to Naqshbandi order. Annemarie Schimmel, *Mystical Dimensions of Islam*, New Delhi: Yoda Press, rpt., n.d., pp. 364-7; Khaliq Ahmad Nizami, 'Naqshbandi Influence on Mughal Rulers and Politics', in *State and Culture in Medieval India*, New Delhi: Adam Publishers & Distributors, 1985, pp. 158-76; Richard C. Foltz, *Mughal India and Central Asia*, Karachi: Oxford University Press,

344 *Situating Medieval India*

1998, pp. 94-7; Muzaffar Alam, 'The Mughals, the Sufi Shaikhs and Formation of the Akbari Dispensation', in *Expanding Frontiers in South Asian and World History: Essays in Honour of John F. Richards*, ed. Richard M. Eaton et al., New York: Cambridge University Press, 2013, pp. 143-63.

14. Qatil, pp. 129-30.

15. Ibid., p. 131.

16. The origin of the Afghans was traced to tribes of Bani Israil that inhabited Syria. During Firaun's persecution, they followed Musa in migrating to Palestine and Egypt. Ishmueel enabled Talut to attain power with the acquisition of a relic (*tabut sakina*). Talut defeated Jalut with the help of Daud. Talut, falling out with Daud, started a reign of terror. Following his repentance, Talut abdicated in favour of Daud and attained martyrdom fighting the infidels. Barkhia and Armia, the posthumous sons of Talut, administered Bani Israil with the help of Daud. Their sons, Asaf and Afghana, inherited the authority and completed the construction of Masjid Aqsa. During the persecution of Bakht Nasr, a section of Bani Israil migrated to Arabia and another to Afghanistan. Khalid bin Walid, a close associate of Prophet Muhammad, fought many battles for Islam. The Prophet honoured Qais (Abdul Rashid) with the title of Pathan and sent him to Afghanistan for propagating Islam among the Bani Israil. Qais had three sons named Sarbani, Batni and Gharghasht. Their progeny, known as Afghans, participated in the Indian expeditions of Muhammad bin Qasim, Mahmud of Ghazni, Muizzuddin of Ghor and Timur of Samarqand. In lieu of their services, the Afghans received governorships and lands in India. Many Afghans migrated to India as traders. Khwaja Niamatullah bin Khwaja Habibullah al-Haravi, *Tarikh-i Khan Jahani wa Makhzan-i Afghani*, Persian text, ed. Syed Muhmamad Imamuddin, Dacca: Asiatic Society of Pakistan, 1960, vol. I, pp. 29-125.

17. Qatil, pp. 133-4.

18. The social base of the trading community was confined to a small group of castes that dominated different regions—Baniyas, Bohras and Parsis in Gujarat, Hindu and Jain Marwaris in Rajasthan, Khatris in Hindustan and Panjab, and Chettis and Komatis on the east coast. Muslim merchants, mostly of foreign origin but settled in India, were important in the trade of Gujarat, Deccan and Bengal. Most merchant groups operated from their home base, but this rule did not apply to Armenians, Gujarati Baniyas and Marwaris and, to a lesser extent, the Khatris. Business deals were mostly confined within the limits of one's caste. Tapan Ray Chaudhury and Irfan

Caste, Creed and Custom 345

Habib, eds., *The Cambridge Economic History of India, vol. I: c. 1200–c. 1750*, Hyderabad: Orient Longman and Cambridge: Cambridge University Press, rpt., 1984, pp. 342-3.

19. Qatil, pp. 134-5.
20. In Multan, the Kambohs were mostly peasants. Originally Hindu, they converted to Islam under the influence of the Suhrawardis. Their association with Shaikh Bahauddin Zakariya generated in them a passion for learning. In the fourteenth century, they became important enough to approach Firoz Shah Tughluq with a complaint against the governor of Multan. In the next century, they supported Yusuf Qureshi as the new ruler. Many Kambohs distinguished themselves as scholars and Sufis. Shaikh Samauddin Kamboh became the patron saint of the Lodi rulers at Delhi. His son-in-law Hamid bin Fazlullah Jamali was elevated as the poet laureate in the court of Sikandar Lodi. Many Kambohs held important positions in the Lodi polity. Iqtidar Husain Siddiqui, 'Social Mobility and Emergence of New Social Groups', in *Delhi Sultanate: Urbanization and Social Change*, New Delhi: Viva Books, 2nd edn., 2016, pp. 89-90.
21. Qatil, p. 35.
22. Ibid., p. 135.
23. Ibid., pp. 134-5.
24. Ibid., pp. 136-7.
25. Ibid., pp. 127-8.
26. Ibid., pp. 96-7.
27. Ibid., pp. 97-8.
28. Ibid., p. 47.
29. Ibid., p. 37.
30. Ibid., pp. 48-9.
31. Ibid., pp. 71-2.
32. Ibid., pp. 74-5.
33. Ibid., pp. 66-7.
34. Ibid., pp. 45-6.
35. Ibid., pp. 48-50.
36. Ibid., pp. 50-2.
37. In the Gangetic valley, the Islamic towns (*qasbahs*) were clustered in the upper Doab and western parts of Awadh. The Sufi shrines, along with the Muslim land grantees, played a crucial role in the development of Bilgram, Makanpur and Karah. Muslim service families, acquiring land rights around the towns, emerged as local gentry. Hindu populace resorted to the sacred tombs for solution to their problems. While Qazis and Muftis handled the

346   *Situating Medieval India*

legal transactions, the towns became flourishing centres for scholars, artisans and office-holders. The three-cornered relation between the state, Muslim law and mysticism persisted through the colonial period. C.A. Bayly, *Rulers, Townsmen and Bazars: North Indian Society in the Age of British Expansion 1770-1870*, Cambridge: Cambridge University Press, 1983, pp. 349-50.

38. Shah Badiuddin Madar (1315-1436) did not figure in the contemporary literature. During the heyday of the Mughal rule, his popularity was reflected in the works of many writers, ranging from Abdul Qadir Badauni to Dara Shikoh. Abdul Rahman Chishti (d. 1683), a Sabiri-Chishti author, has produced a major hagiography entitled *Mirat-i Madariya*. Tracing his evolution as a Jewish scholar and initiation into Islam through Prophet Muhammad, it speaks of his entry into India and encounters with numerous theologians and Sufis. It portrayed Madar as a divinely gifted mystic, who overwhelmed the ruler of Kalpi and neutralized rival spiritual masters. The author has adapted Madar's image for his purpose of strengthening the Chishti order, validating the Mughal policy of religious toleration and undermining the narrow Naqshbandi outlook on religion and state. Muzaffar Alam, *The Mughals and the Sufis: Political Imagination in India 1500-1750*, Ranikhet Cantt: Permanent Black and Ashoka University, 2021, pp. 128-63.

39. Qatil, pp. 98-9.

40. The Madaris, like Avdhut Sannyasis, kept long hair and smeared ash on their bodies. They wrapped iron chains around their heads and necks. Wearing a black turban, they carried a black banner. They had nothing to do with prayers and fasts. They always sat beside a fire and consumed large quantities of cannabis (*bang*). In the excessive cold of Kashmir and Kabul, perfect Madaris did not wear any clothes. According to their claim, Prophet Muhammad entered the narrow gate of heaven only after uttering 'Madar is life' (*dam madar*). It was believed that Badiuddin Madar, arriving in India, overwhelmed a group of Jogis with his miraculous power. Since he established himself at this site (Makanpur), it became a sacred centre for the Madaris. Once a year, they congregated at this place, which was believed to cure blindness and paralysis. Kaikhusrau Isfandiyar, *Dabistan-i Mazahab*, Persian text, ed. Rahim Razazada Malik, Tehran: Kitabkhana Tahuri, 1342 AH / 1983 AD, vol. I, pp. 190-1.

41. Qatil, pp. 101-4.

42. Ibid., pp. 104-8.

43. Ibid., p. 104.

44. Ibid., pp. 75-8.

Caste, Creed and Custom 347

45. Ibid., pp. 88-9.
46. Ibid., p. 86.
47. Ibid., pp. 92-4.
48. Ibid., pp. 69-70.
49. Ibid., p. 71.
50. Ibid., pp. 73-4.

CHAPTER 14

Celebration of Religious Diversity in Agra: Reading the Observations of Nazir Akbarabadi

During the eighteenth century, north India witnessed major transitions at various levels.[1] The decline of the Mughal State hastened the rise of regional powers and invited foreign invasions. Political contestations exerted pressure on social structure, productive activities and commercial networks. As the ruling elites lost power and wealth, the beneficiaries of patronage lost their incomes. The erstwhile Mughal governors established autonomous kingdoms in Bengal and Awadh.[2] South of Delhi, the nascent Jat principality did not last long. The Marathas, having made territorial gains in different parts of India, suffered a major setback owing to their defeat (1761) at the hands of Ahmad Shah Abdali. North of Delhi, the Sikh potentates (*misldars*) created zones of autonomous power, while Ranjit Singh developed a viable kingdom beyond the Satluj. The East India Company spread its tentacles to Delhi and cis-Satluj region. While these political changes unfolded, a considerable vibrancy was seen in the cultural domain. Shah Waliullah, an eminent theologian and prolific writer, initiated a revival of Islamic orthodoxy. Khwaja Muhammad Nasir Andalib and his son Khwaja Mir Dard developed a new Sufi dispensation, which was a fusion of Naqshbandi and Qadiri tenets. Shah Kalimullah Jahanabadi and his disciples imparted fresh impetus to the Chishti order.[3] Urdu poetry scaled new heights owing to the distinctive contributions of Sauda, Dard and Mir. In this context, Nazir Akbarabadi adopted a novel approach to society, religion and culture.

Born in Delhi, Wali Muhammad Nazir Akbarabadi (1740-1830)

Celebration of Religious Diversity in Agra 349

shifted to Agra at the age of 20 and lived here until the end of his life. He adopted the profession of teaching and, freed from seeking political patronage, remained independent of ideological constraints. Proficient in Persian and local Indic dialects, he produced a large corpus of poetry in Urdu. He distanced himself from the elite tradition of literature and identified himself with the common man. His inspiration was traced to indigenous folk tradition as well as Sufism and Bhakti. Some early literary critics held that his poetry pleased only the rustics and, therefore, did not include him in the circle of eminent poets of the period. S.W. Fallon, the author of an Urdu-English dictionary, bestowed fulsome praise on Nazir for his unique contribution to literature.[4] Since then, Nazir's image underwent a positive transformation. A versatile genius, Nazir took interest in a wide range of subjects. A keen observer and avid participant in the contemporary socio-cultural life, he employed a simple language to create vivid images that were often punctuated with humour and satire. Insulated from narrow and sectarian ideologies, he nurtured a wide social outlook. This was manifested in his descriptions of the annual festivals that the Hindus and Muslims celebrated with gusto. In the present study, an attempt is being made to delve into his observations.

Since Nazir's experiences were confined to the city of Agra, it is appropriate to take a close look at the city. Founded by Sikandar Lodi in 1506, it remained the Mughal capital until 1638. Akbar's extensive fort complex enclosed 500 residential and commercial buildings. In the third quarter of the sixteenth century, Agra surpassed Delhi and Lahore in urban growth. In the mid-seventeenth century, it had a population of seven lakhs. A partial Islamic character was seen in its physical appearance and layout, besides the allocation and distribution of non-residential space. Rapid settlement occurred on the west of the Yamuna, both north and south of the fort, particularly on the streets radiating to join the highways. The urban sites acquired their identity from bungalows, gardens, markets, squares, mosques, seminaries, inns and public baths. The shifting of capital to Delhi and change of political masters (Jats and Marathas) did not erode its vibrant economic life. Its rich hinterland, particularly the fertile Doab, supplied provisions

350   *Situating Medieval India*

for feeding its vast populace, 12,000 horses and 4,000 elephants. Transcontinental trade routes converged at Agra from Thatta, Kabul, Qandhar, Bengal, Deccan and Surat. Yamuna, connecting Delhi with Sonargaon, was navigable throughout the year for boats of 100 tons. Agra received luxuries from Gujarat, textiles from Surat and Burhanpur, muslin from Sironj and spices from Deccan. Apart from the famous Biana indigo, Agra produced textiles, carpets, saltpetre, salt, sugar, gum lac, coral, walnuts and drugs. Countless artisans were employed in metallurgy, embroidery and stone carving. The English and Dutch, having established their factories in the seventeenth century, competed for the bulk purchase of indigo and saltpetre, forcing the Mughal emperor to intervene in favour of local traders. From 1670 onwards, the indigo trade declined. Wealthy merchants, working as money-changers and bankers, had operations in major Indian and west Asian cities. The police chief (*kotwal*), working from his office (*chabutra-i kotwali*), maintained order and supervised markets. The judge (*qazi*) tried cases and the censor (*muhtasib*) suppressed religious transgressions.[5]

Nazir, an adherent of the unity of being (*wahdat ul-wujud*), nurtured a passionate love for the Supreme Being. He did not deviate from the basic tenets of Islam. He paid rich tributes to Prophet Muhammad and underscored the significance of the creedal statement (*kalima*) in the life of the Muslims.[6] They bore unlimited reverence for Muhammad on account of being the last of the prophets and receiving the revelation of the Quran. As head of the Muslim community, he illuminated both the earth and heaven. He was privy to divine mysteries, exercising authority over life and death. The sky was impressed at the land that his feet sanctified. The Muslims were not worried about resurrection (*hashr*) as the Prophet was sure to act as intercessor (*shafi*) between them and God. The Muslims were advised to recite the profession of faith (*kalima*), which established the oneness of God and prophethood of Muhammad. It was a pillar of support to the Muslims in both the worlds. It lent lustre to the natural phenomena such as earth, sky, moon, stars and gardens of paradise. It provided light to the Muslims even in the darkness of their graves. It enabled them to face the day of judgement, to get relief from the burden of their sins

Celebration of Religious Diversity in Agra   351

and to face interrogation at the hands of Nakir and Munkir. It enabled the Muslims to travel across the narrow Pul Sirat, to benefit from the Prophet's intermediacy regarding forgiveness of their sins, to gain entry into paradise and enjoy its pleasures. It was the greatest prayer for the Muslims, who had received it owing to the blessings of the Prophet.[7]

Nazir had unbounded reverence for the five holy notables (*panjtan pak*), including Prophet Muhammad, Ali, Fatima, Hasan and Husain. He paid fulsome tributes to the martyrs of Karbala and twelve Imams. Cleansing his interior of impurities, he entrenched them in his heart. In their name, he rotated a rosary of 1,000 beads and raised the Haidari slogan. As a result, his obstacles were removed and the ghosts ran away. Nazir has reserved maximum space to the adulation of Ali. For him, Ali was the light of God, a swimmer in the ocean of spirituality and a shining gem of both the worlds. He was steadfast like the Qutb, while the other stars revolved around him. He was a fountain of the elixir of life (*chashma ab-i hayat*). Possessing immense physical strength, he knocked opponents with bare hands. He pulled down the stronghold of Khaibar in a single attack. Even the sky trembled at the fear of his valour. His authority extended from fish in the ocean to moon in the sky. His relation with Prophet Muhammad was unique. Outwardly appearing as two separate individuals, they were in reality a single body and soul. A person who recognized Ali treated him as an equal of the Prophet. One who perceived any difference between them was doomed. One who died in the love of Ali was assured of a place in heaven. One who nurtured any animus against him went to hell. When Ali was praised, the Kharjis nad Nasibis were wiped out. In the eyes of Nazir, all bounties of heaven were reserved for the five holy entities. Since they were endowed with wondrous powers, they would protect his honour on the day of judgement.[8]

Nazir has taken a keen interest in Krishna's birth and childhood. In his view, God willed these events under favourable stars (*nach-hattar*), so that human suffering was removed. Raja Kansa, the king of Mathura, possessed huge wealth and military resources. Arrogant about his power and invincibility, he threw challenges all around. A man of courage told him that his killer would be born in the

352 *Situating Medieval India*

house of Basudev and Devaki. Kansa, taking the advice of Narada Muni, placed them in a prison. They were provided with all provisions, but suffered captivity under watchful eyes of guards. Whenever a child was born, Kansa killed it without mercy. Krishna was born on the eighth of Bhadon under the sign of Rohini. Devaki asked Basudev to smuggle the child to Gokul without any delay. A reluctant Basudev agreed under his wife's pressure. Owing to a miracle, the guards kept sleeping, while the chains and locks broke up. Basudev reached Gokul before daybreak. He exchanged Krishna with a girl child, who was born to Nanda and Jasodha. Kansa heard about the birth of his killer, but he was helpless against the writ of destiny. In Gokul, a large number of women converged at Jasodha's house, where the birth of Krishna was celebrated with music and dance. Krishna, being divinely gifted, assumed varied forms. His childhood, essentially autonomous, was imbued with deep secrets. In every act, he displayed a strange spectacle (*leela*). Endowed with curly hair and wearing anklets, he jumped into the lap of every beautiful woman. He led a gang of boys in stealing butter and cream. If his hands did not reach the target, he climbed on the shoulders of a companion. If this did not help, he smashed the pot with his flute. When any milkmaid (*guwalan*) caught him, he declared that he was merely removing flies from the curds. If she raised her hand to beat him, he tore her blouse before dashing off. Though these women were upset at his transgressions, they loved him from the core of their hearts. Krishna, facing the ire of Jasodha, exposed the women for their duplicity.[9]

Krishna, in addition to his fondness for butter, spent his time in playing on the flute. The melodious notes (*radhey radhey*) entered the hearts of men and women, many of whom would lose their senses. In fact, they spent anxious hours waiting to hear the lilting notes. When he played his flute in the jungle, animals and birds were enraptured. The cows, grazing in the meadows, stopped in their tracks. Once, he enacted a drama of suspense. Playing with a number of boys on the banks of the Yamuna, he threw a ball into the river and tried to retrieve it. Since he disappeared from sight, a large crowd gathered in consternation. A massive serpent Kali, hissing in ferocity, wrapped itself around Krishna. The boy, displaying

Celebration of Religious Diversity in Agra   353

miraculous power, enlarged his body and overpowered Kali with ease. The multitude was amazed at Krishna's glorious victory. Nazir went on to describe the circumstances of Krishna's marriage. When Krishna stepped out of his childhood, Nanda and Jasodha looked for a beautiful girl from a family of status and wealth. Jasodha sent a group of old women to the house of Birkhbhan for the hand of his daughter Radhika. The girl's mother, feeling socially superior, rejected the proposal. When Krishna went there, Radha was captivated by his looks and music. During her sickness, Krishna appeared in the garb of a physician and cured her. The two were engaged with each other. Nazir, in *Dasam Katha*, composed an account of Krishna's marriage with Rukmini. A daughter of Raja Rukm, she heard the story of Krishna's valiant deeds from Narad Muni. Rukm rejected the match with Krishna, as he was a low caste shepherd. Rukmini sent a letter to Krishna through a Brahmin, asking for his glimpse (*darshan*), as her marriage with Raja Sispal of Chanderi had been fixed. Krishna, riding his chariot, responded to the call and, in a battle, defeated Sispal and Rukm. Baldev, Krishna's brother, overpowered the rest of the army. Krishna brought Rukmini to Dwarka, where the marriage ceremony was held amidst immense fanfare.[10]

Nazir, turning his attention to Panjab, found two saints, Ali bin Usman Hujweri (d. 1073) and Guru Nanak (1469-1539), as worthy of reverence. Though the former was popular as Data Ganj Bakhsh (Bestower of Treasures),[11] Nazir has addressed him as Guru Ganj Bakhsh. The poet prayed that the saint's path might remain permanent and his name might be perpetually inscribed in the collective memory. The saint possessed the power of removing sorrow (*ranj wa malal*) from every heart. When his devotees (*sewak*) called him, he came without fail and made them happy. His devotees were freed from all fears. It was not possible to describe the qualities of his grace (*lutf*). If anyone transformed his heart into Hujweri's abode and kept his sight on his favour, the Sufi distributed silver and gold from his treasure of grace (*ganj-i lutf*). Since the kindness of the Sufi was perennial (*mudam*) and never dried up, a devotee would have no problem taking shelter with him. Therefore, one must nurture the hope of his favour. His patronage was open to all without

354   *Situating Medieval India*

distinction. The devotee was merely required to explain his condition to Hujweri, so that he could benefit from the exalted munificence.[12] Nazir has addressed the founder of Sikhism as Nanak Shah and Baba Nanak.[13] The poet perceived him as an epitome of kindness, who invariably fulfilled the desires of his followers. The Guru, fully aware of the happenings of the world, was a perfect guide (*kamil rehbar*) and shone like a moon in the sky. People keeping the Guru ever in their minds attained happiness through his charismatic power. People who memorized the Guru's teachings found that he came out in their support. When they appealed to the Guru in their sufferings, he arrived in a moment to relieve them. It was not possible to describe the supernatural powers of the Guru. His charisma and generosity were manifest in all the four directions. Since the Guru commanded immense spiritual eminence, his devotees bowed their heads in prayer (*ardas*) and recited God's name (*waheguru*) every moment.[14]

In the eyes of Nazir, Shaikh Salim Chishti was Sultan of both the worlds.[15] A chosen one of God, he was the chief of the Muslim community. He was the head of the kingdom of mysticism (*sardar mulk irfan*). He was the star of the sublime sky and a rosebush in the garden of religion (*gulzar-i din*). Everyone believed him to be a saint who, by his grace, had turned the world in to a garden of elementary school (*bagh dabistan*). A king of kings, he was the centre point of purity (*qibla safa*) and light of the holy Kaaba. He was the guide of the people (*khalqat key rehnuma*) as well as the master of bounty (*sahib-i sakha*). Such was his exalted status that both the king and beggar were subject to his authority. He distributed the gifts of God, as he held the charge of supplies (*mir saman*). All inhabitants of the paradise, including the fairies and handsome lads, were subordinate to him. The aspirants of spiritual advancement treated his door as the holy Kaaba and, therefore, undertook pilgrimage (*ziyarat*) to it, bowing their heads from the core of their hearts. The control of the entire world was under his authority (*zer farman*). Being Sulaiman of the age, he exercised his jurisdiction over human beings and supernatural creatures (*jin wa pari wa insan*). Being the most exalted and dignified of humans, his light was beneficial for the entire humankind. Travellers on the mystical

Celebration of Religious Diversity in Agra   355

path found their destination at his mausoleum (Fatehpur Sikri). He was seen as the eyes and lamp (*chashm wa chiragh*) of the Muslims. The world had become fragrant due to the perfume of his bounty. It was Nazir's earnest hope that the Shaikh would preserve his dignity in the two worlds, as he was the creator of every emotion.[16]

In Nazir's view, Eid ul-Fitr brought more joy than Shab-i Barat and Baqrid (Eid ul-Zuha). People who had acquired pale cheeks due the restrictions of Ramzan were jubilant on seeing the moon of Eid.[17] They got up early and took a bath, which was followed by the cooking of vermicelli pudding. The old and young ate a hearty breakfast, while the boys prepared themselves for going to the Eidgah. People wore clothes of different colours such as red, white, yellow and golden. Those fond of intoxicants crowded into taverns (*mai-khana*) and cannabis dens (*bhang khana*). The distillers did a brisk business, while addicts inhaled hashish (*charas*) filled pipes. If a person got drunk with excess of wine, another expressed joy at the termination of a calamity (*azab*). People drew happiness from eating bread (*nan*), roasted meat (*kabab*) and sweet balls (*laddu*). The lovers met their sweethearts and exchanged Eid greetings in tight embraces. Groups of men congregated in streets, searching for their chosen female friends. Beautiful women, putting on red trousers (*pishwaz*) of a silken fabric, appeared to scatter flowers all around. Wearing attractive blouses (*angiya*) and, beautifying themselves with a variety of cosmetics (*kajal, hina, massi* and *pan*), they were armed to loot young hearts. The men folk, accompanied by their charming companions, visited the Eidgah, where the proceedings included the firing of cannon and special prayers (*dogana*). If people had not lived under the restrictive month long Ramzan fasting, they would not have experienced such happiness that extended down from the king to the beggar. However, the situation was different in case of Nazir, whose beloved failed to come and violated the solemn promise of celebrating Eid ul-Fitr together. The festival brought only sadness to him, as his desires and hopes were shattered. In Nazir's old age, the arrival and departure of Eid ul-Fitr held no meaning. At this stage, he had no choice but to be nostalgic about the enthusiastic preparations for the festival, when he visited the Eidgah with his rose-cheeked beloved.[18]

356 *Situating Medieval India*

In his description of the Shab-i Barat,[19] Nazir has underscored the difference in the manner of celebrations among the rich and poor. In the houses of the rich, semolina dessert (*halwa*) was prepared in sugar, while the poor used jaggery (*gur*) instead. The former were treated as perfect (*poore*) in their devotion, while the poor were seen as imperfect (*adhoore*). The utterly indigent, who could afford neither sugar nor jaggery, merely stared at the dainty dishes that their more fortunate brethren cooked and, thus, felt satisfied. Owing to their lack of means, they were forced to offer the customary prayer (*fatiha*) out of their houses—for father at the river, for maternal grandfather at the oven (*tanur*) of the innkeeper (*bhatiyari*) and for paternal grandfather at the confectioner's shop. On the other hand, such was the power of wealth that the rich could invite even the dead, who appeared to eat the dessert and bread to their fill. The prayer leaders (*mullas*), who were needed to offer prayers for the dead, exposed themselves for their greed. They partook of the dessert at one house and bread at the other, but they did not respond to the invitations from the poor. At night, a large variety of fireworks—*lattu, nabri, chachar, tunta, mehtabi, zarki, anar, hatphool, charkh, hawai, seenk, patakha, chuchundar* and *ghanchakar*—was lit. Fireworks caused accidents in which the victims received burn injuries on their chest, face, eyes and legs. In some cases, the beard and moustaches were burnt. Owing to the fear of accidents, the local administrator (*hakim*) deputed a policeman (*piyada*) to warn the people to take precautions. Though there were people nurturing ill will towards others, yet Nazir prayed for the welfare of all.[20]

In another poem, Nazir has assumed a more sober and didactic tone. He observed that Shab-i Barat emitted light across the world. It conferred eternal happiness on those who remained awake throughout the night in their devotion (*bandagi*) and prayer (*ibadat*). It increased the prosperity of those who distributed charity (*bakhshish*) in the path of God. It taught us to adopt submission towards God and perform good deeds. It persuaded us to avoid negligence towards the Supreme Being and follow the course of generosity. It motivated us to embrace good conduct (*husn amal*), so that we were regarded with beneficial results in the long run (*aqibat*). It showed the right path to all, while reminding us of Amir Hamza.[21]

Diwali, the festival of lights (*ujala*), was marked with merriment and vivacity.[22] All people, cutting across social boundaries and without exception, enjoyed its delights. They gave a fresh coating of clay paste to their houses and spread new mattresses on the floors. In the bazaars of the city, the shops were tastefully decorated. The confectioners (*halwais*) heralded the arrival of Diwali by preparing large stocks of sweetmeats, such as *barfi* and *batasha*. There was a massive increase in the demand for toys, as the sellers did a more brisk business than the confectioners. At night, the lamps were lighted to illuminate (*chiraghan*) the entire surroundings. This light enabled men to appreciate the beauty of faces that were as bright as the flame. The occasion provided an opportunity for the lovers to exchange their feelings of love. They asked their sweethearts to purchase anything of their choice, as they were prepared to give any amount of cash. It was for this day that they had borrowed money and even used fake currency to make their purchases.[23]

The gamblers were overjoyed at the arrival of Diwali, because the lighting of lamps marked the beginning of the annual bout of gambling. In fact, Nazir's account of gambling overshadowed his references to all other aspects of Diwali. A gambling bout opened with the *shagun ki bazi*, i.e. the game of *ganda*, which involved a stake of four cowries. After this, the stakes were progressively increased to three or four *gandas* and rose to even 1,000 *gandas*. Gamblers focused their interest on the amount of gain and loss. People who lost their possessions were forced to mortgage their houses. Some lost all household goods, while others lost the items they had earlier stolen and had brought them out only for the gambling bout of Diwali. A person lost his trousers and was left with a clout (*langoti*). Another person, losing the bangles of his son and ornaments of his daughter-in-law, faced curses from his wife. Instead of showing any remorse, he picked up a violent fight with her. He held her by the hair, threatened to beat her and to remove her ornaments one by one. He went to the extent of declaring, 'I have lost my house. I will not hesitate to lose her at the stake, as the intoxication of Diwali has overtaken me. You are ignorant of the transactions in the game of gambling. In the past, there has been a gambler, who not only lost his trousers and nose

358   *Situating Medieval India*

pin of his wife, but also lost the woman herself.' It was true that some people profited from this indulgence, but a larger number of them met with a miserable end. Nazir maintained that Dussehra brought a lot of happiness and adornment, yet Diwali commanded more of the unique sanctity.[24]

The festival of Holi was unique in many ways.[25] People waited eagerly for its arrival and looked forward to experience the jubilation, colours and music. An atmosphere of joy pervaded every house. As soon it was daybreak, people emerged out of their homes to participate in the festivities and observe the noisy spectacles. Huge crowds filled the streets and bazaars, so that there was no space even for a seed of sesame. It appeared that the roads were closed from all sides. Trays of coloured powder (*gulal abeer*) were ready. Coloured water was packed in a variety of containers such as leather bags, earthen pitchers and metallic pots. Quite visible was the spray pipe (*pichkari*). The most important feature of Holi was rubbing coloured powder on one another with bare hands. Those who maintained distance from others threw coloured water with sprayers. There was so much colour in the air that it assumed the form of smoke. Some people resorted to mischievous pranks in order to push others into embarrassing situations. They threw colour on their victims without warning and ran away to safety. Those caught unawares chased the attackers. In jest, they fell upon each other in a mock wrestling combat, twisting hands, dragging limbs and pulling hair. They also hurled the choicest abuse, so that one called the other as a pimp (*barhwa*). No one felt offended at the transgressions. Everyone preferred to swim in the sea of joy, which was universally understood as the true spirit of Holi. One could hear the sound of a large variety of musical instruments such as *sarangi, rabab, been, mridang, daf, tabla, dholak, tambura, chang, marchang,* and *ghungroo.* The celebration was considered incomplete without the free consumption of intoxicants like wine, cannabis and hashish. Revellers crowded into taverns and, having got drunk, lost their senses and shouted in joy. The festival provided a rare opportunity for women to come out of their seclusions and observe the scene of collective madness. For the men, this was an equally rare opportunity to ogle at the curves of female bodies, particularly when

Celebration of Religious Diversity in Agra   359

these were drenched in coloured water and, as a result, became seductively accentuated. Men felt satisfied only if they managed to rub coloured powder on one of the beauties. The people were aware of the Holi of Braj (Vrindavan, Mathura), where Krishna celebrated the festival with his female companions (*gopis*). However, Nazir asserted that the Holi of Agra remained unsurpassed due to the presence of women in their beauteous glory.[26]

Some people of Agra, including Nazir, visited the brothels in order to enjoy Holi in the midst of music, dance, wine and sex. It was possible to take liberties and release pent up passions in the company of dancing girls (*tawaifs*) and prostitutes (*randis*). The men aimed the sprayers straight at the women's chests, so that they could have a clear view of their upturned breasts through their tight blouses. The women looked unusually attractive owing to their narrow waists and sensuous gestures. The inebriated men felt encouraged to hold them in tight embraces and, in the process, subjected them to kissing and fondling. Some women tried to escape from the clutches of the impassioned men, while others became equal partners in the sexual foreplay and moaned in pleasure. Lying prostrate below their male partners, they enjoyed sexual intercourse and, while allowing their arousal to reach a climax, they expressed their pleasure in unrestrained cries. While narrating and recreating his own sexual escapade in a brothel, Nazir left nothing to imagination. He admitted that, coming out of the place, he fell into a pool of mud on account of his drunken state.[27]

The annual carnival of Baldev (*baldev ji ka mela*) was quite popular in the Agra region.[28] Its main features were enthusiasm, merriment and crowds. A large number of people arrived at the site of the fair from neighbouring towns and villages, employing different modes of transport such as horses, elephants, palanquins and carriages. Some came to pay obeisance to the deity, others to offer prayers and still others to seek remedies for their problems. Since all of them were overflowing with pilgrim's zeal, they felt that God could appear in the forms of Ram, Lachhman, Kachhmachh, Ravan, Narsingh, Narain, Baldev and Krishna. To them, it appeared as if God had descended to observe the delightful scenario and Himself raised the cry of 'Baldev Ji Ka Mela'. A vast concourse of people

360 *Situating Medieval India*

had congregated, particularly from a distance of two leagues up to the temple. Even the tiny sesame seed would not find a place for itself. There was a lot of pushing (*dhakka*) and elbowing. One person was seen fighting with a rival in anger, while another was found missing. Yet everyone was laughing and enjoying. Those who could not find a place in the square and bazaar encamped in the neighbouring jungles and orchards. Women formed a considerable part of the multitude. Wearing colourful clothes and boasting of sharp features, they shot arrows of gaze and used every gesture (*naaz wa ada*) in order to steal hearts. Lovers found the atmosphere ideal for amorous meetings, while some others tried to touch bodies and steal kisses.[29]

As an important feature of the fair, thousands of stalls had been set up to sell a large variety of goods such as flowers, fruits, toys, ornaments (*choori, bangri, naugri, puth, anguthi, challe* and *haar*) and sweetmeats (*laddu, jalebi, perhe* and *gatta*). The traders kept their goods securely tied, though the precaution failed to prevent thefts. A man, holding a stick in hand, chased an alleged thief who ran away with a bundle (*gathri*). At one place, a woman pickpocket (*jebkatri*) was caught, while at another a shop was looted. Sound of music rose up in the sky. Drama troupes (*ras mandals*) sang devotional hymns. Balladeers and mimics provided entertainment. Different forms of poetry—*khand, dohira, kabit* and *kithake*—were recited. The courtyard of the temple was tastefully decorated. Its dome appeared the tallest, the tableaux (*jhankian*) emitted light and curtains looked like spots on the moon. The clothes of the idol, which was the cynosure of all eyes, were changed after short intervals and food was offered to it. A prayer (*aarti*) was held to the accompaniment of musical instruments like bells, drums and cymbals. A special sweet (*prasad*), which was made of sugar and butter, was distributed. Devotees made a beeline to have a glimpse (*darshan*) of the idol. Some pilgrims recited God's name on their rosaries, while some traders offered prostration (*dandaut*). The devotees joined in a chorus to raise, with every breath, a slogan for the glory of Baldev (*jai baldev*).[30]

The night of Janamashtami (*Kanhaiya Ji Ki Ras*) was basically an occasion of joyful fanfare (*farhat wa ishrat*).[31] Large crowds of

Celebration of Religious Diversity in Agra   361

lovers (*mahbub dildar*) gathered to attend the festival, which commemorated the birth of Krishna. Women, with delicate bodies and attired in colourful clothes, arrived to observe the spectacle (*tamasha*). Owing to their convergence, it appeared as if an entire garden of flowers was blooming. All around there was music, happiness and fragrance. It appeared as if an embroidered tapestry of brocade had been spread on the ground. Rhythmic notes of music emerged from the orchestra comprising several musical instruments. The echo of drum (*mridang*) rose to the sky, while the anklets emitted incredible beats (*qiyamat jhanak jhanak*). The centre of attraction was Krishna and his female companions. Wearing a bright scarlet crown (*mukat*) on his head and dressed in a red apparel, Krishna danced in circles with folded hands. His movements and gestures pulled the hearts of onlookers. In addition to his dance, Krishna engaged in playful dalliance with the *gopis*. While displaying his ethereal beauty, he treated the *gopis* in different ways. At one moment, he held one of them and, at another, he released another from his hold. Sometimes, he laughed with them and, other times, he made fun of them. The *gopis*, resembling the fairies from heaven, were attracted to Krishna through the melodies of his flute. They danced around him while focusing their sole gaze on his secret signs (*ramz wa isharat*). Radha stood out among the bevy of *gopis* just as moon outshone the stars. The dance of Krishna and *gopis*, accompanied by divine music, exercised an infectious impact on everyone. Even a poor and helpless man (*bekas gharib*), who had walked all the way during the previous night to see the sacred drama, felt ecstatic without consuming any intoxicant.[32]

Though Rakhi did not match Diwali and Janamashtami in vibrancy and merriment, Nazir did not ignore it. On this occasion, he found that a large variety of *rakhis* was available in the bazaars of Agra. They were made of silken threads of different colours such as golden, green and yellow. Some *rakhis* had shining beads on the top, while others looked like the pomegranate blossoms (*gulnar*). *Rakhis* were available for every person, though the one meant for the chief (*sardar*) was rare. Every handsome man, having tied the *rakhi* on his hand, roamed about in happiness and pride. The

362   *Situating Medieval India*

beautiful ones acquired an additional charm due to the *rakhi*. As they raised their hands in a seductive gesture, the beauty of the *rakhi* merged with that of their hands, henna, fingers and nails. Such a sight, where colours met, was akin to the flowers blooming in a garden. The scenario pierced the heart of onlookers. The nightingale, on seeing them, became enraptured and started picking straws for her nest. The festival of *rakhi* ignited fresh desires in the lovers. On this day, Nazir was sad because the festival was confined to the Hindus. Being a Muslim, he could not participate in it. If he could change his religious identity, he could overcome his deprivation. He wished to wear the sacred thread (*zunnar*) on his body and holy mark (*qashqa*) on his forehead. Thus becoming a Brahmin, he hoped to tie the *rakhi* on the wrist of his beloved. He hoped that she would get the *rakhi* tied with good cheer.[33]

During the monsoon, the level of water rose in the Yamuna and, as a result, swimming became the most important form of recreation. The pastime extended to all without distinction—young and old, high and low, rich and poor, adepts and amateurs, wise and innocent. The participants identified a number of landmarks such as Jharna, Subhan Ka Tanbala, Chattari, Burj Khooni, Dara Ka Chauntara, Mahabat Bagh, Syed Teli, Qila and Rauza. Convivial gatherings (*majlis wa anjuman*) were held at Bagh Hakim and Shivdas Ka Chaman, where sweets and fruits were eaten. In the rising Yamuna, the varied states of water was expressed in local terms such as *khari, chadar, band, nand chakwa, menda, bhanwar, uchhlan, chakar, samet, ghamir, takhta, kassi buchar* and *kurra*. Some people were devoted to swimming, while others were interested in merriment. Large groups of spectators were thrilled on seeing the swimmers. The wide channel of the Yamuna looked like the court-yard of a garden. Some swimmers had faces like the moon. Some others were endowed with fair chests that shone like diamonds. Having tied a clout around their waists, half of their bodies were covered with water and half with sweat. The experts displayed different antics and movements. Some took a long jump into the water, while others dived deep to emerge safe. Some swam along the bank, while others swam across to the opposite bank. Some did not hesitate to go up to the stormy middle (*manjdhar*), while

Celebration of Religious Diversity in Agra 363

others floated on the surface as if they were asleep. Some people enjoyed rides on boats that were of different shapes and sizes. Beautiful girls, while present in the boats, sang and danced. As their ornaments shone in the sun, the voice of singing and echo of musical instruments spread out in the air. People watching the spectacle from the wings engaged in diverse activities. Some flew kites, others held parrots in cages and still others smoked tobacco through pipes. Every moment, slogans were raised for the glory of Krishna, Yamuna, Syed Kabir and a host of spiritual mentors. Nazir, in a special prayer, hoped that all swimmers, including the masters and apprentices, would remain happy until water remained in the Yamuna.[34]

Nazir was anguished at the economic crisis that enveloped the city of Agra in his days.[35] On account of unemployment (*berozgari*), poverty (*muflisi*) spread to all sections of the society. The houses were dilapidated, as the timber beams were replaced with thatched roofs. The basic need of water remained unfulfilled. All workshops had closed down. A large number of artisans, including masters of their craft, longed for the smallest coin (*kauri*). There was no work for weavers, carders, tailors, embroiderers, goldsmiths and blacksmiths. Jewellers, moneylenders and bankers sat idle in their shops as if they were thieves lined up in jail. Merchants, brokers and grocers did not earn anything. Cash boxes were empty. There was no fear of robbers. The local police was no longer bound to produce results. Artists, writers and poets did not craft images of words as they had lost patronage. Writing materials lay waste in shops. Since the prostitutes did not get any customers, they could no longer dream of good clothes and hearty meals. No one saw the performance of jugglers, who roamed about with their drums and pets. Brahmins, Muslim clerics and Pirs did not benefit from the flow of offerings. Gentle men soldiers who had large retinues ceased to get their salaries. Out of job, they sold off their horses and weapons, besides mortgaging their saddles. Some soldiers turned into beggars, while others migrated to the Deccan in search of greener pastures. Beggars, facing starvation, cried in misery. The famed gardens of the city became barren owing to lack of care. Flowers and fruits disappeared, while the fountains and canals dried. Nightingales

364   *Situating Medieval India*

and doves had stopped singing. In these dismal conditions, Nazir could no longer compose poetry as his thoughts also dried up. He could be known by any epithet such as lover, theologian, clerk, mendicant or poet. He prayed that divine kindness would provide the suffering multitudes with employment and food. He belonged to the city of Agra and, due to this emotional attachment, penned these lines.[36]

From Nazir's portrayal of the socio-cultural life in the city of Agra, it emerges that the common people participated in a number of festivals held at regular intervals in a year. The outstanding feature of these festivals was the congregation of vast multitudes at sacred sites for expressing popular devotion. The festivals were rooted in religious traditions going centuries back in time. This religious element served as the foundational principle of their faith. While fulfilling its demands, they were also attracted to elements of physical satisfaction such as music, dance, drama, special foods and sexual freedom. What is equally important, these festivals provided an opportunity to women to emerge from their homely seclusions and participate in the joyous festivities along with their male counter-parts. The festivals encouraged the lovers to meet their sweethearts and express their emotions for each other. They also enabled the people to indulge in what might be seen as vices—gambling, intoxi-cants and fornication—without suffering the qualms of guilt. The people did not see these escapades as vices. Nor did Nazir see them as such. In fact, he was averse to delivering moralistic sermons on cultural preferences. While referring to iconic religious figures, he rose above ordinary divisions. While paying rich tributes to Prophet Muhammad and Hazrat Ali, he nurtured the same sentiments for Lord Krishna, Shaikh Salim Chishti and Guru Nanak. Similarly, he described the diverse festivals—Eid ul-Fitr, Shab-i Barat, Diwali, Holi, Baldev Ji Ka Mela and Kanhaiya Ji Ki Ras—with the same spirit of reverence. He celebrated the entire gamut of human life including the somewhat uncomplimentary aspects. He rejected an otherworldly attitude to human affairs and, instead, focused on the hard physical realities. He underscored the material basis of religious life, highlighting the vulgarity of the rich and misery of the poor. In the deepest recesses of his heart, Nazir was a staunch

Celebration of Religious Diversity in Agra   365

humanist, who had unlimited love for the common man. He showed unconditional faith in the universal spirit of humanism, which remained stubbornly free from considerations of race, class and religion. His inclusive understanding of contemporary social realities went a long way in undermining the rigid sectarianism, which the revivalist leaders like Shaikh Ahmad Sirhindi and Shah Waliullah advocated.

NOTES

1. An earlier version of this paper entitled, 'Inclusive Portrayal of Cultural Patterns in Northern India: Considering Some Observations from the Eighteenth Century', was presented at a national seminar on 'Concept of Social Exclusion and Inclusion in Indian History', Centre for the Study of Social Exclusion and Inclusive Policy, University of Jammu, Jammu, 26-28 March 2014.
2. For political developments in the eighteenth century and the related debates in historiography, see Muzaffar Alam, *The Crisis of Empire in Mughal North India: Awadh and the Punjab 1707-1748*, New Delhi: Oxford University Press, 1986, pp. 1-7; Seema Alavi, ed., *The Eighteenth Century in India*, New Delhi: Oxford University Press, 2002, pp. 1-14; P.J. Marshall, ed., *The Eighteenth Century in Indian History: Evolution or Revolution*, New Delhi: Oxford University Press, 2003, pp. 1-36; Meena Bhargava, ed., *The Decline of the Mughal Empire*, New Delhi: Oxford University Press, 2014, pp. ix-lvi.
3. Saiyid Athar Abbas Rizvi, *Shah Wali Allah and His Times: A Study of Eighteenth Century Islam, Politics and Society in India*, Canberra: Marifat Publishing Company, 1980, pp. 174-202; Saiyid Athar Abbas Rizvi, *Shah Abd al-Aziz: Puritanism, Sectarianism, Polemics and Jihad*, Canberra: Marifat Publishing House, 1982, pp. 75-244; Mohammad Umar, *Islam in Northern India During the Eighteenth Century*, New Delhi: Munshiram Manoharlal and Aligarh: Centre of Advanced Study in History, Aligarh Muslim University, 1993, pp. 26-131; Tabir Kalam, *Religious Tradition and Culture in Eighteenth Century North India*, Delhi: Primus Books, 2013, pp. 23-74; C.M. Naim, *Zikr-i Mir: The Autobiography of the Eighteenth Century Mughal Poet*, New Delhi: Oxford University Press, 1999.
4. Syed Mohammad Abbas, *The Life and Times of Nazir Akbarabadi*, Lahore: Vanguard Books, 1991, pp. 1-6; Ali Jawad Zaidi, *A History of Urdu Literature*, New Delhi: Sahitya Akademi, 1993, pp. 143-4.

366 *Situating Medieval India*

5. Hameeda Khatoon Naqvi, *Urban Centres and Industries in Upper India 1556-1803*, Bombay: Asia Publishing House, 1968, pp. 17-25, 50-64; Tapan Ray Chaudhuri and Irfan Habib, eds., *The Cambridge Economic History of India, vol. I: c. 1200–c. 1750*, Hyderabad: Orient Longman and Cambridge University Press, rpt., 1984, p. 439; I.P. Gupta, *Urban Glimpses of Mughal India: Agra, the Imperial Capital (16th and 17th Centuries)*, New Delhi: Discovery Publishing House, 1986, pp. 18-44; K.K. Trivedi, *Agra: Economic and Political Profile of A Mughal Suba 1580-1707*, Pune: Ravish Publishers, 1998, pp. 136-71.

6. The creedal statement or the profession of faith (*kalima*) comprised 'There is no deity but God; Muhammad is the Apostle of God' (*la alaha ill alah; Muhammadun rasul allah*). The whole sentence does not occur as such in the Quran. The first part (rejection / *nafi*) is in Surat Muhammad (Quran, 47:21), while the second part (affirmation / *isbat*) is in Surat Fateh (Quran, 48:29). It occurred frequently in the Hadis, but more frequently in daily prayers. It was the first of the five pillars of Islam. A Muslim was required to recite it aloud at least once in his lifetime and should understand its meaning. Something similar to it was in use among ancient Arabians and is still recited by Muslims who know it as Talbiyah. Thomas Patrick Hughes, *Dictionary of Islam*, New Delhi: Rupa & Co., rpt., 2007, p. 261.

7. Nazir Akbarabadi, *Kulliyat-i Nazir*, Delhi: Kitabi Duniya, 2003, pp. 382-5. (Hereafter cited as Nazir).

8. Ibid., pp. 392-5.

9. Ibid., pp. 643-51.

10. Ibid., pp. 652-62.

11. Born at Ghazni in the early eleventh century, Ali bin Usman Hujweri (d. 1072) extensively travelled in central and west Asia. At the advice of his mentor Abul Fazl Khattali, he settled in Lahore and, taking the place of Shaikh Husain Zinjani, constructed a mosque. He followed Junaid Baghdadi's path of mystical sobriety, though he was attached to the Hanafi school of jurisprudence. His magnum opus *Kashf ul-Mahjub* (Revelation of the Veiled) explored the theoretical and practical aspects of Sufism, besides the principles of numerous Sufi orders. He was believed to have converted Rai Raju, the deputy governor of Lahore, to Islam. The descendants of this man served as the custodians of Hujweri's shrine till the present. The importance of the shrine as a prominent pilgrim centre has been recorded in the works of Dara Shukoh, Sujan Rai Bhandari and Nur Muhammad Chishti. Surinder Singh, *The Making of Medieval Panjab: Politics, Society and Culture, c. 1000–c. 1500*, New York & London: Routledge, 2019/ New Delhi: Manohar, 2020, pp. 131-48; Anna Suvorova, *Muslim Saints*

Celebration of Religious Diversity in Agra   367

of South Asia: The Eleventh to Fifteenth Centuries, London & New York: Routledge Curzon, 2004, pp. 35-58; Linus Strothmann, *Managing Piety: The Shrine of Data Ganj Bakhsh*, Karachi: Oxford University Press, 2016, pp. 43-69.

12. Nazir, pp. 404-5.

13. Guru Nanak (1469-1538), born in a village of central Panjab, undertook long travels in different parts of the Indian subcontinent and the larger Islamic world. His legacy was preserved in hagiographical accounts (*janamsakhis*) and a corpus of 973 verses in the Sikh scripture. He advocated a loving devotion to a formless God through the Guru's word. He condemned the incompetence of the Lodi regime and Babur's atrocities on the weak. He stood for the uplift of women from their state of inferiority. W.H. McLeod, *Guru Nanak and the Sikh Religion*, Delhi: Oxford University Press, 1968, pp. 148-226; J.S. Grewal, *Guru Nanak in History*, Chandigarh: Panjab University, 1969, pp. 143-286; Harbans Singh, *Guru Nanak and the Origin of the Sikh Faith*, Bombay: Asia Publishing House, 1969; Anil Chandra Banerjee, *Guru Nanak and His Times*, Patiala: Punjabi University, 1971, pp. 148-76; Nikky Guninder Kaur Singh, *The First Sikh: The Life and Legacy of Guru Nanak*, Gurgaon: Penguin Random House, 2019, pp. 101-50.

14. Nazir, pp. 405-6.

15. The family of Salim Chishti (1482-1572), endowed with a connection to Baba Farid and the town of Ludhiana, migrated to Sikri near Agra. He was initiated as a Chishti under Shaikh Ibrahim, a descendant of Baba Farid. During two pilgrimages (*haj*), Salim spent many years in Iraq, Syria, Turkey and Iran. In 1563, he established a hospice at Sikri. Owing to his fame as a Haji and severe austerities, the place evolved as a centre for Sufis, scholars and poor. Salim received the homage of stone-cutters, who quarried stone for the Agra fort and built a mosque near his cell. Akbar, in his quest for a son, shifted the pregnant queen to the Chishti quarters. When Sikri was developed as a capital, a mosque and hospice were built in the complex. On Salim's demise, a beautiful tomb was erected on the site of his new cell. Under Akbar and Jahangir, Salim's descendants were enrolled in the official (*mansab*) cadre. Saiyid Athar Abbas Rizvi, *A History of Sufism in India, vol. II*, New Delhi: Munshiram Manoharlal, 1983, pp. 279-81.

16. Nazir, pp. 402-3.

17. Eid ul-Fitr marked the end of the fasting month of Ramzan. Falling on the first of Shawwal, it followed the sighting of the new moon. The entire community offered the special Eid prayer in an outdoor prayer ground. In

368   *Situating Medieval India*

large cities, it was performed in the congregational mosques. A special alms, called Zakat ul-Fitr, was given at this time. It consisted of a measure of grain for every member of the household or its equivalent in value. It was given directly to the poor. Also known as the lesser feast (Eid ul-Saghir), the festival normally continued for three days. Cyril Glasse, *The Concise Encyclopaedia of Islam*, London: Stacey International, rpt., 2004, p. 205.

18. Nazir, pp. 409-11.

19. It was believed that on this night of full moon, the fate of every human being during the year—prosperity, adversity, health, illness or death—was fixed in heaven and registered in the Book of Life. Also, the Muslims were required to remember their friends and relatives who had passed away. Specially cooked food, particularly buttered bread and sweet rice, was apportioned in the name of the deceased over which a Maulavi or elder of the family read the Fatiha. After this, the food was conveyed to the respective tombs or distributed among the poor. Besides display of fireworks, the Muslims were expected to remain awake during the night to pray for the souls of the dead. Shias attached greater importance to the night, as it was the birth anniversary of Imam Mahdi. They also remembered Hasan and Husain as martyrs. According to belief, the trees held converse at this momentous period. Mrs. Meer Hasan Ali, *Observations on the Mussulmauns of India: Descriptive of their Manners, Customs, Habits and Religious Opinions*, London: Humphrey Milford, Oxford University Press, rpt., 1917, pp. 161-2.

20. Nazir, pp. 407-8.

21. Ibid., p. 409.

22. A number of Vaishnava Puranic myths were associated with Diwali including Sita's rescue and return of Ram to Ayodhya, the triumph of Vamana over Bali and victory of Krishna over Narakasura. In contemporary India, it primarily honoured goddess Lakshmi who was worshipped as a benign force. Adornment of houses with earthen lamps and explosion of fireworks aimed at enticing Lakshmi to get her blessings. Ritualized gambling occurred on the night of the new moon, while businesses treated the occasion as end of the fiscal year. Ganesha as the remover of obstacles and Kubera as the god of wealth shared honours with Lakshmi. A cluster of festivals, Diwali encompassed Lakshmi Puja, Goverdhan Puja and Bhai Duj. Denise Cush et al., eds., *Encyclopaedia of Hinduism*, London & New York: Routledge, 2008, pp. 202-3.

23. Nazir, p. 426.

24. Ibid., p. 427.

25. The Hindu festival of Holi was held in the month Phalgun (February-

Celebration of Religious Diversity in Agra 369

March). An evening before, bonfires were lighted and, sacrificing pieces of coconut, the flames were circumambulated. Next day, everyone engaged in throwing coloured water or powder dyes on each other. The festival marked the reversal of traditional patterns of social authority. Women insulted husbands, students rebuked teachers and children threw rubbish on adults. The origin of Holi was associated with demoness Holika, who ate a child every day. A poor widow was required to offer her only son. At the advice of a Sadhu, the children of the area gathered and abused Holika, who died of shame. Holika seemed to be linked with the demon king Harinayakashipu and child devotee Prahlad. Possibly, this was a part of a process of legitimizing the festival by linking it to a legend involving Vishnu. Denise Cush et al., op. cit., p. 353.

26. Nazir, pp. 415-22.
27. Ibid., pp. 423-4.
28. Baldev, also called Balaram, was the elder brother of Krishna. His mother Devaki, in order to protect him from Kansa, transferred the unborn child to the second queen Rohini, who gave birth to Baldev. Tradition records the adventurous exploits of Baldev. He slew the ape Dvivida who had stolen his weapons and killed demon Dhenuka who had assumed the form of an ass. Fighting with his ploughshare, he forced the Kauravas to give up Krishna's son. Using the ploughshare, he induced river Yamuna to change its course. On his death, the serpent Ananta issued from his mouth and glided to the ocean, giving rise to the myth of his incarnation as the world-snake. As a culture-hero, he was associated with irrigation, viticulture and agriculture, Margaret and James Stutley, *A Dictionary of Hinduism: Its Mythology, Folklore and Development 1500 BC–AD 1500*, Bombay: Allied Publishers, 1977, pp. 37-8.
29. Ibid., pp. 433-6.
30. Nazir, pp. 437-8.
31. The birthday of Krishna was celebrated on the eighth day of the dark fortnight in the month of Shravana. Devotees rose early and spent the day in prayer and meditation, often fasting until midnight. Primary festivities comprised devotional singing and scriptural reading about Krishna's birth and childhood. Midnight, the hour of Krishna's birth, marked climax of the festival with ceremonial worship and devotional songs. Elaborate food items were offered to Krishna and thereafter served to the devotees. Celebrants partook of *darshana* of Krishna's idol, which was elaborately decorated with flowers and ornaments. The *abhisheka* bathing of the idol in fruit juices and milk products was also common. The pastimes of Krishna were enacted in dramas and portrayed in traditional Indian dances. The

370   *Situating Medieval India*

    festival celebrated Krishna's identity as a young cowherd in Vrindavan. Denise Cush et al., op. cit., pp. 386-7.

32. Nazir, pp. 430-1.

33. Ibid., p. 428.

34. Ibid., pp. 431-3.

35. As a poetic genre, Shahr Ashob began in the post-Shahjahan period. Jafar Zatalli was an early example, while he was followed by Mir Taqi Mir, Mirza Rafi Sauda and Shah Hatim. These poets lamented the decline of the elite classes, who could no longer patronize arts. They were forced to shift to medicine, law, trade, bookbinding, theology and even cultivation. However, their eclipse coincided with the rise of low castes (*razal quam*) like weavers, butchers, grocers, vegetable vendors, confectioners, jewellers and bankers. The neglect of urban landscapes was based on personal observations. Yet, these poets could not be true guides to material conditions in cities, both declining and rising. Khurshidul Islam and Ralph Russel, *Three Mughal Poets: Mir, Sauda, Mir Hasan*, New Delhi: Oxford University Press, rpt., 1994, pp. 66-8; Ishrat Haque, *Glimpses of Mughal Society and Culture: A Study Based on Urdu Literature in the 2nd Half of the 18th Century*, New Delhi: Concept Publishing House, 1992, pp. 122-6; Satish Chandra, *The 18th Century in India: Its Economy and the Role of the Marathas, the Jats, the Sikhs and the Afghans*, Calcutta: Centre for Studies in Social Sciences, 1986, pp. 10-1.

36. Nazir, pp. 443-7.

Index

Abdul Malik Isami 18, 36, 48, 292
Abdul Momin Khan 227-8
Abdul Qadir Badauni 122, 346
Abdul Qadir Jilani 333
Abdul Quddus Gangohi 298
Abdul Rahim Juebari 215, 231-2
Abdul Rahman Chishti 276, 281, 346
Abdul Rahman Jami 221, 236
Abdul Sattar 216-17
Abdullah Khan Uzbek 214, 225, 227, 231, 238
Abohar 61, 65, 67
Abu Bakr Tusi 47, 57-8
Abu Hashim Dahbidi 232
Abul Fazl 190, 207-9, 214, 237, 253, 258, 265,
Afghan State 264, 304-5, 312
Afghanistan 9, 38, 63-4, 110, 234, 344
Afghans 21, 35, 38, 190, 214, 242, 293, 305, 322, 326, 328-30, 337, 340, 343-4,
Afrasiyab 18-19
Agra 170, 211, 235, 239, 246, 254-5, 349-50, 359, 363-4, 367
Ahirs 325, 337
Ahmad Chap 39, 44, 49-52, 54, 56
Ahmedabad 248, 262
Ain ul-Mulk Mahru 75, 82, 84-6, 90-6, 98-104, 107, 109
Aitmar Kachhan 39, 42
Aitmar Surkha 39, 42
Aitzaz Ahsan 289
Ajam 335-6
Ajmer 260-2, 275, 281
Ajodhan 57
Akbar 140-4, 146-8, 151-7, 159, 166, 172-4, 176, 178-80, 185, 187-8,

190, 194, 210-11, 214-15, 219, 235, 238-9, 241, 247-51, 253-5, 258, 260-1, 265, 272, 281-2, 294, 306-7, 319, 342-3, 349, 367
Alaghu (Mongol) 47, 49, 80
Alam Lohar 304
Alauddin Ali Ahmad Sabir 316
Alauddin Khalji 25-7, 30, 33-6, 39, 51-4, 63, 91, 98, 104, 106-7, 115, 280
Alberuni 110-13, 115, 117, 133
Ali bin Usman Hujweri 271, 298, 353-4, 366
Aligarh School 265-6
Allahabad 191, 234
Allahabad School 285
Alp Arsalan 9, 11, 13-14
Ambala 174-5, 298
Aminabad 167, 175, 182
Amir Ali Sarjandar 18, 40, 43
Amir Khurd 267
Amir Khusrau 36, 42-3, 50-1, 80, 106, 110, 114-18, 134, 229, 238, 240, 248, 258, 261, 268, 276, 292, 314
Amroha 18, 84, 338
Ananyas 325-6
Arabia 114, 327, 335-6, 344
Arabic 133, 135
Aristotle 117
Arzal 329
Ashiq Husain Jatt 139-40, 154-5, 158, 163, 307
Ashraf 329-30
Ashraf Jahangir Simnani 271
Attock 178, 180
Aurangzeb 186, 252, 282-3, 343

372   *Index*

Awadh 28, 40, 43, 51, 84, 191, 274, 276, 345, 348, 361
Azfar Moin 284
Aziz Khammar 27-8

Baba Farid 57, 68-70, 72, 75, 261, 274, 276, 298-9, 316, 367
Baba Haji Rattan 298
Babu Rajab Ali 139, 146
Babur 78, 164-5, 168, 191, 232, 247, 304, 308, 343, 367
Badakhshan 148, 290
Badaun 28, 43, 47, 57
Baghbacha 167, 182
Baghdad 13-14, 268-9, 320
Bahauddin Zakariya 70, 77, 102, 268, 311, 338, 345
Bahlol Lodi 76-8, 241-2, 293
Bahraich 72, 105, 276-7, 338-9
Bairagis 335, 337
Bakhshu Langah 305
Baldev Ji Ka Mela 359-60, 364, 369
Balkh 213, 234
Balochis 77-8, 264, 305, 312
Banda Bahadur 311, 337
Bangah 311-12, 338-9
Baran 33, 84
Basant 339-40
Batala 160, 253, 298, 311, 321
Batinis 13, 31
Beas 167, 171, 174, 178, 183-4, 187, 189, 305
Begumpura 310
Benares 89, 117, 234, 310
Bengal 38, 87-8, 106, 118, 122, 256, 259-61, 278-9, 284, 348, 350
Bhakkar 70, 85, 169, 235
Bhatinda 39, 57, 76, 293, 298
Bhattis 141-4, 146-7, 152, 155, 157-9, 292, 314
Bhera 164-5
Bhulran 144-5, 157
Bibi Naila (Kadbanu) 61-2, 68
Bihar 89, 276

Bijapur 274, 284
Biranjtan Kotwal 46-7
Bohras 328-9, 343-4
Brahmagupta 114
Brahmins 116-17, 121, 124, 126-9, 137, 142-3, 216, 308-10, 322-4, 326, 332-3, 337, 341-2, 363
Bu Ali Qalandar 212, 298
Bukhara 114, 142, 213, 218, 221, 223, 225-6, 228-9, 233, 237, 241, 303, 343
Bulleh Shah 297-8, 301-2, 317

Cambridge School 263
Central Asia 110, 114, 194, 214-16, 227, 236, 238-9, 343
Chakar Khan Rind 289, 305
Chandarbansis 324-5
Chanderi 51-2
Chenab 95, 168-9, 171, 176, 179, 180-4, 187-8, 291, 303, 305, 312, 314
Chhatris 324-5
China 15, 114-15, 170
Chiniot 142, 144-5, 148, 155-7, 307
Chishtis 266-7, 270-1, 281, 281-2, 298, 335, 348
Christians 12-14, 33, 217

Damodar Gulati 304
Danganah 100, 108
Dara Shukoh 252, 281-2, 346
Deccan 84, 151, 192, 216, 284, 350, 363
Degh 167, 176, 180, 182
Delhi 21, 27, 34-5, 37, 39-41, 43, 45, 47, 49-50, 52, 57-8, 63-9, 73-5, 77, 79, 86, 88-9, 98, 100, 103, 107-9, 114-15, 121, 123-5, 148, 156, 166, 170, 175, 234, 238, 248, 259, 267-70, 272-4, 282-3, 291-3, 307, 311-12, 314, 316, 320-1, 330-1, 333, 337, 348-50
Delhi Sultanate 9, 17, 26, 29-30, 35-6,

Index 373

38, 41, 51, 58, 60, 62, 66-8, 76, 81-2, 90, 97, 102, 106, 110, 118-19, 121, 134, 259, 264, 275, 285, 291-2, 312, 316
Deogiri 27, 51-2, 54, 104
Diplapur 39, 60-3, 65, 67, 69-70, 74, 108, 292-3
Diwali 341, 357-8, 361, 364, 368
Diwan 275-6, 325
Doms 328, 331
Dulla Bhatti 139-60, 289, 296, 306-8, 312, 317
Dussehra 339, 341, 358

Eid ul-Fitr 355, 364, 367

Fakhr Bauni 13, 17-18
Fakhr ud-Daula 15-16
Fakhruddin Kuchi 40, 52, 56-7
Fakhruddin Zarradi 267-8
Farid (Bhatti) 140-2, 146, 149, 152-3, 155, 157, 159
Fariduddin Attar 225, 233
Fasih Khan 219, 224
Fatawa-i Jahandari 9, 21, 26, 29, 34
Fateh Khan Jat 305
Fatehpur Sikri 249, 261, 281, 355, 367
Fazl Jatt 155, 163
Firoz Shah Tughluq 62-3, 65-76, 80, 82, 85-9, 91, 95, 103, 105-9, 120-5, 136, 240, 252, 273
Firozabad 122, 123, 125, 170, 259

Gajpat Rai 88-9
Gakhhars 264, 304-5, 312
Ganga 56, 84, 127, 174, 244, 253
Ganga-Yamuna Doab 63, 120, 123-4, 264
Gangetic Plain 60, 78
Ghaggar 74, 120
Ghazi Malik 60-5, 67-9, 74, 79-81, 105, 292, 314-15
Ghaznavid State 23-5, 31
Ghaznavids 9, 10, 31, 38, 290-1

Ghazni 38, 63, 125, 133, 144, 291, 313-14
Ghiasuddin Balban 9, 13, 17-21, 31, 33, 36, 39-40, 42-6, 51, 54-5, 57-8, 61, 78-80, 94, 115, 210, 291-2,
Ghiasuddin Tughluq 62-3, 69, 268
Ghorids 38, 290-1, 325
Gorakhnath 137, 240, 293, 295, 334
Gosain Jadrup 247
Gugudu 277
Gujarat (Panjab) 169, 181, 185-6, 188, 303, 311
Gujarat (Western India) 28, 73, 86, 103-4, 151, 191, 241, 246-7, 249, 260, 275, 350
Gul Chand 64-5, 292
Gursharan Singh 139, 151-2, 158, 161
Guru Amar Das 309
Guru Angad 309
Guru Arjan 309-10
Guru Gobind Singh 302, 311, 337
Guru Nanak 111, 126, 128-31, 137, 299-300, 308, 320, 335-8, 353-4, 364
Guru Ram Das 309

Hadis (Prophetic traditions) 23, 25, 31, 100, 116, 233, 366
Hafiz Shirazi 218
Hafiz Tashkandi 226, 237
Haibat Khan Niazi 305
Haidar Shaikh 298
Haidaris 58
Haji Ilyas 87-8, 105-6
Hamiduddin Multani 26-7, 35
Hamiduddin Nagauri 267-70
Hanafi School 12-13, 16, 32, 280
Hansi 64, 70-1, 74-5, 290, 311, 316
Hashim Muhammad Dahbidi 223, 239
Hatiya Paik 46-7
Hazrat Ali 351, 364
Hazrat Musa 72, 225
Himalayas 174, 176

Index

Hinduism 293, 322, 334-6
Hindus 26-7, 37, 50, 58, 68, 75, 99, 116, 128, 238, 248, 254, 311-12, 320, 323, 331-6, 338-41, 345, 349, 361
Hindustan 43-4, 217, 259, 270, 324, 326-8, 332-3, 344
Hindustanis 276, 329
Hir 296-8, 303
Hir-Ranjha 180, 302, 304
Hissar Firoza 67-8, 74-5, 120, 292
Holi 340-1, 358-9, 364, 368-9
Humayun 168-70, 230, 246, 260, 285
Husaini Brahmins 335

Ibn Arabi 207, 236
Ibn Battuta 35, 80, 84, 276
Ibrahim Lodi 245
Ibrahim Sharqi 243-4, 259
Ilbaris 33, 38
Imam Abu Hanifa 97
Imam Muhammad Idris 97
Imam Quli Khan 214-15, 223, 234, 239
India 15, 115-17, 133-4, 191, 213, 215, 226, 229-30, 234, 237-9, 241, 246, 260, 270, 278, 326, 329, 342, 344, 346, 348, 368
Indian Muslims 190
Indo-Gangetic Plain 110
Indus 63, 164-5, 169-71, 173, 177-9, 182, 187, 305, 312-14
Iqtidar Husain Siddiqui 8, 29, 38
Iran 14, 31, 216-17, 246, 261, 326-7, 332, 342, 367
Iranis 190, 214, 273
Iraq 15, 31, 254, 261, 367
Iraqis 12, 14
Irfan Habib 8, 20, 29, 265, 285
Ishaq Muhammad 139, 148, 158, 160
Islam 35, 49-50, 58, 67-8, 73, 75, 95, 137, 217, 279-83, 287, 293, 314, 328-9, 333-6, 344, 346, 350, 366

Islam Shah 245, 305,
Islamization 275, 278-80
Ismailis 32-3

Jagat Singh 306
Jahanara 282
Jahandar Shah 166, 183
Jahangir 165, 168-9, 179-82, 188, 191, 194, 209-11, 213-29, 231-5, 237-9, 246-53, 255-6, 258, 260-2, 274, 282-3, 285
Jajnagar 88-9, 106
Jakhbar Jogian 294
Jalaluddin Kashani 46-7
Jalaluddin Khalji 36-54, 57, 80
Jalandhar 162, 255, 262, 311
Jamaluddin Hansavi 58, 316
Jamaluddin Uchi 70, 102
Jammu 292, 306, 314
Janamashtami 340, 360-1
Janjuhas 304, 314
Jasrath Khokhar 76, 289, 292-3
Jats 25, 264-6, 273, 290-2, 310-14, 325, 337, 348-9
Jaunpur 88-9, 241, 243-4, 259-60
Jawanmard Ali Khan 227-8
Jeronimo Xavier 216-17
Jesuits 216-17
Jews 13-14, 33, 217
Jhelam 74, 95, 164, 171, 175-6, 180-2, 184, 187, 252, 291, 314
Jog 293, 295-7, 315
Jogis 117, 240, 293-8, 312, 315, 334-5, 338, 346
Junaid Baghdadi 268, 366

Kabul 63, 156, 167, 175, 179, 181, 214, 247, 252, 293, 346, 350
Kaikhusrau Isfandiyar 294
Kaiqubad 37-8, 40-2, 44, 50, 55
Kaithal 33, 45
Kalals 35
Kalanaur 167, 174, 176, 187, 215, 253
Kalima 351

Index

Kamal Mahiyar 13, 17-18, 20-1
Kambohs 35, 328-9, 343, 345
Kamrup 117, 258
Kangra 106, 167, 192, 258, 292, 305-6
Kansa 351-2, 369
Kara 34, 89, 108
Karam Chand Chauhan 67
Kara-Manikpur 40, 43, 51
Karbala 274, 277-8
Karnal 173, 175
Kashmir 24, 117, 143-4, 156, 167-8, 219, 231, 233, 239, 247, 249, 273, 278-80, 284, 346
Kashmiri Brahmins 332-3
Kayasthas 325-6, 332-3, 341-2
Khalji Revolution 37
Khaljis 21, 33, 35, 36, 38, 40, 43-4
Khalsa 337
Khan-i Jahan 85, 89
Khan-i Khanan 43, 46
Kharals 303
Kharjis 12
Khatirat-i Mutribi Samarqandi 214
Khatris 35, 308-11, 322-5, 331-3, 336-7, 340, 342, 344
Khawaja Abdur Rahim 214, 234, 239
Khoja 327-9
Khokhars 64-5, 291-3, 312, 314-15
Khuldabad 284
Khurasan 9, 12, 14, 16, 31, 64, 100, 112, 114-16, 122, 191, 221, 254, 314
Khurasanis 12-13, 15
Khushwant Singh 289
Khwajazadas 326-7
Khwandamir 169-70
Khwarizm 125, 133
Kilugarhi 40-1
Kishan Singh Arif 139
Koh-i Jud 291-3
Kol 84, 106, 259
Kotwal 243, 254, 350
Krishna 130, 309, 335-6, 340, 351-3, 359, 361, 363-4, 368-70

Kuldip Manak 140, 155, 158, 161-2, 307
Kunbis 325

Ladhi 141, 144-5, 147-8, 152-7, 159-60
Lahore 24-5, 98, 106, 108, 122, 140-3, 145-51, 153, 155-7, 160, 166-7, 171, 173, 175, 180-2, 189, 209, 213-15, 223, 234, 245, 247, 252, 274, 291, 293, 298, 306-7, 311, 317, 349, 366
Laila-Majnun 302
Lakhnauti 52, 79, 87-9, 103, 261
Lal Beg 335
Lal Shahbaz Qalandar 158
Langahs 77-8, 264, 312
Lodis 78, 325
Lohri 139, 158, 307
Lucknow 223, 263, 321, 341
Ludhiana 162, 174-5, 244, 292-3, 367

Machhiwara 167, 174, 187
Madaris 346
Maharishi Balmiki 310
Mahdawis 272
Mahiwal 169, 303
Mahmud Wali Balkhi 191, 215, 234
Majalis-i Jahangiri 216
Makanpur 338-9, 345-6
Maktub Khan 219, 221-2, 229
Malerkotla 76-8, 298, 311, 321
Malik Ali Kotwal 151, 317
Malik Chajju 39-40, 43-4, 52
Malik Fakhruddin 39
Malik Shah 9, 10
Malwa 27, 49, 104, 241, 258-60, 275
Mandahars 45, 291-2, 304
Marathas 265-6, 273, 348-9
Masih ul-Zaman 232, 239
Mathura 234, 255, 351, 359
Mau 305-6
Maulana Alimuddin 115, 119

Index

Maulana Jalali 230-1
Mawra ul-Nahr 221, 232, 237, 327
Medha Khatri 142-3, 148, 306
Meerut 123-4
Mehru Posti 145, 148, 153, 155-6, 158, 307
Minas 292
Mindu Baloch 305
Minhajus Siraj Juzjani 110, 267
Miram Siyah 221-2
Mirasis 141, 158
Mirza Aziz Koka 217
Mirza Hakim 176, 179, 181, 224
Mirza Nizamuddin 144-5, 147-8, 150, 155, 157, 307
Mirzas 303, 326, 330
Mirza-Sahiban 302, 304
Miyan Mir 209, 247, 298
Mohammad Habib 266
Mohan Mandahar 304
Mongols 21, 38, 46, 49, 52, 61-4, 103, 105, 291-2, 314-15
Mote Rai Chauhan 67-8, 292
Mughal State / Mughal Empire 139-41, 146, 150-1, 154-5, 157, 159, 180, 190, 192, 201, 211, 213-15, 233, 238, 252-3, 265-6, 271, 273, 282-3, 305-7, 312, 319, 330, 338, 342, 348
Mughals 144-50, 152, 155-9, 190, 214, 276, 305-6, 322, 325-6, 328-30, 332, 343
Muhammad Ali 218, 223, 226
Muhammad Baqir 190-5, 197, 199, 201-7, 210
Muhammad bin Tughluq 27-31, 34-5, 53, 62-3, 66, 69, 82, 84, 86, 94, 115, 120, 275
Muhammad Hasan Qatil 312, 321-6, 329, 331-9, 341-2
Muhammad Masum 282
Muharram 274, 276, 287, 330, 335
Muinuddin Chishti 247-8, 260, 275
Muizah-i Jahangiri 190-1, 193

Mulla Ali Ahmad 229, 238, 248
Mulla Gadai 249
Mulla Shah Badakhshi 282
Multan 27-8, 39, 43, 46, 60-1, 63-4, 70, 74-8, 82, 85-6, 91-2, 94-5, 100-1, 103, 120, 168, 189, 191, 264, 273, 290, 298, 305, 311-13, 316, 325, 328-9, 337-8, 345
Multanis 108
Muslims 12-14, 44-5, 48, 53, 58, 75, 93, 101, 105, 108-9, 114, 116, 123, 127-8, 136, 209, 229, 235, 254, 259, 277-8, 280, 287, 311-12, 320, 322, 326, 328, 330-4, 336, 338-41, 345, 349-51, 355, 366-7
Mutamad Khan 246, 253
Mutribi Samarqandi 213-19, 221-33, 235
Muzaffar Alam 190, 281, 284

Nadir Shah 183
Nagarjuna 113, 133
Nagarkot 121, 174, 176
Najm Hosain Syed 139, 150, 152, 158, 160-1, 307
Najm Intishar 115, 119
Nakodar 165-6, 175
Nandanah 250, 291
Naqshbandis 215, 235, 238, 260, 272, 281-2, 348
Nasiruddin Mahmud Chiragh-i Delhi 69-70, 82, 240, 266
Nauroz 229-30
Nazir Akbarabadi 211, 348-51, 353-9, 361-4
Nazr Muhammad Khan 214
Niazis 264, 305, 312
Nigaha 320
Nilab 165, 173
Nizam ul-Mulk Junaidi 19, 21
Nizami Chishtis 271
Nizam ul-Mulk Tusi 9-13, 15, 210,
Nizamuddin Auliya 58, 69-70, 72, 75,

Index

377

115, 134, 229, 238, 248, 261, 267-9, 280, 316
Nur Khan 145, 149, 152, 156, 307
Nurjahan 191-2, 218
Nuruddin Baseer 228-9
Nuruddin Rishi 279-80
Nurullah Shustari 274
Nuskha Zeba-i Jahangir 214, 219
Nusrat Fateh Ali Khan 297

Pakistan 152, 154, 162
Pakpattan 68-70, 72, 274, 298, 311, 316
Panipat 69, 173, 175, 298, 311
Panjab 25, 49, 63-5, 69, 76, 78-80, 103, 107, 110, 133, 137, 139, 149, 153-4, 160-1, 167, 169, 179, 184, 188-9, 247, 271, 276, 278, 284, 289, 291-2, 302, 304-7, 311-13, 320, 323-4, 337-8, 340, 344, 353, 367
Panjabi Khatris 322-4, 332, 337
Panjabis 139, 308
Parachas 329
Parahis 311-12, 338
Pasrur 167
Persia 18, 35, 112, 115, 206, 215, 236, 238, 349
Persian 14, 121, 135
Pindi 141-9, 152-3, 156-8, 306-7
Pir Hassu Teli 298
Pirs 278-9
Prince Khurram 234, 256
Prince Nasiruddin Mahmud 19, 106
Prophet Muhammad 25, 45, 73, 86-7, 98-9, 101, 105, 115, 123, 134, 137, 191-4, 217, 226, 236, 277, 283, 293, 298, 350-1, 364
Purab 323-4
Purabi Khatris 324, 332
Puran Bhagat 295-6
Puranas 112, 129, 135
Purbiyas 323-4

Qadiris 348
Qanauj 242, 244, 259
Qanauji Brahmins 325
Qandhar 63, 142, 182, 191-2, 216, 350
Qarmatis 12
Qazi 109, 127, 141, 145, 148, 151, 158, 244, 303, 350
Qiyam Khan 68
Qunduz 213
Quran 23, 25, 30-1, 33, 87, 94, 100-1, 103, 105, 134, 195, 198, 215, 236, 244, 249, 297, 350, 366
Qutbuddin Mubarak Shah Khalji 30, 105, 134
Qutbuddin Aibak 290-1, 314
Qutbuddin Bakhtiyar Kaki 316
Qutbuddin Hasan Ghori 19
Qutbuddin Munawwar 70-1, 74-5
Qutlugh Khan 61

Rachna Doab 140, 142, 158, 306
Rafizis 12-13
Rai Bhiru Bhatti 63
Rai Kalu 61
Rai Sehra 77-8
Raja Basu 306
Raja Takht Mal 305
Rajasthan 49, 63, 247, 260
Rajputs 81, 140, 143, 145, 157, 314, 322-5, 332-3, 342-3
Rakhi 341, 361
Rama 281-2, 336, 339
Ramzan 355, 367
Rana Mal Bhatti 61-2, 67, 81, 292
Ranjha 181, 294, 296, 302-3
Ranthambhor 49, 54, 104
Rasalu 289, 296
Ravi 63, 74, 95, 171, 174, 176, 182, 184, 187, 305
Richard M. Eaton 278-9
Rishis 279
Rizqullah Mushtaqi 241, 244-6, 258, 260

378 Index

Rohilkhand 43
Rohillas 328
Rohtas 177, 305
Ropar 182, 292-3
Roshanara 282
Ruknuddin Abul Fateh 70, 82
Rum 15, 268

Saad Mantaqi 27, 42, 51, 115, 119
Saad ul-Mulk Shihab Afif 61-2
Sabiri Chishtis 271
Sadharan 63, 65, 67-8, 73
Sadhu 63, 65, 68, 73
Sahiban 303
Sahij Rai 292
Saiyid Athar Abbas Rizvi 267, 271-2
Sakhi Sarwar / Sarwar Sultan 311-12, 320, 322, 338
Salar Masud Ghazi 72, 105, 276-7, 312, 322, 338
Salona 341
Salt Range 64, 250, 293-4
Salvahan 295-6
Sama 267-70
Samana 45, 64, 74, 79, 84, 121, 245
Samarqand 125, 213, 218, 221, 223, 225-6, 228-9, 233, 237
Sandal (Bhatti) 140, 142, 146, 149, 152-3, 155, 157
Sandal Bar 140, 147, 150-6, 158, 312
Sanskrit 111, 133
Sant Kabir 126-8, 137, 212, 310
Sant Namdev 309-10
Sant Ravidas 310
Sargdwari 84
Sarsuti 64-5, 70, 74, 98, 121, 292
Sati 254-5, 257
Satluj 120, 163, 167, 171, 174, 182, 187, 305, 314
Satluj-Yamuna Divide 120
Satnamis 265
Seljuqids 16, 31
Shab-i Barat 356, 364
Shafi School 12-13, 16, 32

Shah Abdul Latif 302
Shah Alam 248-9
Shah Badiuddin Madar 346
Shah Daula 167, 180, 185-6, 298
Shah Husain 148-51, 158, 161, 296, 298-300, 302, 307-8, 317
Shah Khwaja 214, 234
Shah Madar 281, 312, 322, 338
Shah Shamsuddin Dariayi 253
Shah Waliullah 348, 365
Shahabad 174, 298, 311
Shahjahan 167, 180, 209, 211, 239, 282-3, 285, 298, 306
Shahr Ashob 370
Shaikh Ahmad Sirhindi 298, 365
Shaikh Alauddin 69
Shaikh Budhan Shattari 241, 246, 260
Shaikh Nuruddin 71, 74-5
Shaikh Raziuddin 102
Shaikh Saddu 312, 322, 338-9
Shaikh Sadruddin 77
Shaikh Salim Chishti 249-50, 261, 354, 364, 367
Shaikh Sharfuddin 69-70
Shaikhs 322, 326-30
Shaikhu 141-3, 147-8, 153, 157, 159-60, 306
Sham (Syria) 268
Shams Siraj Afif 61, 69, 71-5, 80, 82, 106, 108, 122, 124, 240, 258-9
Shamsuddin Iltutmish 18-20, 40, 46, 54, 114, 210, 291
Shamsuddin Turk 27, 35
Shanvi 335
Sharfuddin Ali Yazdi 214, 216
Shariat 25, 44, 47-8, 53, 71-2, 87-8, 93, 100-1, 108, 136, 191-5, 244, 338,
Sharif Ragi 139-40, 156-8, 162, 307
Shattaris 260
Sher Shah 244, 305, 319
Shergarh 298
Shias 12-13, 32, 105, 136, 329, 333-5, 367

Index

379

Shiraz 218, 221
Shorkot 95
Shudras 127-8, 325, 329, 331
Sialkot 167, 185-6, 292, 296
Sidi Maula 46-8, 57
Sikandar Lodi 78, 137, 241, 245-6, 349
Sikandar Tohfa 292-3
Sikhism 308, 353
Sikhs 265-6, 273, 310-12, 320, 322, 336-8, 348
Simon Digby 280
Sind 61, 72, 79, 82, 86, 102, 106, 133, 273, 291, 313, 325
Sind Sagar Doab 164, 168, 291, 304-5
Sipahsalar Rajab 61, 63, 67
Sirajuddin Savi 45
Sirhind 76-7, 121, 165, 172, 174-5, 187, 234, 242, 282, 293, 298
Sirmur 61
Sistanis 38
Siwistan 70, 85, 103
Siyals 181, 303
Siyasatnama 9, 10
Socrates 112
Sodhra 176, 179, 188
Sohal Dev 276
Sohni 169, 303
Sohni-Mahiwal 302, 304
Somnath 113
South Asia 212, 263, 281
South Asian Islam 282-3
Southeast Panjab 60, 74-5, 78, 82
Srinagar 249
Suhan 164-5
Suhrawardis 76, 78, 82, 266-7, 298
Sujan Rai Bhandari 80, 167, 252-5, 258
Sultan Mahmud 11, 12, 16, 23-4, 49-50, 133, 252
Sultan Masud 9, 11, 24
Sultan Muhammad 19-20, 61, 79, 94
Sultan Muizzuddin 94, 106, 290-1
Sultan Nasiruddin Mahmud 46
Sultan Sanjar 49-50
Sultan Tughril 12-13

Sultanpur 166, 174
Sundari 144-5
Sunil Kumar 21, 38, 280, 284
Sunnis 13, 274, 329, 335
Suraj Mal 306
Surajbansis 324-5
Surat 350
Syed Ali Hamdani 280
Syed Jalaluddin Bukhari 73, 82, 101-2, 248
Syed Nasir 67-8
Syeds 87, 90, 102, 244, 322, 326-30, 332-3, 343
Syria 261, 367

Tajuddin Hasan Nizami 114, 291, 314
Tajuddin Kuchi 40, 44, 51, 54, 56-7
Taks 73, 81
Talib Amuli 215
Tanvir Anjum 281, 284
Tarikh-i Firoz Shahi 9, 21, 26, 29, 36, 210
Tashkand 237
Tazkirat ush-Shuara 213
Thanesar 66-7, 74, 97, 292
Thatta 69, 72, 103, 106-7, 122, 350
Tibet 168
Tilak 24-5, 290
Tilla Balnath 177, 293-4, 303
Timur 76-8, 124, 194, 214, 216, 218, 226-7, 237-8, 264, 312, 314,
Tisu Rai 339
Transoxiana 13-14, 31, 64, 213-14, 227, 230, 237, 239
Tughluqs 33, 64, 69, 76, 270, 293
Turan 191, 217-18, 221, 326-7, 342
Turanis 190, 214, 327, 343
Turkey 261, 367
Turkistan 38
Turks 12-15, 38, 64, 128, 237, 314

Ubaidullah Ahrar 330, 343
Uch 74, 70, 73, 82, 99, 102, 248, 292, 298, 311

380   *Index*

Ujjain 113, 134, 247
Umar bin al-Khattab 14, 101
Urdu 349
Uzbeks 214

Vaishnavism 137
Vaishyas 310, 325-6, 329, 332-3
Varahamihira 113-14, 134
Vashistha 281
Vedantis 335
Vedas 128
Vijaynagar 264

W.H. Moreland 265
Wajihuddin Usman Sunami 268-9
Wali Muhammad Khan 213
Waqiat-i Mushtaqi 241
Wazir 11, 15-17, 19, 23-4, 85, 89-90,
    199, 237, 259, 325
White Bein 165

Yahya Ahmad Sirhindi 36, 47, 57, 110
Yahya Khan 183-4, 189
Yamuna 40-1, 56-7, 64, 74, 120, 123,
    170, 173-4, 248, 291, 312,
    349-50, 352, 362-3, 369
Yusuf Qureshi 77-8

Zafar Khan 68, 73
Zafarabad 84
Zakat 100, 108
Zamindars 140-1, 146, 159, 167,
    179-80, 188, 264-6, 292,
    319
Ziauddin Barani 9, 17-18, 20-31,
    33-5, 36-8, 41, 43, 45, 47-8,
    52-4, 56, 58, 82, 84, 98, 120,
    210, 253, 280
Zohra Bibi 277
Zoroastrians 12-13
Zu ul-Nun Misri 73

Printed in the United States
by Baker & Taylor Publisher Services